STERLIN
Test Prep

AP Psychology
Review

4th edition

www.Sterling-Prep.com

4   3   2   1

ISBN-13: 978-1-9475563-3-1

Sterling Test Prep products are available at special quantity discounts for sales, promotions, academic counseling offices, and other educational purposes.

For more information contact our Sales Department at:

Sterling Test Prep
6 Liberty Square #11
Boston, MA 02109

info@sterling-prep.com

Published by Sterling Test Prep

Dear AP student!

Congratulations on choosing this book as part of your AP Psychology exam preparation! Scoring well on AP exams is important for admission to college. To achieve a high score on the AP Psychology exam, you need to develop skills and competence to define and explain psychological concepts, as well as ability to compare and interpret theories and scientific methods. You must also learn to apply knowledge from different theoretical frameworks to analyze a given situation.

This book provides a thorough and curriculum-oriented review of all content areas of AP Psychology course per the College Board's most current AP Psychology outline. The content focused on a targeted and detailed review of all relevant topics, concepts, and psychological theories.

The information is presented in a clear and easy to understand style. This book can be used both as accompanying text during your AP Psychology course and as a review guide before the exam. By using it as your study tool, you will develop the necessary skills and will be well prepared for the AP Psychology course and exam.

The content is developed and edited by highly qualified psychology and sociology teachers, researchers, and clinicians. The content was systematized and organized by education specialists to ensure the adherence to the curriculum and skills outlined by the College Board for the AP Psychology course. All content was examined for quality and consistency by our team of editors who are experts on teaching and preparing students for standardized tests.

We wish you great success in your future academic achievements and look forward to being an important part of your successful preparation for the AP Psychology!

Sterling Test Prep Team

181108gdx

Our Commitment to the Environment

Sterling Test Prep is committed to protecting our planet's resources by supporting environmental organizations with proven track records of conservation, ecological research and education and preservation of vital natural resources. A portion of our profits is donated to help these organizations so they can continue their critical missions. These organizations include:

For over 40 years, Ocean Conservancy has been advocating for a healthy ocean by supporting sustainable solutions based on science and cleanup efforts. Among many environmental achievements, Ocean Conservancy laid the groundwork for an international moratorium on commercial whaling, played an instrumental role in protecting fur seals from overhunting and banning the international trade of sea turtles. The organization created national marine sanctuaries and served as the lead non-governmental organization in the designation of 10 of the 13 marine sanctuaries.

For 25 years, Rainforest Trust has been saving critical lands for conservation through land purchases and protected area designations. Rainforest Trust has played a central role in the creation of 73 new protected areas in 17 countries, including the Falkland Islands, Costa Rica and Peru. Nearly 8 million acres have been saved thanks to Rainforest Trust's support of in-country partners across Latin America, with over 500,000 acres of critical lands purchased outright for reserves.

Since 1980, Pacific Whale Foundation has been saving whales from extinction and protecting our oceans through science and advocacy. As an international organization, with ongoing research projects in Hawaii, Australia, and Ecuador, PWF is an active participant in global efforts to address threats to whales and other marine life. A pioneer in non-invasive whale research, PWF was an early leader in educating the public, from a scientific perspective, about whales and the need for ocean conservation.

With your purchase, you support environmental causes around the world.

Table of Contents

AP Psychology: Exam Information **9**

AP Psychology Strategies **15**

Chapter 1. History and Approaches **19**

    History of Psychology 21

    Theoretical Approaches in Explaining Behavior 27

    Subfields in Psychology 37

Chapter 2. Research Methods **41**

    Types of Research 43

    Statistics 51

    Ethics in Research 57

Chapter 3. Biological Bases of Behavior **79**

    Effects of the Nervous System on Behavior 63

    Effects of the Endocrine System on Behavior 71

    Behavioral Genetics 75

    Influence of Genetics and Environment on the Behavior 79

Chapter 4. Sensation and Perception **81**

    Sensation 83

    Sensory Receptors 87

    Hearing 91

    Vision 95

    Other Senses 103

    Perception 109

Chapter 5. Learning **113**

    Classical Conditioning 115

    Operant Conditioning 119

    The Role of Cognitive Processes in Associative Learning 127

    Biological Processes That Affect Associative Learning 129

    Animal Behavior 131

    Observational Learning 137

Table of Contents (*continued*)

Chapter 6. Cognition and States of Consciousness..**139**

    Attention.. 141

    Cognition... 145

    States of Consciousness.. 155

    Memory... 163

    Language.. 173

Chapter 7. Motivation and Emotion..**177**

    Emotion... 179

    Motivation... 191

    Stress.. 199

Chapter 8. Developmental Psychology...**205**

    Prenatal Development... 207

    Heredity–Environment Issues: Interaction of Nature and Nurture...... 209

    Behavioral Change Throughout Life.. 215

Chapter 9. Personality..**227**

    Personality... 229

    Attitudes.. 237

    Theories of Attitude and Behavior Change.................................. 243

    Self-Concept, Self-Identity; Social Identity.................................. 247

    Self-Presentation and Interacting with Others.............................. 253

Chapter 10. Testing and Individual Differences...............................**257**

    Intelligence.. 259

    Test Design.. 275

Chapter 11. Abnormal Behavior and Treatment..............................**281**

    Understanding Psychological Disorders...................................... 283

    Types of Psychological Disorders.. 289

    Biological Bases of Nervous System Disorders............................ 321

    Treatment of Psychological Disorders.. 325

Table of Contents (*continued*)

Chapter 12. Social Psychology..**329**

    How the Presence of Others Affects Individual Behavior................................321

    Group Decision-Making Processes..337

    Normative and Non-Normative Behavior..339

    Attributing Behavior to Persons or Situations..343

    Processes Related to Stereotypes..345

    Prejudice and Bias..347

    Social Behavior..349

    Discrimination..361

    Elements of Social Interaction..363

    Society and Social Culture..373

    Demographic Structure of Society..385

Appendix

Important Figures in Psychology and Sociology..**397**

Glossary of Terms..**419**

We want to hear from you

Your feedback is important to us because we strive to provide the highest quality prep materials. Email us if you have any questions, comments or suggestions, so we can incorporate your feedback into future editions.

Customer Satisfaction Guarantee

If you have any concerns about this book, including printing issues, contact us and we will resolve any issues to your satisfaction.

info@sterling-prep.com

We reply to all emails – please check your spam folder

Thank you for choosing our products to achieve your educational goals!

AP Psychology: Exam Information

Approximately 260,000 AP Psychology exams are administered per year. The AP Psychology Exam is 2 hours long and includes both a multiple-choice section and a free-response section. Student performance metrics on these two parts are compiled and weighted to determine an overall AP Exam score.

Section	Question Type	Number of Questions	Timing	% of Total Exam Score
I	Multiple-choice	100	70 minutes	66.6%
II	Free-response	2	50 minutes	33.3%

Given the number of questions and the time restrictions per exam section, it is advisable that test-takers plan on devoting no longer than approximately 42 seconds per multiple-choice question and 25 minutes per each free-response question. Following this recommendation should allow for the time needed to answer every question on the exam.

The content of the AP Psychology curriculum and exam is divided into fourteen topics. The table below lists the topics and their approximate presence on the exam. The coverage of the topics on the exam as a whole reflects the approximate weightings.

Topics	Approximate % on AP Exam
History and Approaches	2-4%
Research Methods	8-10%
Biological Bases of Behavior	8-10%
Sensation and Perception	6-8%
States of Consciousness	2-4%
Learning	7-9%
Cognition	8-10%
Motivation and Emotion	6-8%
Developmental Psychology	7-9%
Personality	5-7%
Testing and Individual Differences	5-7%
Abnormal Behavior	7-9%
Treatment of Abnormal Behavior	5-7%
Social Psychology	8-10%

Assessment of Student's Learning on the Exam

The AP Psychology Exam is intended to measure students' grasp of the fourteen major topics covered in the higher education-level course offered through the College Board's Advanced Placement Program (AP). This program presents the opportunity for high school students to obtain college credit ahead of applying for or enrolling in higher education institutions. Students are expected to demonstrate broad knowledge competence on human behavior and mental processes. They should also be cognizant of ethical considerations and be adept at using the scientific method, analyzing biases and evaluating claims. Understanding key terminology and theories is also needed. All terminology, criteria, and classifications referenced by the exam are grounded in the fifth edition of the *Diagnostic and Statistical Manual of Mental Disorders* (DSM-5).

The following are general parameters about the relationship between the components of the curriculum framework and the questions on the AP exam.

The AP Psychology Exam assesses:

- competence defining and explaining a wide range of content grounded in the course topics;

- ability to apply comparison and interpretation skills to course concepts, theories, and scientific methods;

- proficiency in using concepts from different theoretical frameworks or subdomains to analyze a unique scenario;

- capability to design, analyze or critique a research study.

What to Bring to the Exam

A number 2 pencil is required for the multiple-choice section, while a black or blue ink pen is required for the free-response section. Test takers must come to the exam prepared with both writing instruments and clean scratch paper. Calculators are not permitted during the exam. Any computations should be completed either mentally or using paper and pencil. Multi-color markers and pencils are not allowed.

Multiple-Choice Questions

The multiple-choice section consists of one hundred questions with five (A-E) possible answer choices. These questions sometimes require students to respond to data graphs, tables or maps, and they draw upon knowledge required by the curriculum framework. Each question addresses one of the learning objectives for the course. Categorically speaking, the multiple-choice section is composed of three different types of questions: definition or identification questions, cause-and-effect questions, and graphic questions.

Definition or Identification Questions

These questions require test takers to recognize something and then appropriately describe or define it. The following question released by the College Board is an example of a definition/identification question.

Introspection, a research tool used by early psychologists, is a technique which involves:

(A) correlational analyses
(B) machines designed for cognitive analysis
(C) survey methodology
(**D**) self-examination of mental processes
(E) teaching participants to multitask

Cause-and-Effect Questions

These questions require test takers to correctly associate causes with their effects or vice versa. The following question released by the College Board is an example of a cause-and-effect question.

Damage to the cerebellum would most likely result in which of the following problems?

(A) Aphasia
(B) Increased aggression
(C) A loss of vision
(**D**) A loss of motor coordination
(E) A change in personality

Graphic Questions

Graphic questions are identified by their inclusion of a graph, table, map or any other visual material that test takers must refer to in order to answer the question. The following question released by the College Board is an example of this type of question.

EFFECTS OF ADVERTISING
ON ATTITUDE CHANGE

According to the graph above, the greatest degree of attitude change is likely to be produced by which of the following forms of advertising?

(A) Radio only
(B) Newspaper only
(C) Television only
(D) Easy messages in the newspaper and difficult messages on television
(E) Easy messages on television and difficult messages in the newspaper

Free-Response Questions

While the scope of the multiple-choice questions is wide, requiring general psychological knowledge, free-response questions require deeper, more specific knowledge of a given topic. These questions can cover a number of topics and concepts, requiring students to apply what they know in nontraditional ways. They often require the demonstration of higher-order thinking skills. Free-response questions test students' ability to effectively articulate connections among the constructs from the topics.

Categorically speaking, the free-response questions appear on the AP Psychology Exam in two different varieties: hypothetical analysis questions and research study questions.

Hypothetical Analysis Questions

Students might be presented with a hypothetical psychological scenario (e.g., depression, stress) which they must analyze using multiple theoretical framework or subdomain concepts. The following question, which appeared on a past exam and was released by the College Board, is an example of a hypothetical analysis question.

Abram recently graduated from high school and began his first year at a four-year university. Explain with an example how experiencing each of the following in the past may affect Abram's ability to succeed in college.

- Authoritarian parenting style
- Identity versus role confusion
- Unconditional positive regard

Abram's first year was very difficult, and he found that he was not as successful as he would have liked. Explain with an example how each of the following may help Abram be more successful in the future.

- Divergent thinking
- Elaborative rehearsal
- Intrinsic motivation
- Self-efficacy

Research Study Questions

Students may be required to analyze, critique or design a research study to demonstrate their understanding of scientific research principles. The following test item, released by the College Board, consists of several questions based on a research study and is an example of this type of question.

Researchers conducted a naturalistic study of children between the ages of 5 and 7 years. The researchers visited classrooms during class party celebrations. As a measure of hyperactivity, they recorded the number of times children left their seats. The researchers found a strong positive correlation between sugary snacks offered at the parties and hyperactivity. Based on these findings, the researchers concluded that sugar causes hyperactivity.

A. How might the following explain why people may easily accept the conclusion of the study described above?
   - Confirmation bias
   - Availability heuristic
   - Misunderstanding of correlational studies

B. As a follow-up study, the researchers are designing an experiment to test whether sugar causes hyperactivity. For the experiment, please do the following:
   - State a possible hypothesis.
   - Operationally define the dependent variable.
   - Describe how random assignment can be achieved.

C. Based on the results of the follow-up experiment described in Part B, researchers conclude that sugar does not cause any change in hyperactivity.

   - Draw a correctly labeled bar graph depicting this result.

Scoring

The multiple-choice section is graded electronically with points given for each correct answer provided. Missed questions and answers purposely left blank will be considered incorrect and will count against your final score. Therefore, it is important to leave yourself enough time to answer every question on the exam.

The free-response section is cross-evaluated and scored by multiple college faculty members and high school AP teachers participating in the annual AP Reading held each year in June. Fairness and consistency are monitored and enforced during the evaluation process through a system of checks and balances, with all evaluators strictly using shared scoring guidelines. A Chief Reader is also included in the process to ensure scoring standard accuracy.

The raw scores from both sections are then combined in order to arrive at the composite AP score, which is then converted to the AP five-point grade scale (1 to 5). This score is used to signify to colleges and universities the qualification level a student possesses in receiving either college credit or placement.

Composite AP score	Recommendations
5	Extremely well qualified
4	Well qualified
3	Qualified
2	Possibly qualified
1	No recommendation

Not all universities and colleges agree upon the same prerequisite scores; each institution sets its own performance standards, so it is important to check with admissions offices directly to clarify their individual standards. Many universities and colleges will include this on their website. Also, it is advised to refer to the Find Credit Policy Information page which contains a listing of many institutions' qualifying grades (http://collegeboard.com/ap/creditpolicy). Typically, however, composite AP scores of 3, 4 or 5 are considered qualifying scores, allowing the accrual of credit or placement at many participating higher education institutions.

AP Psychology Strategies

The AP Psychology exam is designed to challenge thinking. It is not enough to simply know the facts, however. Competent demonstration of higher-order thinking skills is needed to succeed. In regards to the multiple-choice section, more than simple recall or recognition of fact abilities are required; critical thinking and the ability to link knowledge of a term or concept to other terms or concepts are also needed.

Likewise, the free-response section is more complex than requiring a simple response, and it often demands the communication of understanding connections between concepts and theories by use of analytical and organizational skills. Students must be competent in analyzing, applying and evaluating information.

Both sections challenge students to apply what they have learned to novel situations or combine concepts in nontraditional ways. In preparing for the AP Psychology exam, a number of broad overarching strategies is should be used, such as:

- extensively reading the course textbook(s);

- attending all class sessions;

- possessing a working knowledge of the vocabulary, theories and key concepts of each of the major subfields within psychology;

- familiarity with many of the contributing psychologists and significant research studies (both historical and current) that have shaped our understanding of behavior and mental processes;

- confidence in applying psychological principles and understanding the connections between ideas and theories;

- appreciation of the scientific methods and ethical procedures that produce such knowledge; and

- commitment to least a few months of study time to prepare for the exam.

Multiple-Choice Questions Strategies

- Read all multiple-choice questions carefully. Be sure to do this before looking over the answer choices. It is important to understand exactly what the question is asking for.

- Rephrasing the question can help understand what the question is asking for if the meaning is not immediately apparent. If rephrasing is done, take care not to add extra meaning to the question; assume the existing question is direct and to the point.

- After an answer is selected, quickly return to the question to ensure the selected choice does, in fact, answer the question being asked. Make sure you marked the choice you intended to choose.

- Be aware of the section time limit and endeavor to spend under 42 seconds to answer each question. Devoting your allotted time first to those questions you are more knowledgeable on and confident in answering helps ensure that, if you run out of time, you run out of time on a question you are less confident in answering. Skip time-consuming questions and return to them later if possible.

- If the correct answer is not immediately clear, fall back as best as you can to the process of elimination. Be sure to look at all the possible answer choices before selecting one. Eliminate as many choices as possible. Usually, there is at least one answer choice that is easily identified as wrong. Eliminating even one choice will greatly increase your odds of selecting the correct one. After eliminating the most obvious incorrect choice(s), eliminate any answers that strike you as "almost right" or "half right." You should consider "half right" as synonymous with "wrong." These answer choices are purposely included to catch test takers off guard.

- Use guessing only as a last resort. Always remember that an unanswered question will be guaranteed to lower your score since the score is based only on the number of correct answers provided (incorrect and skipped questions are weighed the same). Therefore, leave nothing unanswered and guess where no other strategies are useful.

Free-Response Strategies

- As with the multiple-choice section, it is crucial to understand exactly what the question is asking; any mental rephrasing done should not result in adding meaning that was not there before. Assume the existing question, as it is written, is direct and to the point.

- It is important to know that this section does not always include a question on experimentation, so do not attempt to turn any question into one based on methodology and set up an experiment.

- You are not bound to answer the questions according to the order in which they are presented. Therefore, it is a good idea to read both questions first and quickly decide which of the two you are more comfortable answering; answer that question first. For example, if you immediately know how to write your response to the second question but not the first, by all means, skip to the second free-response question. This can help you avoid getting bogged down and frustrated, maximizing your time more efficiently.

- It is important to answer questions in their entirety, not just partially. For example, some questions may ask test takers to both identify and explain. Performing only one of these steps is inadequate and will be graded accordingly. A list of the possible actions questions required of test takers includes: *describe*, *discuss*, *explain*, *identify*, *relate* and *show*. It is good practice to underline these directives as you see them so that these expectations are not forgotten or overlooked as you proceed to write your responses.

- Any additional work that goes beyond the question's stated directives does not earn you a higher score or result in extra credit. Therefore, in the interest of time management and keeping the content of your response relevant, answer all questions in their entirety but avoid being tempted into going further.

- Before jumping immediately into writing mode, take a brief moment or two to brainstorm about the questions' topics. You are allowed to jot down notes or outline on scratch paper if this helps your composition process. This often aids in organizing thoughts, which typically leads to the production of a more organized and coherent answer. Key definitions, ideas, examples or names of significant individuals are more often than not useful details to note.

- Keep in mind that there are roughly 25 minutes provided for answering each of the free-response questions. Be sure to find your own balance between the time needed to brainstorm and the time needed to write the response.

- When entering the writing stage, understand a key issue: if the reader cannot read your writing, it cannot be scored. Make an effort to write legibly. If you tend to be a sloppy writer by nature or under pressure, it is a good idea to practice essay writing under a time limit with this in mind.

- A structured essay answer is needed, meaning it should contain complete sentences and paragraphs. Readers will not score answers that deviate from this structure (e.g., outlines, bullet points, etc.). It is also helpful to be aware that a formal introduction and conclusion are unnecessary (but not incorrect); instead, launch directly into answering the question.

- Write the sections of the essay in the order specified in the question. This guarantees a reader-friendly structure, which means they do not have to hunt around to ensure each criterion has been met.

- As you proceed, refer to the required tasks of the question and cross them off as you finish them. This will aid in keeping you on track and prevent leaving out needed components.

- Your written responses should include specific evidence and avoid unsubstantiated claims. Long, meandering responses filled with loosely-related facts regarding specific concepts of phenomena should be avoided. Likewise, contradictions, circular definitions, and question restatements should also be avoided.

- Only include information that is directly relevant and demonstrates the primary points of the argument being made. This information should be presented in a clear and concise manner.

- Terminology should be used correctly. Psychology language and concepts should be included.

- All claims should be directly stated. You do not want the graders to infer or guess how something demonstrates a point. Regardless of whether they correctly guess your intentions or not, you will likely be graded more critically for including ambiguities.

- As you proceed through the free-response section, if a mistake is accidentally made in the answer booklet, simply draw a line through the error (strikethrough) to remedy the issue. Readers will disregard any portion with a single line drawn through it.

- If both questions are completed with time remaining, use it to review each response. Assess if anything else is needed or if anything needs correction. If content needs to be added, draw an arrow off to the side of the page or insert an asterisk (*) and refer the reader to the end of the essay. Make sure to use all the time provided — these thoughtful last-minute revisions can earn crucial points.

Chapter 1

History and Approaches

Since its emergence in 1879, the field of psychology has undergone many changes in its progression to contemporary times. Theories and research methodologies have experienced significant revisions over the many decades. While some areas that are not officially contained in the discipline and originate from its "introspective" past can be labeled as "pseudoscience," real psychology should be recognized as true science because it adheres to rigorous methods employed in the investigation of phenomena as it endeavors to increase understanding of behavior and mental processes. Incorrect perceptions of the actual discipline often originate from the media, not the reality of the field. While being a science, researchers' individual perspectives can influence the approach employed and the resulting explanation of phenomena. Therefore, solid knowledge of major psychological approaches is critical for a comprehensive understanding of the discipline and future practice.

Notes

History of Psychology

Philosophers and scientists have been trying to understand the human mind since the beginning of times. Initially, it was believed that psychological problems were caused by evil spirits, and in 5,000 B.C., trephining (i.e., chipping holes in a patient's skull to allow the evil spirits to escape) was used as a means to treat these problems. As humans became more scientific, so did the understanding of psychological problems.

Perspectives that shaped the development of psychological thought

Science emerges from empiricism (i.e., knowledge coming through experience) and determinism (i.e., cause-and-effect relationships governing events), and while many sciences, including biology, physics, astronomy, and chemistry, developed during the 1600's, psychology developed much later. Early explanations for abnormal behavior often involved supernatural or religious reasoning. What made up the mind was often tied to the soul. While psychology today is empirical and deterministic, prior to the 1600's, psychology's focus was much more philosophical. Thus, while the other sciences really grew in the 1600's, psychology did not become a scientific discipline until the late 1800's.

Painting of a surgeon removing part of a skull (17th century)

Philosophical perspective

Philosophical influences in psychology date back to 430 B.C. when Hippocrates attempted to explain moods, emotions, and behaviors. He theorized that moods, emotions, and behaviors were caused by an excess or lack of body fluids, which he called the humours. Hippocrates believed that these humours were blood, yellow bile, black bile, and phlegm. This theory persisted for many years, though Galen, sometime in the second century A.D., expanded on this theory and allowed for "mixing" of the four humours, which could result in any of nine possible "temperaments." Galen also assigned a temperamental category to each humour: sanguine (blood), choleric (yellow bile), melancholic (black bile), and phlegmatic (phlegm).

Hippocrates, Greek physician

The sanguine temperament is associated with air and is thought to encompass people who are carefree, pleasure-seeking, talkative and sociable. People with this temperament make friends easily and struggle with being forgetful and seeing things all the way through. People with a choleric temperament tend to be excitable, restless and impulsive. This temperament is usually associated with fire. These individuals are known for getting things done efficiently, being strong-willed and good at planning. The melancholic temperament is associated with Earth and is believed to encompass the traits of cautiousness, introversion, and seriousness. People with this temperament are thought to be at risk for moodiness and depression and prefer to do things independently. Those with a phlegmatic temperament are calm, caring, tolerant and private. This temperament is usually associated with water. Individuals with this temperament are likely to be content with themselves, be consistent in habits and have faithful friends.

In the 1600's, Nicholas Culpeper wrote about the humours as governing principles in health that also had astrological correspondences. Culpeper believed that these had an influence on personality and that while some people had only one temperament, others had a mixture, with one temperament being primary and the other being secondary. Several others, including Alfred Adler, Erich Adickes, and Ernst Kretschmer, much later created theories based on four temperaments. These theories helped shape modern conceptions of temperament and personality.

Nicholas Culpeper, English physician

In 1637, René Descartes theorized that animal spirits, produced in the blood, are responsible for causing the body to move and behave. He postulated that the pineal gland was the seat of the soul and directed the animal spirits, as this was the place where all thoughts were formed. He believed that because infants were born with some innate abilities to move, some knowledge had to be inborn in humans. Descartes stated that nerves were hollow tubes filled with animal spirits, which flowed through the body and were responsible for all functioning, including memory and behavior. Descartes's descriptions of animal spirits are remarkably similar to the modern understanding of the nervous system.

Contrary to Descartes, in 1690, the English philosopher and physician John Locke proclaimed that infants are actually born as tabula rasa or "blank slates." He stated that experiences that children have determine the types of adults they become, with their thoughts, emotions, and abilities. Locke postulated that the sources of all ideas are sensations and reflections.

Psychological perspective

In the late 1800's, there was a great deal of research being conducted in laboratories that propelled psychology to becoming a scientific discipline. In the 1850's, Gustav Fechner began to examine sensation and perception, and founded psychophysics (the study of the link between the mental representation of the world and physical work). Fechner asked individuals to hold weights of different mass in each hand and then, while slowly adding equal weights to each hand, would ask individuals to identify which added weight they perceived as heavier. Surprisingly, individuals cited the weight added to the hand initially holding less weight as heavier. Fechner went so far as to develop an equation that calculated the perceived change. He also studied this perceived change phenomenon for loudness and brightness.

Charles Darwin influenced the field of psychology with his *theory of natural selection*. Darwin believed that behaviors, in addition to physical traits, were subject to genetic influence and thus natural selection. Sir Francis Galton, a cousin of Darwin, also believed that behaviors were subject to natural selection and heritability. He purported that genetics explained all the psychological differences among people. Galton began to measure these differences and noted that the closer the relative was to a person, the more similar the traits tended to be.

Galton concluded that the English government should encourage intelligent and/or talented individuals to have children, and people who did not possess these traits (e.g., criminals, those with mental disabilities) should be kept out of the English gene pool. Galton also contributed to what would become the field of psychology by pioneering the use of statistical methods to measure and study behavior. Some of these methods are still used in modern psychology.

Franz Joseph Gall, German Physician and Anatomist

The then growing field of medicine also influenced the development of the field of psychology. Franz Josef Gall created a map of the head, which he used to assign different characteristics such as intelligence, moral character, and other personality traits. In fact, he believed that the shape and bumps on the head were indicative of these characteristics. He referred to his technique as phrenology. While his theory has not withstood rigorous testing, it was important because it was the first theory to assert that different areas of the brain controlled different behaviors and traits, now known as brain localization.

Building on this, Paul Broca and Karl Wernicke, both physicians, identified areas in the brain that do control different areas of speech. Broca had a patient nicknamed Tan, so called because "tan" was the only word he could speak after suffering a stroke, though he could understand speech perfectly well. When Tan died, Broca performed an autopsy and discovered an area in the left side of the brain that was damaged; this area is now known as Broca's Area and is responsible for speech production. Similarly, Wernicke had a patient who had brain damage that resulted in his speaking in made-up or unusual words. When performing the autopsy, Wernicke found another area in the left brain that is responsible for speech comprehension. This area is now known as Wernicke's Area.

Finally, Franz Mesmer inadvertently introduced the concept of psychosomatic medicine. He believed that metallic fluids in the body were the cause of disease and insanity, and by using magnets, he could redirect these fluids. Mesmer also used trance-like states to treat his patients (these "trances" are now called hypnosis). The medical community at large rejected Mesmer's claims, concluding that it was the patients' belief in the treatment that actually caused them to get better; thus, psychosomatic medicine was born.

Notes

Theoretical Approaches in Explaining Behavior

As stated above, many scientists prior to the late 1800's had attempted to explain human behavior, whether philosophically or through actual experimentation. It was not called psychology because the field was not formed yet. However, all had important influences on the creation of the field of psychology and on the different approaches that were taken to explain behavior.

Structuralism, functionalism, and behaviorism in early years

In 1879, Wilhelm Wundt, a German physician, physiologist, and psychologist, established the first experimental laboratory devoted to psychological phenomena. Two years later, he founded the first academic journal in psychology. Wundt believed that the focus of psychology should be to discover the basic mental components of perception, consciousness, thinking, emotions and other mental states and activities. Wundt called his perspective on psychology *structuralism*, as he was primarily interested in the structure (or building blocks) of the mind. Wundt employed a technique known as introspection in his attempts to uncover the basic mental components of the mind. His introspection technique required a research participant to describe in detail what they had experienced when exposed to various stimuli. Wundt believed that these descriptions revealed the building blocks of the mind.

Wundt's structuralism was not without critics. Some scientists were opposed to the use of introspection, stating that it was not a scientific technique. Others noted that people have difficulty describing certain inner experiences. Thus, some of the building blocks might be left out or not accurately defined.

About four years after Wundt established his laboratory, G. Stanley Hall established the first psychological laboratory in the United States at Johns Hopkins University and founded the *American Journal of Psychology*. He was also the first president of the American Psychological Association.

Not far behind Wundt and Hall, William James established his laboratory at Harvard University. James's approach to psychology differed significantly from Wundt's approach. James believed the focus of psychology should be on how behavior functions in allowing people to adapt to their environment, rather than on the mind's structure. For example, James might have been interested in how fear prepares the mind to cope with emergency situations. His approach is referred to as *functionalism*. To study functionalism, James employed a technique called stream of consciousness, where individuals would express their thoughts and reactions to events. James, unlike Wundt, would examine these thoughts/reactions as a continuous flow, rather than breaking them down into fundamental pieces. Functionalism eventually replaced structuralism as the predominant way to think about the mind and behavior.

Wilhelm Wundt, German physician

However, during the first half of the 20th century, psychology in America was not dominated by functionalism, but rather a new approach called *behaviorism*. Behaviorism rejected the notion that the emphasis of psychology should be on the inner workings of the mind. Rather, it was believed that psychology should focus on observable behavior that could be measured objectively.

Edwin Twitmyer was the first to describe the process now known as *classical conditioning*. He set up experiments originally to study reflexes. In his studies, he had a machine that would ring a bell just before it tapped a research participant's patellar tendon (just below the kneecap), causing the individual's kicking reflex to engage. One day, the machine malfunctioned, and the bell rang, but there was no tap to the patellar tendon. Twitmyer observed that the participant's leg kicked anyway. Twitmyer presented his findings at the American Psychological Association Conference, but they received a lukewarm response, likely because they did not fit in with the existing work in psychology in the United States.

Around the same time Twitmyer was conducting his experiments, Ivan Pavlov conducted a series of experiments that revealed dogs could learn to anticipate food at the sound of a bell after the bell-ringing had been initially paired with food. He called this process classical conditioning and eventually won the Nobel Prize for his experiments.

Ivan Pavlov, Russian physiologist

In the United States, John B. Watson continued to emphasize that the focus of psychology should be on changes in the environment that produce observable behaviors. Watson believed that thoughts and other internal events were too subjective and had no place in the science of psychology. Not only were internal events too subjective, but according to Watson, all behavior could be explained through conditioning. Thus, internal events were unnecessary to the study of psychology.

In fact, Watson is famous for saying "give me a dozen healthy infants, well-formed, and my own specified world to bring them up in, and I'll guarantee to take anyone at random and train him to become any type of specialist I might select – doctor, lawyer, artist, merchant-chef and, yes, even a beggar-man and thief, regardless of talents, penchants, tendencies, abilities, vocations and race of his ancestors."

Watson's most famous experiment was with Little Albert, showing that fear could be a conditioned response. Later, Watson was employed in advertising, where he applied behaviorist principles. Today's advertising agencies still use techniques introduced by Watson.

B.F. Skinner, another American psychologist, also believed that only observable behaviors should be studied. Skinner devoted much of his career to studying animals and how they behaved in response to rewards and punishments. Skinner's work was primarily done with animals in boxes (now known as Skinner Boxes), where an animal would be rewarded for a particular response (e.g., pecking a lever in the case of pigeons) and receive nothing for giving undesired responses. Skinner would vary when the reward was given, so the animals could be observed to learn a pattern. Skinner's work led to the formation of the *principles of operant conditioning*. He believed that human behavior was much like animal behavior and is influenced by drives for rewards and motivation to avoid punishment.

Behaviorism was criticized for not allowing any room for free will. Psychologists who were opposed to behaviorism believed humans to be able to use free will and reasoning to make a decision that may be contrary to the innate drive for reward (or motivation to avoid punishment).

Later approaches

Early approaches to explaining behavior focused on using research methods of the existing sciences to understand behavior. Later approaches expanded on this and began using techniques unique to psychology to understand behavior. Further attempts were made to find new ways to explain and treat psychological disorders.

Psychoanalytic/Psychodynamic

The father of psychoanalytic theory, Sigmund Freud, believed that while the conscious mind (i.e., the part of the mind one is aware of) is important, the most important part of the human experience is what is happening in the unconscious mind (i.e., the part of the mind one is unaware of). Freud believed that within the unconscious mind were urges to fulfill sexual and aggressive impulses. He stated that these were usually from early childhood and not remembered by the conscious mind. However, these unfulfilled impulses could exert influence over the individual (e.g., causing an individual to feel depressed, restricting the use of a part of one's body). Freud believed that it was the job of the therapist to uncover these unconscious impulses in order to help the patient cope with them more effectively and eventually decrease the symptoms that were being experienced. Freud's work had little scientific backing, with most of his theory being based on his observations and musings.

A group of psychologists (many of whom were trained by Freud) continued to build on his theory and are collectively known as "Neo-Freudians." The Neo-Freudians helped to shape psychodynamic theory as it is known today. The Neo-Freudians disagreed with Freud's assertion that childhood events determined adult personality and paid greater attention to social factors and the effects of society on personality development.

Carl Jung, a student of Freud's, rejected Freud's view that the unconscious sexual urges were the most important aspect of psychology. Jung instead believed that humans have a collective unconscious, a common set of images, feelings, and ideas inherited from ancestors, and a personal unconscious, which are the experiences, ideas and feelings unique to the individual. Jung believed that the human species have archetypes (universal symbols) that exist in their collective unconscious. He cited art, literature, and religion as evidence of this. For example, the mother archetype can be found in all religions, in many examples of art from all over the world and in many different types of literature. However, there is little evidence to suggest that the collective unconscious actually exists.

Karen Horney is regarded as the first feminist psychologist. She outright rejected several of Freud's notions, including that women have penis envy. She asserted that instead of being envious of the male anatomy, women were envious of the independence, status, and freedom they were often denied. Horney believed that the most important thing in the development of the personality was social relationships. In particular, she believed that the relationship the child has with his/her parents was incredibly important to the development of the personality.

Karen Horney, feminist psychologist

Alfred Adler moved even further from Freud's theory and asserted that humans are primarily motivated by striving for superiority. Adler believed that all humans sought out self-improvement and perfection. Further, because humans are social beings, he thought they were motivated by social interest and desire to improve others. Adler stated that when an adult has not been able to overcome feelings of inferiority developed as a child, that adult has an inferiority complex. He stated that the inferiority complex should be the focus of psychotherapy.

Finally, Erik Erikson believed that the personality continues to develop over one's lifespan. This is radically different from Freud, who believed that the personality is developed by the end of childhood. Erikson proposed a developmental model where the individual has a particular crisis to overcome at each phase in life. Erickson stated it was the outcome of each crisis that determined personality.

Humanistic

Until the 1950's, the view of humans was that there was no free will. Behaviorism posited that humans were a product of classical and operant conditioning, and psychoanalysis had claimed that unconscious urges were responsible for behavior and symptoms. In response to these perspectives, humanistic psychology was created. Two of the major founders, Carl Rogers, and Abraham Maslow, believed that humans did have free will, and rather than the focus being placed on what is wrong with humans (as in psychoanalysis), the focus should be on people striving to be the best they can be. Humanists believed that humans are innately good and strive to lead productive and fulfilling lives. In treatment, Rogers and Maslow both focused on helping individuals grow to their full potential.

Maslow postulated that humans have needs that can be arranged in a hierarchy, with the primary motivation of humans being to strive to become better, to move up the hierarchy. Maslow arranged his hierarchy into a pyramid now known as Maslow's Hierarchy of Needs. Maslow noted that basic needs, such as food, clothing, and shelter needed to be satisfied before the individual could move up to the next level. At the top of Maslow's hierarchy is self-actualization. Maslow stated that all humans strive for this, though few will reach it. Self-actualization is a state where people are fulfilled and have reached their highest potential. Maslow stated that this was unique to every individual.

Rogers, on the other hand, focused on what he called the self and the ideal self. Rogers believed that a person's self-concept (i.e., the perception of who one is) comes from his or her interactions with others. This self-concept also encompasses who one thinks they are (i.e., the self) and who one wishes they were (i.e., the ideal self).

Rogers posited when there is a gap between the self and the ideal self, individuals may demonstrate psychological issues, such as depression. He stated that humans are born with a need for acceptance, sympathy, and love from others, which he referred to as a need for positive regard. Rogers stated that it was the job of the therapist to provide unconditional positive regard to patients who are trying to overcome the gap between the self and their ideal self.

Sociocultural

In the early 1900's, there was an interest in how people influence the behavior of others. Specifically, Norman Triplett focused his research (1898) on social influences and conducted one of the first formal experiments in this area. He found that individuals ride bicycles faster in the presence of others as compared to when they are alone. This work, while published, did not gain much popularity until the 1940's.

Norman Triplett, American psychologist

However, in the 1940's Triplett's research gained traction when research on social influences boomed, with psychologists collaborating with sociologists. This research focused mainly on trying to understand how normal people could become horrific prison camp guards (e.g., in Nazi-controlled Germany), and how propaganda influences people (both were major concerns during World War II). From this collaboration, the field of social and personality psychology was born.

Kurt Lewin is frequently cited as the founder of modern social psychology. His primary research focus was on race relations in the United States. Through his research, he discovered that behavior is a function of the individual and the environment. In other words, Lewin found that because of the differences between individuals and situations, one can expect different behaviors. For example, if a person is typically talkative and outgoing, how might that person act at a wedding? And might that person react differently at a funeral? The answer is likely to be yes, showing that not only are individual personality traits important, but also the situation and the expected behavior.

Contemporary approaches

Contemporary approaches to psychology recognize that there is likely not one reason or explanation for behavior, but that it is likely best explained by a combination of factors. There is greater recognition for how psychology overlaps with the other sciences (e.g., biology) and recognition of the many different things can be meant when one says they study "psychology."

Evolutionary

As biology has gained a greater understanding of genetics and genetic influences on health, illness, traits, etc., psychologists have begun to look for genetic explanations for behavior and personality. Evolutionary psychologists seek to find how behavior is influenced by genetic inheritance. For example, one explanation for why humans sleep at night instead of during the day is because their eyes do not see well in the dark. By being inactive and lying still during the night, humans had a greater chance of survival. If they were up wandering around at night, they may step off the edge of a cliff or get devoured by a predator.

Biological

Advances in biology and neurology have allowed for a more biological perspective in psychology. In clinical neuropsychology and behavioral neuroscience, there is an emphasis placed on the biological factors that cause psychological disorders and/or determine behavior. For example, it is known that there are structural changes in the brain in patients with schizophrenia (e.g., increased ventricle size). A clinical neuropsychologist is interested in studying how these structural changes contribute to the symptoms of the disorder. A behavioral neuroscientist may be interested in how emotions are related to physical sensations in healthy individuals and/or individuals with a disorder.

Cognitive

As stated previously, behaviorism was the predominant approach during the first half of the 20th century in the United States. However, psychologists in Europe, focused on thought and thought processes, created the field of cognitive psychology. Hermann Ebbinghaus is credited as completing the first studies focusing on memory. Using himself as his research subject, he memorized lists of made-up words and then tried to recall the lists at different times. Ebbinghaus plotted his results in what he called "forgetting curves." These forgetting curves showed that most of what is learned is forgotten quickly, but then forgetting slows and whatever information remains is retained.

Hermann Ebbinghaus, German psychologist

Biopsychosocial

The biopsychosocial approach is perhaps the newest approach in psychology. Psychologists who ascribe to this model place an equal emphasis on the biological, psychological and sociocultural factors that influence health and illness. The biological factors can include brain structure, hormones, and drug effects. The psychological considerations are thought processes, emotions, personality, and experiences. Sociocultural factors include gender, ethnicity, family, peers, one's culture, etc. For example, when considering the causes of depression, one might consider family history, neurotransmitters and any history of brain injury, which are all biological explanations of depression.

For psychological explanations of depression, it would be important to consider what a person is telling themselves (e.g., "I am worthless"). Sociocultural factors to be considered in depression include family support, personality characteristics, and recent bereavement. All three of these categories of factors could be contributing to symptoms of depression for an individual.

Subfields in Psychology

The subfields in psychology are defined by the questions they seek to answer about behavior.

Biological

Individuals who work in biological psychology seek to find connections between biological factors (e.g., brain structure, hormone levels, neurotransmitters) and behaviors and/or illness behaviors. These psychologists often receive advanced training in neuroscience and biology to help them understand these factors and their interactions with behavior.

Clinical

Clinical psychologists are interested in the diagnosis and treatment of psychological disorders. Some clinical psychologists opt to study psychological disorders either in addition to or in lieu of actually treating psychological disorders.

Cognitive

The subfield of cognitive psychology is concerned with higher mental processes. These individuals study processes such as memory, reasoning, decision making, thinking, language and problem-solving.

Counseling

Counseling psychologists, similar to clinical psychologists, can provide treatment. However, these psychologists tend to focus more on educational, social and career adjustment problems, rather than psychological disorders.

Educational

Educational psychology is devoted to the study of human learning. Within this field, how humans learn, retain information and the role that individual differences play are studied.

Developmental

The subfield of developmental psychology focuses on how humans grow and change from conception to death. Areas of growth and change that are studied include thought processes, physical development, morality development, sense of self and emotions.

Experimental

Experimental psychology examines several processes including sensation and perception, learning, thinking, and memory. Research in this subfield may be done with humans or animals.

Human factors

Human factors psychology focuses on applying psychology principles to work environments. Topics such as ergonomics, safety, product design, and human-computer interaction are considered by human factors psychology. Goals tend to be to increase efficiency and safety in work environments.

Industrial–organizational

Individuals in the industrial-organizational psychology subfield focus on human behavior in the workplace. Industrial-organizational psychologists are often hired by companies to apply psychological theories to workplace situations to increase productivity, employee satisfaction, safety, and well-being.

Personality

Personality psychology seeks to examine the consistency in human behavior over time. This subfield also examines the traits and characteristics that differentiate one person from another.

Psychometric

The subfield concerned with psychometrics is concerned with psychological measurement including theory and technique.

Social

Social psychology seeks to understand how people's behaviors, thoughts, and feelings are affected by others. The "others" may actually be present, imagined to be present, or implied to be present.

Notes

Chapter 2

Research Methods

Psychology should be regarded as an empirical discipline since knowledge is developed through conducting research. Moreover, the specific phenomenon being investigated determines the research method used by psychologists. Experimental and correlational research approaches, as well as surveys, naturalistic observations and case studies, each bring their own advantages and disadvantages in relation to the context. Control of variables is important throughout this process. Regardless of the chosen research method, a number of ethical guidelines govern their design and professional psychologists must adhere to these guidelines when they design their research. Reasonable conclusions are derived through proper and quality research design, which establishes validity. Experiments are often utilized for ascertaining phenomenon causes and effect. The resulting data provides the grounds for theory development, which can then be used in the treatment of mental and behavioral problems. This data can be interpreted using both descriptive and/or inferential statistics; understanding how, why and to what effect is critical.

Notes

Types of Research

Psychological research is used to better understand the behavior of humans and animals. Psychology is a science, and therefore, research in psychology follows the scientific method and uses both quantitative (nomothetic approach) and qualitative methods (idiographic approach) to generate and evaluate hypotheses about human behavior and cognition. All branches of psychology can have a research component to them. Research psychology is contrasted with applied psychology. Psychology draws on scientific knowledge from other fields to help explain and understand psychological phenomena.

While both qualitative and quantitative methods are used, there are differences between the data that are obtained by these two methods. *Qualitative research* requires a broad spectrum of observational methods, including exploratory statistics, structured interviews, and participant observation to enable the gathering of rich information unattainable by classical experimentation.

For example, if a researcher wishes to better understand what students' level of satisfaction is with their teachers, they may ask students an open-ended question like "What do you like and what do you dislike about Mr. Smith's teaching style?" Needless to say, this researcher will likely receive a vast array of answers in the form of words or sentences. The researcher will then work to categorize students' answers into subgroups or themes. These themes help researchers understand which areas emerge more often. This information can be used to increase student retention and satisfaction, provide information to teachers about their areas of strength and weakness and perhaps used by the administration in making promotion decisions.

Unlike qualitative research, *quantitative research* involves using numbers to describe the data received. A researcher might be interested in knowing how many hours adolescents spend watching television each day. Thus, he might go to a local high school and ask each student enrolled to provide a response to the question: "How many hours per day do you watch television?" However, instead of providing students with an open-ended question to which they can say anything, he provides them with the following options: 1 hour, 2 hours, 3 hours, 4 hours, or 5 or more hours per day. Each student will select only one of these responses, thus allowing researchers to know the exact number of each student's television-viewing habits. Quantitative research provides numbers that can be analyzed. Researchers might want to know demographic information, such as how many members are in the family, their ages or how many pets they have.

Different research methods have been developed in psychology to address the need for asking different types of questions regarding human cognition, behaviors, and emotions. There are four main types of research designs in psychology: experiments, correlational studies, survey research, and clinical research. Each of these four research designs has its advantages and limitations, which is why it is not uncommon in the field to use a mixed research design when testing complex hypotheses and developing theories. One may wonder how to choose the appropriate design. Skilled researchers will first develop their hypothesis and then let their question dictate and inform the most appropriate research design, depending on the goal of the question. Each subsection below provides an overview of the strengths, weaknesses, and purpose of the design. An example of each design is provided. It is important to point out that each of these studies has the potential to contribute to the understanding of psychological phenomena.

Experiments

Experiments are the most favored form of design in contemporary research. Experiments are unique in that they provide the only research design where one of the variables is controlled or manipulated in order to observe an outcome on another variable. Therefore, this type of design can establish a cause and effect relationship between two variables. For example, a researcher might want to know whether playing violent video games causes aggression in children. In order to understand causation, researchers must create or manipulate the conditions that they want to study in two or more groups of people and then measure their outcome of interest. The example below will be used to discuss an experimental design in more detail.

Example: Dr. Smith wants to know whether video games cause aggression in children. Thus, he chooses two video games (Hitman and Call of Duty). He recruits children ages ten through twelve to participate in his study, and ninety people sign up for his study. As each person signs up, they are randomly assigned to one of three conditions: A) the Hitman condition, B) the Call of Duty condition, or C) a control condition with children playing a non-violent video game called Tetris. After having each child play three hours of Hitman, Call of Duty, or Tetris, the researcher will give each child a measure he developed called the Video Aggression in Children Inventory. This inventory will rate on a scale of 1-5 how much aggression a child shows. The researcher will further obtain child and parent-report data regarding the number of violent acts (e.g., hitting, kicking, biting or other acts in which the child intentionally causes pain to another person) the child engages in throughout the week after playing the video games.

The above example portrays an experiment that includes several elements essential to experimental research. The first is *random assignment* to conditions. This means that Dr. Smith cannot simply choose who he wants to place in each condition. The random assignment refers to the fact that Dr. Smith must randomly designate each child into condition A, B, or C. Subjects in an experiment are randomly assigned to either the experimental (sample group) or the control group (comparison group). The sample group must be representative of the target population, or the group of people (or animals) to which scientists want to be able to generalize their study findings.

It is extremely important that subjects are randomly assigned to different experimental conditions because Dr. Smith wants to make sure there is no difference between the people in the different conditions. This is of utmost importance because if the independent variable in the experiment has an effect on the dependent variable, one cannot assume that it is because the people in the conditions were different.

Researchers can do this through several methods, such as randomization tables or pulling choices out of a hat. Basically, each participant has to have an equal chance of being put into any of the three conditions. The reason for this is to make all conditions as equitable as possible, and to eliminate differences that might occur if the assignment was not random (e.g., children who usually play video games could group together in the same condition, the researcher could divide them by age and fail to account for age differences in aggression related to video gaming, etc.).

In the design above, there are several variables that are important to point out. A *variable* is a factor or a set of related events that can have one or several levels. For example, if education is the variable, levels can be divided by the type of degree obtained (i.e., high school, bachelor's, master's, doctorate) or video game types (excessive violence, some violence or non-violent). There are a few types of specific variables that are important in understanding experimental designs—independent variables, dependent variables, and confounding variables.

The first is called the *independent variable* (IV). The independent variable is the variable that the researcher manipulates. In the above example, it is the video game condition (either A for Hitman, B for Call of Duty, or C for the non-violent Tetris control group). The *dependent variable* (DV) is the outcome measure, or what needs to be measured. In this example, it is the level of aggression that the child displays, which is measured in three ways: 1) through the use of the Video Aggression in Children Inventory, 2) child-report data on the number of violent acts in the following week, and 3) parent-report data on the number of violent acts the child engaged in the subsequent week after viewing the video games.

Another essential variable to consider is *confounding variables.* When a variable is confounded, the variable becomes linked to something else and therefore one cannot propose an association between the IV and the DV because one does not know if the IV (or whatever other factors confounding the IV) had an effect on the DV. Confounding variables can be at least partially prevented from entering the experimental design by appropriately assigning participants randomly (with a method representing the flip of a coin). If this is accomplished, experiments are the best method to predict cause-effect relationships.

Mainly, confounding variables are characteristics or other things that might cause differences between the two groups. These should always be minimized if they can be foreseen. What confounding variables can be identified in the example? One example of a confounding variable might be how and where the children were recruited. If the researcher recruits primarily from video game stores or school gaming clubs, he might get a larger sample of children who play video games frequently than occurs in the natural population. This might lead to an elevated estimate of aggression. Other confounding variables may include experimenter bias (which occurs when researchers unintentionally affect the outcome of their research) or participant bias.

Limitations of experimental designs

Although experiments provide precision and a controlled environment, experiments sometimes lack *ecological validity,* or the extent to which the experiment represents realistically how humans behave in natural settings. Another limitation is that some human conditions, such as experiencing physical violence trauma, cannot be simulated or studied under an experimental design because they are detrimental to the participants and unethical. Furthermore, it is unknown whether manipulations set up in a laboratory setting will generalize to real-world situations. Lastly, confounding variables may prohibit valid conclusions from the data. Therefore, it is imperative that researchers think about potential confounds prior to commencing any type of research study.

Strengths of Experimental designs

Experimental designs are the only kind that enable scientists to examine a cause and effect relationship between two or more variables. Researchers can control variables of their choice and examine the outcome.

Quasi-Experimental Design

A quasi-experimental design is like an experiment, except in this type of design at least one of the components of a true experiment is missing (i.e., random selection, random assignment, controlled IV). An example of quasi-experiments can be seen in psychological studies studying peer-interactions within daycares or violence inside prisons; in these cases, human behavior is being studied in natural settings providing more ecological validity but less internal validity.

Correlational studies

Correlational studies examine the association between two variables that cannot be controlled experimentally. In other words, there is no manipulation of any of the variables being studied. However, researchers can describe the relationship among variables, use this data to make predictions and examine or create hypotheses. Causal relationships are very difficult to prove using a correlational design because researchers cannot control the independent variable.

An example of a correlational study would be trying to find if there is an association between caffeine intake in the morning and reported higher levels of focus in a sample of college students. In this case, since the amount of caffeine intake by each student is not controlled, one would only be able to report an association, or tentative relation, between levels of alertness and caffeine intake, and not a cause-and-effect relation. Similar to true experiments, random selection and sampling of participants also take place in correlational studies.

Example: A researcher wants to know whether a person's weight is related to their height. He cannot randomly assign people to weigh a certain amount, so he chooses a correlational design. He randomly selects 100 people to participate and asks them each to report their weight and height. He then examines the data and discovers that there is a systematic relationship between the two variables, namely that people who weigh more tend to be taller.

An example of a correlational study would be trying to find if there is an association between caffeine intake in the morning and reported higher levels of focus in a sample of college students.

Limitations of Correlational Designs

This type of design cannot be used to determine causality, and therefore can only provide insight into the magnitude and types of relationships that exist. In addition, there is also the possibility that some other random variable caused the relationship since the experimenter is unable to control all variables.

Strengths of Correlational Designs

They can be used to describe relationships as they occur in daily life and can be used to predict future events or behavior.

Survey research

Survey research includes obtaining information from subjects through self-report questionnaires or interviews. Self-reports usually intend to assess beliefs, feelings, values, attitudes. There are many kinds of survey methods used in the field of psychology. One of the most common types of methods involves using the 5-point Likert Scale, where respondents rate their answers from 1 to 5, with 1 usually being the weakest, and 5 being the strongest level of agreement or disagreement with a particular statement.

The next most common method is using a true/false response paradigm. Finally, survey methods also include focus groups and qualitative interviews, where the researchers ask open-ended questions, trying to get as much information from the participants about a specific topic as possible.

Example: One of the most widely known examples of survey research is the U.S. Census. This survey occurs every ten years and attempts to describe various demographics of the entire American population. Researchers will ask questions such as age, family size, what type of job one does, how much they earn and where they live. This data is then used to help policymakers allocate funding and resources. An example that is more psychology-related may be when a clinical psychologist wants to know how many immigrants suffer from PTSD (post-traumatic stress disorder). Since she knows that many countries have underdeveloped mental health care systems, she develops a questionnaire to give to newly arrived immigrants asking about any symptoms of PTSD. Her questionnaire asks questions such as whether they experienced or witnessed any traumatic event, whether they have unwanted flashbacks or recollections of the event, and so forth. Then she determines whether their symptoms meet the criteria for PTSD based on the current Diagnostic and Statistical Manual-5th edition.

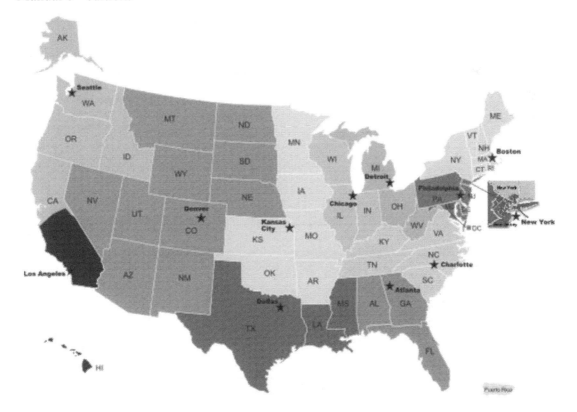

U.S. Census Bureau Regions

Limitations of Survey Research

Survey designs allow for quick polling of various individuals. However, this may lead to sampling errors, such as oversampling of a certain age group or ethnicity, which may influence the results that are obtained. Another issue is that questions may be misunderstood, and participants may guess at the answer. Furthermore, participants' response bias (answering in a certain way, hoping to please the researcher) may influence the results. Sometimes people may be in a hurry and answer the questions without reading all the choices or the entire question. An example of this is when participants consistently pick the middle option, regardless of the question.

Strengths of Survey Research

Survey research allows psychologists to gather vast amounts of descriptive information both quickly and inexpensively. They may telephone or hand out questionnaires, which helps keep costs down.

Clinical research

Clinical research is used to assist in determining the effectiveness and safety of different types of treatment or medications intended to be used with humans. It can be used to examine which components of a treatment work best for which client. The basic premise is that a proposed treatment, whether intended to prevent a disease or to treat a disorder, has to assist in decreasing the symptoms the person describes. Clinical research differs from clinical practice in that not all treatments are yet established. Through clinical research, experimenters are able to compare new treatments to established ones in order to examine feasibility and effectiveness. Clinical research is most frequently carried out in large medical schools or hospitals.

Statistics

After collecting data using one of the above methods, it is important for researchers to describe and make inferences about what that data means. This is done through the use of descriptive and inferential statistics. Descriptive statistics are used to describe the data that was obtained. Inferential statistics, on the other hand, are mathematical procedures that are employed to assist psychologists in making inferences regarding the meaning of the data.

Descriptive

While statistics may seem intimidating at first, descriptive statistics are quite basic and are easy to understand. There are three main descriptive statistics that students should familiarize themselves with: measures of central tendency, measures of variability and correlation coefficients.

The three measures of *central tendency* are the mean, the median, and the mode. These are used to describe the one score that is most representative of the entire group of numbers. As an example, one asks four friends how long they studied for a statistics exam; their responses in hours are: 1, 3, 3, 5.

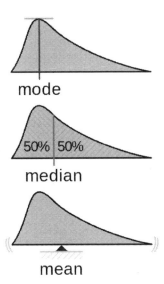

The *mean* of a group of numbers refers simply to the mathematical *average*. It is calculated by summing all the scores in the distribution and then dividing by the total number of scores. In this example, adding $1 + 3 + 3 + 5 = 12$. Then, 12 is divided by 4 since there are four numbers in the sample. Thus, this sample has a mean of 3.

The mean of the sample is typically denoted by the letter *M*. The mean has several characteristics that should be noted. First, since the mean includes all scores in a distribution, changing one number will result in a change in the mean. This can result from adding or taking away a score. Furthermore, if a constant value is added or subtracted to each score in the distribution, the same constant must be added or subtracted from the mean. Similarly, if one multiplies or divides the scores by a constant value, the mean will also change in the same way. These rules may be useful if one needs to change the units of measurement (e.g., changing from how many hours students spent studying to how many minutes they spent).

The *median* is the score that is exactly in the middle of the distribution; in fact, it divides the distribution equally so that 50% of subjects have scores at or below the median. Another way to think of the median is that it finds the midpoint of a group of scores and divides the group into two groups of the same size. In order to find the midpoint in a sample with odd numbers, arrange the sample in ascending order (i.e., 1, 2, 3, 4, 5). In this example, 3 is the median because 1 and 2 are below it and 4 and 5 are above it. But what if the sample is even? In that case, still list the numbers in ascending order (i.e., 1, 3, 3, 5), then take the middle two numbers and divide them by 2 (3+3/2 = 3). Thus, 3 is the median.

The median offers several advantages over the mean. First, if the distribution has an extreme score or a skewed distribution, the median should be used because the mean is susceptible to changes in one score. For example, if five people are asked their average salary and one person is a billionaire, his answer is considered an extreme score and would skew the distribution away from what the other four people earn. But if one uses the median, they will find the middle number to represent the group, so this outlier will not affect the representation of the distribution. Furthermore, if an ordinal scale was used, then the median is always preferable to the mean.

The *mode* refers to the score in the distribution that occurs most frequently. In the previous example (1, 3, 3, 5), the number 3 is the score that occurs most frequently. Thus, 3 would also be the mode. Distributions can have one, two or even more modes. Suppose everyone in class was asked what their favorite color is, and the results were: 10 blue, 10 green, 9 pink, 8 orange, 5 red. The data would have a bimodal distribution because both blue and green occur the most often. The mode can be used to report the findings from data that was collected using a nominal scale (i.e., favorite restaurants, major in college, etc.).

Means and medians can be shown on a line graph, bar graph or histogram, depending on the scale of measurement.

Measures of variability include the range, the interquartile range and the standard deviation of a group of numbers. These measures of variability are used to describe how close together or how far apart scores are in a distribution. If all scores in a data set were exactly the same, there would be no variability. However, it is uncommon to have no differences in the data researchers obtain. Some phenomena will have little variability (i.e., the number of hands each person has), while others will vary greatly (i.e., response time in answering test questions). Variability serves two main purposes: to describe the variability or differences of the distribution and secondly to explain the degree to which an individual's score is representative of the entire distribution.

Range refers to the difference between the highest and lowest scores in the data set. For example, if someone asked everyone in a room to report their ages, they would simply subtract the youngest person's age from the oldest person's age. That would be the range of the data. While the range is likely the easiest way to describe how spread out the scores in a distribution are, it fails to account for all the numbers in the middle. Imagine that the room chosen to poll was at a birthday party for a grandmother, who just turned 100 years old. Also present is the niece, who just turned one and is the youngest member at the party. The range would be 100-1, which equals 99; this does not inform on the average age of people at the party. Rather, it uses the two extreme scores of the youngest and oldest person and ignores all the other scores. This is especially problematic when there are outliers in a distribution, as it often does not accurately describe the variability. Thus, the range is also the most unreliable way to measure variability since it relies solely on two extreme scores.

The *interquartile range*, unlike the range, ignores extreme scores and focuses solely on the range covered by the middle 50% of the distribution. The following list of numbers corresponds with the number of jeans each person in a class owns: 1, 2, 3, 4, 5, 6, 7, 8. In order to locate the interquartile range, one must first identify the boundary at which 25% of the scores fall below and label that Q1 (or quartile 1). The line would be drawn in between the 2 and the 3. Next, the boundary at which 25% of the numbers fall above would be identified and labeled Q3 (or quartile 3). The line would be drawn in between 6 and 7. Thus, the middle 50% would fall between 3 and 6. The simplest way to calculate the interquartile range is to draw a type of graph called a histogram, which is basically made up of boxes depicting each score on a number line.

Standard deviation (SD) is a widely used measure of the variability or dispersion. It shows how much variation there is from the "average" (mean). The practical value of understanding the standard deviation for a set of values is in appreciating how much variation there is from the "average" (mean). In general terms, the standard deviation tells a researcher how far from the mean the data points tend to be. A low standard deviation indicates that the data points tend to be very close to the mean, whereas high standard deviation indicates that the data are spread out over a large range of values.

The standard deviation of a statistical population (complete population), a data set, or a probability distribution is the square root of its variance:

$$\sigma = \sqrt{\frac{(x_1 - \mu)^2 + (x_2 - \mu)^2 + \cdots + (x_N - \mu)^2}{N}}$$

where σ is the standard deviation, $x_1, x_2, \ldots, x_N$ are values from a finite data set, μ is mean and N is number of values in the data set.

Sample standard deviation is used when the data is obtained by random sampling from some parent population and the denominator is reduced by one:

$$s = \sqrt{\frac{\sum_{i=1}^{N} (x_i - \overline{x})^2}{N - 1}}$$

where *s* is the sample standard deviation, $\{x_1, x_2, \ldots, x_N\}$ are the observed values of the sample, $\overline{x}$ is the mean value of these observations, and *N* is the number of observations in the sample. Standard deviation has the same units as the data points.

For example, the average height of adult males in the US is about 70 inches, with a standard deviation of around 3 inches. This means that most men (about 68% percent, assuming a normal distribution) have a height within 3 inches of the mean, or between 67 and 73 inches (i.e., one standard deviation above and below the mean) and almost all men (about 95%) have a height within 6 inches of the mean or between 64 and 76 inches (2 standard deviations). Three standard deviations account for 99% of the sample population being studied, assuming a normal distribution (bell-shaped curve). If the standard deviation was zero, then all men would be exactly 70 inches tall. If the standard deviation was as large as 10 inches, then men would have much more variable heights, with a typical range of about 60 to 80 inches within one standard deviation.

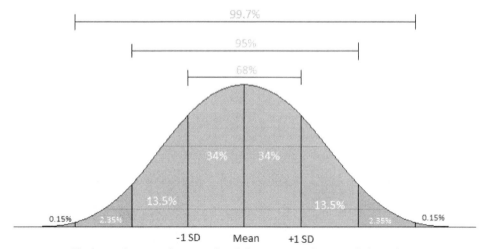

Bell-shaped curve for standard deviation of normal distribution

Correlation coefficients refer to the co-relationship between two variables. This helps to understand how strongly variables are related to each other. A positive correlation can mean either that the variables both increase or decrease together simultaneously. A negative correlation, on the contrary, means that one variable decreases while the other one increases. Correlation coefficients are used to measure the relationship between the two variables and can range from +1.00 to –1.00. The positive and negative signs indicate whether there is a positive or negative correlation. The actual number shows the strength of the correlation.

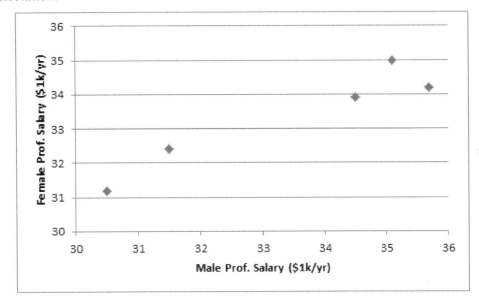

Scatter plot showing strong positive correlation

A weak correlation of +.03 might be obtained if comparing people's height with their IQ score, as these two variables are not related. However, a much stronger correlation of about +.83 would occur if one looked at the relationship between height and weight. This is because as people's height increases, they tend to weigh more. It is rare in psychology to have a perfect +1.00 or –1.00 correlation, the strongest possible correlation.

Additionally, just because a strong correlation predicts how one variable will function, correlation does *not* imply causation. One variable may not be causing the change in the other, and it is important to remember that correlations cannot be used to imply causation. Typically, scatter plots are used to represent the relationship between the two variables.

Inferential

Inferential statistics are used to assist researchers in applying information gathered from samples to entire populations. Since it is typically impractical (i.e., too costly, too time-consuming) to sample an entire population, researchers rely on samples to answer their questions. If, for example, a researcher is trying to determine if a new anxiety treatment works, he/she would select a sample from the population and administer the new treatment to the sample. To find out if the treatment works, he/she must somehow compare the level of anxiety in the treated sample to the level of anxiety in the whole population. He/she must determine whether there is a noticeable difference between the two groups.

One way researchers examine differences between populations and samples is through the use of a statistic called a z-score. An individual whose z-score falls around 0 (or population mean) is fairly representative of the population. An individual who scores in the extreme regions (+2.00 or −2.00) is statistically different from the rest of the population. These types of statistics are used in the assessment and reporting of intelligence. A person's overall score means very little until it is compared with the mean of the population.

Ethics in Research

Ethics in psychological research cover a broad array of topics. First, it is the assurance of the ethical treatment of human beings and animals who participate in psychological research studies. Secondly, it ensures the accurate and fair conducting of research and reporting of research findings. Since ethics generally rely on values and morals, as opposed to facts, it can be difficult to differentiate right from wrong. In other words, there is a large gray area in what is considered ethical and unethical. In order to account for this, a number of ethical issues, guidelines, and practices were developed to help guide psychologists in understanding ethical versus unethical research.

Ethical issues that inform and constrain research practices

A number of ethical issues inform and constrain research practices. These include informed consent, respect for privacy, the storage and collection of confidential data, the training of the research team and the correct and accurate reporting of results. As discussed below in more detail, it is imperative that informed consent is provided to research participants. This enables them to understand the risks and benefits of a project and decide whether they would like to be involved.

Informed consent must be written in such a way that the procedures and involvement of the individual are clear and understandable. Any questions the participant has should be addressed at that time. It is important to understand that there is a power difference between the research subjects and researchers. This is especially true in the case of underrepresented groups, such as those whose native language is not English, children, or minorities.

It is important to maintain awareness of how the data is collected and stored. Psychologists must agree to maintain confidentiality and use extreme precautions when storing personal and sensitive data. This may mean de-identifying information so that if the data were stolen, no identifiable information would be available. Often, researchers use a code or a number instead of a person's name to decrease the likelihood of identification. Researchers are also required to train their research team to maintain high ethical standards. This may include training programs through university institutional review boards (IRB) or through online programs.

Ethical and legal guidelines

Ethical guidelines are provided by a number of psychological organizations, the federal government, and local and institutional review boards. These guidelines became necessary after the unfair treatment of human beings was discovered. In such instances, humans were subjected to take part in risky medical or psychological studies without their consent or understanding of the study. For example, during World War II, the Nazis forced prisoners to take part in medical experiments that they conducted.

APA Guidelines on Research with Humans

The American Psychological Association (APA) put out a lengthy document that describes a psychologist's role in protecting the welfare of human and animal subjects. The first portion, called General Principles, calls upon researchers to both respect and protect the civil and human rights of individuals. As such, they are required to obtain approval for the research prior to commencing studies, and they must agree to conduct their research study without varying from the approved research protocol. This means that they must not add in other aspects or change their methods without first obtaining approval to do so. This ensures that there is oversight in the research and that the researcher cannot make a unilateral decision as to what is ethical.

Another major portion of the document discusses the importance of providing informed consent to research participants. Researchers are required to inform prospective participants about the purpose of the research study, how long the study will last and what the procedures will entail. At the same time, they must inform the participant that they have the right to refuse participation, to decline any portion of the study, or to withdrawal from the study after it has begun. Researchers must indicate whether they foresee anything that may influence a participant's willingness to be in the study (i.e., discomfort from a medical procedure, potential loss of confidentiality, feeling uncomfortable due to the nature of questions asked, etc.).

Also included in the informed consent are any potential benefits and risks. Lastly, participants are provided with the contact information for whom to contact with questions about their involvement or rights. Informed consent must always be obtained prior to beginning research, unless the study involves only observation in public places or the use of archival data, which will not lead to the identification or harm of individuals. Psychologists are permitted to compensate research participants for their time and travel but must avoid excessive financial or material inducements so that they avoid coercion of subjects.

Researchers are required to inform prospective participants about the purpose of the research study, how long the study will last and what the procedures will entail.

APA guidelines also discuss the role of deception in research. In general, researchers should avoid the use of deception if there is another method to answer their question. However, if psychologists have determined that non-deceptive procedures are not available, they may use deception if there is a significant scientific or educational value that can be gained from their study. Yet, regardless of the importance, psychologists are not allowed to deceive subjects regarding research topics that may cause physical pain or high levels of emotional distress. After a study in which deception was used, researchers are required to inform participants that deception was used and that they are permitted to withdraw their data if they so choose.

Lastly, researchers are required to debrief research participants. During the debriefing, participants must be allowed to ask questions about the information, nature, and results of the study. Researchers should correct any misunderstandings that the participant has regarding their role or the aims of the study. If psychologists become aware that involvement in research has harmed someone in an unforeseen way, they must take appropriate steps to minimize the harm as well as report the unforeseen harm to a governing board (e.g., the IRB at their university).

During the debriefing, participants must be allowed to ask questions about the information, nature, and results of the study.

The federal government also provides a number of guidelines. For example, the Department of Health and Human Services offers guidelines for the ethical standards of research subjects. Most academic research is guided through IRBs which must consist of a minimum of five members, including one community member who has a non-scientific interest. Scientists must also be represented on the team. Generally, IRBs require a research proposal that includes the description of the proposed project, whether human or animal subjects will be used, how informed consent will be obtained, and debriefing information. Often, the IRB asks for copies of any forms that will be given to participants, such as informed consents, questionnaires or other measures and debriefing information. State and local boards may also develop their own rules and regulations for conducting research.

Please, leave your Customer Review on Amazon

Chapter 3

Biological Bases
of Behavior

Understanding the links between biology, physiological processes and behavior is essential for the study of psychology. In pursuit of this understanding, extensive research has been conducted on the brain using evolving brain imaging technologies. Through this, important discoveries have been made concerning the structures and associated functions of different brain regions. Insights have also been gained concerning the functions of the central and peripheral nervous system. Other research discoveries brought to light the structures, functions, and importance of neurons. Neuroscience aids psychologists and psychiatrists in developing an understanding of how an excess or deficit of certain neurotransmitters is connected to the occurrence of physical conditions and mental disorders (e.g., Parkinson's disease, dopamine deficiency), as well as how certain pharmaceutical agents act in their patients.

Notes

Effects of the Nervous System on Behavior

Behavior is the internally coordinated responses (actions or inactions) of living organisms (individuals or groups) to internal and/or external stimuli. Behaviors can be either innate (instinctual) or learned. Behavior can be regarded as any action of an organism that changes its relationship to its environment. Behavior provides outputs from the organism to the environment.

The brain and behavior

The brain consists of outer grey matter or cell bodies and inner white matter, called axons. It is divided into three major regions—forebrain, midbrain, and hindbrain. The brain has four ventricles, including two lateral ventricles. The vertebrate brain is located at the anterior end of the dorsal tubular nerve cord. The cerebrum is associated with the two lateral ventricles, the diencephalon with the third ventricle and the brain stem and cerebellum with the fourth ventricle.

The informational pulses executed in the nervous system allow people to perform their daily functions. The processing of information takes place in the central nervous system (CNS), a highly developed mass of nerve cells. The brain can override spinal reflexes, for example, jerking away from getting a vaccine.

The central core of the brain is formed by the diencephalon (where the third ventricle is located), consisting of the thalamus, a collection of several large nuclei, and the hypothalamus — the master command center for neural and endocrine coordination. The hypothalamus forms the floor of the third ventricle and is found below the thalamus and next to the pituitary gland.

The hypothalamus is responsible for maintaining homeostasis and is involved in many regulatory functions, such as osmoregulation and thermoregulation. It is an integrating center that regulates hunger, sleep, thirst, body temperature, water balance, and blood pressure. It controls the pituitary gland and thereby serves as a link between the nervous and endocrine systems. The hypothalamus is also responsible for the secretion of ADH (Anti-Diuretic Hormone) via its neuro-secretory cells.

The thalamus consists of two masses of grey matter on the sides and roof of the third ventricle. It is the last portion of the brain for sensory input before the cerebrum. It is a central relay station for sensory impulses traveling up from the body or from the brain to the cerebrum. Except for smell, it channels sensory impulses to specific regions of the cerebrum for interpretation. Lastly, the pineal gland, which secretes the melatonin hormone, is located in the diencephalon.

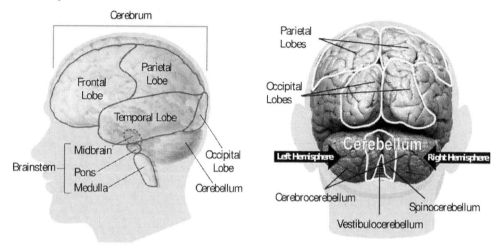

Generalized structure of the human brain

Forebrain

The forebrain lies above the brainstem and the cerebellum and is the most advanced of the brain regions in evolutionary terms. It is the largest and the most important region of the brain and is divided into several components responsible for several activities. The forebrain receives sensory input from the midbrain and hindbrain and regulates their output. The largest component of the forebrain is the cerebrum.

The cerebrum, also called the *telencephalon*, makes up most of the forebrain and is responsible for the higher thought processes necessary for learning and memory, language, speech, intelligence, and creativity. It is the last center receiving sensory input and carrying out integration to command motor responses. The "grey matter" of the outer part of the cerebrum is the cerebral cortex, the center that receives information from the thalamus and all other lower parts of the brain. The inner portion of the cerebrum consists of white matter.

The *cerebrum* has two hemispheres connected by the *corpus callosum*, a thick nerve bundle. Each hemisphere is divided into lobes, which include: the frontal lobe (involved in conscious thought and voluntary skeletal muscle movement), the parietal lobe (involved in integrating sensory information related to temperature, touch, pressure and pain), the temporal lobe (involved in processing auditory information and smell) and the occipital lobe (involved in processing visual information).

Midbrain

The midbrain is a collection of cell bodies that receive incoming signals from the spinal cord and various parts of the brain. The midbrain is involved in smooth movement, temperature control and integration of visual and auditory motor reflexes. The brainstem consists of the midbrain, pons and medulla oblongata. It contains the reticular formation, a bundle of axons responsible for motor functions and cardiovascular and respiratory control. Besides acting as a relay station for tracts passing between the cerebrum and spinal cord or cerebellum, the midbrain has reflex centers for visual, auditory and tactile responses.

The *brainstem* connects the brain to the rest of the central nervous system by connecting the cerebrum to the spinal cord. This part of the brain is evolutionarily the oldest structure and smallest region of the brain, one that has developed over time into the two other components. It is primarily concerned with life support and basic functions such as movement, while more advanced processes are left to more evolved areas of the brain.

Hindbrain

The hindbrain, located in the posterior part of the brain, regulates organs below the consciousness level. In humans, it regulates lung and heart functions, even when people are asleep, and also coordinates motor activity.

The *pons* functions with the medulla to regulate breathing rate. The pons contain bundles of axons traveling between the cerebellum and rest of the CNS. The pons has reflex centers concerned with head movements in response to visual or auditory stimuli. The *medulla oblongata* lies between the spinal cord and the pons, anterior to the cerebellum. It contains vital centers for regulating heartbeat, breathing and vasoconstriction. It contains reflex centers for vomiting, coughing, sneezing, hiccupping and swallowing. It contains nerve tracts that ascend or descend between the spinal cord and the brain's higher centers.

The *cerebellum* is separated from the brain stem by the fourth ventricle. The cerebellum is in two portions and is joined by a narrow median portion. The cerebellum integrates impulses from higher centers to coordinate muscle actions, maintain equilibrium and muscle tone and sustain normal posture. It receives information from the eyes, inner ear, muscles, etc., indicating body position; it integrates that information and sends impulses to the muscles to maintain balance. The cerebellum assists in the learning of new motor skills, such as sports or playing the piano.

The human hand takes up a large proportion of the primary motor area. Ventral to the primary motor area is a pre-motor area that organizes motor functions before the primary area sends signals to the cerebellum.

Lateralization of cortical functions

Most evidence of lateralized brain function stems from understanding how brain damage affects performance on cognitive tasks. Paul Broca, a 19th-century neurologist, first studied a patient's inability to produce speech following brain damage. His first patient was Leborgne, who understood most of what was said to him and though he could only utter the word "tan," he was able to drink and eat, leading Broca to discard the theory of motor impairment. Leborgne's brain was damaged in the lower rear portion of the frontal lobe, lower front portion of the parietal lobe and the upper part of the temporal lobe. Broca concluded that frontal lobe damage affected speech production. *Aphasia* is referred to as the partial or total loss of ability to articulate ideas due to brain damage. *Broca's Area* refers to the lower rear portion of the frontal lobe, adjacent to the motor cortex.

Paul Broca, neurologist

Korbinian Brodmann examined brain cells with different strains that are made to recognize chemical differences between various areas. Brain areas defined by cytoarchitectonic characteristics are known as *Brodmann's area*. There are 52 recognized Brodmann's areas in the brain.

In 1871, Carl Wernicke reported a different sort of language disorder, called *Wernicke's aphasia*. Wernicke's aphasia is characterized by fluent excessive speech, made-up words and a lack of comprehension despite an intact hearing capacity.

Women are more vulnerable to aphasia after significant damage to the frontal lobe. Men are more vulnerable to aphasia after damage to the parietal and temporal lobes. There are similar sex differences in *apraxia*, or impairment in voluntary movement.

Carl Wernicke, German psychiatrist

In the Wernicke-Geschwind model, Broca's area stores the motor representation of speech while Wernicke's area stores the auditory representation of speech sounds. These areas are connected by a fiber tract known as the *Arcuate fasciculus*. This model is now considered oversimplified.

Methods used in studying the brain

Electroencephalogram (EEG) measures electrical brain activity by using sensors (electrodes).

Computerized tomography (CT) uses computer-enhanced X-rays to produce images of specific brain regions.

Magnetic Resonance Imaging (MRI) uses magnetic fields, which produce clearer and more detailed images than CT scan images.

Functional MRI (fMRI) portrays the differences in activity in various brain regions.

Positron Emission Tomography (PET) tracks radioactive markers that have been injected into the bloodstream.

Neuronal communication and its influence on behavior

A neuron consists of a cell body and branching fibers. A neuron consists of dendrite fibers that receive information and axon fibers that pass the information along to other neurons and various muscular glands. The *myelin sheath* is a layer of fatty tissue that insulates the axons and increases the speed of transmission of their impulses. An action potential is initiated when the excitatory signals minus the inhibitory signals go above and beyond the threshold value or the minimum intensity. An action potential is started by the movement of positively charged ions in and out of the channels in the axon's membrane after receiving these signals. Overall, nerve cells communicate by firing other nerve cells.

Influence of neurotransmitters on behavior

Neurotransmitters are the chemical messengers released in the brain that allow communication between neurons. At least 50 different neurotransmitters have been identified. Neurotransmitters have the ability to excite or inhibit neurons. Acetylcholine, norepinephrine, dopamine, serotonin, and gamma-aminobutyric acid (GABA) are the most common neurotransmitters. Each of these neurotransmitters can have a direct or indirect effect on neurons in specific parts of the brain, which in turn affects behavior. Acetylcholine and norepinephrine are considered excitatory neurotransmitters, while serotonin and GABA are considered inhibitory neurotransmitters and dopamine may act as either, depending on where it acts and which receptor site it binds to.

Schizophrenia is a severe mental illness that is caused by gene-environment interactions leading to psychopathology. Schizophrenia causes disturbances in thinking, emotional reactions and behaviors. Schizophrenia is characterized by positive symptoms or psychotic behaviors (e.g., delusions and hallucinations) and negative symptoms (e.g., flat effect, inability to experience pleasure and lack of engagement in daily activities). *Chlorpromazine* and *Clozapine* are medications that block dopamine receptors in the brain to ease the symptoms of the disease and aid the patient in being functional.

Depression affects about 3.5% of the human population. In depression, there is an excess of inhibition signals that control mood, thought, pain and various other sensations. In order to treat depression, antidepressants are utilized. These antidepressants affect norepinephrine and serotonin levels in the brain and aid in the correction of abnormal neurotransmitter activity.

The widely used drug *Prozac* is a selective serotonin reuptake inhibitor (SSRI) that reestablishes the level of serotonin needed to function at a normal level. SSRI's inhibit the reuptake of excess serotonin at the synaptic gap, in turn increasing neurotransmitter activity in the synaptic cleft. This increased serotonin activity helps alleviate depressive symptoms.

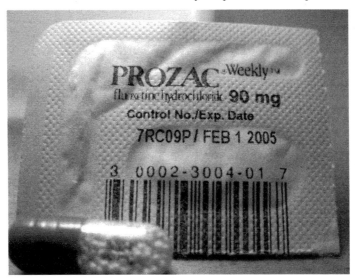

Alzheimer's disease affects about four million Americans. This progressive brain disease causes memory loss and dementia, and eventually, the affected individuals cannot properly care for themselves. It is caused by the loss of cells that secrete acetylcholine in the basal forebrain. The basal forebrain is the portion of the brain that controls for sensory and associative information processing and motor activities. Currently, there is no known treatment for this disease.

Generalized Anxiety disorder (GAD) causes excessive worry, which in turn interferes with daily tasks and functioning. Research has portrayed generalized anxiety disorder as involving many neurotransmitter systems in the brain, including norepinephrine and serotonin.

Attention-deficit/hyperactivity disorder (ADHD) causes hardships in areas of attention, overactivity, impulse control, and distractibility. Dopamine and norepinephrine imbalances are strongly related to ADHD.

Notes

Effects of the Endocrine System on Behavior

Recently, there has been much interest in the area of *behavioral endocrinology*, the study of the interaction between hormones and behavior. Hormones are similar to neurotransmitters but are able to travel much farther throughout the body. Hormones mainly influence behaviors involving aggression, mating, and parenting.

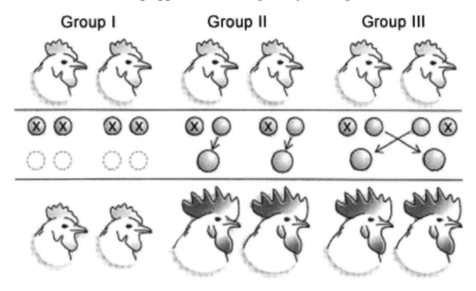

In what is considered the first endocrinological experiment, Arnold Berthold castrated three groups of birds. The first group was castrated, and their testes were discarded. The second group also had their testes removed, but one of each birds' own testes was re-implanted into their abdominal cavity. The birds in the third group had their testes removed and had one testis from a different bird transplanted into their abdominal cavities. The birds in the first group were smaller than average and did not engage in typical rooster behavior. The birds in the second and third groups were of average size and engaged in all typical rooster behaviors. Berthold concluded that there were no specific nerves that direct testicular function and proposed that there must be a "secretory blood-borne product," which is now referred to as hormones.

Testosterone is an androgenic steroid hormone believed to influence aggressive and assertive behaviors. One piece of evidence often cited for this claim is that males who tend to produce more testosterone are generally more aggressive than females, even across different species. In humans, males produce ten times more testosterone than women and are convicted of violent crimes at a similarly higher rate, although some argue that this is due to socialization. During puberty, when blood concentrations of androgens rise, aggressive behaviors tend to increase.

Additionally, researchers have found that males and females who have heightened levels of testosterone smile less than their low-testosterone counterparts, which suggests that testosterone is implicated in dominant behavior, which is distinct from aggressive behavior.

Estrogens are a group of hormones often associated with female sexual and reproductive development. Although present in males, estrogens exist at much higher rates in females. They are believed to play a role in sexual behavior, as well as in mental health and eating patterns. In non-human mammals, a peak in estrogen induces estrus prior to ovulation. Female non-human mammals have no mating desire when not experiencing this peak in estrogen.

Estrogen is also believed to play a role in mental health, although the exact influence and mechanisms are unknown. Mice that displayed obsessive compulsive-like rituals decreased these behaviors when their estrogen levels were raised. Women suffering from postpartum depression have also displayed symptom reduction after estrogen levels were stabilized. Estrogen has also been theorized to influence eating behaviors, particularly binge eating behaviors. Estrogen replacement has been shown to suppress binge eating in female mice. Symptoms in women with bulimia nervosa fluctuate in relation to their menstrual cycle, suggesting that estrogen levels may play a role in this disorder.

Cortisol is a steroid hormone associated with fight-or-flight behavior. Levels of cortisol generally increase after a stressor is presented. Cortisol increases blood pressure and blood sugar levels and suppresses the immune system. Cortisol redistributes glucose to the brain and major muscles during a fight-or-flight situation. This can be seen as an adaptive process as individuals experiencing this fight-or-flight response are able to behave quickly and efficiently in order to ensure survival.

Oxytocin is a peptide hormone that triggers lactation and social bonding. It is thought to be particularly influential in parenting behavior. Female rats receiving antagonists after giving birth do not behave in the typical maternal way that rats that are not given antagonists do. Administration of oxytocin has also been shown to increase bonding toward individuals with similar characteristics. Oxytocin is also important for forming monogamous pair bonding in certain animals.

Testosterone, estrogen, cortisol, and oxytocin are just a few of the many hormones that are believed to influence behavior. In the animal kingdom, some hormones have been found to play a key role in specific behaviors. For example, sea slugs have an egg-laying hormone (ELH) that causes them to lay eggs. ELH directly excites the reproductive tract and causes egg expulsion, even if the sea slug has not mated. The process of molting is also directly controlled by hormones. Behaviors like these are considered to be instinctual, as they are innate and inherited.

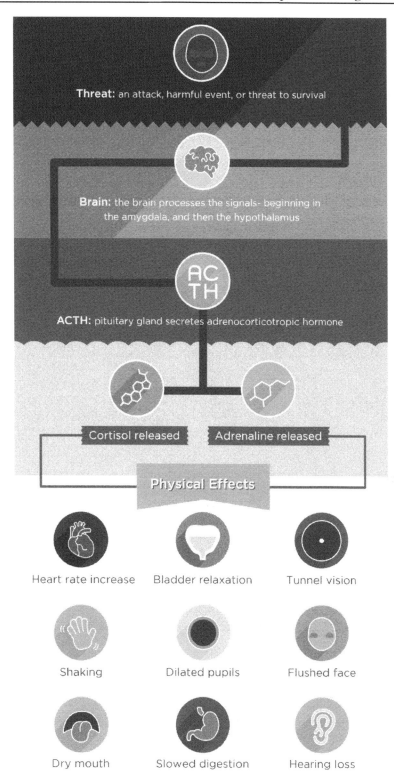

The fight-or-flight response

Notes

Behavioral Genetics

Temperament, heredity, and genes

Temperament refers to aspects of personality that are believed to be innate (rather than learned) due to their emergence in infancy. Temperament also appears to be persistent throughout childhood and adulthood. *Behavioral genetics* is the study of the genetic factors underlying differences in temperaments. Genetic factors are determined through the examination of *heredity*, the transmission of traits and characteristics from parent to offspring. These traits and characteristics are controlled by *genes*, or functional units comprised of DNA that provide instructions for the creation of proteins.

Behavioral geneticists ask *mechanistic questions* that are answered by describing how an organism is biologically organized and equipped to behave. In order to determine the effects that genes may have on temperament, twin studies have been conducted to assess for temperament differences in individuals with the same genetic makeup (DNA), or identical twins.

It has been concluded that if identical twins are raised in dissimilar environments, as in the case of adoption, but share certain traits, those traits likely result from the influence of their shared genetic makeup and not the environment. Children who have been adopted can also be compared to their adoptive parents in order to better determine the role of environment on temperament. Studies using this method, however, have been criticized because there is evidence that most environmental influence is exerted by peers rather than parents.

Studies of migratory birds provided early evidence for the idea that behavior has a genetic component. In an experiment conducted by Andreas Helbig, German blackcaps were found to fly southwest to Spain and northwest Africa, while Austrian blackcaps were found to fly southeast to Israel and northwest Africa. Helbig hypothesized that if this behavior was genetically controlled, hybrids of the two birds would fly an intermediary path. Indeed, hybrids in a funnel cage left directional marks intermediate to the parent birds' flight paths.

Adaptive value of traits and behaviors

Adaptive value refers to the extent to which a trait, behavior or characteristic positively affects an organism's chance of survival. *Behavioral ecology* is the study of behavior that seeks to explain how specific behaviors increase fitness. *Behaviors*, as mentioned before, are the coordinated responses of organisms to internal and external stimuli and can be regarded as any action of an organism that changes its relationship to the environment. Since genes influence behavior, behavior can evolve over time. Behavioral ecologists examine behavior by asking *survival value questions* that attempt to determine how a certain behavior may help animals exploit resources, avoid predators or secure a mate.

Altruistic behaviors have been observed across many species. *Altruism* is defined as the behavior of an organism that benefits another at its own expense. While altruism may not initially appear to be an adaptive property, it has a genetic benefit known as *inclusive fitness.* Inclusive fitness refers to the reproductive success of an individual plus that of its close relatives. In other words, altruism can be explained on the basis that it helps relatives who are capable of reproducing to survive. Squirrels, for example, will often sound an alarm when a predator approaches, putting themselves at risk to save many of their relatives.

Kin selection is an instance of inclusive fitness, which combines the number of offspring produced with the number an individual can produce by supporting others, such as siblings. Kin selection is the evolutionary strategy that favors the reproductive success of an organism's relatives, even at a cost to the organism's own survival and reproduction. Kin altruism is altruistic behavior whose evolution is driven by kin selection. Examples include honey bees that do not reproduce but leave that function to their relatives, and adoption of orphans within animal populations.

Social behavior is also adaptive for many species. Some animals are largely solitary and join with a member of their species only to reproduce, while others pair, bond and cooperate in raising their offspring. The study of social behavior from an evolutionary biological perspective is known as *sociobiology.* Sociobiology is based on a reproductive cost-benefit analysis of the value of living in a society made up of members organized in a cooperative manner extending beyond sexual and parental behavior.

There are both benefits and costs to living in a social group. Societies will only evolve if the benefits in terms of reproductive success outweigh the disadvantages. Social groups such as herds, flocks, and schools provide concealment and defense against predators, thus increasing the chances of survival of the organisms within them. Packs are also adaptive, as they enable members to work together to trap prey. Lions, for example, work together to catch larger prey, such as buffalo.

Packs are also adaptive, as they enable members to work together to trap prey.

Within social groups, *dominance structures* are also adaptive, as they minimize fighting over food and mates. In a dominance structure, dominance is determined by a confrontation where one animal gives way to another. Similarly, *agonist behavior* (aggression and submission) is adaptive and originates from competition for food, mates, and territory. Agonistic behavior is ritualized so injuries and time spent in contests are minimized. The possession and defense of territory, known as *territoriality*, is also adaptive as it ensures adequate food and a place to mate.

The mate selection process can also be viewed through a behavioral ecological lens. The reproductive behavior of males and females is related to their anatomy and physiology in an adaptive way. Males, for example, produce sperm in great quantity and compete with other males to inseminate as many females as possible. Females who produce few eggs are selective about their mates. Evidence suggests that this selectivity promotes survival because females tend to select males with adaptive traits. This idea is known as the *good genes hypothesis*. An alternative hypothesis, known as the *run-away hypothesis*, asserts that females choose traits that are desirable because they are initially adaptive, but that these traits can become exaggerated until they become a handicap. One such example is selecting a mate due for brightly colored feathers, but bright coloring will often make an organism easily found by a predator.

Interaction between heredity and environmental influences

Genetic and environmental factors always combine to produce behavior. It appears that on average, genetics and the environment exert an equal influence on an organism's behavior. It is important to note that these influences vary by trait and are difficult to quantify.

One illustration of the bidirectional nature of genes and the environment is the etiology of phenylketonuria (PKU). PKU is a form of intellectual disability that results from the abnormal breakdown of the amino acid phenylalanine. PKU is controlled by a single gene. It was found that infants with this gene who were fed a diet low in phenylalanine did not develop an intellectual disability. This example illustrates the importance of the interaction between genes and the environment, rather than the individual influence of each. Gene-environment interaction models have been proposed for most, if not all, psychopathologies.

A recent hypothesis about the nature of depression, called the orchid/dandelion hypothesis, states that there are groups of children who can survive any good or bad environment with little consequence because of their genetic makeup. This group of children is known as the "dandelions," which are able to grow anywhere. The second group, known as the "orchid" group, is hypothesized to excel when placed in positive environments but become depressed when placed in poor environments. This hypothesis also provides an explanation for how genes contributing to depression have survived evolution. Children with this environmental sensitivity are hypothesized to often thrive when placed in positive environments, making it likely that their genes will be passed on.

Influence of Genetics and Environment on the Behavior

Regulatory genes and behavior

A central dogma of biology states that there is a segment of DNA (called a gene) which codes for ribonucleic acid (RNA), which then codes for one out of 20 amino acids, which are the building blocks of proteins. Proteins are considered the intermediate point between genes and behavior. *Regulator genes* are genes that are involved in controlling the expression of one or more genes. About 95% of genes are regulator genes and do not code for proteins. Regulation can occur during transcription, post-transcription, and translation. Gene regulation does not necessarily have a direct effect on the genetic code itself, but rather regulates how proteins are coded.

Gene expression and gene regulation are modulated by environmental factors. The mapping of the human genome (30,000 genes) has helped in the recognition of the modulatory factors in gene expression. One field of interest that examines the interaction between nature and nurture is *epigenetics*. More specifically, epigenetics is the study of changes in gene expression as a result of environmental factors. A recent study showed that childhood abuse can have an effect on genetic expression, highlighting the implications of parental care on the epigenetic regulation of hippocampal glucocorticoid receptor expression.

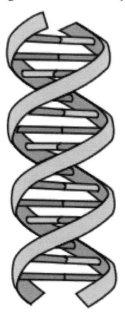

DNA molecule

Genetically based behavioral variation in natural populations

Even within a species, genetic and behavioral variation can be observed. The feeding behavior of garter snakes is one such example. Steven Arnold tested garter snakes from different geographical locations and found that inland garter snakes only fed on frogs and fish, refusing to feed on slugs. The coastal population of garter snakes, however, readily fed on slugs. When a hybrid garter snake was born, it showed an intermediate acceptance of slugs. Smell receptors and tongue flicks were indicated as physiological differences that underlie this behavior. Behavioral variation is caused by the interaction between genes and the environment. Behavioral variation can also be affected by epigenetics, various molecular factors that change gene expression but do not change the DNA sequence itself.

Chapter 4

Sensation and Perception

Sensation is the effect of environmental stimuli on sensory organs. Perception is a cognitive process and effect of sensory input interpretation; further, it can be dramatically shaped by top-down and bottom-up processing. Combined, sensation and perception provide the basis for which every organism is aware of its environment. Furthermore, senses share common properties, which are best understood through the understanding of thresholds, adaptation, and transduction. The senses are varied themselves and likewise, each possesses their own particular structures and functions. For example, vision is processed by the eyes and brain, while hearing is processed by the ears and brain. Insights into perception can be explored, such as color vision theory and pitch perception. An added complication to matters is the fact that the brain is capable of constructing its own reality, and illusions can exert a powerful effect on perception.

Notes

Sensation

Psychophysics

The field of psychophysics was founded in the mid-1800s by Gustav Theodor Fechner, a German physicist, psychologist, and philosopher. His experiments not only started the field of psychophysics but also the broader field of experimental psychology. *Psychophysics* is described as the quantitative study of the relationship between physical and psychological events. More specifically, it refers to the study of stimuli and the resulting sensations and perceptions that they bring about in an organism. The main areas of study within psychophysics are threshold, Weber's law, signal detection theory, and sensory adaptation.

Threshold

Threshold is the intensity that must be exceeded for a reaction or phenomenon to occur. *Sensory threshold* broadly refers to the weakest stimulus that can be detected by an organism 50% of the time. *Absolute threshold* is the weakest stimulus that can be detected at a certain percentage (often 50%) of the time when there is initially no stimulus present. A typical hearing test, for example, plays beeps at increasing volume levels. The test-taker is instructed to indicate when he or she first hears a beep. A hearing test of this variety seeks to measure the test-taker's absolute threshold for hearing, which is why there is initially no sound.

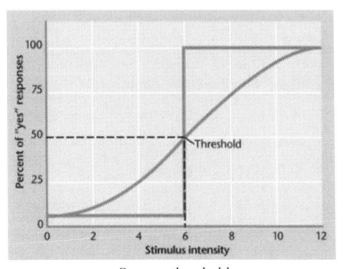

Sensory threshold

Differential threshold refers to the level at which an organism can perceive a change in an already-detected stimulus and detect it half of the time. An example of this occurs when one notices an increase in the temperature of a room. The point at which this temperature difference is detected subtracted by the original temperature is the differential threshold. In other words, the differential threshold is the magnitude of the change in intensity between the original stimuli and the final stimuli. *Terminal threshold* refers to the upper limit at which a stimulus can no longer be detected. For example, if one were to touch a hot stove, pain would likely be felt instead of heat, because the terminal threshold for temperature has been exceeded. The highest pitch that a person can hear is the terminal threshold for pitch.

Weber's law

Originally proposed for weightlifting, *Weber's law* (named after German physician Ernst Heinrich Weber, founder of experimental psychology) posits that the differential threshold for an individual is dependent on proportion, not amount. For example, if a weightlifter notices when one pound is added to the ten-pound weight that he was lifting, then according to Weber's law, he would notice when two pounds are added to a twenty pound weight. For this reason, Weber's law is often called the *law of just noticeable differences*.

Weber's law was later applied to sensation. Although it does not hold completely true for sound or for very high or low-intensity stimuli, Weber's law is generally accurate for sight, touch, taste, and smell. One common experiment in which Weber's law is generally found to be supported involves having a test subject judge two lines, with one line longer than the other. This is then repeated with an even longer set of lines. Findings show that the difference in these larger lines must be proportional to the difference of the smaller lines in order for participants to notice that one is longer. The proportion of change necessary to notice a difference varies for each individual.

	Left is shorter	Right is longer
Obvious	—	——
Less obvious	—————	—————
Hard to distinguish	———————	———————

The same holds true for other senses as well. A dog, for example, is able to detect much more subtle changes in smell than a human is able to.

Signal detection theory

Signal detection theory aims to uncover the internal and external mechanisms that contribute to sensation and perception. Specifically, it posits that the detection of a given stimulus is partly dependent on the intensity of the stimulus. For example, a loud noise is more likely to be detected than a soft noise, and a temperature change of 10° F is more likely to be detected than a change of 2° F.

Signal detection theory also proposes that the psychological state of the individual or animal experiencing the stimuli will also have an effect on how it is perceived. For example, someone who is walking alone at night in a bad neighborhood will likely experience a soft noise as subjectively louder than if they had heard the same noise during the day. This theory is significant because it notes that our perception can be influenced by our past experiences and expectations.

Signal detection theory has applications for researchers who seek to understand more about sensation through lab experiments. These researchers will often begin perception experiments with a *signal detection test*. In each trial of the test, a stimulus will either be presented to or withheld from a participant. The participant is instructed to indicate whether or not he or she perceived a stimulus at each trial. Through repeated trials, a *receiver operating characteristic* curve can be plotted, providing information to the researchers on the detection of various stimuli. This curve provides a unique baseline for each individual participant and allows researchers to study perception more accurately.

Sensory adaptation

Sensory systems are constantly recalibrating based on the environment. This ability to recalibrate is referred to as *sensory adaptation*. Sensory adaptation most often occurs when a constant stimulus is presented over time, and receptors respond by decreasing their sensitivity to the stimulus. This ability of receptors to adapt is found in all types of sensory receptors, with the possible exception of pain receptors.

One does not generally notice the sensation of clothes on the skin because skin receptors have adapted to this constant stimulus by reducing their sensitivity. Similarly, a friend's house may have a specific smell associated with it, but often the people living in the house are unable to detect it because they have been sensing it for a long time and their olfactory receptors have adapted to it.

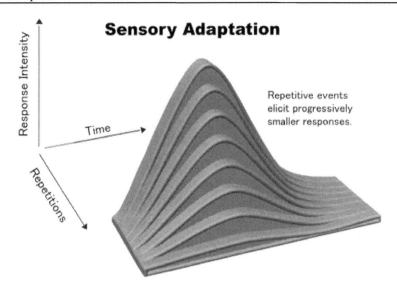

Sensory Adaptation

Response Intensity

Time

Repetitions

Repetitive events elicit progressively smaller responses.

Sensory adaptation can also be observed in the visual system. When in the dark, the concentration of the light-sensing chemical in the rods and cones in the eye will increase. This leads to increased sensitivity and the ability to see better. Dark adaptation occurs in cones within about ten minutes, while rods can take up to thirty minutes to become fully adapted.

Sensory Receptors

Sensory systems code for four different aspects of a stimulus. The first aspect of a stimulus is *type*, or modality. This means that the stimulus is primarily coded for by the kind of receptor that it activates. For example, taste is coded for by taste receptors, while smell is coded for by odor receptors.

The second aspect of a stimulus is *intensity*. An increased stimulus results in a larger receptor potential, leading to a higher frequency of action potential. Stronger stimuli affect a larger area and recruit a larger number of receptors.

The third aspect of a stimulus is *location*, which is coded for by the site of the stimulated receptor. The precision of location, called *acuity*, is negatively correlated with the amount of convergence in ascending neural pathways, size of the receptive field and overlap with adjacent receptive fields. Response is highest at the center of the receptive field since receptor density is highest there. Acuity can be increased by *lateral inhibition*, a process by which excited neurons reduce the activity of neighboring neurons.

The fourth aspect of a stimulus is *duration*. Duration is coded for by two types of receptors: rapid adapting receptors and slow adapting receptors. *Rapid adapting receptors* respond quickly at the onset of a stimulus, but slow down gradually during the remainder of the stimulus. *Slow adapting receptors* maintain their response at or near the initial level of firing through the full duration of the stimulus. Rapid adapting receptors are critical for signaling rapid change, while slow adapting receptors are important for signaling slow changes.

Types of sensory receptors

Sensory receptors are nerve endings that respond to an internal or external stimulus. Sensory receptors can be classified by three methods: receptor complexity, location, and type of stimulus detected. An example of more complex receptors are the encapsulated nerve endings that have physical specialization, while less complex receptors are free nerve endings consisting of dendrites, whose terminal ends have no specialization.

Exteroceptors are receptors that are found at or near the surface of the skin and respond to stimuli occurring on the surface of the body. Exteroceptors code for tactile sensations as well as for vision, hearing, smell, and taste.

Interoceptors respond to stimuli occurring inside of the body and are located in visceral organs and blood vessels. Receptors within the GI tract, for example, carry signals to the brain relating to feelings of hunger. Interoceptors are associated with the autonomic nervous system. *Proprioceptors* respond to internal stimuli occurring in skeletal muscles, tendons, ligaments, and joints, and can detect the position of a body part in space.

When classifying receptors by the type of stimuli they detect, receptors fall into five categories.

The first type of receptors, *mechanoreceptors*, respond to touch and pressure. Mechanoreceptors can be either rapid adapting or slow adapting receptors.

The second type of receptors, *photoreceptors*, responds to light.

The third type of receptors, *thermoreceptors*, responds to temperature and temperature changes. One type of thermoreceptor responds to increases in temperature, while another responds to decreases.

The fourth type of receptors, *chemoreceptors*, respond to taste, smell and changes in blood chemistry. Chemoreceptors are found universally in all animals, and chemoreception is thought to be the most primitive sense.

The fifth type of receptors, *nociceptors*, responds to pain and tissue damage.

Mechanoreceptors	• Respond to touch and pressure
Photoreceptors	• Respond to light
Thermoreceptors	• Respond to temperature
Chemoreceptors	• Respond to taste, smell, and changes in blood chemistry
Nociceptors	• Respond to pain and tissue damage

The skin contains many of these receptors close to the surface (i.e., the boundary between the dermis and the epidermis). However, mechanoreceptors that respond to pressure are located deeper in the dermis.

Proprioceptors, mechanoreceptors, photoreceptors, thermoreceptors, chemoreceptors, and nociceptors are all examples of *somatic sensors,* and they make up the *somatosensory system.*

Sensory pathways

A *sensory unit* is made of a single neuron and its receptor endings. When stimulated, a sensory unit brings about activity in its neuron's receptive field within the brain. For example, when the receptive field of one of the retina's cells is stimulated, associated neurons in the visual cortex of the occipital lobe are activated so that the sensory input can be interpreted.

In order to do this, specific pathways are needed for each of the senses and types of stimuli. Sensory information is carried through the spinal cord to higher levels of the brain through *ascending pathways*. Via these pathways, information from taste cells is transmitted to the parietal lobe, information from the eyes is transmitted to the occipital lobe, and information from the ears is transmitted to the temporal lobe.

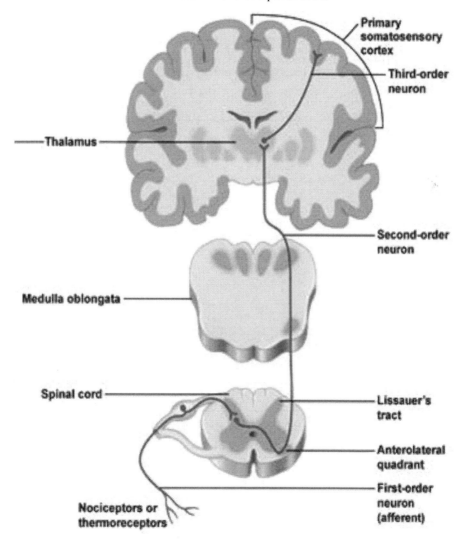

For sensations concerning touch, the three major ascending pathways are the posterior column pathway, the anterolateral pathway, and the spinocerebellar pathway.

- The *posterior column pathway* carries fine touch, vibration, pressure and proprioceptive (position of body parts) sensations from the skin and joints. Information is transmitted to the postcentral gyrus of the cerebral cortex via first-order, second-order and third-order neurons.

- The *anterolateral pathway*, also called the spinothalamic tract, carries sensations of pain, temperature, and poorly localized touch. Information in this system flows from the skin through the ventral posterolateral nucleus in the thalamus to the somatosensory cortex of the postcentral gyrus. The spinothalamic tract consists of two adjacent pathways: an anterior pathway and a lateral pathway. The anterior pathway carries poorly localized touch sensations, while the lateral pathway carries information about pain and temperature.

- The *spinocerebellar pathway* carries sensations concerning limb and joint position. This information is obtained by the Golgi tendon organ and muscle spindles, which then convey the information to the cerebellum.

Posterior column pathway	• Carries fine touch, vibration, pressure, and proprioceptive sensations • Information is sent to the postcentral gyrus of the cerebral cortex
Anterolateral pathway	• Carries sensations of pain, temperature, and poorly localized touch • Information is sent to the somatosensory cortex of the postcentral gyrus
Spinocerebellar pathway	• Carries sensations concerning limb and joint position • Information is sent to the cerebellum

Hearing

Ear structure and function

The human ear is made up of three main parts: the *outer ear*, the *middle ear*, and the *inner ear*. The outer ear is what most people think of when they think of an ear. It consists of the pinna and the auditory canal. The *pinna*, also known as the auricle, is the visible part of the ear outside of the head. Its role is to direct and amplify sound waves. The *auditory canal* is the opening of the ear, lined with fine hairs that filter the air. The auditory canal also contains modified sweat glands that secrete earwax to guard against foreign matter.

The middle ear cavity is filled with air and contains three small bones known collectively as *ossicles*. These bones are the *malleus* (hammer), the *incus* (anvil), and the *stapes* (stirrup). The ossicles convert the vibrations of the *eardrum*, or tympanic membrane, into waves of fluid in the inner ear. The auditory (eustachian) tube extends from the middle ear to the pharynx to equalize the inside and outside ear. The *oval window*, or vestibular window, is a membrane-covered opening that separates the middle ear and the inner ear.

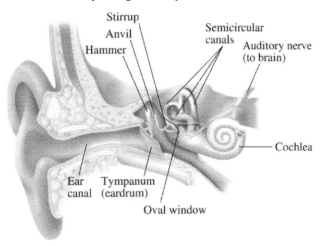

The inner ear contains the *bony labyrinth*, which is a hollow cavity in the temporal bone of the skull. The bony labyrinth is comprised of two main functional parts: the cochlea and the vestibular system. The *cochlea* is spiral shaped and houses the cochlear duct, which contains the *organ of Corti*. Within the organ of Corti are hair cells called *stereocilia*. Afferent neurons from these hair cells form the *cochlear nerve*. The upper compartment of the cochlea is the *scala vestibuli*, a fluid-filled cavity that conducts sound vibrations to the *cochlear duct*. The cochlear duct transforms this vibrational energy into electrical energy and sends signals to the brain. The *vestibular system* of the bony labyrinth is composed of three semicircular canals that are perpendicular to one another and are critical for the sense of balance.

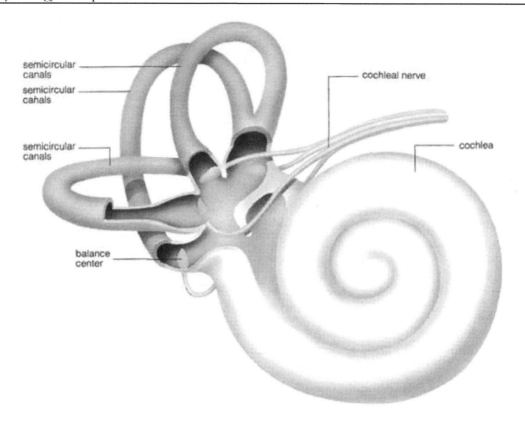

Sensory reception by hair cells

The process of hearing begins when sound waves enter the auditory canal, hitting the tympanic membrane (eardrum) and causing it to vibrate. These vibrations then move to the ossicles. Sound is amplified about twenty times by the size difference between the tympanic membrane and the oval window. The stapes strikes the membrane of the oval window, passing pressure waves to the fluid in the cochlea.

When the stapes strikes the membrane of the oval window, pressure waves move from the vestibular canal to the tympanic canal and across the *basilar membrane*, the base for these hair cells, causing the round window to bulge. This excites the stereocilia, which bend from the vibration of the basilar membrane. This bending generates nerve impulses in the cochlear nerve that travel to the brain stem.

Auditory processing

When nerve impulses traveling from the cochlear nerve into the brainstem reach the auditory areas of the cerebral cortex, the information is interpreted as sound. This occurs via the *primary auditory pathway*, which starts in the cochlea and moves through the vestibulocochlear nerve to the superior olivary complex. A neuron then carries the message to the *mesencephalon*, a structure that forms a major component of the midbrain. The message is then finally received by the primary auditory cortex.

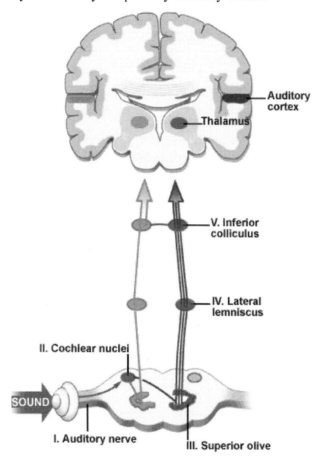

The organ of Corti is varied in structure so that different areas are sensitive to different pitches. The organ of Corti's narrow base detects high pitch, while the wide tip detects low pitch. The nerve fibers from these different regions lead to slightly different activations in the brain, producing the sensation of pitch. Sound volume is detected by the magnitude of vibrations. Increased stimulation of receptors is interpreted as louder, while decreased stimulation is interpreted as softer. Tone is detected by the brain based on the distribution of the hair cells that are stimulated, allowing a person to differentiate the sound of a piano from that of a violin, even if the two instruments are playing the same tune at the same volume.

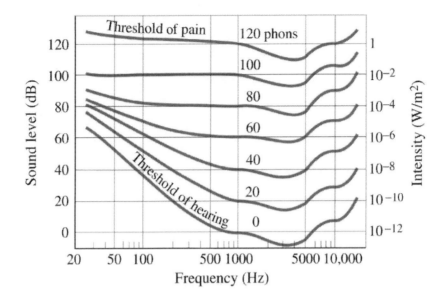

Vision

Eye structure and function

The human eye is an elongated sphere measuring 2.5 cm in diameter. Although many people tend to think of it as similar to a camera, the eye is a considerably more complex network of interconnected parts. The eye itself is contained by the *orbit*, a pear-shaped structure that is formed by several bones. The *sclera* is the outer, white fibrous layer that covers most of the eye for protection. The *cornea* is the transparent part of the sclera at the front of the eye. It can be conceptualized as the "window of the eye." The cornea focuses light on the retina and acts as a protective covering.

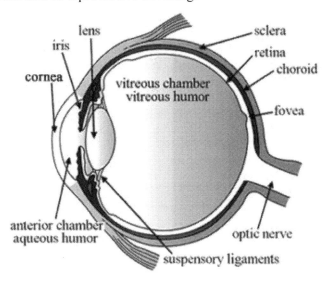

The *pupil* is the black circle in the middle of the eye that dilates and constricts in response to changing light levels in the environment. The size of the pupil determines the amount of light that can enter the eye. The dark brown inner layer of the eye is the *choroid*, which contains blood vessels and pigments that absorb stray light rays. The choroid thickens to form a ring-shaped ciliary body which becomes the *iris*. The iris can be recognized as the pigmented area of the eye that surrounds the pupil. The iris controls the amount of light allowed into the eye by dilating and constricting the pupil using the papillary sphincter and dilator muscles. Stimulation of the sympathetic nerves dilates the pupil to let in more light when the environment is dark, while stimulation of the parasympathetic nerves constricts the pupil to allow in less light when the environment is bright.

The *lens* sits behind the iris and aids in focusing refracted light onto the retina. It also divides the eye into two chambers: the aqueous humor and the vitreous humor. The *aqueous humor* nourishes the cornea and fills the anterior cavity. Blocking of outflow of the aqueous humor results in increased pressure in the eye, or *glaucoma*. The *vitreous humor*, which is jelly-like and protects the shape of the eye, fills the posterior cavity.

The lens focuses light onto the retina by thickening (to focus on nearby objects) and thinning (to focus on distant objects). The *retina* is a thin layer of tissue that sits behind the lens and is responsible for interpreting visual stimuli. The retina contains blood vessels and cells that sense light. Specifically, it contains the *fovea centralis*, the area that produces color vision in daylight. Considerable processing occurs in the retina before an impulse is sent to the brain.

People who are able to see objects well when they are close but not when they are far away are said to have *myopia*, or nearsightedness. This is often due to an elongated eyeball that focuses a distant image in front of the retina. A new treatment called radial keratotomy surgically cuts and flattens the cornea to correct this issue. People who are able to see objects well when they are far away but not when they are close are said to have *hyperopia*, or farsightedness. This is often due to a shortened eyeball that focuses images behind the retina. *Astigmatism* occurs when the cornea or lens is uneven, causing images to become blurry. *Cataracts* occur when the lens becomes opaque due to new cells forming within it. Light can then no longer enter through the lens. If (due to age) the lens loses its elasticity and can no longer assume a spherical shape, near vision is lost. This type of vision loss is called *presbyopia*.

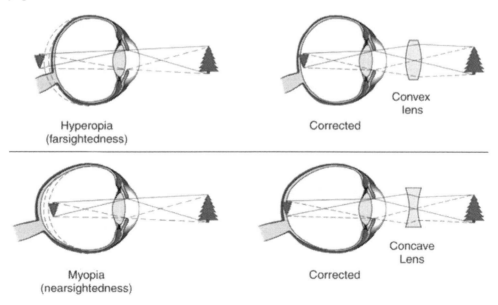

Hyperopia (farsightedness) | Corrected — Convex lens

Myopia (nearsightedness) | Corrected — Concave Lens

Light receptors

Vision begins when light becomes focused on photoreceptors in the retina. *Photoreceptors* are cells that sense light. In their simplest form, photoreceptors only detect the presence and intensity of light. In humans, however, they are much more complex. Photoreceptors are located on the back of the retina, which picks up photons of light via the 130,000,000 rods and cones situated on it. Photoreceptors are able to sense light because they contain *photopigments*, which absorb light. There are four types of photopigments: rhodopsin, blue-sensitive pigment, green-sensitive pigment, and red-sensitive pigment.

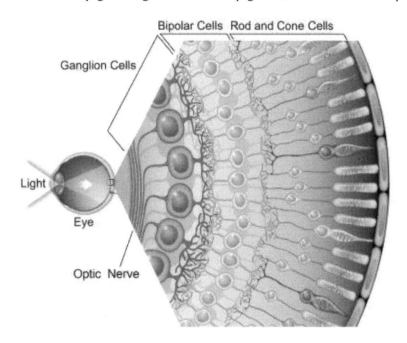

These photopigments are contained within two types of photoreceptors: rods and cones. Rods and cones both have an outer segment that is joined to an inner segment by a stalk. The outer segment contains stacks of *lamellae*, membranous disks with many molecules of rhodopsin. *Rhodopsin* molecules contain the protein *opsin* and the pigment molecule *retinal*, also called the chromatophore molecule, derived from vitamin A.

Cones are responsible for sharp vision and color vision. They are primarily located in the *macula*, a highly sensitive area of the retina. Specifically, they are contained in the *fovea*, an area within the macula. There are three kinds of cones that contain blue, green or red pigment. These pigments are all composed of rhodopsin and opsin, with varying structures of opsin allowing for the absorption of different wavelengths of light. Combinations of cones are stimulated by intermediate colors; the combined nerve impulses are interpreted by the brain as one of 17,000 hues. Humans and other primates are the only animals that have this ability for color vision.

Rods are responsible for peripheral and night vision. Rods are more sensitive to light than cones but do not provide as detailed of an image or detect color. When a rod absorbs light, rhodopsin splits into opsin and retinal, leading to the closure of ion channels in the rod cell plasma membrane. This produces signals that result in impulses to the brain. Rods are grouped outside of the macula in the periphery of the retina.

Visual image processing

Light rays enter the eye through the cornea which bends them due to its curved surface so they can freely pass through the pupil (the opening in the center of the iris with the ability to dilate and constrict depending on how much light is passing through). Light rays then pass through the lens. The shape of the lens is controlled by the *ciliary muscle*, which relaxes when viewing distant objects, causing the lens to flatten. The lens becomes rounder when viewing near objects where light rays must bend to a greater degree. This change is called *visual accommodation*. Once light rays have passed through the lens, they pass through the vitreous humor. Light rays are then focused onto the retina. Due to refraction, the image on the retina is inverted 180 degrees, which is later corrected in the brain.

Once light has been sensed by rods and cones within the retina, this sensory information needs to be transmitted to the brain so that it can be translated into vision. The retina has three layers of neurons that transmit this information: the rods and cones near the choroid, bipolar cells, and ganglion cells. Since only rod and cone cells are sensitive to light, light must penetrate through the ganglion cells. When a rod absorbs light, rhodopsin splits into opsin and retinal, leading to a cascade of reactions and the closure of ion channels in the rod cell plasma membrane. This stops the release of inhibitory molecules from the rod's synaptic vesicles, which in turn starts signals that result in impulses to the brain.

Rods and cones synapse with bipolar cells, creating a hyperpolarization that activates the retinal (the pigment molecule) and causes it to change its shape. After retinal is activated, it changes back to its resting shape and the photoreceptor cell is depolarized. Bipolar cells then pass the information to ganglion cells. Through this process, integration occurs. Many rods can synapse with a single ganglion cell, resulting in indistinct vision. Each cone, however, only synapses with one ganglion cell, resulting in clear vision. There are more rods and cones than nerve fibers leaving ganglionic cells. If all the rod cells in a receptive field are stimulated, the ganglion cell is weakly stimulated or remains neutral. If the center of the receptive field is lit, the ganglion cell is stimulated. If only the edges of the receptive field are lit, the cell is inhibited.

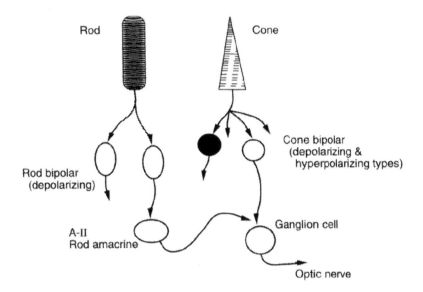

Visual pathways in the brain

Historically, visual perception was believed to encompass only what was seen by the eye externally. It was believed that these external stimuli directly produce a perception in the brain. However, from the discoveries of science, it is now known that this is not the case. Information from the eye is simply a physiological process; significant processing of the signals that the eye receives occurs in the brain.

In order for these signals to reach the brain, the ganglion cells produce an action potential. This is the first step in the pathway from the eye to the brain. Axons from the ganglion cells come together to form the optic nerve. The *optic nerve* is a pathway that crosses to the opposite side of the brain at the point known as the *optic chiasm*. Thus, information stemming from the right side of the visual field is sent to the left half of the brain, and information stemming from the left side of the visual field is sent to the right half of the brain.

The area where the optic nerve passes through the retina lacks rods and cones, and is known as a *blind spot*. The brain combines information from both eyes in order to compensate for this blind spot. Information from the optic nerve travels through the optic tract and terminates in the lateral geniculate nucleus in the thalamus. This information is then sent from the thalamus to the visual cortex in the occipital lobe. Here, a visual association area compares new visual information with old information.

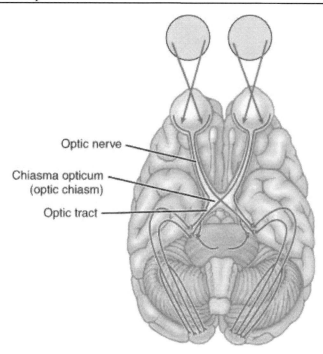

Once visual information has been transmitted through this pathway, the brain is able to process the inverted image from the retina and make it appear upright. The brain also combines the two images from each eye to form a 3D image, which is used to judge distance.

Parallel processing

Parallel processing refers to the brain's ability to process stimuli of differing quality simultaneously. This helps us to perceive the world in a unified way, rather than in disjointed pieces. In vision, information is divided into color, motion, shape, and depth. Each of these components is analyzed individually by the brain. This new information is compared with stored memories to better identify the stimuli that are being processed. These four components (color, motion, shape, and depth) are then integrated to form a complete image without analyzing each component individually. It is hypothesized that before these separate processes become integrated, they are stored as memories to aid the brain in recognizing the image.

Parallel processing is rooted in cognitive psychology, which studies mental functions and views the brain as a complex computer. The concept of parallel processing can be applied beyond sensation to the other processes within cognitive psychology: attention, memory, perception, language, and metacognition.

Feature detection

Feature detection is the brain's way of filtering visual information for important objects or organisms. Feature detection can also be conceptualized as a way of focusing on common elements across different instances of an object. For example, if someone sees ten cats, each a different size and color, they will still know that they are all cats. Similarly, one can identify the letter "a" below, regardless of the font it is in.

$$a \; a \; \alpha \; a \; a \; a \; a$$

It is hypothesized that this process is done via *feature detectors*, specialized neurons in the visual cortex that code for certain features such as lines, angles, and movements. Feature detection occurs for different features simultaneously, making it a type of parallel processing. Feature detectors pass information to higher level brain cells, which then process this information to form a complete image. An alternative hypothesis to feature detectors proposes that groups of cells, rather than individual cells, work as a network to detect for certain features.

Notes

Other Senses

Somatosensation

Somatosensation refers to the broad sensory system of touch, specifically temperature, pain, vibration, and body position; the types of receptors that are part of the somatosensory system include nociceptors, thermoreceptors, proprioceptors and mechanoreceptors, as previously described.

In general, a somatosensory pathway has three long neurons. The first neuron's cell body is in the dorsal root ganglion of the spinal nerve. The second neuron's cell body is in the spinal cord or the brainstem. The axons of these neurons cross to the opposite side of the spinal cord or brainstem and usually terminate in the thalamus. The third neuron usually has its cell body in the ventral posterior nucleus (VPN) of the thalamus, and it ends in the lateral postcentral gyrus in the parietal lobe of the cerebral cortex, which is where the processing aspect of somatosensation primarily occurs.

Taste

The sense of taste is very useful from an evolutionary perspective. Foods that are potentially harmful tend to taste bitter, while high-calorie foods tend to taste sweet, thus increasing an organism's chance of survival. This sense begins with *taste buds*, as they contain the receptors for taste. Taste buds are primarily located on the tongue, specifically along the walls of *papillae*, small elevations on the surface of the tongue. Isolated taste buds are also present on the surfaces of the hard palate, pharynx, and epiglottis. They are contained by *epithelium*.

Taste buds contain multiple taste cells, each of which open at a taste pore. Here, particles of food that have been dissolved in saliva come into contact with taste receptors. Taste receptors are able to detect five elements of taste: sweet, sour, salty, bitter and umami (i.e., savory). Taste buds for these elements are concentrated in particular regions of the tongue, and these elements are organized into independent pathways. The brain appears to take an overall weighted average of taste messages to form the perceived taste.

Taste is considered a form of *chemoreception*, because chemical signals are transduced into action potentials. Elongated taste cells contain hair-like *microvilli* that bear receptor proteins. These receptor proteins are able to sense certain chemicals. The microvilli then release neurotransmitters to send signals to the brain. Primary sensory axons for taste run through the facial nerve, the glossopharyngeal nerve and the vagus nerve. This information is primarily transmitted to the gustatory cortex in the neocortex. Taste information then moves through the thalamus and is received by two regions of the frontal lobe: the insula and the frontal operculum cortex.

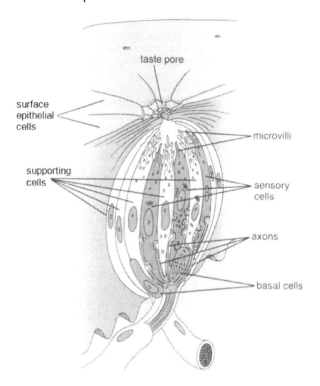

Smell

Olfactory cells/chemoreceptors that detect specific chemicals

Olfactory cells are modified bipolar neurons located in the *epithelium* (mucus membrane) on the roof of the nasal cavity. Olfactory cells are a form of chemoreceptor because they detect chemicals. Humans have about 40 million olfactory cells that can detect over one trillion different odors. Olfactory cells are covered in tufts of long, non-motile cilia that contain receptor proteins for an odor molecule. Each olfactory cell contains only one type of odor receptor. It is believed that there are approximately 1,000 different types of odor receptors.

When chemicals enter the nostrils, they become trapped in the mucus of the nasal cavity where they then dissolve. These molecules then bind to receptors on the cilia, causing cell depolarization and creating an action potential. Axons of olfactory receptor cells of the same specificity synapse together. Information is then passed to the olfactory cortex located within the limbic system through a specific pathway in the brain.

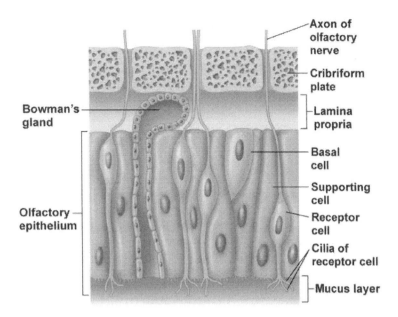

The sense of smell is also supplemented by the sense of taste, as the same substances often stimulate the receptors for both taste and smell. When one loses the sense of taste while sick with a cold, this is often due to losing the sense of smell.

Pheromones

Pheromones are chemicals secreted in sweat and other bodily fluids and have influence beyond the body of the organism secreting them. In many animals, pheromones play a crucial role in behavior, particularly in the areas of sex, fear, and food. Pheromones have been found to play a role in mate attraction; some organisms can release pheromones that attract potential mates from over two miles away. Pheromones also play a role in territory marking; dogs and cats are known to do this by spraying their pheromone-filled urine on objects.

There is research to suggest that pheromones also influence human behavior. A widely known study conducted by Martha McClintock suggested that the menstrual cycle of women could be sped up or slowed down, depending on what pheromones the women were exposed to. The methodology of this study has, however, been called into question. It has also been hypothesized that women prefer the smell of men who have genetically coded immunity (i.e., innate immunity) that is different from their own because this would result in having more disease-resistant children. Pheromones in non-human animals are detected by olfactory membranes, as well as by the *vomeronasal organ*. In adult humans, the vomeronasal organ appears to be shrunk or absent, suggesting that if humans are able to sense pheromones, it is through the regular olfactory process.

Olfactory pathways in the brain

The olfactory pathway is not yet well understood, however, it is known that once sensory information has been detected by the cilia, it gets transferred to the olfactory bulb through openings in the *cribiform plate*, a part of the skull located at the top of the nasal cavity. The *olfactory bulb* is located at the base of the brain and is in direct contact with the limbic system. The limbic system is involved in adrenaline flow, emotion, behavior and long-term memory.

It is hypothesized that the olfactory bulb's connection with the limbic system is the reason smells are often associated with strong emotions and memories. Information in the olfactory bulb is moved through the lateral olfactory tract to the primary olfactory cortex. Information then travels through the thalamus, where interneurons communicate this information to the orbital-frontal cortex, which is where conscious smell perception occurs.

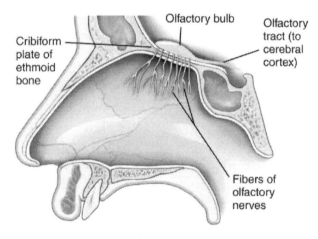

Kinesthetic sense

The *kinesthetic sense* refers to the body's perception of its position, including the movement of joints, muscles, and tendons. Even when one's eyes are closed, the brain is able to sense where different parts of the body are. This is due to the kinesthetic sense, also called *proprioception*. The kinesthetic sense provides constant feedback to the brain of what the muscles in the body are doing. Much of this information is subconscious and out of awareness.

Proprioceptors are receptors that provide sensory information about joint angle, muscle length and muscle tension. Information from the body is transmitted from these proprioceptors to the parietal cortex of the brain, where information about the position of body parts can be interpreted. The channel through which this transmission of information occurs has yet to be discovered, although it is hypothesized to be a similar pathway to that of touch.

Vestibular sense

The *vestibular sense* refers to the awareness of balance and spatial orientation. Sensory information for this sense primarily originates in the inner ear, but visual and propioceptive information is also used. The processes for the sense of balance can be divided into dynamic equilibrium and static equilibrium. *Dynamic equilibrium* refers to the rotational movement of the head and utilizes the semicircular canals. The enlarged bases of the canals are called *ampullas*. Fluid within the canals causes the stereocilia of the hair cells to bend. This information is then carried by the vestibular nerve to the brain.

Static equilibrium involves vertical and horizontal movement and is detected when the head moves with reference to gravity. Static equilibrium utilizes the utricle and the saccule by the *maculae* (specialized mechanoreceptors) within them. The *utricle* and the *saccule* are small membranous sacs that contain hair cells. The utricle is sensitive to horizontal movements, while the saccule is more sensitive to vertical movements. Small carbon granules that rest on a gelatinous membrane that contains hair cells are displaced when movement occurs. This bends the hair cells and indicates the direction of movement.

Information from both static equilibrium and dynamic equilibrium hair cells is transmitted to the parietal lobe. There, it is integrated with sensory information stemming from other areas of the body. This integration provides a complete sense of movement and balance.

Notes

Perception

Bottom-up/Top-down processing

Both bottom-up and top-down processing are strategies used by the brain to understand stimuli. *Top-down processing* occurs when perceptions are formed by working from a larger concept to more specific information. Top-down processing is also known as concept-driven processing and often occurs outside of conscious awareness. When one sees an image or word that is incomplete (e.g. the image below), but is able to fill in the missing details, this is a form of top-down processing. Top-down processing also has applications in the realm of sensation. For example, if a boy walks into a pizza shop and smells something ambiguous, he will likely identify it as the smell of pizza because of his expectations. When expectations or prior knowledge influence perception, top-down processing is occurring.

Bottom-up processing can be conceptualized as occurring in the direction opposite to top-down processing. This process starts with sensory information and then moves to higher level processing. Bottom-up processing is also known as data-driven processing. If one accidentally places their hand on a hot stove, the reaction will be to pull away quickly without making a conscious decision to do so. Because processing moved directly from the stimulus (pain) to action, bottom-up processing has occurred.

There is much debate surrounding the degree to which sensory systems rely on top-down processing verses bottom-up processing. Researchers have thus turned to neurobiology in an attempt to answer these questions. Although much is still unknown, certain areas of the brain have been found to have more bottom-up connections and others more top-down connections. The primary visual cortex is believed to contain mostly bottom-up connections. The *fusiform gyrus*, part of the temporal lobe and the occipital lobe, is believed to be involved in top-down processing.

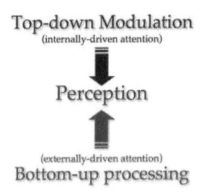

Perceptual organization

The environment we live in is three-dimensional, and thus we need a three-dimensional approach to understand it. Therefore, the three dimensions of height, width and depth must be measured by the eyes. Organisms are only able to conceptualize these properties by processing sensory information within the brain. For example, the brain uses many rules and principles to determine the depth of an object.

One rule concerns *relative size*, meaning that smaller objects tend to be perceived as farther away. *Interposition* means that objects that block other objects are usually perceived as closer. *Relative clarity* is the principle that states objects that have a clear image are perceived as closer than objects that have a hazy image. Objects that are higher in the visual field also tend to be perceived as farther away. *Parallel lines* appear to converge with distance, giving the perception of depth. The brain also uses shading to inform depth perception; dimmer objects often seem farther away.

The brain also uses rules and principles to determine the motion of an object. The images of objects that are traveling towards the eye appear to grow, while the images of objects that are traveling away appear to shrink. The *phi phenomenon* is an optical illusion whereby one perceives a continuous motion between separate objects flashing at a certain speed.

The process of identifying a form despite a brand new image being displayed on the retina is referred to as *form perception*. During visual processing, information is formatted to draw out relevant and detailed information from a stimulus. Although this process is not fully understood, it is believed to occur in the areas of the brain known as the ventral and dorsal streams.

The brain is also able to perceive objects as unchanging, even when the retinal image changes. This ability is known as *constancy*. For example, people are able to identify their friends even when seeing them at different angles and do not think they have transformed into different people just because they have turned around.

Gestalt principles

Gestalt is a German term that translates to shape or form. Within psychology, Gestalt usually refers to an organized or unified whole. The basic principle guiding Gestalt psychology is the idea that the whole is greater than the sum of its parts, thus emphasizing top-down processing. Gestalt psychology seeks to understand how organisms perceive meaning out of apparently meaningless stimuli, particularly visual stimuli. Several Gestalt principles have been proposed to describe the ways in which humans perceive "wholes" from parts. The Gestalt principles are generally broken up into categories of similarity, continuation, closure, proximity and figure.

The *similarity principle* proposes that when an image is made up of similar elements, these elements will be integrated into groups and each group will be perceived as a single unit. The *principle of continuation* asserts that groups that are aligned with each other tend to be perceived as wholes. The *closure principle* states that even when an image is incomplete, if enough of the image is present, the mind will be able to fill in the gaps and the image will be perceived as whole. The *proximity principle* proposes that when items are close to each other, they tend to be perceived as one group. The *figure principle* refers to the tendency to differentiate an object from its surroundings by perceiving the object as a figure and the surroundings as background.

Please, leave your Customer Review on Amazon

Notes

Chapter 5

Learning

Changes in behavior can be categorized as either learned or unlearned. In explorations of the differences between the two types of behavior change, conversations about learning are evoked. This process can be categorized as classical conditioning, operant conditioning and observational learning. Biological bases of behavior expose the predispositions for learning. Common examples of these phenomena can be recognized in the everyday situations of pet training (operant conditioning) and phobia development (classical conditioning). Concerning classical and operant conditioning, there is a multitude of associated concepts of acquisition, contiguity, contingency, discrimination, extinction, generalization, punishment, reinforcement and spontaneous recovery. Research involving cognition in learning and animals' biological predispositions toward learning has contributed heavily to the field.

Notes

Classical Conditioning

Classical conditioning is a type of learning that occurs when a conditioned stimulus is paired with an unconditioned stimulus to produce a conditioned response. In classical conditioning (as opposed to operant conditioning), there is no voluntary or conscious control over whether or not a behavioral response occurs following the pairing of stimuli. Behaviors conditioned through a classical conditioning procedure are not maintained by consequences, but rather by the continuous association of specific stimuli.

Neutral, conditioned and unconditioned stimuli; conditioned and unconditioned responses

Learning is defined as a durable change in behavior brought about by experience. *Associative learning* occurs when an organism learns that events are connected, or when a response becomes associated with a particular stimulus. In one form of associative learning, *classical conditioning*, a stimulus that initially had no response associated with it becomes paired with a stimulus that elicits a response. This pairing results in the stimulus that initially had no response eliciting the same response as the stimulus it was paired with.

Classical conditioning was accidentally discovered by Ivan Pavlov, who was originally studying the digestive system of dogs. He found that after repeated pairing of a bell ringing and food, the dogs he studied started to salivate at the sound of the bell, even when there was no food.

In this experiment, the food was the *unconditioned stimulus*, because it elicited a response from the dogs naturally; this response did not have to be learned. Salivation at the presentation of food was the *unconditioned response*, as it also did not have to be learned. The sound of the bell changed from a *neutral stimulus* to a *conditioned stimulus* through the learning process. Salivation in response to the bell is the *conditioned response*, as it had to be learned through conditioning. Note that behaviors learned through classical conditioning are not maintained by their consequences, but rather by paired associations.

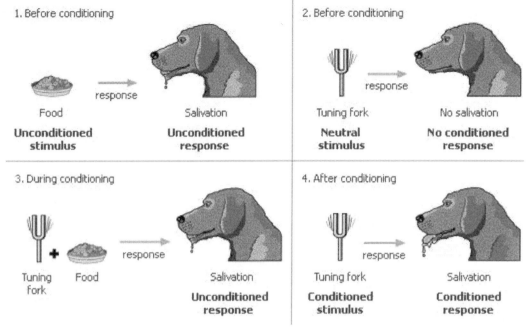

1. Before conditioning

Food
Unconditioned stimulus

→ response

Salivation
Unconditioned response

2. Before conditioning

Tuning fork
Neutral stimulus

→ response

No salivation
No conditioned response

3. During conditioning

Tuning fork + Food

→ response

Salivation
Unconditioned response

4. After conditioning

Tuning fork
Conditioned stimulus

→ response

Salivation
Conditioned response

Classical conditioning

The classical conditioning process also plays a large role in the development of phobias and anxiety. In a famous experiment often called the "Little Albert" experiment, Watson and Rayner demonstrated that classical conditioning could be used to make a previously neutral stimulus elicit a phobic reaction in humans. Little Albert was a nine-month-old infant who showed no response to a white rat at the beginning of the experiment. He did, however, start to cry whenever a hammer was struck against a steel bar. Over seven weeks, the white rat and loud noise were repeatedly paired. At the end of the seven weeks, Little Albert displayed a fear response to the white rat, even when the loud noise was not present. In this example, the white rat was originally a neutral stimulus and became a conditioned stimulus. Crying in response to this conditioned stimulus was the conditioned response. Albert's crying in response to the loud noise (unconditioned stimulus) was the unconditioned response.

During *forward conditioning*, learning occurs at the fastest rate. In forward conditioning, the start of the conditioned stimulus comes before the start of the unconditioned stimulus in order to signal that the unconditioned stimulus will follow. Delay and trace conditioning are two examples of forward conditioning. In *delay conditioning*, the conditioned stimulus is active and is overlapped with the activity of the unconditioned stimulus.

During *trace conditioning*, the conditioned stimulus and unconditioned stimulus do not overlap. Rather, the conditioned stimulus begins and ends before the unconditioned stimulus is active. The period of time with no stimulus is known as the *trace interval*, observed, for example, when a buzzer sounds for five seconds and a second later a puff of air is shot into an eye and the person blinks. After multiple pairings of the buzzer and the puff of air, the person will blink at the sound of the buzzer itself.

In *simultaneous conditioning*, the conditioned stimulus and unconditioned stimulus are active and inactive at the same time. Following the above example, ringing the buzzer and blowing a puff of air at the same time would mean the conditioned and unconditioned stimulus have coincided.

Simultaneous conditioning

In *second-order* and *higher-order conditioning*, a two-step process is involved. The first step involves presenting a neutral stimulus, or conditioned stimulus (1), which then comes to signal an unconditioned stimulus through forward conditioning. Then, a second neutral stimulus, or conditioned stimulus (2), is paired with the conditioned stimulus (1), and comes to produce its own unique conditioned response. For example, bell ringing is paired with food until the sound of the bell elicits salivation. If a light is then paired with a bell, the light will also elicit salivation. The sound of the bell is the conditioned stimulus (1), food is the unconditioned stimulus. The light becomes the conditioned stimulus (2) once it is paired with the conditioned stimulus (1).

In *backward conditioning*, the conditioned stimulus immediately follows an unconditioned stimulus. Here, the conditioned response for the conditioned stimulus proves to be inhibitory. This occurs because the conditioned stimulus acts as a signal that the unconditioned stimulus has ended, rather than as a signal that the unconditioned stimulus is about to surface. Here, the puff of air into an individual's eye could be followed by the sound of the buzzer.

Temporal conditioning is when an unconditioned stimulus is presented at regular time intervals. Conditioning is said to have occurred successfully when the conditioned response tends to occur shortly before each unconditioned stimulus. Here, an organism's biological clock comes into play and serves as the conditioned stimulus.

In the *zero contingency procedure*, the conditioned stimulus is paired with the unconditioned stimulus; however, this unconditioned stimulus can be present at other times. If this occurs, it is assumed that the unconditioned stimulus can occur without the presence of the conditioned stimulus. Consequently, the conditioned stimulus does not predict the unconditioned stimulus per se, the conditioning does not occur, and the conditioned stimulus does not necessarily produce a conditioned response. This finding suggests that the component of associate learning known as *prediction*, rather than the pairing of a conditioned and unconditioned stimulus, precedes conditioning. This finding had a great impact on later conditioning research.

Processes: acquisition, extinction, spontaneous recovery, generalization, discrimination

In classical conditioning, *acquisition* refers to the period of time when the conditioned response is first established and gradually strengthened. Acquisition occurs at the first instance that an organism displays a conditioned response to a previously neutral stimulus. *Extinction* is the process of a conditioned response being decreased or discontinued. In classical conditioning, extinction occurs when a previously conditioned stimulus is no longer paired with an unconditioned stimulus. Once Pavlov discontinued the bell ringing and food pairing, for example, the dogs stopped salivating in response to the sound of the bell.

Spontaneous recovery refers to the re-emergence of a previously extinguished conditioned response after a period of rest. This renewed conditioned response is usually much weaker than the conditioned response before extinction. Spontaneous recovery sometimes occurs when the organism is returned to the environment in which the conditioned response was acquired. *Stimulus generalization* is said to occur if stimuli similar to the conditioned stimulus elicit the same conditioned response. This occurs when the similar stimuli are not themselves conditioned. In the Little Albert experiment, for example, Little Albert developed a fear not only of white rats, but of all furry animals, including cats and dogs.

Stimulus discrimination refers to the ability to differentiate between a conditioned stimulus and other similar stimuli. For example, if Pavlov's dogs had not salivated in response to a novel bell sound, this would be a form of stimulus discrimination.

Operant Conditioning

Operant conditioning is another type of associative learning, in which an individual's behavior is modified by its antecedents (i.e., before trained behavior) and consequences. It is distinguished from classical conditioning (respondent conditioning), because operant conditioning deals with the reinforcement and punishment to change behavior. Operant behavior operates on the environment and is maintained by its antecedents and consequences, while classical conditioning deals with the conditioning of reflexive (reflex) behaviors, elicited by prior associations.

Operant conditioning was originally studied by Edward Thorndike and was popularized by B.F. Skinner, known for his experiments on lab rats. Operant conditioning focuses on the antecedents and consequences of behavior, and their effect on the rate of behavior. Operant conditioning is used widely in applied behavior analysis, an evidence-based therapy primarily used for children with autism and in the treatment of anxiety disorders.

Types of reinforcement: positive, negative, primary, conditional

Reinforcement can be defined as anything that increases a behavior. Reinforcement is not related to the intention of the person attempting to change a behavior. For example, if a teacher praises a student in class for always turning in their homework on time and this behavior subsequently decreases, the praise acted not as a reinforcement, but a punishment. Similarly, a teacher who does not allow a student to go outside for recess after the student is disruptive in class would be reinforcing the disruptive behavior if the student becomes more disruptive.

Positive reinforcement involves the addition of a stimulus after a behavior occurs to increase the behavior. Positive reinforcement occurs when a child is presented with a sticker every time he or she raises a hand in class, as long as the hand-raising behavior increases.

Negative reinforcement involves taking away a stimulus to increase a behavior. For example, a teacher may cease teaching when a child in class starts to throw a tantrum. If the tantrum-throwing behavior increases in response, it can be said that the tantrum-throwing behavior was negatively reinforced by the removal of the lesson. In positive and negative reinforcement, the words positive and negative do not mean good or bad but refer to the presentation or removal of a stimulus.

Dog training using positive reinforcement

Primary reinforcers are reinforcers that are naturally reinforcing for an organism, such as food, water and pleasure. *Conditioned reinforcers* are reinforcers that are not naturally reinforcing for organisms. These stimuli become reinforcing by being associated with primary reinforcers via classical conditioning. If a student receives a token for good behavior in class and is able to turn in the token for candy, the token will likely become a conditioned reinforcer, as it becomes associated with receiving candy.

Before picking out a specific reinforcer, the *Premack Principle* should be taken into consideration. This principle states that when choosing a particular reinforcer, the person who is receiving the reinforcer must be considered. If a child likes to eat chocolate ice cream but hates going to dance class, the parent can use chocolate ice cream as the reinforcer to make the child go to dance class. In other words, more probable behaviors reinforce less probable behaviors.

Reinforcement schedules:
fixed-ratio, variable-ratio, fixed-interval, variable-interval

The rate at which a behavior occurs depends largely on when it is reinforced. There are four main types of reinforcement schedules: fixed-ratio, variable-ratio, fixed-interval and variable-interval.

On a *fixed-ratio schedule*, a reinforcer is presented after a behavior occurs a set number of times. For example, on a fixed-ratio schedule, a rat receives a food pellet after pushing a lever ten times. A fixed-ratio schedule of reinforcement results in a steady increase in behavior, with a brief pause after each reinforcer is delivered.

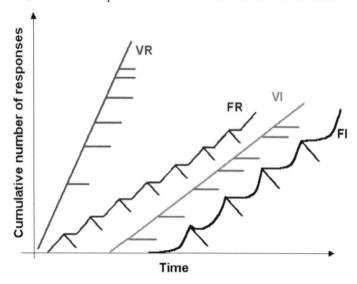

On a *variable-ratio schedule*, a behavior is reinforced after an unpredictable number of responses. For example, a rat receives a food pellet after pushing a lever ten times, then after five times, then again after four times. On a variable-ratio schedule, behavior increases rapidly at a steady rate. Lottery games are often based on this schedule of reinforcement.

On a *fixed-interval schedule* of reinforcement, a reinforcer is presented following a behavior after a fixed amount of time has passed. For example, a rat receives a food pellet the first time he presses a lever after a one-minute interval has elapsed. Receiving a paycheck after working for two weeks is also an example of a fixed-interval schedule of reinforcement. Fixed-interval schedules are considered the weakest schedule of reinforcement.

On a *variable-interval schedule* of reinforcement, a reinforcer is presented after the first response, following a variable amount of time. For example, a rat is presented with a food pellet after pushing a lever after one minute, then again after two minutes, and again after three minutes. This reinforcement schedule results in a steady increase in behavior.

Processes of shaping and extinction

Shaping refers to the process of reinforcing small approximations of a desired behavior. Shaping is used when a desired behavior does not occur or occurs less frequently than desired. When shaping a behavior, the desired behavior is broken down into small steps, which are then reinforced individually. Shaping is often used in dog training and for teaching children with autism to speak. When teaching a pet to spin around, a pet trainer starts by positively reinforcing head-turning behavior. Once the dog is consistently turning its head, the trainer then only rewards the dog for turning its head and taking a step. Once the dog is doing that consistently, the trainer only rewards the dog for turning its head and taking two steps, etc. Reinforcement of the small steps that make up spinning in a circle continues until the dog spins in a full circle. When teaching a child with autism to say the word "cookie," a behavioral therapist would reinforce after the child makes a "c" sound, then a "coo" sound, then a "cook" sound, and finally would reinforce only after the child says the word "cookie."

Extinction Graph

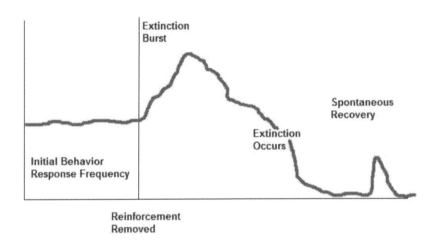

Extinction in operant conditioning is the process of stopping the reinforcement of a previously reinforced behavior. Note that extinction for operant conditioning differs from extinction for classical conditioning. In order for extinction to be effective, all reinforcement of the undesired behavior must be stopped. Thus, in a clinical setting, it is important to make sure that parents and teachers are made aware of the extinction process. Shortly after the start of the extinction process, an *extinction burst* will occur. An extinction burst is a temporary increase in the undesired behavior.

The concept of an extinction burst was accidentally discovered by B.F. Skinner when a pellet dispenser jammed in an experiment that involved a rat pressing a lever to receive food. Skinner found that the rat initially pushed the lever at a greater rate when it stopped receiving reinforcement. After a while, the lever pressing behavior declined, and eventually stopped altogether.

B.F. Skinner, American psychologist

When using extinction to get a dog to stop begging for food at the dinner table, all members of the family must be willing to stop giving the dog food or else a variable schedule of reinforcement will be created, and the behavior will be strengthened. Initially, the dog will increase the begging behavior. After the extinction burst has reached its peak, the begging behavior will begin to decline and eventually stop altogether.

Punishment

Punishment can be defined as anything that decreases a behavior. As with reinforcement, whether or not something is considered punishment is dependent solely on its effect on the rate of behavior. *Positive punishment* occurs when a stimulus is added, and a behavior subsequently decreases. Receiving a speeding ticket can be considered a form of positive punishment, as long as speeding behavior subsequently decreases. *Negative punishment* occurs when a stimulus is removed, and a behavior subsequently decreases. Taking away a child's television after they swear is a form of negative punishment.

Behavior analysts and animal trainers tend to avoid using punishment, as it has been hypothesized to increase aggression and may lead to the emergence of other problematic behaviors. When punishment is used in behavior analysis or animal training, it is usually done only when extinction alone has failed to reduce a behavior. Punishment is generally used in conjunction with the reinforcement of an *incompatible behavior*. For example, a teacher who has a child in her class who hits the classmates sitting next to him may punish hitting behavior while reinforcing hand-folding. Also, note that successful punishment may become negatively reinforcing for the punisher.

	Positive (+) To add, present, provide	Negative (-) To remove, take away
Reinforcement - behavior INCREASES in the future	**Positive Reinforcement** A stimulus is **PROVIDED** contingent on the behavior which leads to an **INCREASE** of behavior in the future.	**Negative Reinforcement** A stimulus is **REMOVED** contingent on the behavior, which leads to an **INCREASE** of behavior in the future.
Punishment - behavior DECREASES in the future	**Positive Punishment** A stimulus is **PROVIDED** contingent on the behavior, which leads to a **DECREASE** of behavior in the future.	**Negative Punishment** A stimulus is **REMOVED** contingent on the behavior, which leads to a **DECREASE** of behavior in the future.

Positive vs. negative reinforcement/punishment

Trial-and-error learning is a form of operant conditioning that combines both punishment and reinforcement. If a response is desirable, the organism will increase this behavior (reinforcement). If a response is undesirable, the organism will avoid this behavior (punishment).

Escape and avoidance learning

Escape learning is a type of learning that occurs when an individual performs a behavior to terminate an aversive stimulus. Escape behavior then becomes negatively reinforced as it increases in rate due to the removal of a stimulus. Escape conditioning is believed to play a large role in the maintenance of many psychopathologies.

Individuals with social anxiety may, for instance, leave (escape) a highly social environment, resulting in the removal of the anxiety. Although this reduction in anxiety may seem temporarily beneficial, the escape behavior becomes reinforced and is more likely to recur in the future.

Avoidance learning is a type of learning that results from escape behavior. If a signal is given before the aversive stimulus is activated, the organism will learn to proactively engage in escape behavior. For example, a person with social anxiety who has learned to escape highly social and anxiety-producing situations may begin to avoid these situations altogether.

Avoidant behavior is self-reinforcing, meaning that the reinforcer (relief) occurs whether or not the aversive stimulus is actually avoided. Since avoidance learning is self-reinforcing, avoidance behavior will often perpetuate without an intervention. Thus, *exposure therapy* might be used for the individual with social anxiety who now avoids all social situations. Exposure therapy involves exposing the individual to the previously avoided stimuli with the intention of breaking the pattern of escape, thus decreasing the fear response.

Table Comparing Two Forms of Associative Learning

	Classical Conditioning	**Operant Conditioning**
Response	Involuntary, automatic	Voluntary, operates environment
Acquisition	Associating events where the conditioned stimulus announces the unconditioned stimulus	Associating response with a consequence (reinforcer or punisher)
Extinction	Conditioned Response decreases; conditioned stimulus is repeatedly presented alone	Responses decrease when reinforcement stops (after initial temporary increase)
Cognitive processes	Individuals develop the expectation that conditioned stimulus signals the arrival of unconditioned stimulus	Subjects develop the expectation that a response will be reinforced or punished. They also exhibit latent learning without reinforcement
Biological predisposition	Natural predispositions constrain what stimuli and responses can easily be associated	Organisms best learn behaviors similar to their natural behaviors; unnatural behaviors instinctively drift back toward natural ones

Notes

The Role of Cognitive Processes in Associative Learning

As mentioned before, there are two types of associative learning: classical conditioning and operant conditioning. Both classical and operant conditioning are under the category of behavioral psychology. *Behaviorism* deals with observing behavior and its corresponding consequences. Behaviorism views the mind as a "black box" that is never taken into consideration. On the other hand, *cognitive psychology* takes a completely different approach. In cognitive psychology, the brain is taken into consideration and the discipline's main focus is to study how thoughts affect people's views and behavior. Cognitive psychologists do not think learning is solely due to stimulus pairing and reinforcement, although they acknowledge these two factors are components of the learning process.

For example, scientist Wolfgang Kohler observed that when his chimp was given the challenge of reaching a fruit hanging from the ceiling, the chimp was eventually able to reach the fruit using various props that were in the room. The chimp stacked boxes to get within reach of the fruit, and then used a stick to obtain it. In this case, the chimp combined and used previously learned behaviors to solve the problem.

In this case, the chimp combined and used previously learned behaviors to solve the problem.

Insight learning describes when previously learned behaviors are suddenly combined in innovative ways. For the chimp, stacking the boxes and using the stick were reinforced because the chimp was able to obtain the fruit every time. When a new situation was presented where the fruit was completely out of reach, the chimp was able to combine the two reinforced behaviors in a unique way to obtain the desired result of retrieving the fruit.

Another day-to-day example for humans is taking a different route while driving and getting stuck in traffic. Similarly, insight learning can be observed when someone is trying to hang a picture up on the wall and pulls a chair over to where the picture needs to be placed, gets on the chair, and proceeds to place the picture on the desired part of the wall.

This phenomenon can also be seen in the opposite light, where previously unseen behavior can come into play when necessary. This process is called *latent learning.* In latent learning, something is learned but is not expressed as an observable behavior until it is required. For example, a child who is driven to school by her parents every day learns the route to school. One day when her parents are not able to drive her to school, the child is able to successfully navigate her way to school independently using a bike.

Conditioning does not only refer to behavioral learning. In operant conditioning, certain behaviors are reinforced, and the probability of that behavior being repeated increases. Cognitively, the reinforcement provides the expectation of a future reinforcer. Thinking prospectively is involved in this particular type of learning. Expectation might also be present in stimulus generalization. For example, if students are rewarded for raising their hand before speaking in one class, they may begin to expect this behavior to be reinforced in all other classes.

Biological Processes That Affect Associative Learning

Learning is a change in behavior due to experience. There are many outside factors that can affect learning, but it is constrained biologically. For example, chimpanzees are able to communicate only via sign language, but not vocally because they do not have fully developed vocal cords. Associative learning is understood through the use of stimuli that are essential for the organism's survival. Not all reinforcers are equally effective.

Another example of this mechanism is food aversion. If someone becomes nauseous after eating chocolate, even though the cause of nausea might not be solely due to the chocolate, he or she will develop a strong aversion to the taste and smell of chocolate. The aversion to chocolate goes against the principles of associative learning because it occurs after one instance, and the aversion lasts for a long period of time, sometimes indefinitely. Different research groups have tried to condition organisms to associate the feeling of nausea to other factors like sound and light, but thus far they have not been able to do so. It is argued that learning occurs more rapidly if it is biologically relevant to the organism.

Learning is a process that causes physical changes to the central nervous system. Different parts of the brain are involved in learning different things. The cerebellum, for example, is responsible for learning motor tasks and the amygdala is involved in learning fear responses.

Learning and memory are interconnected as various synaptic connections form following memory formation. New incoming information is initially stored as a *short-term memory,* lasting from seconds to hours, and then can be permanently transformed into *long-term memory* via a process called *consolidation.*

Notes

Animal Behavior

Sensitive Periods

In humans and animals, certain behaviors must occur during a *sensitive period*, or critical period, in order to be learned. *Imprinting* is one such form of learning associated with a sensitive period. Imprinting is a phase-sensitive type of learning (learning occurring at a particular age or life stage) that is rapid and independent of the consequences of behavior.

For most animals that imprint, the sensitive period occurs within 13-16 hours of life. For example, chicks, ducklings, and goslings follow the first moving object that they see after they hatch. These animals usually imprint on their mother but have the ability to imprint on any moving organism or object, including humans.

Song learning in birds also involves a sensitive period. Work by Peter Marler shows that young birds learn to sing in part from older birds. Songs heard outside of the sensitive period have no effect on the birds. The brains of these birds are primed to respond to acoustic stimuli during the sensitive period; the birds are even able to learn other species' songs due to the strength of social influence during this time.

In humans and animals, vision is also learned during a critical period. The parts of the brain that process vision develop from signals stemming from the eyes. One experiment showing this involved sewing one eye of a cat shut immediately after birth. Only vision in the open eye developed; the sewn-up eye did not develop normally and was unable to sense visual stimuli. In humans, it is important to treat babies that are born blind as soon as possible to ensure that the critical period for vision is not missed.

Cycles of behavior

Daily cycles of behavior are known as *circadian rhythms*. These include any biological processes that tend to reoccur every 24 hours. Circadian rhythms have been observed widely in cyanobacteria, fungi, plants, and animals. These rhythms are driven by a *circadian clock*, an internal mechanism that receives input from external cues and provides output that regulates behavior. The circadian clock is driven primarily by input from sunlight but is also affected by temperature, eating and drinking patterns and social interactions.

Nocturnality is a pattern of animal behavior characterized by activity during the night and sleeping during the day. Nocturnal creatures generally have certain adaptations that allow them to thrive on this sleep pattern. These animals often have highly developed senses of hearing, helping them to avoid predators and communicate. They also often have larger corneas to allow for more light to enter their eyes in the dark.

Communication

Communication is any action by a sender that influences the behavior of a receiver. Often, these signals benefit both the sender and the receiver. The four types of communication used by animals are chemical communication, auditory communication, visual communication and tactile communication.

The four types of communication used by animals are chemical communication, auditory communication, visual communication and tactile communication.

Chemical communication stems from signals that are chemicals, such as pheromones, urine, and feces. A *pheromone* is a chemical that is released to cause a reaction in another member of the same species. Pheromones that trigger reversible behavioral changes are called *releaser pheromones*, while those that cause long-term behavioral changes are called *primer pheromones*. Chemical communication is often used in mating and territory marking. Female moths attract males with tail gland pheromones, while cats mark their territory with urine.

Auditory communication is communication stemming from sound. Auditory communication is faster than chemical communication and can be modified by volume, pattern, duration, and repetition. Like chemical communication, auditory communication is often used in mating and for marking territories. Whale songs, for example, have six basic themes for mating and group identification. Birds also have various songs for distress, courting and marking territory. Language is the ultimate auditory communication, and complex language is restricted to humans. Non-human primates are limited to about 40 vocalizations with limited meaning. Chimpanzees cannot advance beyond the level of a two-year-old child, even when raised in an environment identical to that of an infant. Grammar also appears to exist exclusively in humans.

Visual communication is used most often by animals that are active during the day. Visual communication is generally used in defense and courtship displays. These displays are generally exaggerated and always performed in the same way to ensure the meaning is clear. Visual communication between males makes use of threat postures, which may prevent fighting. These behaviors include baring of teeth to display aggression and lying in a supine position to display submission. Visual communication is also used in animal courtship through dancing. In bees, visual communication is used to convey information about food sources. A bee that has located a good source of pollen returns to the hive and performs a dance indicating the distance and direction of the source from the hive.

Tactile communication occurs when one animal touches another. Tactile communication is used for feeding, mating, and grooming. Gull chicks peck at their parent's beak to display hunger and to prompt the parent to feed them. Male leopards will nuzzle the female's neck to stimulate her willingness to mate. In primates, grooming is used to clean the skin or coat of another and also helps to create social bonds.

Tactile communication is used for feeding, mating, and grooming.

Many animal species have mate-selection rituals referred to as "courtship." These can involve a combination of chemical, auditory, visual and tactile communications (e.g., complicated dances, touching, vocalizations, displays of beauty or fighting prowess). Most animal courtship occurs out of sight of humans and is often the least documented of animal behaviors.

Learned Behaviors

Non-associative learning occurs when a particular organism is exposed to only one type of stimulus. It reflects the relatively permanent change in the strength of a response towards a single stimulus due to repeated exposure to that particular stimulus. It is considered the simplest way of learning. The two major types of non-associative learning are habituation and sensitization.

A *habit* is a behavior that is performed continuously and repeatedly until it becomes automatic. Habituation in a certain sense takes the same course of action. *Habituation* is defined as a learned behavior that allows animals to disregard meaningless stimuli by diminishing a response to a frequently repeated stimulus. It is stimulus specific. There are two types of habituation, including *short-term habituation* and *long-term habituation.* Short-term habituation lasts a few minutes or hours. The stimulus is presented at relatively short intervals, for example, every 15 seconds. The response to the stimulus decreases quite quickly with repetition. The response strength recovers after a period of time without any type of stimulus.

Long-term habituation lasts for days or weeks. It involves short-term habituation that is induced repeatedly, with a long period of time between each short-term habituation session. The individual remains habituated to the stimulus for days or even weeks. Habituation differs from extinction because the behaviors that decrease in extinction are learned, while the behaviors decreased in habituation are innate. Sea anemones, for example, will disregard repeated "feeding" stimulation with a stick.

Sensitization is where an individual becomes more responsive to the stimulus with each repeated presentation of the stimulus. Instead of having the ability to tune out the stimulus or avoid reacting in general, the stimulus tends to have a more profound effect. For example, when someone is trying to fall asleep, the sound of water dripping from a faucet becomes more difficult to ignore. Sensitization may also cause an individual to respond strongly to similar stimuli. For example, as an individual leaves a rock concert and an ambulance passes by with its loud siren, the siren might seem louder than usual and more painful to the ears, as the individual's ears have become sensitized to the rock music. Sensitization is only temporary and does not cause any long-term behavioral changes.

Insight learning is a form of learning involving reason and rationality. Insight learning is a form of problem-solving that occurs suddenly through understanding the relationship between different aspects of a problem. Insight learning involves a sudden realization that is distinct from cause-and-effect problem-solving. Apes presented with a problem requiring them to use objects in new ways in order to receive food are believed to use insight learning to solve the problem. Insight learning manifests as a spontaneous occurrence and is a noteworthy phenomenon in the learning process.

Spatial learning is a form of associative learning that refers to the process by which animals encode information about their environment. In spatial learning, animals associate attributes of a landmark with reward. Wasps, for example, are able to associate pine cones with the location of their nest and become lost when the pine cones are removed.

Innate Behaviors

Innate behavior, also called instinct or inborn behavior, is the inherent inclination of a living organism towards a particular complex behavior the organism is "programmed to do." The simplest example of an instinctive behavior is a *fixed action pattern*, in which a very short to medium length sequence of actions, without variation, is carried out in response to a clearly defined stimulus. Any behavior is instinctive if it is performed without being based upon prior experience (that is, in the absence of learning) and is an expression of innate biological factors.

Inherited behaviors develop because they increase fitness across generations. In mammals, care for offspring by female parents is believed to be an innate behavior. Some innate behaviors require maturation, making them appear learned. Birds, for example, appear to fly through observational learning but in laboratory settings are able to fly on their first try even without seeing another bird fly. In this example, the flight behavior is innate, but the ability to fly requires physical maturation.

Fixed action patterns, or behavioral patterns, are behaviors that are always performed in the same way and are elicited by a sign stimulus. Behavioral patterns are believed to be innate, although recent research has called this belief into question; many behaviors formerly thought to be fixed action patterns are found to have developed after practice. One example of a behavioral pattern occurs in Kelp gull chicks, who beg for food from parents by pecking at a red spot on their mothers' beak. In a lab setting, the chicks at first will peck at any beak model but later will only peck at models resembling the parents. This suggests that behavior patterns are not completely innate.

Notes

Observational Learning

Most advanced organisms, including humans, do not only learn through direct experience. *Observational learning* is another form of learning relevant to humans and animals. In observational learning, learning occurs through observing the behavior of others. *Observational learning* can also be called social learning or vicarious learning and is the learning that occurs by watching and imitating others.

Observational learning was identified in 1961 in an experiment conducted by Albert Bandura. In this experiment, children in one group observed an adult playing aggressively with a bobo doll; children in another group observed an adult playing non-aggressively with the same doll. Children in the group who had observed the adult playing aggressively with the doll were much more likely to play aggressively than those in the other group. Another study found that monkeys born in a laboratory do not express a fear of snakes until they are shown a video of other monkeys showing a fear response to snakes.

Modeling

Modeling is a basic mechanism of observational learning. Here, the observer sees the action being performed by another individual. As time passes, the same observer imitates that particular action. Children usually engage in an activity like "playing house" or playing "superhero." Most children play the role of mom or Superman based on the models they have observed. An adult's appearance is modeled after the appearance of other members of society; for example, an adult's dress, walk, and talk are all similar to that of his or her acquaintances.

Modeling is not just limited to humans. Lions are involved in modeling as well. Lionesses take their cubs out when they go hunting, and the cubs observe and are then able to hunt based on what they have observed.

Biological processes that affect observational learning

Mirror neurons

Mirror neurons have been identified in various parts of the brain, including the premotor cortex, supplementary motor area, primary somatosensory cortex, and the inferior parietal cortex. In monkeys, mirror neurons fire when the monkey performs a particular task, as well as when the monkey observes another monkey performing a task. Humans also have mirror neurons, although their exact function is still unknown. Some argue that mirror neurons are activated by connecting the sight and action of a particular movement; essentially, they are programmed to mirror. Other researchers believe that mirror neurons aid in observing and eventually helping us imitate observed actions. Disorders of the mirror neuron mechanism are speculated to be related to autism spectrum disorders.

Role of the brain in experiencing vicarious emotions

It is stated that mirror neurons in humans are involved in *vicarious emotions.* Vicarious emotions include emotions like empathy. Empathy is known as the emotional reaction that is based on another person's emotional condition or understanding of the other person's experience from within the other person's frame of reference.

Applications of observational learning to explain individual behavior

Observational learning connects humans, as humans are social organisms. Humans form and behave like each other throughout development; however, this mimicking is not without flaws. Individual differences are present between humans and animals. Various personality differences and psychological disorders can affect the phenomenon of observational learning. Most of the research on observational learning has focused on violence, suggesting that observing violence can increase the overall behavioral pattern of violent acts in society. However, individuals who observe violence do not always turn out to be violent, and cognitive processes play a central role in how individuals use or choose not to use what they learn through observation.

Chapter 6

Cognition and
States of Consciousness

How people learn, remember, retrieve information and then use it in communication and problem-solving — cumulatively known as cognition — is a critical question to explore in psychology. Consciousness is another topic that figures prominently into discussions of sense-making. Of primary importance is first understanding what it encompasses and then examining the various states of consciousness, such as sleep and sleep cycles, dreams, hypnosis, circadian rhythms, and psychoactive drug effects. Arriving at a definition of consciousness can be a tricky task at best. Methods that researchers can employ to facilitate this endeavor include the construction of individual definitions that are then utilized to explore the states of consciousness and many associated concepts.

Notes

Attention

Attention is a state of focused awareness on a subset of the available perceptual information. It is the ability to focus on a task and concentrate. It refers to the allocation of processing resources.

Selective attention

Selective attention poses a difficulty in attending to more than one activity at the same time. Trying to attend to one task over the other requires the use of selective attention. This can be seen clearly through the classic *Stroop effect*, in which participants asked to identify the ink color of the word describing another color (e.g., when the word "blue" is printed in red) are slower and more prone to errors than when the word and the ink color match. This occurs because reading is an automatic process and color naming is a controlled process. The automatic process of reading interferes with the participant's ability to selectively attend to ink color.

In the dichotic listening task, the participants listen to two messages simultaneously. One message goes to each ear. As they listen, they are asked to ignore one of the messages and repeat back the words from the other message. Not much processing occurs with the unattended message. However, participants are able to identify the message as a human voice or noise and whether the voice was male or female, but the information is limited. They cannot tell what language the voice was speaking, and they cannot report any of the words spoken, even if the same word was repeated over and over again.

The Treisman's Shadowing study highlights that humans cannot attend to multiple stimuli at once. It shows what exactly can draw attention, such as hearing an individual's name in the unattended ear. However, when attention is drawn to the unattended ear, information is lost from the attended ear. This phenomenon is known as the *cocktail party effect*. Essentially, it is not possible for someone to attend to more than one task at a time without one of the activities suffering.

The *Bottleneck theory* describes the bottleneck mechanism that limits the amount of information that can be attended to simultaneously. It controls what information gets through, what is selected, and when the selection occurs.

The phenomenon known as the "cocktail party effect" occurs when information is lost from the attended ear because attention is drawn to the unattended ear.

Researcher Donald Broadbent proposed that in early selection, physical characteristics of messages are used to select one message for further processing, while all other information is ignored.

Anne Treisman proposed that in *attenuation*, physical characteristics are used to select one message for full processing, and other messages are only partially processed.

Researchers J. Anthony and Diana Deutsch proposed that in *late selection* messages get through, but that only one response can be made.

The Treisman and Geffen experiments tested both attenuation and late selection. The tasks of dichotic listening and detecting target words in either channel (where an individual taps upon detection) were both performed. It was found that detection is much worse in the unattended channel, thus supporting the attenuation principle. In late selection, detection should not be a problem, since all the information gets through to the subject.

Divided attention

As mentioned before, it is difficult to attend to more than one stimulus at once. *Interference* occurs when an individual tries to attend to two stimuli at the same time and makes multiple responses, rather than making one response to multiple stimuli.

The *capacity theory* states that there is a limited amount of cognitive resources available to be able to properly conduct mental tasks. Nonetheless, theories suggest that even with multiple resources available, only one cognitive process can occur at a time.

Automatic processing does not require divided attention. An example would be driving a car, listening to the radio and carrying on a conversation at the same time. Controlled processing, on the other hand, requires divided attention.

The *feature integration theory* is a theory on attention and perceptual processing. Sometimes individuals process all parts of a scene in parallel, or at the same time, involving divided attention. Other times, individuals process parts of the scene serially, one at a time, requiring focused attention, overall a more demanding kind of processing that is required when objects are more complex. These two types of processing were tested.

Different types of stimuli were incorporated to test these two different types of processing. The isolated factors used were TIY and the combination factors used were TIZ. Triesman and Gelade hypothesized that if isolated features were involved in divided attention, targets could be identified in parallel with fillers, and if combination features were involved in focused attention and targets could be identified serially with the fillers, then the reaction times for isolated features should be less than the reaction times for conjugation features. They found that TIY had a reaction time of 800 ms and TIZ had a reaction time of 1200 ms. Theoretically, these results provide support for the feature integration theory. People must focus attention on a stimulus before they can synthesize it into a meaningful pattern. Individuals must focus their attention on complex incoming information, including visual and auditory stimuli, in order to synthesize it into a meaningful pattern.

Notes

Cognition

Information-processing model

The *information-processing model* describes how the human mind translates sensory information. This model compares the mind to a computer information processing system. The mind carries out a string of mental computations based on various mental representations. Incoming information is exposed to processes well beyond simple stimulus-response patterns. The mind is involved in bringing in the information through attention mechanisms, working memory processes that actively manipulate the incoming information, and long-term memory that passively holds the incoming information for future use. As children grow, their brains develop as well, leading to higher order processing and sensory-driven responses to incoming information. This model focuses on a continuous pattern of development, rather than having distinct steps like Piaget's theory of cognitive development.

Cognitive development

Piaget's stages of cognitive development

Jean Piaget's theory of cognitive development states that there are specific stages that children go through in which their intellect and ability to understand relationships evolve. The stages outlined by Piaget are in a fixed order for all children, regardless of their country of origin, ethnicity or native language. However, the age range at which children achieve them is flexible and can vary from child to child.

Jean Piaget, Swiss developmental psychologist and philosopher

The *Sensorimotor Stage* occurs between birth and the age of two years. During this period, infants begin to understand the information entering their senses and their ability to interact with the outside world evolves. The child learns to manipulate objects even though he or she is not able to understand and process the permanency of the objects when they are not within the realm of present sensory perception. In other words, once an object is removed from the child's view, he or she is not able to understand that the object still exists. Towards the end of this stage, children are able to achieve the concept of *object permanence.* For example, after object permanence has developed, when a mother leaves the room, the child understands that she will probably return, giving the child a sense of security.

The second stage of Piaget's theory is known as the *Preoperational Stage.* This phase starts when a child achieves object permanency. The age range for this stage is from two to seven years old. Language development occurs quite rapidly in this stage. Here, the child learns how to interact with his/her environment through the use of words and images. *Egocentrism,* which refers to children's belief that everyone sees the world in the same manner that they do, is a distinctive part of this stage. Children in this stage do not understand different perspectives and possess the notion that inanimate objects have the same ability they do to perceive visuals, feelings, sounds, and touch.

Another major focus in this stage of development is *conservation*, which refers to the ability to understand that quantity does not change even if the shape changes. For example, if a short and wide glass of water is poured into a tall and thin glass, the child in this particular stage will perceive that the taller glass has more water because of its greater height. This occurs because the child is not capable of understanding the concept of reversibility and is only able to focus on a single aspect of a stimulus, a phenomenon known as *centration.*

The third stage of Piaget's cognitive development theory is the *Concrete Operations Stage.* This stage involves children from the ages of seven to about twelve. At this stage, there is a slow decrease in *centristic thought* and an increased ability to focus on more than one aspect of a specific stimulus. The child at this stage is able to process the concept of grouping, knowing that small dogs and large dogs belong to the same animal category. Another example is that pennies, quarters, and dollar bills are all part of the larger category of money. This concept of grouping can only be applied to concrete object(s). Other objects that have not been seen or touched remain elusive since the ability of abstract thinking has yet to develop.

The fourth and final stage of Piaget's cognitive development theory is the *Formal Operations Stage.* Children at this stage are from the age of twelve and up. At this stage, the child starts to develop a more abstract view of the world. They are able to apply the concepts of reversibility and conservation to both real and imagined situations. They have a more holistic understanding of the world and the concept of cause and effect. When children enter their teenage years, they are able to develop their own view of the world around them. Most children reach this particular stage, but those that do not are usually referred to as having lower intellectual capacities.

Cognitive changes in late adulthood

In Piaget's theory of cognitive development, the onset of formal operational thinking is thought to proceed up to the age of twenty-five. Expanding on these findings, researchers have focused on the cognitive development that occurs after this age. The *constructive development framework (CDF)* states that the development of post-formal operational thinking in an adult is exemplified mostly by the presence of dialectical thinking.

Dialectical thinking entails the search for the truth through reasoned argumentation. The framework consists of four distinct classes of thoughts, including the process, context, relationship, and transformation.

The *process* class of thought describes the way in which things in our systems come up, evolve, and then eventually disappear. The *context* is the class of thought that describes how things are part of the structure of a larger, stable, and more organized whole. The contextualization of distinct parts within a whole gives rise to various points of view. The *relationship* class of thought describes how things that are part of a larger whole are related, and the nature of their common ground. Finally, the *transformation* class of thought describes how living systems are involved in constant development and transformation (which potentially is a synthesis of the previous form of organization) and are subject to influencing human agency.

In late adulthood, cognition tends to become more focused, and the elderly make the most of their cognitive abilities through goal-oriented processing. Older individuals tend to focus on activities that take minimal cognitive effort but produce maximum results in order to conserve cognitive resources. As individuals enter late adulthood, their memory begins to fail and they have a difficult time remembering events, names, and complex concepts. Although their problem-solving abilities deteriorate with time, their decision-making abilities are usually faster and more focused. Older adults who continue to engage in stimulating their minds through conservation and educational activities tend to experience a slower decline in cognitive abilities than those who remain stagnant.

Role of culture in cognitive development

Lev Vygotsky developed a sociocultural theory of cognitive development, which states that children's cognitive skills evolve from interactions with the culture surrounding them, involving their parents, teachers, and other members of their community. To be able to comprehend the role of culture in cognitive development, Vygotsky proposed that it is imperative to study cognitive development from the views of four interrelated perspectives, including the micro-genetic, ontogenetic, phylogenetic, and socio-historical frameworks.

The *micro-genetic framework* refers to development over short periods of time—minutes and seconds. The *ontogenetic* is associated with changes over a lifetime, and *phylogenetic* refers to changes over evolutionary periods. The *socio-historical framework* refers to changes that have occurred in an individual's culture over time, such as variations in values, norms, traditions, tools, and technology.

Lev Vygotsky, Soviet psychologist

There are two principles of cultural influence in Vygotsky's theory. The first principle states that cultures vary widely in the kinds of institutions and settings they offer to facilitate children's development and in how they assess their cognitive development. The second one is that unless these variations are considered part of the child's cultural contexts, the child's cognitive development is seriously underestimated.

Vygotsky suggested that children are born supplied with necessary mental functions. These functions include memory, sensation, perception, and attention. These mental functions are in turn influenced by the culture they are subjected to, and the culture transforms the functions into new mental processes and higher cognitive abilities over time.

Initial cognitive competence comes from interactions with adults and other knowledgeable people within the child's culture. The myriad tasks a child must learn, such as learning and speaking a new language, are far too complicated to learn in isolation. Vygotsky proposed that most tasks are learned through guidance and encouragement from the culture surrounding the child. That is, the child's cognitive development is influenced and shaped as the child participates in cultural activities and observes adults engaging in those cultural activities.

According to Vygotsky's theory, children's cognitive development is enhanced through the right interactions. For example, a structured learning environment, in which the child is provided with aid and instruction that are uniquely parallel to the child's current abilities, can fuel development. Cooperative and interactive learning exercises are vital during this process, as is monitoring the child's progress very closely. As the child gains more ability, more cognitive responsibility should be given to the child. Unlike Piaget's theory, which emphasizes that peers are the major change agents in a child's cognitive development, Vygotsky's theory proposes that adults are the most important source of guidance.

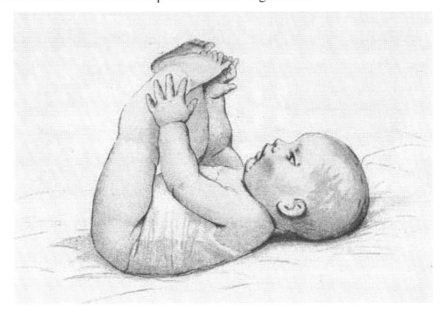

In Vygotsky's theory, children's cognitive development is enhanced through the right interactions, in which they are provided with aid and instruction that are appropriate to the child's current abilities.

Influence of heredity and environment on cognitive development

As with other kinds of development, cognitive development results from the combination of heredity and environmental forces. *Heredity* is the set of inherited developmental instructions transmitted from parent to offspring via the genetic code. The *environment* includes external surroundings and social and cultural influences. The interaction between heredity and the environment can be visualized as a set of paths for development. In the earlier stages of life, development is heavily based on heredity. As life goes on, the number of path options increases, and the influence of the environment also increases.

It is difficult to accurately distinguish the influences that heredity and the environment have on human characteristics. Individuals who possess a similar genetic makeup, such as close relatives, usually also live in similar environments. Consequently, when similarities in IQ are seen within one family, it is hard to differentiate whether these similarities arose from heredity or the environment. However, after extensive research, it has been found that both heredity and the environment play a key role in cognitive development and intelligence.

Many researchers say that heredity sets the upper and lower bounds of an individual's IQ. Physical and behavioral experiences that affect an individual's quality of life may also affect their intellectual development. Many researchers argue that the environment determines IQ. Historically, the race and intelligence controversy has encouraged discrimination against members of minority groups, reinforcing separate social classes and affecting the general understanding of cognitive development. Individuals in lower social classes have historically been deprived of learning resources, parental assistance, role models, and privacy for studying. However, it cannot be concluded that all minorities score lower on IQ tests. Further, twin studies have found that IQ is at least partially inherited, and identical twins seem to have similar IQ scores even when raised separately.

Biological factors that affect cognition

The hippocampus plays a vital role in the creation of memories. Researchers like Eric Kandel and his colleagues have shown that individuals with a damaged hippocampus lose the ability to form explicit memories but can form implicit ones.

Eric Kandel, Austrian psychologist and neuroscientist

There is evidence that the amygdala plays a central role in the storage of emotional memories. This has been concluded because it is now known that some emotions are used to prove experiences. That is, certain memories have emotional significance and are remembered better or are harder to forget. For example, individuals with post-traumatic stress disorder (PTSD) have problems getting rid of traumatic memories because they are heavy emotional experiences.

The Clive Wearing study was designed to research the effects of brain damage on memory. The procedure was to examine Clive's case of amnesia through both qualitative and quantitative processes. The qualitative process consisted of interviews with Clive's wife, Deborah. Deborah Clive was asked about her husband's amnesia, and she described Clive writing in his diary, "9:00 AM just woke up," and several moments later writing, "9:01AM just woke up," demonstrating his severe case of amnesia.

In Clive's case, the MRI showed that there was damage to the frontal and temporal lobes, however, the most affected part of his brain was the hippocampus, where the functions of memory and learning are localized. Through the qualitative interviews, it was discovered that memories are distributed in several parts of the brain and not just the hippocampus. For example, Clive could still play the piano, which illustrated that the areas of the brain related to procedural memory and the cerebellum were not affected.

The HM research study was performed by Milner and Scoville. The purpose of the study was to figure out how brain damage affected memory. The doctors removed tissue from the temporal lobe, including the hippocampus. The incisions were made across the forehead to pull the skin back, directly exposing the specific area of the brain. The entire hippocampus was pulled out, including the amygdala and some white matter tracts leading to and from the temporal lobe.

Patient HM suffered from anterograde amnesia, and he was unable to recognize the faces of the people he met. He could carry on a normal conversation but did not recognize people who visited him on a regular basis. He could read and re-read the same books without knowing he had already seen them. HM could recall information acquired in his life, but he could not create new memories.

Corkin analyzed an old MRI, which revealed that there were missing parts of the temporal lobe, the hippocampus and surrounding areas of HM's brain. These areas are involved in specific neurotransmitter pathways in memory, including acetylcholine, which plays a vital role in learning and episodic memory. The hippocampus plays an important role in transforming episodic memories from short to long-term memories. Since HM was able to retain some memories, it was concluded that the hippocampus does not store these memories but processes them. The medial temporal region within the hippocampus is central for long-term memory storage of knowledge, as well as for the use of this knowledge in everyday situations. The fact that HM and other people with amnesia have deficits in some types of memories but not in others is taken as evidence that the brain has multiple memory systems supported by multiple brain regions.

Cortisol is a stress hormone that is produced in the adrenal glands in response to psychological and physiological stress. However, during long-term stress, too much cortisol is released, affecting not only immune functioning, but also memory processing. Too much cortisol can stop the brain from forming new memories or accessing already existing memories.

Sapolsky performed a study that demonstrated that prolonged stress can damage neurons in the hippocampus, but this can be reversed if normal levels of cortisol are restored. However, long-term stress can cause irreversible damage.

Robert Sapolsky, American biologist

Lupein and colleagues followed a group of elderly people for a period of five years to study the effect of cortisol on memory. They found that the cortisol levels were too high in about 30% of the group of elders in their study. That is, the elderly exposed to high levels of cortisol had more memory loss and greater atrophy of the hippocampus.

Problem-solving and decision making

Types of problem-solving

There are different strategies for solving problems. One such strategy is *trial and error*. For other problems, an *algorithm*, or a step-by-step process, is used. Another strategy is using *heuristics*, or mental shortcuts. With some problems, a combination of these various strategies is used to formulate a solution. For example, while changing a tire, an algorithm strategy is used until an individual notices that a wrench that is needed is missing.

In the meantime, other tools will be used, and the best possible solution will be sought out using the strategy of trial and error. These problem-solving strategies are used consciously at certain times and unconsciously at others. Individuals might not be actively thinking about a certain problem, but while in the shower or participating in other mundane activities, the individual might get a spark of knowledge or inspiration, normally known as *insight.*

Approaches to problem-solving

The *Gestalt Theory* states that problem-solving occurs through a flash of insight. It was noted that insight occurs when a problem solver transitions from a state of not knowing to a state of knowing. During insight, problem solvers envision the problem that enables the solution. The Gestalt psychologists came up with ways to conceptualize what insight really is. Insight involves constructing a schema where all the respective parts fit together. Additionally, it involves sudden reorganization of different visual information to make it fit together to solve the problem. It also involves restating the problem in a simpler manner, thus making it easier to solve. It removes various mental blocks and finds a mental analog, or similar problem, which the problem solver already knows how to solve.

The *information processing theory* states that a problem can be represented as a problem space, or a representation of the initial state, goal state, and all possible intervening states and a search heuristic. This process is seen as a strategy for moving through the problem space from one state of the problem to the next. The problem begins in the initial given state, where the problem solver applies an operator that generates a new state, and so on, until the goal state is reached. For example, a common search heuristic is means-ends analysis, where the problem solver seeks to apply an operator that will satisfy the problem solver's current goal; if there is a constraint that blocks the application of the operator, then a goal is set to remove that constraint. The information processing theory informs educational programs aimed at teaching strategies for problem-solving.

Barriers to effective problem solving

Fixation is another obstacle in problem-solving. Fixation is the inability to see a problem from a fresh perspective. Fixation occurs due to a *mental set*. A mental set is the tendency to fixate on particular solutions that have worked in the past, even though these solutions may not be adequate for the current problem. Another type of fixation is known as *functional fixedness*. This is the tendency to perceive the functions of objects as fixed and unchanging.

Heuristics and biases

Humans are not always careful and logical when making decisions. Usually, humans do not put in enough time and effort while making decisions; they write off the problem or situation at hand as trivial, lack the time necessary to solve the problem, or can find no clear and logical path to solve it.

Oftentimes, mental shortcuts or heuristics are used to increase the efficiency of making a decision. Mental shortcuts are helpful most of the time but can lead to errors in judgment. The *representativeness heuristic* is the tendency to think about the likelihood of a particular event occurring based on typical mental representations of those events. The *availability heuristic* is the tendency to make judgments based on how readily available the information is in a person's memory. If the memory is readily available, a person might think that the idea is more common than it actually is.

Belief bias is the tendency to judge arguments based on personal beliefs rather than using sound logic. Once preexisting beliefs are formed, they become resistant to change through a phenomenon known as *belief perseverance*. Belief perseverance is the tendency to cling to beliefs despite the presence of contrary evidence.

A *confirmation bias* is a barrier in problem-solving that occurs when individuals tend to search for information that supports the individual's preconceived notions, rather than information that disproves them. This bias prevents individuals from looking at the given problem from multiple perspectives. A person is most likely going to approach the problem through their biased perspective. In this sense, the decision that is made will most likely be erroneous. That is, having a one-sided view rather than a holistic view of the situation and might lead the problem solver to an incorrect solution.

Through a frequent utilization of intuitive heuristics and a tendency to confirm preconceived notions, *overconfidence* may develop. Overconfidence refers to an overestimation of the accuracy of knowledge and judgments. Individuals can also be influenced by how the information is *framed*. For example, people usually buy the meat in the grocery store labeled as 75% lean versus the meat labeled as 25% fat.

States of Consciousness

Consciousness is an individual's awareness of everything going on within himself and his surroundings. It is the selective attention to information and the processing of one thing at a time.

Pre-consciousness is information that we are not aware of, but that can still be accessed if attention is directed to it. *Unconsciousness* consists of information we cannot access, including primitive beliefs and patterns that drive behavior.

Alertness

Alertness is the state of active attention by means of high sensory awareness, such as being watchful and prompt to meet danger or emergency, which often manifests itself in being quick to perceive and act. This is related to both psychology and physiology. A lack of alertness is seen in a number of conditions, including narcolepsy, attention deficit disorder, chronic fatigue syndrome, depression, Addison's disease, and sleep deprivation. Pronounced lack of alertness can be graded as an altered level of consciousness.

People who have to be alert during their jobs, such as air traffic controllers or pilots, often face challenges maintaining their alertness. Research shows that for people engaged in attention-intensive and monotonous tasks, retaining a constant level of alertness is rare if not impossible. If people employed in safety-related or transportation jobs have lapses in alertness, this "may lead to severe consequences in occupations ranging from air traffic control to monitoring of nuclear power plants."

Sleep

Stages of sleep

The Circadian rhythm is a metabolic thought process that follows a particular pattern. There are five recognized stages of sleep. It takes approximately 90-100 minutes to pass through all five stages. The brain's waves change according to the specific stage of the sleep cycle one is in. The first four stages of sleep are known as NREM, and the last stage of sleep is known as REM sleep.

Stage one is experienced as one is falling asleep. It is a transition stage between being awake and being asleep. It usually lasts for about one to five minutes in duration and occupies approximately 2-5% of a normal night of sleep. In this stage, the eyes begin to roll slightly. It consists mostly of *theta waves*, which are slow-moving high amplitude and low frequency. Additionally, there are brief periods of alpha waves, which are similar to those that are present while awake.

Stage two follows stage one and is considered to be the baseline of sleep. This stage is part of the 90-minute cycle and occupies approximately 45-60% of sleep.

Stages three and *four* are considered *delta*, or slow wave, sleep and may last for about 15-30 minutes in duration. They are considered slow wave sleep because brain activity slows down dramatically from the *theta rhythm* of stage two to a much slower rhythm called *delta*, and the height (amplitude) of the waves increases dramatically. Contrary to popular belief, it is delta sleep that is the deepest stage of sleep, not REM. Additionally, it is the most restorative. It is delta sleep that the sleep-deprived brain craves first and foremost. In children, delta sleep can occupy up to forty percent of all sleep time, and this is what causes children not to wake up or stay in the "dead asleep" state during most of the night.

Stage five is considered *REM sleep*. REM is an abbreviation for "rapid eye movement." This is a very active stage of sleep. It composes about 20-25% of a normal night of sleep. A person's breathing, heart rate, and brain wave activity quicken. In this stage, vivid dreams can occur. From REM a person returns back to stage two of sleep. During REM, the body is essentially paralyzed. The genitals become aroused. Morning erections are from the final REM stage. Babies tend to be in REM more than adolescents and adults.

In children, delta sleep can occupy up to forty percent of all sleep time.

Sleep cycles and changes to sleep cycles

The 90-100-minute cycles are considered the sleep cycles. The *adaptive theory of sleep* proposes that animals and humans evolved sleep patterns to avoid predators by sleeping when predators are most active. The *restorative theory* proposes that sleep is necessary to the physical health of the body and serves to replenish chemicals and repair cellular damage.

An EEG machine is usually used to measure stages of sleep. As an individual lies awake and relaxed before they sleep, their EEG shows slow alpha waves.

Sleep and circadian rhythms

The circadian rhythm is a human's 24-hour biological clock, which can be negatively affected by changes in one's normal patterns of behavior such as tiredness after long periods of travel, known as jet lag. A human's body temperature and awareness changes throughout the day and night, therefore, it is often advised to take a test or study during one's circadian peaks. Jet lag can negatively affect rhythms. If all light cues and clocks are hidden, humans will adapt to a 25-hour day; however, bright lights can reset an individual's natural clock. The suprachiasmatic nucleus, pineal gland, and the hormone melatonin all affect circadian rhythms. The hypothalamus is a small section of the brain that influences the glandular system. The suprachiasmatic nucleus is the internal clock that tells individuals to wake up and fall back asleep.

Dreaming

Dreams are a sequence of images, emotions, and thoughts that pass through a sleeping person's mind. The *manifest content* is the remembered story line of a dream, while the *latent content* is the underlying meaning of a dream. Under Freud's *wish fulfillment theory*, dreams are the key to understanding our inner conflicts. They bring to light the ideas and thoughts hidden in one's unconscious mind. The theory poses that dreams represent wish-fulfilling attempts, where one acts out their unconscious desires. This theory also touches upon latent and manifest content, where manifest content is the literal storyline of the dream and latent content is the unconscious meaning of it. The ego protects individuals from information in the unconscious mind, referred to as "protected sleep."

Sigmund Freud, Austrian neurologist and founder of psychoanalysis

The *Information processing theory* states that dreams act to sort out and understand the memories that one experiences during the day. REM sleep does increase after stressful events. The *Activation- Synthesis Theory* is part of the physiological function theories and states that during the night, the brainstem releases random neural activity, and dreams may function to make sense of that activity.

REM rebound is the tendency for REM sleep to increase following REM sleep deprivation. When a person has not had a good night of sleep for a week and then proceeds to sleep for ten hours in a row, that person will then tend to dream more frequently.

The term *daydreaming* is used frequently in contemporary society. The question scientists ask is why humans take part in such an activity. It has been suggested that daydreaming aids humans in preparing for future events, it nourishes their social development and can act as a substitute for impulsive behavior.

Sleep-wake disorders

Insomnia refers to a recurring problem in falling or staying asleep. Insomnia is not defined by the number of hours one sleeps every night. It affects about 10% of the population.

Narcolepsy is characterized by uncontrollable sleep attacks. One suffering from this disorder lapses directly into REM, usually in times of stress or joy. This disease affects less than .001% of the population.

Sleep Apnea refers to a sleep disorder characterized by temporary cessations of breathing during sleep and consequent momentary reawakening. It is as common as insomnia. This disorder affects attention, memory, and energy levels and prevents deep sleep. Overweight men tend to be at a higher risk of being affected by sleep apnea.

Night terror is a sleep disorder that is characterized by high arousal and a sensation of being terrified. It occurs in stage four, early on in the night. These arousals are often not remembered.

Sleepwalking or *somnambulism* is a sleep disorder that affects 10% of all humans at least once in their lives. It occurs most often during deep, non-REM sleep, usually in stage three or four sleep, early on in the night. Some symptoms or features of sleepwalking include ambulation or moving about during sleep. The onset of this disorder typically occurs in pre-pubertal children. It is quite difficult to arouse the person during an episode and is usually followed by amnesia. Other medical and psychiatric disorders can be present, but do not account for the condition. The ambulation is not due to other sleep disorders such as REM sleep behavior disorder or night terrors. Fatigue persists, and stress and anxiety levels are high during this time.

The sleepwalking activity may include just sitting up and appearing awake while actually being asleep, getting up and walking around, or complex activities such as moving furniture, going to the bathroom, dressing, and undressing, and similar activities. Some individuals even drive a car when they are asleep. The episode can be very brief, lasting a few seconds, or can last up to thirty minutes or longer.

One common misconception is that a sleepwalker should not be awakened. It is not dangerous to awaken a sleepwalker; however, if awoken the person will be confused and/or disoriented for a short time upon awakening. Another major misconception is that a person cannot be injured when sleepwalking. Actually, injuries caused by instances of tripping and loss of balance are common among sleepwalkers.

Hypnosis and meditation

Hypnosis is comparable to relaxation where the two components of physical and mental health must be addressed together. Most researchers are in agreement that hypnosis is a very deep state of relaxation, where the mind is more focused and the connection between one's thoughts, emotions and behaviors are more vivid. Contrary to popular belief, hypnosis is not magical and cannot cause individuals to do anything against their judgment or moral beliefs.

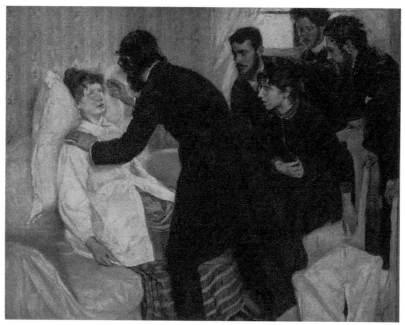

Painting of a hypnotic session

A hypnotherapist is a licensed professional who uses hypnosis as part of the treatment regimen for various psychological disorders. It is mostly never used as the primary form of treatment but is most beneficial when used with relaxation and talk-therapy for a more comprehensive treatment plan.

Posthypnotic amnesia is forgetting events that occurred while under hypnosis. The *posthypnotic suggestion* claims that a hypnotized person behaves in a certain way after hypnosis ends. The *role theory* states that during hypnosis, people act out the roles of a hypnotized person because they are expected, suggesting that hypnosis is a social phenomenon. *Hypnotic suggestibility* states that individuals have the ability to be hypnotized, and this ability tends to be higher in people who have rich fantasy lives, can focus intensely on a single task for a long time, and follow directions well.

The *state theory* states that hypnosis is an altered state of consciousness. The *dissociation theory* was conceptualized by Ernest Hilgard, where he hypothesized that hypnosis causes a voluntary split in consciousness. One level responds to the suggestions of the hypnotist and the other level retains awareness of reality. In the ice water bath experiment, subjects in a state of hypnosis felt pain but did not report it. This experiment suggested the presence of a hidden observer. In other words, there seems to be a level of our consciousness that monitors what is happening, while another level obeys the hypnotist.

Meditation is a very powerful mechanism as it helps in turning off the mind and quieting one's thoughts. True meditation is the cessation of all thoughts. If the goal is simply to relax and turn off the mind, then meditation is a useful tool to ease stress and anxiety.

Consciousness-altering drugs

Types of consciousness-altering drugs and their effects on the nervous system and behavior

A psychoactive drug is a consciousness-altering chemical that affects mood and perception. These drugs are found in food and drinks including chocolate, coffee, soda, alcohol, and even over-the-counter drugs such as Aspirin, Tylenol, and cold and cough medications. These drugs affect consciousness by influencing the function of neurotransmitters at the synapses of the central nervous system.

Some psychoactive drugs are agonists and mimic the functionality of a neurotransmitter; some are antagonists and block the action of a neurotransmitter; and some work by blocking the reuptake of neurotransmitters at the synapse. *Tolerance* is caused by a physiological change when more of the same drug is needed for the same effect, failure to increase dosage accordingly can lead to symptoms of withdrawal. Psychoactive drugs include depressants, stimulants, and hallucinogens.

Depressants slow down body and cognitive functions. *Stimulants* arouse body and cognitive functions. *Hallucinogens* distort perceptions or evoke sensation without any sensory input.

Alcohol is an example of a depressant as it slows down the sympathetic nervous system. It also disrupts memory processing and reduces self-awareness. Alcohol is associated with almost 60% of all crimes. From a macro perspective, it is considered the worst legally available and readily accessible substance.

Barbiturates are also depressants and act as tranquilizers. They are usually taken to sleep yet reduce REM sleep. When this drug is taken with other drugs, a synergistic effect can occur.

Another example of depressants is *opiates.* This drug is derived from the poppy plant and acts as the agonist for endorphins. Opiates are physically addictive as they rapidly change brain chemistry and create tolerance and withdrawal symptoms. Examples of opiates are heroin and morphine. Addiction comes quickly, and withdrawal symptoms are severe.

As previously stated, stimulants speed up body and cognitive processes. Specifically, they affect the autonomic nervous system and produce a sense of euphoria. Caffeine, cocaine, amphetamines, and nicotine are all examples of stimulants. Stimulants tend to disturb sleep, reduce appetite, increase anxiety, and cause heart problems.

Hallucinogens cause changes in the perception of reality. These changes include sensory hallucinations, loss of identity, and vivid fantasies. LSD, peyote, psilocybin, mushrooms, and marijuana are all examples of hallucinogens. LSD is associated with PTSD and schizophrenia.

Reverse tolerance occurs when the second dose is less than the first but can cause greater effects and can linger in the body for weeks.

Drug addiction and the reward pathway in the brain

One key pathway in understanding the effects of drugs on the brain is called the *reward pathway.* The reward pathway involves many parts of the brain, including the ventral tegmental area, the nucleus accumbens, and the pre-frontal cortex. When activated by a rewarding stimulus like food, water, and sex, information travels from the ventral tegmental area and then up to the pre-frontal cortex.

Cocaine provides a prime example of how drugs interfere with the normal activity of the brain. When an individual snorts, smokes, or injects cocaine, it travels to the brain via the bloodstream. Even though it reaches all areas of the brain, its euphoric effects are controlled in a few specific areas, especially in areas associated with the reward pathway.

Information is transmitted in the brain through the process of neurotransmission through neurotransmitters. An example of a neurotransmitter is dopamine. Under normal conditions, dopamine is released by a neuron in the synapse and binds to specialized proteins, known as dopamine receptors, on the neighboring neuron. After the signal is sent to the neighboring neuron, dopamine is transported back to the neuron from which it was released by another specialized protein known as the dopamine transporter.

Drugs of abuse are able to negatively affect the process of neurotransmission. Cocaine, for example, blocks the removal of dopamine from the synapse by binding to the dopamine transporters. This results in a build-up of dopamine in the synapse, which causes the continuous stimulation of receiving neurons, probably responsible for the euphoria experienced by cocaine users.

Memory

Memory refers to the persistence of learning over time through storage and retrieval of information.

Encoding

Process of encoding information

Encoding is the processing of information into the memory system. There are two ways of encoding information, *automatic processing,* and *effortful processing.* Automatic processing is the unconscious encoding of incidental information. Space, time, and word meanings are all encoded without effort. These can become automatic with practice. Effortful encoding requires conscious effort. *Rehearsal* is the most common effortful processing technique. After a good amount of rehearsal, what was effortful may become automatic.

There are various factors that one must keep in mind when thinking of encoding. The *next-in-line effect* states that individuals rarely remember what has been said or done if it has occurred either immediately preceding or proceeding one's need to use information. Information acquired minutes before falling asleep is rarely remembered, however, information gained an hour before sleep is well remembered. Taped information played while one is sleeping is registered by the ears but is not remembered.

The *spacing effect* states that individuals encode better after studying or practicing over time.

The *serial positioning effect* describes an individual's tendency to recall the first and last items in a list.

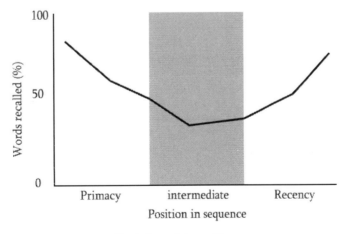

Serial position effect

There are three types of encoding, semantic, acoustic, and visual encoding. *Semantic encoding* refers to the encoding of meaning, such as the meaning of words. *Acoustic encoding* refers to the encoding of sounds, especially the sounds of various words. *Visual encoding* is the encoding of picture images. After extensive research studies, it has been found that semantic encoding is the most effective for ascertaining meaning.

The *self-reference effect* states that individuals remember things better when they are used to describe themselves. One example of this phenomenon can be seen with the use of adjectives.

Processes that aid in encoding memories

There are many tricks that exist to enhance the encoding process. One of these tricks is the use of imagery or mental pictures. Another one is known as chunking. *Chunking* is the organization of items into familiar, manageable units. Often these processes occur automatically.

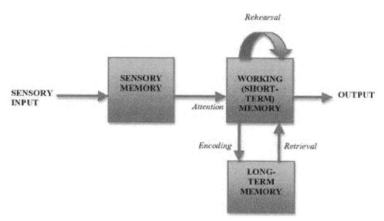

Model of memory systems

Storage

Types of memory storage

Memory storage is the retention of encoded material over time.

Sensory memory is the first stop for any external stimuli. It contains all of the information processed by the senses for less than a second. In George Sperling's experiment, he flashed a 3×3 grid for one-twentieth of a second to participants. These participants had to recall one of the rows immediately afterward. It was indicated which one to remember by a matched tone. Participants were able to recall everything perfectly. This experiment suggested that the entire grid system must be held in sensory memory for a split second.

Iconic memory is a momentary sensory memory of visual stimuli, a photograph-like quality lasting about a second. There is also an *echoic memory* for auditory stimuli. Even when not paying attention to someone, an individual can still recall the last few words said in the past three or four seconds. Not all information in sensory memory is encoded into short-term memory. Selective attention determines which sensory images get encoded.

Short-term or working memory holds everything an individual is currently thinking. If the individual does not use short-term memory, it usually fades within 10 to 30 seconds. Working memories refer to the memories that individuals are currently working with and are aware of. The capacity is limited to seven items. Individuals are able to recall digits better than letters.

Long-term memory is an individual's permanent storage system. It is unlimited, and once the information is there, it usually remains indefinitely. Memories do not reside in a specific part of the brain and are not electrical. *Episodic memory* is memories of specific events stored in sequential order. *Semantic memories* contain the general knowledge of the world and are stored as facts, meanings, or categories. *Procedural memory* is the memory of skills and how to perform them, which are stored sequentially, and are difficult to describe with words. *Explicit memories* are conscious memories of facts or events. *Implicit memories* are unintentional, and individuals might not even realize that they have them. An *eidetic* or photographic memory is very rare and seems to use very powerful and enduring visual images.

Semantic networks and spreading activation

The *semantic network theory* states that the way in which the brain forms new memories is by connecting their meanings and context with meanings already in memory. *Spreading activation* is a method for searching associative networks, neural networks or semantic networks. The process is initiated by labeling a set of source nodes, such as concepts in a semantic network, with weights or "activation" and then iteratively propagating (i.e., spreading) that activation to other nodes linked to the source nodes. Activation may originate from alternate paths and terminate when two alternate paths reach the same node. However, brain research shows that several different brain areas play an important role in semantic processing.

Retrieval

Recall, recognition, and relearning

Retrieval refers to getting information out of a memory so that an individual can utilize it.

Recall is the retrieval of a memory through the use of external cues. These external cues can be logical structures, partial memories, narratives or clues. An example of this can be observed when an individual is taking an exam; this involves remembering parts of the information and then reconstructing the rest based on partial memories.

Recognition is the process of matching a current event or fact with something already in memory. Here, an individual identifies information after experiencing it again. An example of this is when an individual takes a multiple-choice exam since they must recognize the right answer from a group of answer choices. *Re-learning* is the process of learning something that has already been learned. This usually makes it simpler to understand and retrieve information in the future and can eventually strengthen memories.

Retrieval cues

Retrieval cues carry forward the recovery of memories that have been lost. A cue can be an object or a scene that reminds an individual of something related. For example, when trying to memorize the parts of the brain, it is quite helpful to actually use a brain model with parts that can be disassembled and reassembled; since auditory, visual, and tactile sensations are identified as cues.

Cued recall is a process that research psychologists use to study these effects. Subjects are usually given pairs of words to study. The experimenter then gives the participant one word to cue the recall of the word it was paired with. The stronger the link between the words, the better the subjects will recall the specific pair.

When mental and physical cues are not immediately available to generate them independently, a fruitful strategy is to take cues from hierarchies, associations, and schemas, which, as mentioned before, are the various ways in which the information is organized in long-term memory. Retrieval cues are the most important for prospective memory, or memory about a future event.

The role of emotion in retrieving memories

In a mood-congruent memory, there is a greater likelihood of recalling an item when the person recognizes the mood that he or she was in when the event occurred. For example, depressed people will most likely recall sad memories from the past. Moods also affect how an individual interprets other people's behaviors. *State-dependent* memory refers to the recall of events encoded while in particular states of consciousness.

Processes that aid retrieval

Priming is a mechanism many people use to aid in retrieving information. The term priming refers to the activation of associations in our memory. The *priming effect* takes place when individuals respond faster or better to an item if a similar item preceded it. The priming effect is mostly considered involuntary and is considered an unconscious phenomenon. The priming effect consists of repetition priming and semantic priming.

Repetition priming refers to the fact that it is easier and quicker to recognize a face or word if an individual has recently seen that same image or word. *Semantic priming* refers to the fact that it is easier and quicker to recognize someone if we have just seen someone closely associated with that person.

There are many factors that affect retrieval. One of these factors is the order in which the information is presented. The *primacy effect* states that individuals are more likely to recall items that are at the beginning of a list. The *recency effect* is demonstrated by an individual's ability to recall items at the end of a list. The *serial position effect* suggests that the recall of a list is affected by the order of items.

The *context effect* helps individuals put themselves in the same context that they experienced when encoding the information. *The tip of the tongue phenomenon* is the temporary inability to remember information. *Flash-bulb memories* are powerful because of the relevance of the concurrent events encoded as contextual information along with the memory.

William James, the first psychologist to identify the tip of the tongue phenomenon

Déjà vu is that eerie feeling of having experienced something before. During this phenomenon, the current situation cues a past experience similar to the present one, tricking the mind into thinking that they are the same.

Forgetting

In *encoding failure*, we fail to encode information in an adequate manner. Consequently, the information never enters long-term memory. In *retrieval failure*, the memory is encoded and stored, but cannot be accessed.

In *motivated forgetting*, we revise our own personal narratives consciously or unconsciously. One example of this mechanism is *repression.* In psychoanalytic theory, repression is the basic defense mechanism that banishes anxiety-arousing thoughts, feelings, and memories from consciousness.

Aging and memory

Normal aging is associated with a decline in memory and is referred to as age-related memory loss or age-associated memory impairment. Through various studies comparing the effects of aging on the different types of memory, including semantic memory, episodic memory, short-term memory, and priming, it was found that episodic memory is the most impaired as a result of normal aging. Some types of short-term memories are also impaired.

Source information is a type of episodic memory that is impaired with aging. This type of information involves where and when the information was learned. Knowing the source of the information can be very helpful in daily decision making. Episodic memory is supported by networks spanning frontal, temporal, and parietal lobes. The interconnections within the lobes are known to enable distinct aspects of memory. Whereas the effects of grey matter lesions have been extensively studied, less is known about the interconnecting fiber tracts. With aging, degradation of white matter structure has emerged as an important general factor, further focusing attention on the critical white matter connections. Additionally, associative learning, a component of episodic memory, is also affected by aging.

Several reasons have been proposed as to why the elderly use less effective ways to encode and retrieve. One reason is disuse, which poses that adults tend to not use memory strategies as they move further away from the educational system. Another reason is the *diminished attentional capacity hypothesis*, which postulates that older people engage in less self-initiated encoding due to reduced attentional capacity. The third reason proposed is the lack of *memory self-efficacy* older people experience such as losing confidence in their own memory performances, in turn leading to poor results.

A postmortem research examination of five brains of elderly people classified as "super aged," having above average memory, presented a possible biological explanation for memory deficits in aging. The study found that these individuals had fewer fiber-like tangles of tau protein than those seen in typical elderly brains. However, a similar amount of amyloid plaque was found.

Memory dysfunctions

Alzheimer's disease is a progressive neurodegenerative disease in which connections that mediate the cell-to-cell communication in the brain are completely lost. It is the most common form of dementia.

Wernicke-Korsakoff syndrome is a severe neurological disease caused by thymine or Vitamin B_1 deficiency. It is usually associated with heavy alcohol consumption. Its symptoms include oculomotor malfunctions, cerebellar dysfunction, and altered mental states. It is also characterized by severe amnesia, disorientation, and frequent confabulation, or making up of information to compensate for poor memory retrieval. Those suffering from the syndrome also have impaired short-term memory and experience difficulty learning new information or tasks.

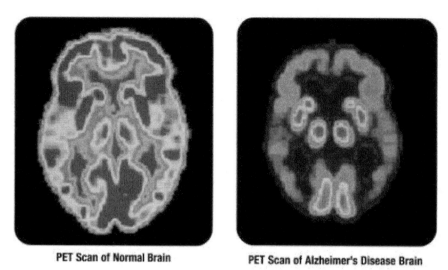

PET Scan of Normal Brain   PET Scan of Alzheimer's Disease Brain

PET scans of a healthy brain versus the brain of a person with Alzheimer's disease

Decay

Decay occurs when a person does not use a memory or its connections for a long period of time. The *re-learning effect* suggests that relearning information takes less time and effort than learning it.

Below is the Ebbinghaus Forgetting Curve.

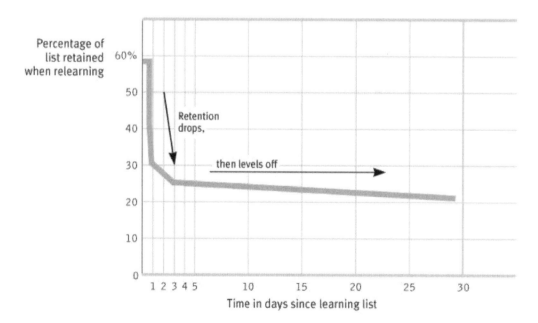

Interference

Interference occurs when information in memory competes with what someone is trying to actually recall. *Retroactive interference* is the learning of new information that interferes with the recall of older information. *Proactive interference* occurs when older information interferes with the recall of information learned more recently.

Memory construction and source monitoring

People tend to alter their memories as they encode or retrieve them. Their expectations, schemas, and environment may alter their process of memory formation and retrieval.

Source amnesia refers to the inability to recall the origin of an event that has been experienced, heard or read about, or imagined.

Source monitoring is an unconscious mental test that humans tend to perform in order to determine if a memory is real and accurate, comes from a dream, or is imagined. Individuals use many sources to determine the source of a memory or an idea. Physical, linguistic, and categorical information about people and objects is used to determine reality in certain situations, such as determining that the person we see walking towards us is a longtime friend and not a character from a movie.

External source monitoring focuses on sources that are in an individual's environment. An example of this would be recalling which professor gave an exam yesterday. *Internal source monitoring* is focused on internal factors, such as when individuals try to distinguish between what they said out loud and something they thought to themselves.

Source monitoring errors can occur for many reasons, such as brain injury, aging, depression, and cognitive biases.

Changes in synaptic connections underlying memory and learning

Neural plasticity

Neural plasticity refers to the formation of neural connections. It allows neurons to repair, regrow, and adapt after injury or disease. This process varies by age. There is a rapid formation of neural connections in children and it is ongoing throughout life. Neural plasticity is affected by heredity and the environment.

Memory and learning

Memory and learning are closely related to one another. Memory is the acquired information and learning refers to the acquisition of knowledge or skill. Memory and learning are interdependent.

Long-term potentiation

Long-term potentiation (LTP) is the signal transmission that strengthens the response of the post-synaptic nerve cells by forming additional synapses. It is an essential phenomenon for neural plasticity. The early phase occurs in the first hour or so, and CaMKII and PKC are activated. This is independent of protein synthesis. The late phase requires gene transcription in the postsynaptic cell. New gene transcription and mRNA translation occur, and the number of AMPA receptors increases, which in turn increases the size of the synaptic connection (this depends on protein synthesis).

The process of long-term potentiation starts with the rapid stimulation of CAI neurons in the hippocampus. Glu and D-serine bind to NMDA receptors. Ca^{2+} flows into the cell and Ca^{2+} binds to calmodulin. CaMKII is activated, which phosphorylates AMPA receptors. Permeability of Na+ ions increases, which increases the cell's sensitivity to depolarize. Gene expression and protein increases, and finally synaptic connection strengthens.

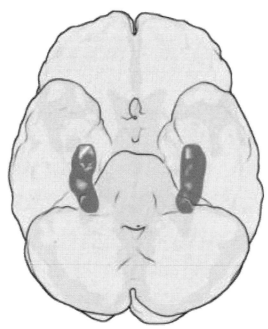

Long-term potentiation was first discovered in the hippocampus of the brain (darkened spots in above image)

Language

Phonemes are the smallest unit of sound used in language. The English language has about 44 phonemes. *Morphemes* are the smallest units of meaningful sound represented as words or parts of words. Overall, language consists of phonemes that make up morphemes, which then add up to words. Syntax refers to the order in which words are spoken or written.

Independent of what language they are first exposed to and use, babies all go through the same stages of language development. *Babbling* is the first stage and occurs around six months of age. It represents experimentations with phonemes. Babies in this stage can produce any phoneme in any type of language. The next stage is called the *holophrastic stage*. In this stage, babies speak in single words, also called holophrases. The third stage of language development is known as *telegraphic* speech. In this stage, toddlers combine the words they can say into simple commands. The meaning is clear, but there is no syntax present. In the beginning stages of development, children often begin to learn grammar and syntax rules by misapplying them.

Theories of language development

The Learning perspective argues that children imitate what they see and hear and learn from punishment and reinforcement. The main theorist involved in the learning perspective is B.F. Skinner. Skinner stated that adults shape the speech of children by reinforcing the babbling of infants that sound most like words.

The Nativist perspective states that humans are biologically programmed to gain knowledge. The main theorist involved with this school of thought is Noam Chomsky. Chomsky proposed that all humans have a *language acquisition device (LAD)*. The language acquisition device contains knowledge of grammatical rules common to all languages. It also allows children to understand the rules of whatever language they are listening to.

Chomsky also developed the concepts of transformational grammar, surface structure, and deep structure. Transformational grammar is the grammar that transforms a sentence. Surface structure includes words that are actually written. Deep structure is the underlying syntactic representation of a sentence.

Noam Chomsky, American linguist and scientist

The *Interactionist Theory* states that language development is caused by a combination of both social and biological factors. The interactionists believe that language learning is heavily influenced by the desire of children to communicate with others. The interactionists believe that children are born with very powerful brains that mature slowly and predispose them to acquire new understanding that they are motivated to share with others.

The main theorist involved in the interactionist theory is Vygotsky. Interactionists focus on Vygotsky's model of collaborative learning. *Collaborative learning* is the idea that conversations with older people can help children both cognitively and linguistically.

Influence of language on cognition

Individuals can think in words, but more often than not, the thinking occurs in mental pictures. The *linguistic relativity hypothesis* proposed by psychologist Benjamin Whorf states that the structure of human language affects the way in which an individual conceptualizes their world. Basing it off the concept that every language describes and conceptualizes the world in its own unique way, the hypothesis states that an individual's mother tongue limits their cross-cultural understanding.

Every human language portrays the values of the place and culture from which it came, and various philosophers and linguists have long debated how this affects and shapes the mentality of the people who speak a different language.

Brain areas that control language and speech

The left hemisphere of the brain is responsible for language and speech. The left hemisphere is the dominant hemisphere, and the right hemisphere plays a role in interpreting visual information and spatial processing. In about one-third of the individuals who are left-handed, speech functions are located on the right side of the brain. These left-handed individuals may need more complex testing to determine if their speech center is on the left or right side prior to any surgery in that particular area.

Aphasia is the impairment of language affecting production, comprehension, reading, or writing due to brain injury. It is most commonly caused by stroke or trauma.

Broca's area is located in the left portion of the frontal lobe. If this area of the brain is damaged, the individual will have difficulty moving the tongue or facial muscles to make the sounds of speech. The individual can still understand spoken language, but has significant hardship in speaking and writing, especially within specified lines. This is called *Broca's Aphasia*.

Wernicke's Area is located in the left temporal lobe. Damage to this area causes *Wernicke's Aphasia*. The affected individual may speak in long sentences that have no meaning, add unnecessary words, and even create new words. They can make speech sounds but have difficulty understanding speech, and therefore are unaware of their mistakes.

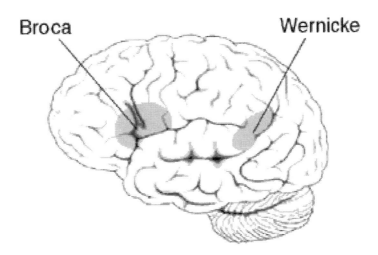

Broca's and Wernicke's areas

Please, leave your Customer Review on Amazon

Notes

Chapter 7

Motivation and Emotion

To better understand emotion, researchers focus their efforts on exploring the influence of biological and cultural factors, as well as the motivation of biological and social factors. Human behavior that illustrates theories of motivation can be divided into primary and secondary motives to offer more insight. Behaviors can be triggered by the influence of environmental cues and neural/hormonal mechanisms involved in various motivational states. Conflicting behaviors and motives are also a topic revealing the complex processes at play. In analyzing the link between physiology and experienced emotions, established theories of James–Lange, Cannon–Bard, Schachter–Singer and opponent-process theories offer interesting and sometimes divergent explanations.

Notes

Emotion

Three components of emotion

The exact definition of emotion is debated among experts in the field. Broadly, *emotions* refer to states of mind arising spontaneously in response to a stimulus. Emotions differ from *moods* in that emotions are typically short in duration and have a clear cause, while moods can last for an extended period of time and are not always in response to stimuli. *Affect* refers to the experience of emotion in a short time span. Affect also describes an individual's expression of emotion. Psychologists have typically studied emotions as they relate to three domains: cognition, physiology, and behavior.

Cognitive component

The cognitive component of emotions refers to the thoughts that arise during an emotional experience. Research suggests that cognitions have a bidirectional relation with emotions; certain thoughts can cause an emotional experience, and the emotional state of a person can influence what thoughts they have. For example, thinking about an upcoming test may lead to a feeling of anxiety. Additionally, anxiety can lead a person to think about all of the details of the worst-case scenario in different situations.

In cognitive therapy (CT), individuals with various psychopathologies are instructed to evaluate their cognitions and analyze the emotions that result from them. Aaron Beck, recognized as the father of cognitive therapy, termed cognitions that contribute to negative emotions as "automatic thoughts." Cognitive theorists propose that reflection on these automatic thoughts can reduce their effect on emotions.

Physiological component

The physiological component of emotions refers to changes in the body that occur during an emotional experience. These responses are typically brought about by changes in the sympathetic and parasympathetic nervous systems. Changes in the endocrine system also contribute to the physiological aspects of emotions.

Common physiological responses that correlate with emotional experiences include changes in heart rate, blood flow, facial expression, and pupil dilation. Emotions may not have unique physiological patterns; for example, fear and excitement share the same physiological responses. The physiological responses associated with emotions prepare an individual's body to engage in a specific kind of action. Fear, for example, is associated with pupil dilation, which allows the eye to take in the maximum amount of visual information in an emergency.

Behavioral component

Emotions can be described as states of behavioral readiness. Although emotions are not the cause of behaviors, their presence increases the likelihood that certain behaviors will occur. For example, anger is correlated with aggressive behavior and anxiety is correlated with avoidant behavior. The behavioral component accounts for the adaptive nature of emotions.

The behavioral component of emotions also refers to the outward expression of emotions. How people perceive emotional cues and experience of others influences how they interact with them. For example, when someone looks angry or acts in an aggressive manner, others may be more likely to stay away from that person.

Universal emotions

There is much debate over how many basic emotions exist and what those emotions are. Emotions are typically organized according to the facial expressions that coincide with them. Theories classifying human emotions typically suggest that there are between four and eight basic emotions. Research done by Paul Ekman in Papua New Guinea showed that emotions and their representation as facial expressions are consistent across cultures, suggesting they are innate rather than learned responses. Ekman originally identified six basic emotions present across all cultures and labeled them *universal emotions.* Contempt was added later as the seventh universal emotion.

Paul Ekman, American psychologist

Fear

The emotion fear occurs when there is a perceived threat of danger. Fear is associated with the fight-or-flight response, which involves escaping from or defending against the perceived threat. Physiologically, fear is associated with the activation of the sympathetic nervous system, resulting in an increased heart rate, rapid breathing, muscle tension and constriction of blood vessels. Fear is primarily associated with the amygdala. It can be easily conditioned in humans and animals; some theorize that this is why phobias are so common.

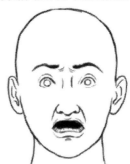

Fear is associated with anxiety, which arises when threats are perceived to be uncontrollable or unavoidable. Anxiety is also used to describe chronic worry not associated with a specific stimulus. Both fear and anxiety are viewed as subjectively negative emotions.

Anger

Anger is often viewed as a negative emotion by both subjective reports and social appraisal. Physical correlates of anger include increased heart rate, blood pressure, adrenaline levels and blushing. Note that the physiological response for anger is similar to that of fear; some theories propose that anger is used to unconsciously mask fear.

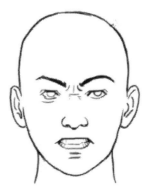

Anger is often felt when one's boundaries have been violated or when reality does not line up with expectations. Behaviorally, anger is associated with aggression, which refers to overt action intended to harm another individual. Anger is also associated with increased risk-taking. Relaxation skills are often taught to reduce anger levels in individuals who have trouble with anger management.

Happiness

Happiness is a pleasurable emotion that results from the attainment of a subjective goal. Happiness is often associated with higher levels of energy and sociability.

Physiologically, happiness is associated with lower levels of cortisol and an increased heart rate. Dopamine is also believed to play a role in the regulation of happiness.

A recent discipline in psychology, called *positive psychology*, is concerned with the study and promotion of happiness. Research stemming from this field suggests that approximately 50% of an individual's happiness is genetically determined. Martin Seligman, an American psychologist, theorized that humans are happiest if they possess five measurable elements of well-being: positive emotion, engagement, relationships, meaning and achievement (PERMA).

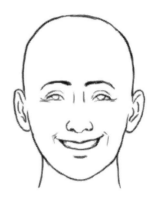

Surprise

Surprise, the briefest of all the emotions, results from experiencing an unexpected event. When experiencing surprise, one's attention is directed to the unexpected event. After the initial reaction, surprise changes to a different emotion depending on the cause of the surprise. If the surprising stimulus is a spider, for example, surprise will likely be followed by fear. If the surprising stimulus is finding a twenty-dollar bill, surprise will likely be followed by happiness.

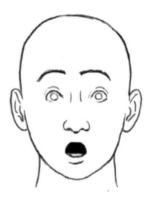

Physiologically, surprise is a startle response. It is not necessarily experienced as pleasant or unpleasant. Surprise is associated with activation of the sympathetic nervous system only when the unexpected event is deemed threatening.

Contempt

Contempt is a social emotion that is felt when one believes to be superior to someone else. Behaviorally, contempt is characterized by the rejection or exclusion of the other party. Contempt is often felt when another person is viewed as easily controllable and when there is a lack of intimacy between the two parties. Contempt is often felt in conjunction with anger or may follow anger. There is evidence that this emotion is used for regarding the actions of others as incompetent.

Contempt was not originally identified by Paul Ekman as a universal emotion and was added to the list at a later date. Findings on contempt are less clear than findings on other emotions, causing some experts to be skeptical of contempt's status as a universal emotion.

Disgust

Disgust is believed to be a rejection response that protects the body from potentially harmful contaminants. In North Americans, nine domains that elicit disgust have been identified: food, body products, animals, sexual behavior, death, gore, poor hygiene, interpersonal contamination, and moral offenses.

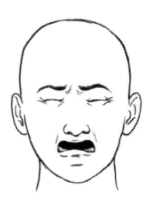

Studies have found that females are typically more sensitive to disgust than males. It has been hypothesized that disgust is a defensive emotion that emphasizes the line between human and animal. Another hypothesis proposes that disgust is a food-related emotion that evolved to protect humans from disease. Interestingly, some of the nine domains that have been found to elicit disgust can be viewed in terms of their pathogenic natures.

Sadness

Sadness is primarily associated with a perceived loss and is often described as a "sinking" feeling. Behavioral correlates of sadness include becoming lethargic, withdrawn and isolated. Physiologically, sadness is not fully understood but has been found to be associated with a decrease in heart rate. Chronic sadness can lead to poor cardiovascular health and increase the chances of dying after a heart attack.

Excessive sadness is characteristic of depression. One type of treatment for depression, cognitive therapy, focuses on the cognitive components of sadness in order to reduce its intensity. Someone receiving cognitive therapy for depression would be taught to recognize cognitions that contribute to sadness (e.g., "I'm not good at anything") and come up with evidence to contradict these thoughts. They are then taught to replace cognitions associated with sadness with more neutral thoughts (e.g., "I am good at some things, I can improve in the areas I am not yet as good in.")

Adaptive role of emotion

Emotions play a functional role in the lives of humans and other animals. As early as 1872, Charles Darwin theorized that emotions evolved and adapted over time. Since then, a body of research has developed to detail how specific emotions evolved and what their functions are. Different emotions prepare the body for behavior in various ways. Emotions like fear and anxiety allow the body to react automatically. For example, if a car swerves onto the sidewalk, individuals on the sidewalk will most likely move out of the way as a result of their fear response and not due to any thought processes per se.

Charles Darwin, English naturalist and geologist

Individuals typically avoid stimuli that result in negative emotions by seeking out situations that are associated with positive emotions. In this way, positive emotions like joy, pride, and happiness serve as motivators for future behavior. Individuals will repeat behaviors associated with positive emotions. For example, emotions provide intrinsic rewards for adaptive behaviors, such as finding food and having sex.

Emotions and emotional expression are also crucial interpersonally. In humans, the emotional cues of others greatly influence our interactions with them. In one study demonstrating this, infants were placed on safety glass with a visual cliff in the middle of the surface. The infants' mothers stood at the opposite side of the visual cliff and were instructed to display fear, sadness, anger, interest or joy. Approximately 75% of the infants crossed when the mother displayed joy or interest; none of the infants crossed when the mother displayed fear.

Theories of emotion

James–Lange theory

The James-Lange theory of emotions was proposed by psychologist William James and physiologist Carl Lange independently. This theory states that physiological responses to stimuli act as the basis for emotions. Thus, emotion is viewed as a secondary response to a physiological trigger. According to this theory, the brain receives input regarding muscle tension, heart rate, perspiration, and other physiological processes and then interprets these responses as a particular emotion. This theory proposes that emotions are the subjective experiences of physiological reactions. Thus, James and Lange believed that without physical arousal, emotions would not exist.

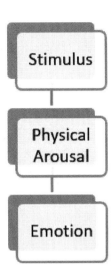

Cannon–Bard theory

The Cannon-Bard theory of emotions was proposed by William Cannon and his doctoral student Philip Bard. Cannon and Bard disagreed with the James-Lange theory and proposed that emotions and physiological reactions occur simultaneously as separate entities. Cannon and Bard believed that the James-Lange theory did not account for people being physiologically aroused without experiencing any emotions, such as when exercising. Since different emotions can have the same physiological arousal pattern, Cannon and Bard believed that physiological arousal cannot precede emotions, but that the two must exist separately. For example, fear and anger have almost identical physiological profiles but are experienced as different emotions.

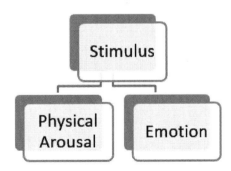

Cannon and Bard also cited research on animal behavior to support their theory. Dogs who had their spinal cord and vagus nerves separated from the rest of their bodies showed no change in emotional behavior, suggesting that emotions are not just physiological responses.

William Cannon, American merchant and politician

Schachter–Singer theory

The Schachter-Singer theory of emotions was devised by researchers Stanley Schachter and Jerome E. Singer. It states that emotions result from the interaction of cognitive and physiological factors. Cognitions thus provide a framework within which an individual can understand his or her physiological response.

Work by Stanley Schachter showed that individuals will label a state of physiological arousal based on the cognitions available to them (via prompts and suggestions). Additionally, individuals will not label cognitions as emotions if physiological arousal is absent. This suggests that both a state of physiological arousal and cognition to interpret this state must be present for an individual to experience an emotion.

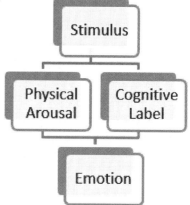

This theory emphasizes the role of past emotional experiences. According to this theory, past experiences of emotion provide a framework for individuals to label their emotions.

The role of biological processes in perceiving emotion

Brain regions involved in the generation and experience of emotions

Basal ganglia are groups of nuclei found on the sides of the thalamus. They are connected to the thalamus in the limbic system. The basal ganglia play a key role in cognitive function by enabling various cognitive and emotional programs to be stored in other cortical areas.

The o*rbitofrontal cortex (OFC)* is involved in the decision-making aspect of emotion. More specifically, it controls an individual's engagement in reinforced and punished behaviors. It is also involved in motivational behavior such as eating and drinking. Damage to the orbitofrontal cortex is often associated with impulsivity, suggesting that this area modulates goal-directed behavior.

The *prefrontal cortex (PFC)* is associated with the experience and regulation of emotions. It is believed that the prefrontal cortex integrates cognition and emotion. Individuals with depression display abnormally low activity in their prefrontal cortex.

The *ventral striatum* is activated by stimuli associated with reward. This area is the primary site of rewarding feelings elicited by dopamine. The insular cortex, or *insula*, is linked to the social emotions of disgust and empathy. It is also involved in the processing of others' emotions. The insula is believed to process physiological information to form an experience of emotion. The insula is also integral to experiencing pain and conscious desire. Though typically associated with motor control, recent research has indicated that the *cerebellum* may be central to the regulation of emotions.

The role of the limbic system in emotion

The structures within the *limbic system* are directly related to emotion. The *amygdala* is composed of two round structures that are involved in emotions and motivation. Specifically, it is associated with fear and aggression. The amygdala has also been linked to the fear-conditioning process. It is responsible for the activation of the sympathetic nervous system, resulting in the fight-or-flight response and increased arousal.

The *thalamus* primarily relays information from one part of the brain to another. Lesions on the thalamus are associated with difficulties in emotional reactivity due to the thalamus' connections with other parts of the limbic system. Additionally, the thalamus is involved in the regulation of sleep.

The *hypothalamus* is located below the thalamus and is involved in the expression of emotions. Like the amygdala, the hypothalamus is involved in the processing of fear. Specifically, the hypothalamus is involved in defensive behaviors resulting from fear.

The *hippocampus* is primarily involved in the creation of new memories and is easily affected by long-term stress. Atrophy of the hippocampus has been found in patients suffering from post-traumatic stress disorder, schizophrenia, and depression.

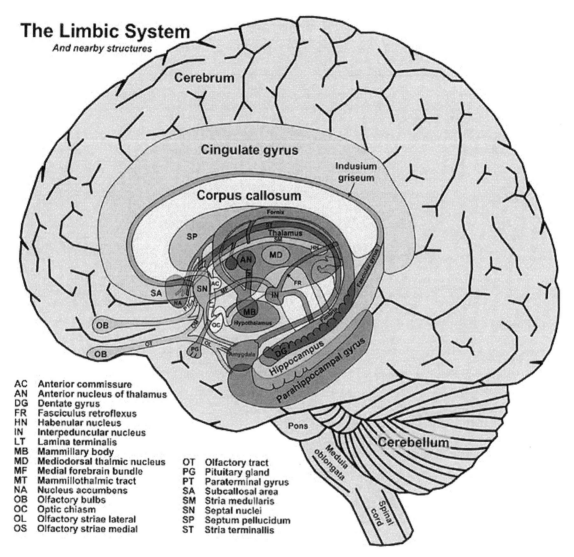

AC	Anterior commissure
AN	Anterior nucleus of thalamus
DG	Dentate gyrus
FR	Fasciculus retroflexus
HN	Habenular nucleus
IN	Interpeduncular nucleus
LT	Lamina terminalis
MB	Mammillary body
MD	Mediodorsal thalmic nucleus
MF	Medial forebrain bundle
MT	Mammillothalmic tract
NA	Nucleus accumbens
OB	Olfactory bulbs
OC	Optic chiasm
OL	Olfactory striae lateral
OS	Olfactory striae medial

OT	Olfactory tract
PG	Pituitary gland
PT	Paraterminal gyrus
SA	Subcallosal area
SM	Stria medullaris
SN	Septal nuclei
SP	Septum pellucidum
ST	Stria terminallis

Limbic system

Emotion and the autonomic nervous system

The *autonomic nervous system* (ANS) is part of the peripheral nervous system and regulates the functions of organs within the body. Responses of the autonomic nervous system are involuntary and often occur without conscious awareness. The autonomic nervous system is involved in the regulation of heart rate, respiratory rate, sexual arousal, digestion, and pupillary response.

The autonomic nervous system is divided into the sympathetic nervous system and the parasympathetic nervous system. Both branches are constantly activated to maintain homeostasis. The *sympathetic nervous system* is associated with the fight-or-flight response. For example, the sympathetic nervous system dilates the pupils in order to increase the amount of light entering the eye. This branch of the nervous system also increases blood flow to the muscles by increasing heart rate and dilating the skeletal muscles. The sympathetic nervous system also inhibits digestion, making the body more efficient during an emergency. The bronchioles in the lungs also become dilated, allowing the body to take in more oxygen at once. These responses all prepare the body to take action, whether it is fight or flight. The sympathetic nervous system is also associated with fear, stress, and surprise.

Conversely, when the *parasympathetic nervous system* is activated, blood pressure decreases, heart rate slows down, and digestion is promoted. The parasympathetic nervous system is associated with relaxation and tranquility.

	Parasympathetic *Body at rest*	**Sympathetic** *Emergency situations*
Eyes	Constricts pupils	Dilates pupils
Heart	Beats more slowly	Beats faster and stronger
Lungs	Constricts airways	Relaxes airways, which lets you breathe more deeply
Digestion	Stimulates digestion	Inhibits digestion
Muscles	Reduces blood flow to skeletal muscles	Increases blood flow to skeletal muscles

Physiological markers of emotion (signatures of emotion)

Emotions are characterized by the physiological responses associated with them. These responses are functional and prepare the body to engage in different types of behaviors. These physiological reactions result from the interaction between the peripheral nervous system, endocrine system, limbic system and other areas in the brain.

Anger, for example, is characterized by its association with the sympathetic nervous system. Thus, when experiencing anger, an increase in blood pressure and heart rate can be expected. This response prepares the body for aggressive behavior like attacking and defending.

The physiological responses of individual emotions are not unique. For example, anger and fear are characterized by similar central nervous system arousal; when experiencing both emotions, heart rate, perspiration and blood pressure increase. This suggests that emotions are more than just their physiological markers.

Recent theories of emotions have conceptualized physiological responses as existing on a continuum. These theories sort emotions by how they are distributed among two or more dimensions. Wilhelm Wundt, the father of modern psychology, proposed that emotions can be described on three dimensions: how pleasurable they are, how arousing they are and how straining they are. Most modern theories incorporate valence (i.e., the emotional value associated with a stimulus) and arousal as two dimensions of emotions.

Wilhelm Wundt, father of modern psychology

Motivation

Motivation is a need or desire that energizes and directs behavior. More specifically, it is involved with the initiation, guidance, or maintenance of goal-directed behaviors. The term motivation is derived from the Latin word *movere,* meaning to move. Motivation theories explore the processes that explain why and how human behavior is activated, considered one of the most important areas of study in the field of organizational behavior. Despite the extensive amount of research conducted in this area, there exists no unified, universally accepted theory of motivation. So far, research on motivation found it to be multidimensional, dynamic, fluctuating; it can be modified or influenced by social interactions and is a key component for change.

Factors that influence motivation

Factors that influence motivation can be intrinsic (internal) or extrinsic (external), and they can have biological underpinnings and sociocultural influences. Several theories of motivation have been proposed, each focusing on a different aspect of, or reason for, what motivates goal-oriented behavior. Early theories of motivation focused on instincts, and psychologists suggested that humans were programmed to behave in specific ways as a response to motivational cues. However, in the early twentieth century, researchers began to examine the possibility of different explanations for differential motivation in individuals.

Although some psychologists such as Freud decided to focus on internal drives, others, such as Bandura, decided to focus on external factors and the effect of learning from the environment, and how individual behavior is influenced by reinforcement contingencies. Lastly, other psychologists took a third route, examining cognitive processes, and how cognitive schema about the past and the future influence behavior, motivating individuals to behave a certain way. Since there are many theories of motivation suggesting the influence of several different factors, all these factors have been categorized into two major schools of motivation theories: the content theories of motivation and the process theories of motivation.

The content theories, also known as needs theories of motivation, represent the earliest theories in the field and suggest that needs are the primary factors affecting motivation. An example of this type of theory would be Maslow's hierarchy of needs model. Conversely, process theory of motivation talks about how human needs change.

Instinct

According to the evolutionary perspective on motivation, behaviors are not made consciously, but rather have an instinctual base. *Instincts,* or impulses, represent the capacity of an organism to carry out complex behaviors automatically, without conscious awareness. Instinctual theory assumes there are innate, automatic, involuntary forces and unlearned behavior patterns that are present when elicited by certain stimuli. For example, cats tend to arch their backs when faced with an imminent threat.

Many examples of instinctual behavior can be observed in humans. Most instinctual behaviors can be observed in the form of reflexes in human babies, such as a sucking response in an attempt to obtain food, a crying response to express distress or some need, a grasping response while exploring objects in the environment, and the ability to convey feelings and thoughts through body language, even unconsciously. Although there is a premise that instinctive behaviors are hereditarily based, they also seem to be influenced by the forces of natural selection.

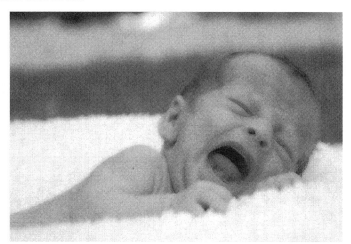

Most instinctual behaviors can be observed in the form of reflexes in human babies, such as crying to express distress or some need.

Arousal

According to the optimal arousal perspective, individuals are motivated by attempting to reach an optimal state of arousal or activation. Supporting this theory, research has found that individuals perform best at a moderate level of arousal. An example of arousal theory in humans can be observed in introverts and extroverts, where the level of arousal may affect whether a person is motivated to interact with others or not. That is, it is believed that extroverts have a lower level of cortical arousal and are therefore more likely to seek arousal than their introverted counterparts. Introverts, however, are believed to have higher levels of cortical arousal, and therefore do not require as much external stimulation from their environment. The critics of arousal theory argue that one of the major limitations of this model is that it can only focus on internal influences of behavior and can provide us with only half the picture.

Drives

The drive reduction theory suggests that drives and needs motivate behavior. A drive is a specific state of arousal following a physiological need. Negative feedback systems exist to maintain homeostasis between drives and needs. This theory proposes there are two types of drives—primary drives and secondary drives. Primary drives are innate drives that result from biological needs. Secondary drives are learned and result either from operant conditioning or from associations formed with primary reinforcers.

An example seen in humans is when we feel hunger simply through smelling or seeing food, even if we have just eaten. Supermarkets tend to utilize this insight through providing food samples, or making food within the supermarket, so the smell might motivate people to buy it. Critics of drive-reduction theory argue that the theory only focuses on observing the internal physiological environment, yet external factors, as we know, also play a major role in motivation. Similarly, another limitation of this theory is that it does not explain some human behavior, usually driven by curiosity, which tends to expose humans to danger and does not necessarily result in drive-reduction.

Needs

A need is a factor required because it is essential for the individual and tends to be satiated following a drive or behavioral response that is goal-oriented towards meeting this need. Maslow proposed that our needs are prioritized from physiological, to biological, social and ultimately spiritual. Biological needs include food, water, oxygen, sleep, hygiene, sexual and stress release. Safety needs include need for security, comfort, and peace of mind. Attachment needs refer to the need to belong, affiliate, love and be loved. Esteem needs refer to the need for self-efficacy, self-esteem, and sense of worthiness, and respect from others. Cognitive needs include the need for knowledge and understanding. Self-actualization needs include the need to develop, fulfill one's potential and to have meaningful goals and be able to fulfill them in life. Transcendence is a more recently acknowledged need, and refers to the need for spirituality, religion or identification with a higher being or source of guidance.

Theories that explain how motivation affects human behavior

Drive reduction theory

Physiological need creates an aroused tension, which is referred to as the drive that motivates an organism to satisfy the need. The need is usually to maintain homeostasis. Individuals are not only pushed by their needs but are pulled by their incentives; which are positive or negative environmental stimuli that motivate behavior.

Incentive theory

Incentives are the stimuli that individuals are drawn to due to learning. They learn to associate some stimuli with rewards and others with punishment. Individuals are motivated to seek rewards and tend to refrain from behaviors associated with no rewards or negative consequences. Put differently, individual differences in behavior across settings and people have underlying value systems traditionally associated with certain incentives and/or rewards.

A classic example of incentive theory in humans is the drive towards the incentive of monetary compensation or recognition. That is, people tend to go to work and try to excel at what they do because they want to receive remuneration or recognition from others; regardless of whether the task at hand is unpleasant, the incentive fuels the behavior. Nonetheless, not all incentives provide enough motivation necessary for individuals to take action, as people may not place the same value on different kinds of rewards or incentives and might not be motivated enough to engage in unpleasant tasks. That is, social, cognitive and physiological factors can all play a role in what an individual finds motivating or not.

Another caveat to this theory is that people must be able to believe the reward is obtainable in order for it to be a motivating factor. For example, if a runner does not believe he will be able to meet the marathon requirements on time, he might find it so difficult to attain this goal that it is not realistically attainable and will consequently not put any effort into achieving the goal.

Other theories

Cognitive-based theory of motivation focuses on the intrinsic (internal) or extrinsic (external) motivating factors that influence an individual's decision making and behaviors. Research has shown intrinsic motivating factors to be more effective at motivating certain behaviors. This theory proposes that motivation is not innate but is rather a result of a persistent set of behavioral patterns resulting from interaction with different environmental stimuli. Similarly, there is a high emphasis on expectations regarding the possible outcomes of goal-directed behavior. One type of cognitive motivation theory is the *expectancy-value theory*, which posits that the amount of effort a person puts in a task depends on the degree to which the person expects to succeed in said task. Therefore, the value of a task is considered along with attainment value, intrinsic value, and costs.

The *need-based theory* on motivation was proposed by Maslow, and focuses on the human hierarchy of needs, from physiological needs ascending through to self-actualization. According to Maslow's theory of motivation, needs higher up in the hierarchy cannot be met before needs lower in the hierarchy have been met.

Derivatives of the needs theory have evolved with time to include the ERG theory proposed by Clayton Alderfer and the Two-Factor theory, proposed by Frederick Herzberg. *ERG theory* is a modification of Maslow's theory; instead of five needs that are hierarchically organized, Alderfer proposes that basic human needs can be grouped into three categories: Existence, Relatedness, and Growth.

Paralleling Maslow's theory, existence corresponds to physiological and basic safety needs, relatedness corresponds to social needs and the need for belonging, and growth corresponds to self-actualization and esteem. This theory is a bit more flexible than Maslow's original theory, as it recognizes that more than one need can operate at a specific time and does not rank these needs in any particular order.

Next, the *Two-Factor theory* proposed by Herzberg focuses on what satisfies and dissatisfies individuals, especially in the workforce. The factors affecting satisfaction were labeled "hygiene" factors, which characterize the environment in which an individual works. Hygiene factors include working conditions, salary, safety, on-the-job security and quality of supervision. Concrete examples of hygiene factors include instances of sexual harassment in the workplace, lack of a constant temperature in the office, or inappropriate levels of background noise. If these factors are kept at appropriate levels, or if the environment is "hygienic," according to this theory, workers are more likely to be motivated to work.

Biological and sociocultural motivators that regulate behavior

Researchers believe that some forms of behavior may be motivated by the integration of both biological and sociocultural factors. For example, one model that explains how these interactions can become faulty is the diathesis-stress model, which has been proposed in an attempt to describe behavior as a product of innate predispositions and environmental stress. Specifically, this model states that a person is more likely to suffer an illness if he or she has a particular vulnerability or diathesis and is under a high level of stress.

Diathesis factors that have been highly researched include individual psychological characteristics such as impulsivity and hostility, biological vulnerabilities such as cardiovascular reactivity, and environmental characteristics such as low socioeconomic status and an unstable family environment in childhood. Other common motivators that affect behavior and are influenced by biological and sociocultural forces are hunger, sex drive, and substance use.

Hunger

The brain (i.e., the ventromedial and paraventricular nuclei of the hypothalamus), the endocrine (i.e., leptin and insulin) and digestive systems are involved in the regulation of hunger motivation and the behavioral act of eating. Sociocultural factors regulating the hunger motivation include factors such as appeal, availability and time.

The brain and the endocrine and digestive systems are involved in the regulation of hunger motivation and the behavioral act of eating.

Sex drive

Biological factors involved in the regulation of motivational processes involved in sex include visual and olfactory senses, as well as the regulation of testosterone, estrogen, oxytocin, and vasopressin. Sociocultural influences include the cultural beliefs associated with sex, age and emotions.

Substance Addiction

Biological factors influencing substance abuse include genetics and biochemical reactions within the limbic system. Sociocultural factors include self-perception and esteem, emotion-regulation abilities and stress, and societal influence.

Biological factors influencing substance abuse include genetics and biochemical reactions within the limbic system.

Notes

Stress

Like emotion, the exact definition of stress is debated. One widely used definition refers to stress as an acute threat to homeostasis. Stress is thus viewed as a response to change. Stress can be either negative or positive. *Eustress* is positive stress that is motivating to an individual. Winning the lottery, for example, would result in eustress. *Distress* refers to negative, unpleasant and overwhelming stress experienced by an individual. Distress causes anxiety and is usually experienced in response to an event that individuals believe they are unable to cope with.

Acute stress refers to intense stress that lasts for a short period of time and involves the fear response. Chronic stress refers to stress that persists over time. Chronic stress has been linked to numerous physical ailments.

The nature of stress

Appraisal

The appraisal view of stress was developed primarily by Richard Lazarus. This model views stress as a combination of stressors in the environment and an individual's cognitive response to these stressors.

The appraisal process is divided into two stages according to the Lazarus model. In the *primary appraisal* state, a quick initial evaluation of the situation or event is given. This evaluation assesses for threat. The three appraisals that can result from this primary state are that the situation is *irrelevant*, is *positive* or is *threatening*. This primary appraisal state is adaptive because it is concerned only with the organism's survival.

In the *secondary appraisal* stage, individuals evaluate their ability to adapt and cope with the situation. According to the appraisal model, the primary and secondary appraisals interact in order to form an emotional response. For example, if the situation is perceived as threatening in the primary appraisal stage, but individuals believe they have the resources to cope with the threat, their stress levels will be less than if they determine that a situation is threatening and believe that they do not have the necessary resources to cope with the threat.

Cognitive *reappraisal* refers to the process of changing an emotional response by changing the thoughts associated with the stressor. For example, an individual who fails a test may initially believe that this failure will threaten his or her future plans (primary appraisal) and that he or she will not get a good grade (secondary appraisal). Reappraisal for this individual would involve viewing the test in the larger scheme of things and taking a more neutral stance on the topic. Cognitive reappraisal is a central aspect of many types of therapy, including cognitive behavioral therapy.

Different types of stressors

Stressors are typically organized into three categories: microstressors, personal stressors, and cataclysmic events. *Microstressors* refer to small stressors that are encountered daily. Examples of microstressors include spilling a drink on one's clothes, interacting with an irritating co-worker and being stuck in traffic. Microstressors can include *ambient stressors*, which are chronic low-grade stressors, such as pollution and overcrowding.

Microstressors refer to small stressors that are encountered daily, such as being stuck in traffic.

Personal stressors refer to big changes and milestones that occur in an individual's life. Common personal stressors include moving somewhere new, the birth of a child, the loss of one's job and sudden changes in finances.

Cataclysmic events (e.g., floods, earthquakes, hurricanes) and catastrophes (e.g., large-scale industrial explosions, terrorist attacks) are unexpected stressors that occur on a large scale and affect many people at the same time.

A recently identified form of stress is technostress. *Technostress* refers to stress relating to the use of technology. People are said to experience technostress when they are unable to adapt to the use of technology.

Effects of stress on psychological functions

In the early years of development, experiencing acute and chronic stress can be detrimental to an individual's mental health. Exposure to personal stressors during childhood (e.g., abuse or marital conflict) is associated with personality disorders, poor school performance, anxiety, depression, and antisocial behavior. Exposure to cataclysmic events during childhood is associated with depression and has been linked to the development of post-traumatic stress disorder. Chronic stress experienced in childhood is associated with anxiety and depression.

During adulthood, stress has been linked to the development and maintenance of most psychopathologies. Stressful life events have been shown to precede depressive episodes and the onset of anxiety disorders. Research shows that stress is also related to the onset of schizophrenia, as well as any relapses that may occur.

Stressful life events have been shown to precede depressive episodes and the onset of anxiety disorders.

Exposure to a traumatic stressor often results in the development of post-traumatic stress disorder, which is characterized by nightmares, anxiety, and hypervigilance.

Substance abuse disorder is also associated with chronic stress. Some models of addiction view substance abuse as a method of coping with overwhelming distress. Interventions targeting stress reduction have been shown to be successful in reducing relapses in individuals with substance abuse disorders.

Stress outcomes/response to stressors

Physiological

Acute physiological responses to stressors include an increase in cortisol levels, adrenocorticotropic hormone (ACTH) levels, and heart rate. These responses prepare the body for defense or to flee.

Chronic stress is associated with negative health outcomes across a variety of diseases. Overexposure to cortisol and other stress hormones is believed to be the cause of these negative health effects. Chronic stress is associated with digestive problems, including irritable bowel syndrome, the worsening of ulcers and gastroesophageal reflux disease (GERD). Heart disease and insomnia have also been linked to chronic stress.

Emotional

Common emotional responses to stress include depression, anxiety, and anger. Research suggests that how an individual interprets a stressor determines what emotions they will experience. People tend to experience depression in response to a stressor if they determine that they are unable to cope with it. People typically experience anger in response to a stressor when they determine that they will fight the stressor. Fear and anxiety are experienced when individuals determine that they will flee from the stressor. Exhaustion often occurs following an acute stress response.

Behavioral

People under chronic stress often engage in unhelpful coping strategies in an attempt to reduce their stress levels. Among these unhealthy coping strategies are smoking, drinking, drug use and binge eating. These behaviors contribute to the physical effects of stress.

Self-injury is also viewed as a negative response to stress under some theoretical models. In these models, individuals who engage in self-harm are theorized to have a lower distress tolerance. Recent research has supported this idea by showing that individuals who engage in self-harm show higher physiological reactivity when performing a distressing task.

Managing stress

Several techniques have been identified to help individuals reduce and manage stress. One technique, called diaphragmatic breathing, involves breathing to inflate and deflate the abdomen rather than the chest. This is done on counts of five for each inhalation and exhalation. Diaphragmatic breathing has been shown to reduce stress levels and is often taught to individuals with panic disorder as part of a treatment plan.

Progressive muscle relaxation (PMR) involves systematically tensing and relaxing certain muscles. This is believed to promote awareness of muscle tension and allows individuals engaging in PMR to practice reducing their muscle tension. PMR has been shown to improve sleep, increase energy and lower physiological indicators of stress (i.e. salivary cortisol).

Exercise has also been shown to help individuals reduce stress. Studies suggest that exercise can decrease fatigue, improve alertness and aid in sleep. In addition, exercise has also been shown to temporarily relieve symptoms of anxiety and depression. Regular exercise may also help prevent the development of these disorders.

Holistic approaches to stress management often incorporate aspects of spirituality. Spirituality gives our lives context and can be found in both religious and secular communities. It may reduce stress by providing a sense of meaning and purpose. Spirituality also enables individuals to give up control and acknowledge that much of life is outside of any one person's control.

Exercise has been shown to help individuals reduce stress.

Recent research has indicated meditation and mindfulness as powerful tools for combating stress. During meditation and mindfulness, attention is focused on thoughts, emotions, physical sensations, external stimuli or a certain phrase. Mindfulness promotes non-judgmental awareness focused on the present moment. Often, breathing is used to "anchor" oneself in the present moment. Mindfulness and meditation can reduce stress and increase positive emotions. They are often used in clinical settings with individuals who ruminate constantly or are excessively anxious.

Chapter 8

Developmental Psychology

Developmental psychology deals with the behavior of organisms from conception to death and examines the processes that contribute to behavioral change throughout the lifespan. The major areas of emphasis in the course are prenatal development, motor development, socialization, cognitive development, adolescence, and adulthood.

Notes

Prenatal Development

Effects of Nutrition, Illness and Substance Abuse

Poverty has been known to have a negative influence on prenatal care and development. Women of lower socioeconomic background tend to have children at a younger age, which is correlated with lower birth weights. Additionally, it is believed that these women do not have access to sufficient education and are less likely to be aware of the risks of smoking, consuming alcohol and drug use during pregnancy. It is said that women between the ages of 16 and 35 possess a healthier constitution for a fetus in comparison to those under 16 or over 35. Women in the first age range usually have fewer complications during pregnancy and birth. The over-35 age range can pose a risk for longer delivery time, which can sometimes result in the death of the mother or the fetus. They also run the risk of pre-term labor. Premature babies of younger mothers have a higher risk of neurological disorders. Down syndrome is a major risk for infants born to mothers over 40 years old. Miscarriage is a high risk for younger mothers and mothers over 35.

Maternal drug use occurs when drugs ingested during pregnancy are metabolized in the placenta and are ultimately transmitted to the fetus. With the use of drugs or narcotics, there is a higher risk of birth defects, low birth weight and a higher rate of death or stillbirth. Additionally, the chemicals within the drugs can cause the newborn to be addicted to them as well. Marijuana can stunt fetal growth rate and result in a premature delivery. Heroin can cause interrupted fetal development, stillbirth, numerous other birth defects, and miscarriages. Other fetal abnormalities that can result are facial and head size abnormalities, as well as gastrointestinal abnormalities.

Additionally, the risk of *sudden infant death syndrome (SIDS)* increases and there can be dysfunction in the central nervous system as well as neurological dysfunction, such as tremors, sleep problems and seizures. Similarly, the use of cocaine puts the fetus at risk of being stillborn or premature. It can also result in low birth weight, motor dysfunction and overall damage to the central nervous system.

The use of alcohol can cause disruptions in the fetus' brain development, cell development, and organization and the maturation of the central nervous system. Additionally, the use of alcohol can lead to organ defects in the heart and many other major organs. The brain can also be affected, which could lead to learning impairments. Alcohol use during pregnancy increases the risk of the onset of behavioral problems, mental problems, and facial abnormalities in the newborn, as well as increasing the risk of miscarriage and stillbirth. *Fetal alcohol syndrome (FAS)* is a developmental disorder caused by too much alcohol intake during pregnancy. Children affected by fetal alcohol syndrome have a vast array of facial and cognitive defects.

During pregnancy, if an expectant mother smokes, the fetus is exposed to nicotine, tar and carbon monoxide. Nicotine causes blood flow to the fetus to decrease, as it constricts the blood vessels. Carbon monoxide causes oxygen flow to the fetus to be reduced. The decreased levels of blood and oxygen flow can result in a stillbirth, low birth weight and sometimes an ectopic pregnancy. Additionally, there is an increased risk of SIDS, miscarriages and premature birth. Researchers have also found an association between smoking during pregnancy and asthma in childhood.

If a mother contracts a disease, the placenta does not always have the ability to filter out these pathogens. Babies can be born with ventral diseases transmitted by the mother. Proper nutrition is necessary to produce a healthy fetus. The lack of iron can cause the fetus to develop anemia, the lack of calcium can cause poor bone and teeth formation and the lack of protein can cause a smaller fetus and mental retardation. The exposure to various environmental toxins in pregnancy has led to higher rates of miscarriage, sterility and different birth defects. These toxins include lead, mercury, and ethanol.

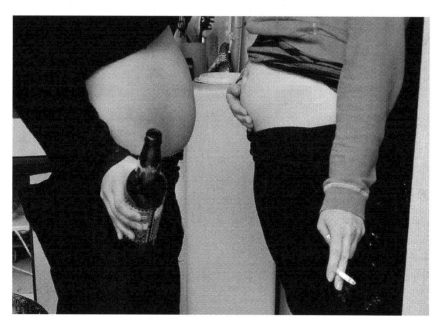

Smoking and drinking during pregnancy are linked to adverse effects on the fetus

Heredity–Environment Issues: Interaction of Nature and Nurture

Nature refers to heredity, while nurture refers to environmental experiences during development. Some researchers argue that humans are "pre-wired," while others argue that life experiences and parenting determine the course of human development.

Parenting styles' influence on development

The *authoritarian* parenting style sets strict standards to guide children's behavior; there is no discussion about the rationale behind them and punishment is used more than reinforcement. Children with authoritarian parents tend to be less trusting of others and are more withdrawn from their peers. The *permissive* parenting style is characterized by parents who do not set clear guidelines for their children; the rules are constantly changed and are not usually enforced. Under this parenting style, it is easy for children to get away with almost anything and they tend to have emotional issues and problems with self-control and appear to be more independent.

The *authoritative* parenting style is characterized by parents who set consistent standards for their children. The standards are reasonable and explained and the parents encourage their children's independence, and praise as often as they punish. Their children are more socially capable and perform better academically. *Uninvolved parenting* is characterized by few demands, low responsiveness, and very little communication. These parents fulfill their children's basic needs but are usually detached from their lives. In very extreme cases, these parents may reject or neglect the needs of their children.

Motor development

Reflexes are innate, automatic responses to specific stimuli. There are a number of reflexes that humans are born with. The *rooting reflex* occurs when children are touched on the cheek and as a result turn their head and seek to put the object in their mouth. The *sucking reflex* is when an object is placed in the baby's mouth and the baby proceeds to suck on it. The *grasping reflex* occurs when a baby tries to grasp an object that is placed on his or her hand or foot. The *moro reflex* is when startled babies fling out and then retract their limbs, making themselves as small as possible. The *Babinski reflex* is when a baby's foot is stroked, and the baby spreads out his or her toes. These reflexes are lost later in life.

Five-and-a-half-month-olds engage in the motion of *rolling over*. The motion of *standing* occurs eight or nine months after birth. Finally, being able to *walk* alone tends to occur fifteen months after birth. The effect of the environment on motor development is slight.

Maturation of cognitive abilities

Jean Piaget worked for Albert Binet, who was the creator of the first intelligence test. Piaget noticed that children of the same age gave similar answers to the test questions. His hypothesis proposed that children think in similar ways that differ from the way adults think. This led to the *theory of cognitive development*, which states that children view the world through cognitive schemata. These are a set of cognitive rules that humans use to interpret the world. For example, during *assimilation* humans incorporate their experiences into their existing schemata. In contrast, when the information violates their schemata, humans tend to accommodate and change their schemata in order to incorporate the new information.

There are four stages of thinking. The first stage is the *sensorimotor stage*, which occurs from birth to age two. During this stage, individuals explore the world through their senses. Behavior is governed by reflexes until individuals develop their first cognitive schemata. A major challenge is the development of *object permanence*, or understanding that objects continue to exist even when they are out of the individual's sensory range.

The *preoperational stage* occurs from the ages of two to seven. Object permanence prepares individuals to use symbols to represent real-world objects. This stage is the start of the onset of language development when the first words are spoken, yet individuals are still limited in the ways they think about the relationships between the characteristics of objects. During this stage, individuals are egocentric in thinking and can only see the world through their perspective.

The next stage of cognitive development is known as *concrete operations*, occurring from the ages of eight to twelve. Individuals learn to think more logically about complex relationships between different characteristics of objects and the concept of conservation is developed, as well as the realization that properties of objects remain the same even when their shapes change. Examples include volume, area, and numbers.

The next stage of development is *formal operations*, which occurs from the age of twelve to adulthood. Individuals gain metacognition, which is the ability to think about thinking, and the ability for abstract reasoning begins to develop. An individual in this stage can start to form hypotheses. Additionally, individuals can manipulate objects in their minds without physically seeing them and can contrast ideas in their minds without real-world correlates.

The preoperational stage occurs from the ages of two to seven.

With every theory comes unsought criticism. Piaget's critics argue that he underestimated children. For example, it has been found that many children go through stages much faster than others and enter them earlier than Piaget had thought. Also, it is argued that Piaget's test relied too heavily on the use of language and that his results were biased in favor of older children.

The *Information Processing Model* is a more continuous alternative to Piaget's stage theory. It states that an individual's ability to memorize, interpret and perceive gradually develops as individuals age, and not in stages. This model could explain some apparent cognitive differences that Piaget attributed to different cognitive stages.

Sex and gender's influence on socialization and other aspects of development

The Biopsychosocial theory focuses on the biological aspects of the nature and nurture mix that produces gender roles. This theory posits that culture plays a part in the roles associated with each gender - and even proposes that women have a larger corpus callosum - which in turn may affect how the brain hemispheres communicate. Freud's *Psychodynamic Theory* proposed the Oedipus and Electra complexes, which describe that during gender development children come to realize that they cannot overcome their same-sex parents for attention from the other parent. As a result, children tend to identify with the same-sex parent.

Sigmund Freud and his mother

The *Social-Cognitive Theory* focuses on the effects of society and an individual's thoughts about gender on role development. Social psychologists look at how individuals react to boys and girls differently. Cognitive psychologists focus on the internal interpretations made about gender-role related messages as individuals receive these messages from the environment. In the *gender-schema theory*, messages about gender are internalized into cognitive rules about how each gender should behave.

Temperament and other social factors

Various researchers that focus on the role of nature in development believe that every child is born with a set of characteristics, defined as *temperament* by researchers Thomas and Chess in 1977. These characteristics, in turn, affect the response of the child's caregiver and ultimately mold the child's future personality traits. Three different dimensions have been proposed to characterize temperament. The first dimension is *negative emotionality* and includes irritability, negative mood, inflexibility and high intensity as negative reactions. The second dimension is *self-regulation* and includes persistence, non-distractibility, and emotional control. The third dimension, *approach/withdrawal, inhibition* or *sociability,* includes approaching new situations and people or withdrawing from them.

According to this theory, the relatively "easy" child is adaptable, playful and quite responsive to adults. These children usually get a great deal of attention in the early stages of development because their interactions are pleasant and reinforcing. The "difficult" child is fussy, difficult to calm down and has problems eating and sleeping; as a result, they provide little positive reinforcement to their caregivers. The "slow to warm up" child is slow to adapt. Adults who are in contact with such a child are rewarded by the positive behavior usually found in the "easy child," but it takes longer to elicit this behavior.

Temperament is usually stable over time. However, recent research has suggested specific factors that affect temperament, including gender, children's participation in out-of-home care and parental characteristics. Research has also shown that inhibited girls are more likely to change than inhibited boys, and that children who receive outside child care become less inhibited over time. Parents who are over-controlling tend to have children who will remain inhibited over time.

Notes

Behavioral Change Throughout Life

Stages of Life

Psychological maturation can be thought of as stages through which humans pass after birth and throughout their lifespan. The stages of the life course can be categorized as infancy, toddlerhood, early childhood, middle childhood, adolescence, adulthood, middle age and old age.

Infancy is typically viewed as the first year of life. Newborns typically measure between fourteen and twenty inches at birth and weigh somewhere between five and a half to ten pounds. Infants spend a large portion of their first year sleeping and are capable of deciphering distinct units of sound in speech, eventually beginning to babble.

According to Piaget's theory of cognitive development, young infants are capable of simple reflexes (e.g., using their mouth to suck, closing their hand around an object that touches their palm and following movement with their eyes). At around six weeks of age, infants are also able to imitate some actions using their bodies (e.g., waving their hand), and they enter into the phase of first habits and primary circular reactions. By four months, infants have entered into the phase of secondary circular reactions, meaning they are able to grasp a desired object and repeat actions such as opening and closing a book. Around eight months to twelve months, infants increase their ability to coordinate hand and eye movements.

Toddlerhood typically refers to children from the time they turn one-year-old to their third birthday. This stage is characterized by the child's increased mobility, as walking typically occurs during the toddler years. Children reach other important developmental milestones during the toddler years, including physical growth, the development of both gross and fine motor skills, and improved vision, hearing, speech, and social relationships.

Toddlerhood represents a part of the life cycle during which children begin to experience greater control over their movements (e.g., running and climbing during play), greater ability to draw, greater ability to use utensils to feed themselves, greater ability to see both near and far and greater ability to communicate through hearing, speaking and playing with other children. At this age, children are able to take turns and also engage in imaginary play.

After age two, children typically experience a decreased need for naps, tend to have an increased vocabulary and often begin toilet training. Children in toddlerhood may also experience separation anxiety when they are separated from a caregiver. Frequently, children at this age will want to assert their independence through temper tantrums or by saying "No!"

Childhood is generally divided into early childhood and middle childhood. Early childhood occurs prior to children entering school, so they are still in the play stage of their lives. Early childhood begins with toddlerhood and ends around age seven to eight. Children in this stage remain highly dependent on caregivers for emotional bonding. Middle childhood begins around the time children enter first grade. Children in this stage become more independent and increase their peer friendship network.

Adolescence is a transitory stage between childhood and adulthood. Adolescence is typically the time when teenagers go through puberty, leading to sexual maturity. During adolescence, both primary and secondary sex characteristics develop. Primary sex characteristics include reproductive organs that grow and become functional. Secondary sex characteristics include body hair, deepening of the voice (in boys), breast development and the menstrual cycle (in girls). Females tend to develop faster than males. In addition, adolescents develop better processing speed, selective attention, memory, and metacognition.

Some recent research suggests that more children are experiencing puberty prior to adolescence. Adulthood cannot be defined purely by an individual experiencing puberty, so the end of adolescence and entrance into adulthood has no definite age. Rather, it varies by cultural, biological, individual and familial beliefs and experiences. Legally, an adolescent is still considered a minor, yet adolescents strive for the increased independence that characterizes the adult years.

As mentioned previously, the beginning timing of the beginning of *adulthood* varies, but generally occurs when a person experiences sexual maturity or has reached the age of majority. Adults, in contrast to children and adolescents, are regarded as independent and self-reliant, and are responsible for their own actions and care. This is the time in the life course when an individual may begin to establish a career and/or a family. There is no absolute agreement on which ages constitute the middle-age stage, but it is roughly thirty-five through sixty-five. *Old age* is considered to be age sixty-five until death. When an individual reaches old age, they may become more physically and mentally frail and dependent on caregivers.

Physical and cognitive changes as people age

Development refers to age-related changes that occur over a person's lifespan. Developmental theorists and researchers are interested in exploring these changes and identifying age-related milestones that correspond to them. Developmental theories of identity formation focus on the evolution of distinct aspects of an individual's personality.

The most well-known theories of identity development are Freud's psychosexual development theory, Erikson's psychosocial development model, Vygotsky's theory of sociocultural development, Kohlberg's model of moral development and present-day theories of gender development. These theories typically focus on a specific aspect of development and are made of stages that build upon each other sequentially.

Developmental models have been criticized for drawing hard boundaries between different stages; in actuality, identity development typically occurs gradually over time. In *continuity,* individuals develop steadily from birth to death. In *discontinuity*, development occurs in distinct steps and the rate is variable. *Stage theories* are discontinuous theories of development.

Freud's psychosexual development model

One of the best-known theories of development is Freud's theory of *psychosexual development*. According to Freud, children become fixated with certain erogenous zones in order to decrease anxiety and satisfy their libido, or sexual drive. The first stage proposed by Freud is the *oral phase*. This phase lasts from birth to one year of age. During this stage, the mouth is the focus of libidinal gratification, particularly in the form of breastfeeding.

The second stage of psychosexual development, according to Freud, is the *anal stage*. This stage lasts from one to three years of age and is characterized by potty training. The third stage of psychosexual development is the *phallic stage*. During this stage, the genitalia is the erogenous zone for the child. This stage lasts from three to six years of age. According to Freud, it is during this stage that children become aware of their bodies and of the sexual differences between males and females. Freud proposed that during the phallic stage, an Oedipus complex emerges in boys. Carl Jung proposed that an Electra complex emerges during this stage in girls. The Oedipus complex is associated with castration anxiety, and the Electra complex is associated with penis envy.

The fourth psychosexual stage identified by Freud is the *latency stage*. This stage lasts from the age of six until puberty. During this stage, sexual feelings are dormant and there are no erogenous zones. The final stage of psychosexual development is the *genital stage*. This stage lasts from puberty until death. As with the phallic stage, the erogenous zone associated with this stage is the genital area.

Stage	Ages	Focus of Libido	Major Development	Adult Fixation Example
Oral	0 to 1	Mouth, tongue, lips	Weaning off of breastfeeding or formula	Smoking, overeating
Anal	1 to 3	Anus	Toilet training	Orderliness, messiness
Phallic	3 to 6	Genitals	Resolving Oedipus/Electra complexes	Deviancy, sexual dysfunction
Latency	6 to 12	None	Developing defense mechanisms	None
Genital	12+	Genitals	Reaching full sexual maturity	If all stages were successfully completed, then the person should be sexually matured and mentally healthy

Erikson's psychosocial development model

Erik Erikson was a neo-Freudian who believed in the basics of Freud's theory but adapted it to fit his own observations. According to Erickson, the psychosexual stage theory contains eight stages. Erickson thought that personality was profoundly influenced by experiences with others.

Psychologist Erik Erikson

Erik Erikson developed an eight-stage model of development throughout the lifespan. Erikson's stage theory is often referred to as the *psychosocial theory of development*. Each stage is associated with a virtue, psychosocial crisis, and existential question.

The *first stage*, characterized by hope, lasts from birth until two years of age. The psychosocial crisis is basic *trust vs. mistrust*. During this stage, the infant questions whether or not caregivers can be trusted. The existential question during this stage is: "Can I trust the world?" Erikson believed that mistrust could develop during this stage if caregivers did not meet the child's basic needs or provide a secure environment. In this first stage, babies need to learn that they can trust their caregivers to fulfill their needs and that their requests are effective. Consequently, a sense of trust or mistrust remains throughout life.

The *second stage* of development, according to Erikson, is characterized by will and lasts from the ages of two to four. The existential question asked by the child is: "Is it okay to be me?" As this stage emerges children gain control over their eliminative functions (potty training is an early effort at achieving autonomy). The two conflicting forces during this stage are *autonomy vs. shame and doubt*. Caregivers who encourage their children to develop their own interests allow them to develop a sense of autonomy. Caregivers who restrict their children or are too demanding during this stage may instill a sense of shame and doubt in their children. In this stage, toddlers learn to control their temper tantrums. If they learn to control themselves and their environment, they will appropriately develop will-power and learn to control their bodies and emotional reactions in response to various social challenges.

The *third stage*, according to Erikson, is characterized by an *initiative vs. guilt* conflict and occurs during preschool years. The existential question asked by the child during this stage is: "Is it okay for me to do, move and act?" The value associated with this psychosocial stage is purpose. During this stage, children develop the ability to plan and carry out behaviors. If caregivers and teachers support a child's efforts, according to Erikson, the child will develop initiative and independence. If trust and autonomy are achieved, natural curiosity about one's surroundings develops, and individuals start to ask questions often. If curiosity is encouraged, individuals feel comfortable expressing their constant curiosity. Erikson theorized that if caregivers and teachers do not support a child's efforts during this stage, the child will develop guilt feelings regarding his or her desires and will not express their sense of wonder.

The *fourth stage* in Erikson's model is competence. The conflict in this psychosocial stage concerns *industry vs. inferiority*. This stage lasts from five years old until the age of twelve. Children in this stage become aware of themselves as individuals and develop self-confidence. According to Erikson, children who are praised for their efforts during this stage develop a sense of industry; children who are ridiculed develop a sense of inferiority about their capabilities and experience anxiety about performance.

The *fifth stage* of psychosocial development occurs between the ages of thirteen and nineteen, when the main social task is to discover what social identity individuals are most comfortable with. This stage is characterized by *identity vs. role confusion* conflict. During this stage, adolescents are concerned about how they appear to others. The existential question asked by the child during this stage is: "Who am I and what can I be?" Different roles are tried out. In an *identity crisis*, if adolescents are not able to figure out a sense of self, they might have another identity crisis later in life.

The *sixth stage* identified by Erikson is characterized by a conflict of *intimacy vs. isolation*. This stage occurs during young adulthood and is associated with the virtue of love. The existential question asked during this stage is: "Can I love?" or "Will I be loved or will I be alone?" Individuals in this stage gain intimacy through romantic relationships and marriage, or they may experience a sense of isolation when they are unable to form these relationships. Erikson believes that individuals also become isolated due to fear of rejection. Young adults try to figure out how to balance time and effort between work, relationships and the self. The patterns that are chosen become relatively permanent.

The *seventh stage* occurs in middle adulthood and is characterized by care. The existential question asked by individuals in this stage is: "Can I make my life count?" This stage is characterized as *generativity vs. stagnation*. According to Erikson, individuals who raise a family or make a social contribution during this stage will experience a sense of generativity. A person who does not contribute to society is theorized to experience a sense of stagnation. In this stage, individuals look critically at their life path. They try to ensure that their lives are going the way they want and if not, they try to change it either by controlling others or by changing their identity. In a midlife crisis, individuals tend to see this as the last chance to achieve their goals. Kubler Ross developed a theory about the stages of grief and coping with death. The stages include (in order) denial, anger, bargaining, depression and finally acceptance

The *eighth* (final) *stage* is characterized by the conflict of *integrity vs. despair* and occurs from late adulthood until death. According to Erikson, individuals in this stage ask themselves the existential question "Is it okay to have been me?" People in this stage look back on their life and accomplishments. If they are satisfied, they can stand out from their society and offer wisdom. If they are dissatisfied, they may sink into despair over lost opportunities.

Erikson's Stage Theory in its Final Version			
Age	**Conflict**	**Resolution or "Virtue"**	**Culmination**
Infancy (0-1 year)	Basic trust vs. mistrust	Hope	Appreciation of interdependence and relatedness
Early childhood (1-3 years)	Autonomy vs. shame	Will	Acceptance of the cycle of life, from integration to disintegration
Play age (3-6 years)	Initiative vs. guilt	Purpose	Humor; empathy; resilience
School age (6-12 years)	Industry vs. inferiority	Competence	Humility; acceptance of the course of one's life and unfulfilled hopes
Adolescence (12-19 years)	Identity vs. confusion	Fidelity	Sense of complexity of life; merging of sensory, logical, and aesthetic perception
Young adulthood (20-25 years)	Intimacy vs. isolation	Love	Intimacy; isolation from lack of relationships or fear of rejection
Middle adulthood (26-64 years)	Generativity vs. stagnation	Care	Caritas, caring for others, and agape, empathy and concern
Old age (65-death)	Integrity vs. despair	Wisdom	Existential identity; a sense of integrity strong enough to withstand physical disintegration.

Vygotsky's sociocultural theory of development

According to Russian psychologist Lev Vygotsky, individuals learn and develop through active interaction with their environment. His theory of development is known as the *social development theory*. Vygotsky was particularly concerned with the role of social interaction in cognitive development.

Vygotsky believed social learning was crucial to cognitive development; he proposed social learning precedes an individual's development. According to this theory, the environment largely shapes an individual, particularly in how the individual will think and what they think about. According to Vygotsky, infants are born with four mental functions they are able to develop through social interactions. These four *elementary mental functions* are attention, sensation, perception and memory.

Vygotsky also created the concept of a *More Knowledgeable Other* (MKO), which refers to a person who has a better understanding of a concept than the learner. The presence of a more knowledgeable other allows for a *zone of proximal development*. This zone refers to tasks that can be done by an individual when they receive help from a more knowledgeable other.

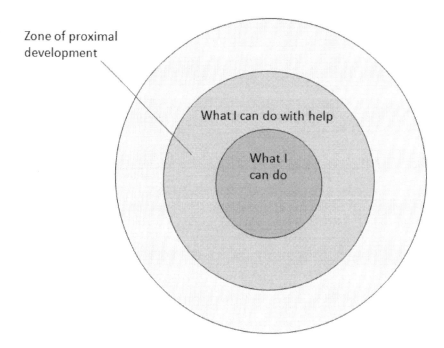

Piaget's stages of cognitive development

Jean Piaget, a Swiss psychologist, proposed that children think differently than adults and progress through four stages of cognitive development. Piaget's model is biologically based; as the child matures, they move on to the next developmental stage. Piaget believed that children go through all four of the stages and that none of the stages can be skipped. He also believed that all children go through the stages in the same order, although they may progress at different rates.

The first stage of development proposed by Piaget is the *sensorimotor stage*. This stage occurs roughly between birth and two years of age. During this stage, infants acquire knowledge about the world through manipulation of their sensory experiences and intelligence is limited to basic motor and sensory information. An important feature of this stage is learning object permanence. *Object permanence* refers to the understanding that objects exist even when they cannot be observed. To study this, Piaget hid toys under a blanket while a child was watching. Piaget then observed whether or not the child would look for the toy under the blanket. Piaget found that children develop object permanence at around eight months old.

Piaget found that children develop object permanence at around eight months old – the understanding that objects exist even when they cannot be observed.

The second stage of development, according to Piaget, is the *preoperational stage*. This stage lasts roughly between the ages of two and seven. During this stage, children do not yet understand logic and are unable to mentally manipulate information. This stage is also characterized by engagement in pretend play. Children in this stage are unable to take on viewpoints of others and believe that others share the same viewpoints as them. This is known as *egocentrism*. To study this concept, Piaget used a *three mountains task* to determine at what age children are able to take on viewpoints of others. In this experiment, three model mountains were placed in front of a child. A doll was placed in various positions surrounding the mountains. Only at the ages of seven and eight were children able to identify the viewpoint of the doll as different from their own viewpoint.

The third stage proposed by Piaget is the *concrete operational stage*. This stage occurs between the ages of seven and eleven. During this stage, children think rigidly and logically. At this stage, children acknowledge that other people have different viewpoints than them. Hypothetical and abstract thinking has not yet developed at this stage.

The fourth stage of cognitive development is the *formal operational stage*. This stage starts around eleven years of age and continues throughout an individual's development. During this stage, children can use hypothetical and abstract thinking. Individuals in this stage also develop the ability to think about thinking, or *metacognition*. At this stage, children develop the ability to use both deductive and inductive reasoning.

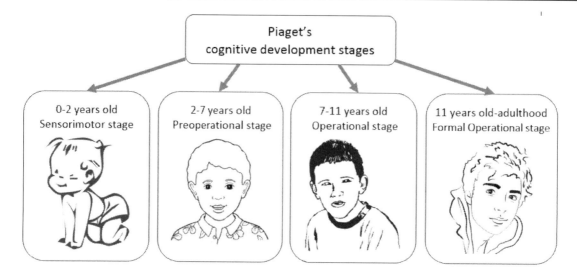

Moral development

Lawrence Kohlberg's stages of moral development

Lawrence Kohlberg was a psychologist who described how humans have the ability to reason about ethical situations that occur in life. Kohlberg proposed to discuss moral dilemmas in schools to stimulate moral reasoning among school children. He integrated moral dilemma discussion into the curricula of humanities and social studies classes. Through these and other studies, Kohlberg found that moral discussion increases moral reasoning and works best if the individual is in discussion with a person who is using reasoning that is one step above their own.

Kohlberg proposed a theory of moral development consisting of six stages. The first two stages are considered the pre-conventional stages. The first stage is the obedience and punishment orientation. According to Kohlberg, individuals in this stage display moral behavior in order to avoid punishment. The second stage is the self-interest orientation. In this stage, individuals display moral behavior only when they will benefit from it.

The third and fourth stages are considered the conventional stages. The third stage is characterized by interpersonal accord and conformity. Individuals in this stage display moral behavior due to social norms. The fourth stage is characterized by an authority-respecting and social order-maintaining orientation. Individuals in this stage are concerned with obeying an authority and contributing to order within their society.

The fifth and six stages are considered post-conventional stages. The fifth stage is the social contract orientation. Individuals in this stage view laws as social contracts and believe that laws should sometimes be changed in order to benefit the greatest number of people. The sixth stage is driven by universal ethical principles. Individuals in this stage use abstract reasoning in order to determine the validity of laws and make moral decisions.

Other theories of moral development

In the *Heinz dilemma*, Heinz must make a moral choice about whether to steal a drug he cannot afford to save his wife's life. The responses to this moral dilemma include pre-conventional, conventional and post-conventional responses. The pre-conventional response stage, often experienced by young children, emphasizes making the decision that will most likely avoid any type of punishment. During this type of response, moral reasoning is limited to how the choice affects the decision-maker.

The conventional response looks at the moral choice through the eyes of others and the decision is made based on how others will view the decision-maker after making the decision. The conventional response stage attempts to follow the conventional standards of right and wrong. The post-conventional response involves moral reasoning. It examines the rights and values involved in each choice and allows the decision-maker to define the ethical principles involved. In this type of moral reasoning, the morality of societal rules is examined, not just blindly accepted.

Carol Gilligan criticized Kohlberg's theories, arguing that his model was based exclusively on the responses of boys. According to Gilligan's research, boys have a more absolute view of what is moral, while girls will pay more attention to situational factors. However, recent research does not support Gilligan's theory of gender differences in moral development.

Please, leave your Customer Review on Amazon

Notes

Chapter 9

Personality

Human development of enduring behavioral and personal characteristic patterns can be explored through a series of major theories (e.g., behavioral, humanistic, psychodynamic, social cognitive, trait). Discussion of various associated personality assessment techniques is also fruitful in bolstering understanding. The *self* refers to the thoughts and beliefs individuals have about themselves. The notion of self is complex and multifaceted; it includes gender, racial and ethnic identities, as well as beliefs about the individual's ability to accomplish tasks and exert control over different situations. The notion of self develops over time and is shaped by a variety of factors, including society, culture, individuals and groups, and unique experiences. How people view themselves influences their perception of others, and by extension, their interactions with them.

Notes

Personality

Personality is defined as individual characteristic patterns of thinking, behaving and feeling. The study of personality focuses on examining how the various parts of an individual become integrated and understanding the individual differences in personality traits.

Theories of personality

Some of the major theories of personality attempt to understand, explain or predict personality characteristics, depending on their specific focus. The most well-known theories attempting to understand the differences and commonalities among people include the psychoanalytic theory of personality, and the humanistic, trait, social, biological and behaviorist theories. As a result, the study of personality can only be understood under each umbrella theory, as consensus is yet to be established.

Psychoanalytic perspective

Freud's early exploration of the unconscious involved using hypnosis and free association techniques. *Free association* is the concept of being relaxed and relating whatever comes to mind. The mental dominoes of the patient's past are then revealed through the process of psychoanalysis. There are three components in Freud's personality structure that interact with each other: the id, the superego, and the ego.

The *id* is the unconscious energy that drives us to satisfy sexual and aggressive drives; it operates on the pleasure principle, demanding immediate gratification. The *superego* is the part of the personality that represents the individual's internalized ideals, based on the individual's standards of judgment or morals. The *ego* is the executive control system of the conscious mind, responsible for mediating the desires of the id and the superego, which is known as the *reality principle*.

Freud constructed a map of the stages of psychosexual development, believing that personality develops during childhood and is highly influenced by unresolved, unconscious problems occurring in early childhood. He believed that children passed through a series of psychosexual stages. The id focuses its libido, or sexual energy, on different erogenous zones.

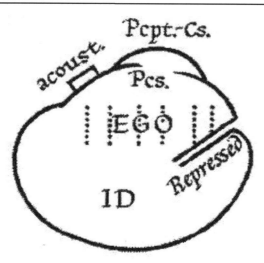

Freud's diagram of the ego and the id

The *oral stage* occurs from the ages of 0 to 18 months. The pleasure center is in the mouth. The activity that persists during this stage includes sucking, biting, and chewing. The *anal stage* occurs between 18 and 36 months. The pleasure in this stage is focused on bladder and bowel control. The *phallic stage* occurs between the ages of 3 and 6 years old. During this stage, the genitals are considered the primary pleasure zone. During this stage, children cope with incestuous feelings; the Oedipus and Electra complexes are formed.

The *latency stage* occurs from age six until the child reaches puberty. There is a dormant sexual feeling that forms. This is also called the "cooties" stage (when the libido and sexuality are hidden in the unconscious and children want to primarily hang around with other children of their age and gender) and it lasts until the *genital stage* (between puberty and death), in which there is a maturation of sexual interests.

Fixation is a lingering focus of pleasure-seeking energies persisting from an earlier psychosexual stage. Orally fixated people may need to chain smoke or constantly chew gum. Anally fixated people can either be anal expulsive or anal retentive.

Defense mechanisms are unconsciously designed by the ego to redefine reality and reduce anxiety.

There are seven types of defense mechanisms.

- *Repression* refers to banishing anxiety-driven thoughts deep into the unconscious. According to Freud, one example can be observed when individuals do not remember lusting after their parents.

- *Regression* is when a person is faced with anxiety and retreats to a more infantile stage, or patterns of behavior used earlier in development. An example would be thumb sucking on the first day of school.

- In *reaction formation*, the ego switches unacceptable impulses into their opposites. For example, when individuals choose to be rude to someone they are interested in romantically.

- *Projection* refers to disguising personal threatening impulses by attributing them to others. For example, sometimes individuals think that their spouses intend to cheat on them when in reality they are the ones considering cheating on their spouses.

- *Rationalization* offers self-justifying explanations in place of the real, more threatening, reasons to explain our actions. For example, when a person doesn't get into an aspired college of choice, they might react by saying, "I didn't want to go there anyway, it's too far from home."

- *Displacement* shifts unacceptable impulses toward a safer outlet. For example, instead of yelling at an instructor, an individual may take his anger out by yelling at his girlfriend.

- *Sublimation* refers to re-channeling unacceptable impulses into more acceptable or socially approved activities. For example, feelings of aggression or violence may be channeled into aggressive sports play.

In order to assess an individual's unconscious mind, methods of hypnosis or free association, as well as projective tests, are most commonly used. Projective tests are personality tests that provide ambiguous stimuli designed to trigger projection of people's inner dynamics.

The Thematic Appreciation Test (TAT) is a projective test designed to help people express their inner feelings through stories they are asked to make up about a series of deliberately ambiguous scenes. The Rorschach inkblot test is the most popularly used projective test. In this test, a set of ten inkblots are designed to identify people's inner feelings when they're asked to interpret what they see in the inkblots.

Neo-Freudians are psychologists who adopted some of Freud's theories and built upon them. Some of the famous names in this group include Alfred Adler, Karen Horney, and Carl Jung. Alfred Adler stated that childhood is important to personality, yet he argued that focus should be on social factors and not on sexual ones. Next, Adler posed the inferiority complex theory, stating that human behavior is driven by their efforts to conquer inferiority and to feel superior.

Karen Horney's theory talked about childhood anxiety. She theorized that childhood anxiety is related to feelings of helplessness and a dependent attachment. This, in turn, triggers the constant yearn for love and security. She argued against Freud's penis envy concept.

Carl Jung put less emphasis on social factors and focused on the unconscious. Jung theorized that all humans have a collective unconscious, which is a shared or inherited source of memory that evolved the history of our species.

Carl Jung, Swiss psychiatrist and psychoanalyst

Humanistic perspective

The main principles of the humanistic perspective include that people are innately good, are able to determine their destinies through free will, and are motivated to self-actualize and reach their full potential. According to this framework, there is an important positive correlation between self-concept and self-esteem. Self-concept is a person's global feeling about the self. Abraham Maslow and Carl Rogers were the founding fathers of humanistic psychology. Maslow hypothesized on the hierarchy of needs and suggested that self-actualization is at the top of the hierarchy.

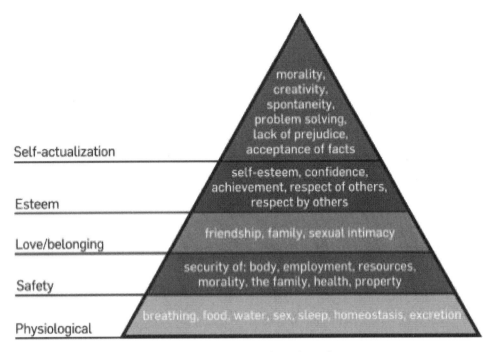

Maslow's hierarchy of needs

Similarly, Carl Rogers' self-theory posed that people need unconditional positive regard as a means to self-actualize. *Unconditional positive regard* is defined as the acceptance and support for a person regardless of what the person does or says. The main criticism of these humanistic theories is that they are overly optimistic and lack objectivity. *Determinism* is the belief that what happens is dictated by what has happened in the past, a concept fully supported by psychoanalysts and behaviorists. In contrast, this perspective does not support the existence of free will.

Trait perspective (Dispositional)

A trait is defined as a characteristic of behavior or a disposition to feel and act a certain way. According to this theory, there are three types of traits that define an individual's personality. First, *cardinal traits* are dominant throughout an individual's life to the extent they become identified by them, as they shape and dominate an individual's behavior.

Next, *central traits* act as the foundation of personality and are represented by varying levels of certain characteristics among individuals. For example, how intelligent or considerate someone is would be an example of their central traits. *Secondary traits* are associated with preferences or attitudes and tend to be expressed only in certain situations.

The Big Five Personality Theory proposes that there are five broad dimensions of personality that can be used to describe personalities. According to this theory, traits are stable and persist over time. Personality traits are at least partially attributed to genetics, apply cross-culturally and predict other individual attributes.

The five-factor model (FFM) consists of openness, conscientiousness, extraversion, agreeableness, and neuroticism.

- *Openness* refers to being imaginative or practical, having a variety of experiences or routines, and independent thinking or conforming.

- *Conscientiousness* refers to being organized or disorganized, careful or careless, and disciplined or impulsive.

- *Extraversion* refers to being sociable or aloof, fun-loving or sober, and affectionate or reserved.

- *Agreeableness* refers to being soft-hearted or ruthless, trusting or suspicious, and helpful or uncooperative.

- *Neuroticism*, or emotional stability, refers to being calm or anxious, secure or insecure, self-satisfied or self-pitying.

Extraversion refers to being sociable or aloof, fun-loving or sober, and affectionate or reserved.

Personality inventories are questionnaires aiming to gauge different aspects of personality. The NEO-FFI3 screener personality inventory is intended to measure the big five domains of personality. The Minnesota Multiphasic Personality Inventory (MMPI) is the most widely used personality test. Although it was originally used to identify psychopathology, it is now used for screening purposes, making differential diagnoses and aiding in treatment plan development. The person-situation controversy deals with the question of whether traits are stable or change over time. Research studies have noted that traits change according to the situation.

Social cognitive perspective

The social cognitive theory emphasizes self-efficacy, observational learning, and the interaction between contextual influence and cognitive processes. This perspective falls under the umbrella of behaviorism. Behaviorism, as introduced by Watson, supports a direct and unidirectional pathway between stimulus and response, with human behavior seen as a simple reaction to external stimuli. The social cognitive theory focuses on how individuals interact with their environment and how observing others influences behavior.

Reciprocal determinism describes the interpenetrative relationship between personality and social and environmental factors. The social cognitive perspective states that different people choose different environments. For example, the friend's individuals frequently hang out with, the places they frequently visit, and the music they listen to are often chosen by individuals following their own disposition. Consequently, after choosing an environment, individuals are reciprocally influenced, or shaped, by said environmental factors.

Biological perspective

Hippocrates believed that personality was determined by the relative levels of four humours in the body. The humours or fluids he described were blood, yellow bile, black bile, and phlegm. Hippocrates was one of the first people to recognize the biological underpinnings of personality. Heritability is a measure of the percentage of a trait that is inherited. Little evidence exists regarding the influence heritability has on specific personality traits.

Temperament is an emotional style and characteristic way of dealing with the world. Infants seem to differ immediately at birth due to their innate differences in temperament. Temperament has been known to influence personality development.

Another famous theory of personality related to biology was first proposed by William Sheldon, who later became known as the pioneer of somatotype personality. The theory of somatotype personality associated certain personality traits with different body types. There were three body types in this theory: endomorphs (fat), mesomorphs (muscular) and ectomorphs (thin).

Behaviorist perspective

The behaviorist theory states that personality is determined by an interaction between the individual and their learning experiences or surrounding environment. That is, reinforcement contingencies promote and shape personality development. Therefore, individuals can alter their personalities by changing the environment. The behaviorist perspective, first proposed by B. F. Skinner, refutes the belief that we must change our inner selves before we can experience a personality change. Critics of this theory highlight its failure to recognize the importance of cognition in personality development.

Situational approach to explaining behavior

Personalities help create situations to which individuals then react. For example, a counter-productive example of this would be to give someone the cold shoulder if we believe they are angry at us; in doing so we create or exacerbate the suspected behavior. This theory follows the stimulus-response-consequence model.

Personal control is the sense individuals have of control over their environment, rather than the control that their environment has over them. *External locus of control* refers to the perception that chance or outside forces beyond one's personal control determine one's fate. *Internal locus of control* is the perception that one controls one's own fate.

Learned helplessness refers to the hopelessness, or passive resignation, an animal or human learns when they are unable to avoid repeated aversive events.

Attitudes

Generally, people like to believe that they form their own opinions or attitudes about people, objects, and ideas. However, psychologists have found that these attitudes are influenced by groups around us to a greater degree than most of us would like to admit. Social psychologists have been studying this phenomenon for quite some time and have found just how important outside actors are in forming our attitudes and opinions.

Components of attitudes

To understand how our attitudes are influenced, we first have to understand what exactly attitudes are. An attitude is a set of beliefs (either favorable or unfavorable) toward a person, place, or another object. Attitudes are comprised of three components (cognitive, affective and behavioral) that interact with one another to perpetuate the attitude. The *cognitive component* is what the person thinks about the topic. For example, "My boss is always forgetting what I tell him. My boss is a real jerk." The *affective component* of the attitude is the feeling or emotion associated with the attitude. For example, "Every time I see my boss I feel angry." Finally, the *behavioral component* of the attitude is the action that is taken. For example, "I'm currently applying for other jobs within my company, so I can get a different boss. I also try to avoid my boss as much as possible." The components of the attitude will result in an overall approach toward the object, person, etc.

The link between attitudes and behavior

It is not surprising that attitudes and behavior are connected. In the above example, the attitude toward the boss is causing the individual to apply for new jobs and avoid the boss as much as possible. However, what would happen if the individual actually spent more time with their boss? Might the attitude change?

Processes by which behavior influences attitudes

After spending time with the boss, the individual in the example may actually discover that he is a single father and incredibly overworked and overwhelmed. Upon learning this, the attitude about him being a jerk because he forgets what the individual tells him might change. Thus, in this example, the attitude changed as a result of the change in behavior. This is one example of how behaviors may have an influence on attitudes. However, there are other ways behavior can influence attitudes.

One of these processes is known as the foot-in-the-door phenomenon, named after door-to-door salesmen who believed that if they could get one foot in the door, the homeowner would not be able to turn them away. The foot-in-the-door phenomenon states that you should first ask for a simple request and once this has been agreed to, you should follow up with a more substantial request. For example, outside of the voting center someone might ask a person to sign a petition, so a candidate may run for a particular office. Once you sign it, you may then be asked to volunteer several hours of your time to help this candidate's campaign.

The opposite of this is known as the door-in-the-face technique. With this technique, you start by asking for a substantial request, and then, when it's rejected, you follow up with a simple request that is likely to be accepted. For example, one might ask their neighbor to watch their 9-month-old baby for the weekend while they take a trip. When the neighbor says no, they may then ask the neighbor to watch the baby for 2 hours while they go to the grocery store. The idea is the neighbor is so relieved about not being pressed to undertake a demanding task that they will be happy to help with a simpler one.

Another process where behavior can influence attitude is role-playing. This was most famously observed in Stanley Zimbardo's Stanford Prison Study. In this study, a group of men was randomly assigned to be either prison guards or prisoners in a mock prison set up by Dr. Zimbardo in the basement of a building at Stanford University. The "prisoners" were arrested by local police and "booked" into the prison. The "guards" were given uniforms and essentially given free rein to run the prison. After approximately one day, some of the "guards" began acting brutally toward the "prisoners." The study, which was supposed to last 2 weeks, was ended after only 6 days due to the sadistic behavior of the "guards" and the extreme distress of the "prisoners."

This study is cited most frequently when discussing how role-playing affects attitudes. All of the participants in this study were average, emotionally stable, law-abiding American males, and it was due to the flip of a coin that one was assigned to be a prisoner or a guard. The result of playing these roles over a matter of days caused a severe shift in behavior in both the guards and prisoners. The attitude of the guards was to perceive the prisoners as inferior, and the attitude of the prisoners was to believe that they were inferior. Thus, the role-playing significantly influenced the attitude of the guards, prompting acts of sadism, and influenced the attitude of the prisoners, prompting submissiveness.

Another case where attitude can appear to change, though it usually doesn't, is in the case of self-presentation. In this scenario, an individual will profess attitudes that match his or her actions to avoid feeling foolish. There is usually awareness that a discrepancy exists between the presented attitude and the true attitude. However, the behavior, though contrary to the true attitude, is assumed to help one appear consistent.

Processes by which attitudes influence behavior

It is reasonable to assume that attitudes will always predict behavior. However, a study by Richard LaPierre demonstrated that this isn't always the case. In 1934, LaPierre drove through the U.S. with a Chinese couple and stopped at over 250 restaurants and hotels. They were only refused service once. Sometime later, LaPierre surveyed the owners of the restaurants and hotels about their attitudes toward Chinese people, specifically asking if they would serve Chinese people in their place of business. Ninety-two percent stated that they would not serve Chinese people. In this study, clearly the attitude did not influence actual behavior. Most of the owners admitted to racial bias (i.e., the cognitive and affective components of attitude), but did not take action when actually confronted with serving the Chinese couple (i.e., the behavioral component of attitude).

Subsequent studies have focused on determining the circumstances of when attitude will predict behavior. One of the biggest problems with attitudes predicting behaviors is that oftentimes people are not honest about their attitudes, especially if there is a negative social consequence for holding a given attitude. For example, an individual may have a negative attitude toward a specific racial group; however, expressing this negative attitude may be socially unacceptable. Thus, the individual may try to hide their true attitude. In order to minimize this, social psychologists have created the bogus pipeline paradigm, where a person is connected to wires and electrodes and told that the apparatus will measure whether or not they are telling the truth. In reality, the wires and electrodes are not measuring anything. Still, this increases the probability that the subjects will be honest in their attitudes, making prediction of behavior more accurate.

Related to this, asking about specific attitudes, rather than general ones, will help predict specific behavior. For example, if one asks generally about religious attitude, one is unlikely to predict whether someone will attend church next weekend (a very specific behavior). However, they would be able to predict the total number of many different religious behaviors over time (general behaviors). The more specificity with which we can identify an attitude, the better we can predict specific behaviors.

Social psychologists have created the bogus pipeline paradigm, where a person is connected to wires and electrodes and told that the apparatus will measure whether or not they are telling the truth.

The presence of other external factors or conditions can also impact whether attitudes affect behavior. In other words, one's attitude is more likely to affect behavior if there are no other external factors involved. For example, an individual may not want to volunteer at a food bank because their attitude is that people should find gainful employment if they want to eat. However, if that person's close friends decide to volunteer at a food bank as a group, the individual may engage in the volunteering behavior. The external force of peer pressure influenced the behavior in this case, not the attitude.

Closely related to this is the desire to conform to a particular group behavior. In one study, a group read about a proposed law to pay unemployment benefits. Half of the group was told that it was a Democratic-backed proposal, while the other half were told it was a Republican-backed proposal. Among those who were told it was Democratic-backed, those who identified as conservative said the proposal was too expensive, while liberals supported the proposal. However, among those who were told the proposal was Republican-backed, conservatives approved of the proposal, while liberals said the pay was not high enough. In this study, the participants demonstrated behavior (i.e., deciding whether or not to support the proposal) based on the political party of their preference, and not the proposal's content itself. This is an example of how belonging to a group influences attitude and thus behavior.

We know that similar findings occur in the "real world" if two conditions are met. First, the individual must identify with the group. For example, someone with few ties to or no opinion on politics is unlikely to have a strong attitude about a politically charged topic. The second condition is that the issue needs to be somewhat ambiguous. For example, people usually have strong feelings about abortion, but how much government assistance one should receive each month is a bit more ambiguous.

The Theory of Reasoned Action is another model used to try to predict behavior from attitude. This theory, created by Icek Ajzen and Martin Fishbein, purports three constructs: behavioral intention, attitude and subjective norm. Attitude and subjective norm combined determine behavioral intention. Behavioral intention, in turn, is the strength of the intention to perform a behavior. In other words, a person's behavior is determined by the attitude and how others would perceive him/her for engaging in that behavior. Through research, it has been found that the most relevant application of this theory is in consumer behavior. The theory (and associated mathematical formula) seem to predict consumer behavior very well.

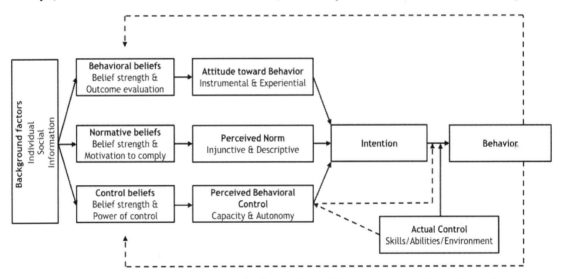

Reasoned Action Approach, a psychological model to explain and predict behavior

Finally, not all attitudes are created equal. The stronger the attitude is, the more likely it will predict behavior. Research has shown that individuals with a strong attitude have spent more time learning about the object of the attitude. This learning process serves to solidify the attitude and makes it not only difficult to change but a better predictor of behavior. Also, individuals with strong attitudes are more likely to have experience with and/or be involved with the object of the attitude. Again, these experiences serve to strengthen the attitude and serve as a stronger predictor of behavior.

Cognitive dissonance theory

At times, our attitudes, beliefs, and behaviors do not correspond with one another. One can have two competing thoughts or beliefs, resulting in a state of tension existing within that individual. Because this tension is uncomfortable, the individual will try to reduce it. For example, a high school senior may want to attend Harvard. He may believe that Harvard is the only school worth attending if one is going to go to college and therefore spends all of his time studying and trying to get good grades. But when he applies, he is rejected by Harvard. Thus, there is tension between his goals and the reality of the situation. As a result, the high school senior may downplay how much he wanted to attend Harvard and proclaim that "there are better schools out there anyway." In this way, the high school senior reduces the tension. This is known as cognitive dissonance theory.

Cognitive dissonance occurs when there are two competing thoughts (i.e., cognition) or two thoughts that are inconsistent with one another (i.e., dissonance). The dissonance is uncomfortable, and therefore the individual makes attempts to lessen it. Cognitive dissonance is important to the study of attitudes and behavior because changes in attitudes due to cognitive dissonance have an impact on behavior.

A child might want to purchase a gift for his mother. When he goes into the store to purchase the gift, he discovers he does not have enough money. However, knowing that this is all his mother wants, he steals the gift. The child may have two thoughts: "I stole the gift" and "stealing is wrong." These two thoughts are in conflict with one another and thus dissonance occurs. In order to resolve this dissonance, two things could happen: 1) he could return the gift to the store and admit his wrongdoing, or 2) he could think "stealing may be a bad thing sometimes, but when it is done to help someone, it's not really that bad." The latter, a change in cognition, would serve to reduce the dissonance while still allowing for the behavior (i.e., stealing the gift).

Theories of Attitude and Behavior Change

How attitudes form and change is not completely understood. However, research has led us to two theories, the Elaboration Likelihood Model and the Social Cognitive Theory. Further, we have been able to identify several factors that affect attitude change.

Elaboration likelihood model

The Elaboration Likelihood Model is a theory of persuasion for attitude change. It states that there are two routes to persuasion: the central route and the peripheral route. The central, or direct, route involves the individual gathering information to form their attitude. Individuals gather evidence and use logic to form their attitude over time when using the central route. If an attitude change occurs, it tends to be resistant to change over time and predictive of later behavior. Most of us would like to believe that our attitudes derive from the utilization of the central route; however, research has shown that many of our attitudes are formed through the peripheral route.

The peripheral route involves quick judgments based on positive or negative cues. Often, there is limited evidence and very little time is taken to research and logically think about the object of the attitude. The peripheral route involves a number of vague impressions, emotions and the characteristics of the message (as discussed below) when forming the attitude. One example of the peripheral route is the foot-in-the-door phenomenon (see above).

Which route is taken is dependent on two important factors: motivation and ability. Motivation is the desire to process the message and may be affected by personal relevance and already existing attitudes. Ability is the actual capability for critical evaluation of that message and is influenced by distractions and familiarity with the message.

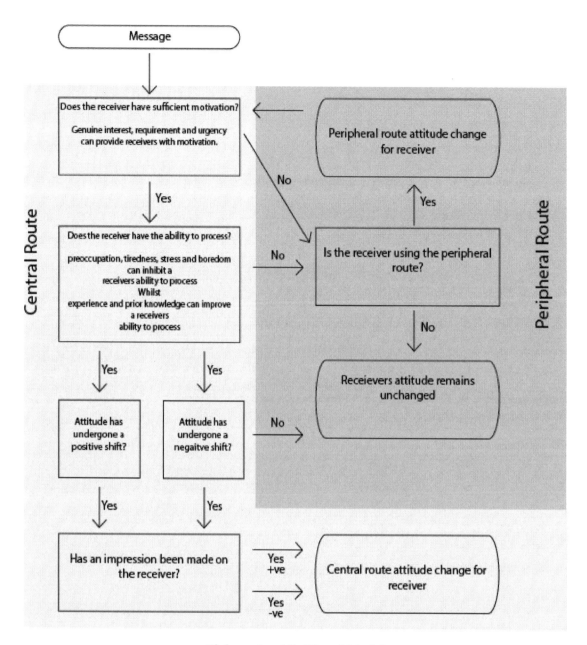

Elaboration Likelihood Model

Social cognitive theory

Social Cognitive Theory was developed by Albert Bandura and posits that an individual learns through observing others. We now know that individuals can learn behaviors and even attitudes by observing others in the media, during social interactions and in other experiences with external actors. In this way, humans do not have to test the results of behaviors on their own; they can learn what the consequences will be through observing others.

If an individual sees a desired consequence as a result of another having a particular attitude or behavior, there is a greater likelihood that the individual will emulate that attitude or behavior. For example, if a celebrity goes on television and states that he or she lost a great deal of weight by eating food at a certain fast food chain, someone watching this commercial may change their attitude toward that chain and now decide that it is a healthy way of eating.

Albert Bandura, psychologist

Factors that affect attitude change

There are many factors that affect our attitude change and the ease at which we change our attitudes. One of these is the message source. Our willingness to change our attitude based on what someone says depends partially on the characteristics of that person (i.e., the communicator). We are more likely to change our attitude with communicators who are more attractive, are perceived to be trustworthy and/or are perceived as experts in the given topic.

Not only is the communicator important, but so is the message content. Two-sided messages, where the communicator's message as well as the opposing viewpoint are presented, are generally more effective than one-sided messages, where only the communicator's message is presented. This is assuming that the viewpoint of the opposing side can be easily refuted. The characteristics of the target of the message also influence whether or not an attitude change will occur.

Even after the message has been delivered by the communicator, the characteristics of the target will determine if the message will change attitudes. Previous research has shown that less intelligent people are easier to persuade than more intelligent people. Gender differences also seem to exist, but they are small. When these differences are found, women are more easily persuaded than men, especially when they have little background on the topic. However, men and women are equally likely to change their private attitude.

As described above, changing one's behavior can also change their attitude. In the case of the Stanford Prison Study, the guards' attitudes began to shift, and they engaged in the brutal treatment of the prisoners. Likewise, after a few hours of "acting" like prisoners, the prisoners' attitudes began to shift, and they started to see the guards as powerful oppressors and themselves as inferior to them, bringing about a change in their behaviors (i.e., they became more submissive).

Finally, individuals with similar attitudes often form groups; sometimes these groups are formalized and other times they may be friends who share similar attitudes. Regardless, when members of the group discuss their attitudes with members of opposing groups, the original attitudes tend to become stronger and more solidified. This is referred to as group polarization, a situation where the discussion serves to make the attitudes members of the group hold more pronounced or polarized.

Self-Concept, Self-Identity; Social Identity

The role of self-esteem, self-efficacy, and locus of control in self-concept and self-identity

Self-concept and self-identity were first identified by psychologists Carl Rogers and Abraham Maslow. Self-concept and self-identity refer to beliefs people hold about themselves and their abilities. Beliefs in three domains have been found to greatly influence a person's overall self-concept: self-esteem, self-efficacy, and locus of control.

Self-esteem refers to the level of worth a person believes they possess. People with high self-esteem see themselves as valuable and are accepting of themselves. They are typically confident and optimistic about the future. People with low self-esteem view themselves negatively. Individuals with low self-esteem tend to be highly self-critical and sensitive to criticisms from others. They typically have low self-confidence and are pessimistic.

Self-efficacy refers to one's belief in their ability to reach a goal. Self-efficacy is concerned with the level of competence a person believes they possess for a particular task. For example, someone who believes they are able to quit smoking possesses high self-efficacy, while someone who believes they will never be able to quit possesses low self-efficacy. Research shows that the level of self-efficacy a person has about a given task influences both their level of success on that task and the likelihood that they will start the task. People with high self-efficacy are more likely to take risks than those with low self-efficacy and are able to recover more quickly from setbacks. People with low self-efficacy avoid challenging tasks and lose confidence in their abilities when faced with a setback.

Locus of control refers to individuals' beliefs about how much they can control the events that affect them. Individuals with an *internal locus of control* feel that they are able to control many of the events affecting them. They are more likely to take responsibilities for their actions and circumstances than those with an external locus of control.

People with an *external locus of control* tend to blame outside forces like luck or chance for their circumstances. This often leads to feeling hopeless when faced with challenges. Locus of control lies on a continuum; most people fall in between an internal and external locus of control. Locus of control has been found to become more internal with age and varies by culture.

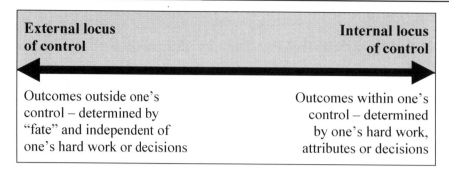

Different types of identities

A person's *social identity* refers to their psychological relationship to particular social categories. Social identity is primarily based on groups that an individual belongs to. Research suggests that a person's social identity is influenced by their race or ethnicity, gender, age, sexual orientation, and class. These factors often interact with each other to form a person's self-identity. *Intersectionality* occurs when an individual belongs to two or more social groups or categories at the same time.

Race refers to physical distinctions like skin color and eye shape and is now believed to be a social construction. *Ethnicity* refers to distinctions based on national origin and culture, including language, relation, and place of origin. A person's racial and ethnic background can influence how they perceive themselves. Racial and ethnic identities are passed down from earlier generations.

Ethnic identity is believed to typically develop during adolescence. Jean Phinney proposed a model for adolescent ethnic identity development that breaks up this process into three stages. In the first stage, an adolescent's ethnic identity is unexamined. Many theorists believe that adolescents from a dominant culture stay in this stage and do not form a sense of ethnic identity. During the second stage, *moratorium*, adolescents search for the meaning of their ethnicity. In the third stage, adolescents have come to feel secure about their sense of ethnic identity; their ethnic identity becomes an integral part of their self-identity.

Psychologist William Cross proposed a model for *racial identity* development, particularly black identity development, which is made up of four identity statuses. The first stage is referred to as *pre-encounter*. During this stage, individuals are unaware of their race and the effects their race has on others. During the *encounter* stage, individuals have an encounter that leads to the examination of their racial identity. Following the encounter stage is the *immersion* stage, where individuals explore their racial identity, particularly through interaction with individuals of the same race. In the final stage, *internalization and commitment*, individuals have formed a secure sense of racial identity. Individuals who have completed this stage are able to form positive relationships with individuals who share their racial identity and those who don't.

Gender is a social category that refers to attitudes and behaviors that a culture associates with a particular biological sex. *Gender identity* refers to a person's subjective experience of their own gender, typically as male or female. When an individual's gender identity and biological sex are incongruent, they may identify as transsexual or transgender.

Sexual orientation refers to a person's sexual identity in relation to the gender to which they are attracted. Sexual orientation is typically organized into four categories: heterosexuality, homosexuality, bisexuality, and asexuality. Stigma is often associated with homosexuality, bisexuality, and asexuality. *Sexual identity* refers to how individuals think of themselves in terms of who they are sexually attracted to and may or may not align with sexual orientation. Contemporary models of sexual identity have acknowledged its formation occurs in both sexual minorities and majorities.

Age identity refers to a person's inner experiences of their age and the aging process. Research on age identity has found that older individuals tend not to feel old. Researchers have suggested that this is due to self-continuity and self-enhancement. *Self-continuity* refers to the desire to remain the same over time, while *self-enhancement* refers to maintaining a positive self-image. In the United States, those with older age identity report lower levels of life satisfaction. Since societies often associate aging with decline, older individuals may wish to identify as younger. Thus, differences in age and age identity are less pronounced in Asian cultures, where age is less associated with decline.

Research on age identity has found that older individuals tend not to feel old. Researchers have suggested that this is due to self-continuity and self-enhancement.

Social class refers to divisions in society in which individuals are classified by wealth, education and occupation. The three most typically discussed social classes are the working/lower class, middle class, and upper class. The social class a person belongs to has wide-ranging effects and may become a part of their identity. Individuals from the upper class are typically able to send their children to better schools, and individuals from the lower class may come to believe that getting a good education is beyond the means of their class. Being in a lower social class also has negative health consequences. In addition, people from lower classes often receive poorer quality healthcare than the upper classes.

Influence of social factors on identity formation

Gender development

Gender is a social construct that forms over time. Gender identity development begins at a young age, forming between the ages of three and six. Some theories of gender development break the formation of gender into three stages. In the first stage, toddlers learn about the socialized characteristics of gender. In the second stage, gender consolidates and becomes rigid. This typically happens between the ages of five to seven. In the third and final stage, socially defined gender roles become more relaxed for the individual.

Gender schema theory was developed by Sandra Bem as a cognitive theory for the development of gender within a society. Gender schemas are sets of gender-related beliefs held by an individual that influence their behavior. Bem believed that these schemas are formed by children's observations of the behaviors of males and females within society. Bem proposed that gender identity is formed primarily from being sex-typed at an early age. *Sex-typed* refers to the acquisition of sex-appropriate preferences and behaviors.

A social-learning theory approach to gender development focuses on the role of parents and caregivers in an individual's acquisition of gender identity. This approach was first proposed by Walter Mischel. According to Mischel, parents reward their children for engaging in gender-appropriate behavior. For example, a boy might be praised for taking an interest in fixing cars, and a young girl might be praised for wearing a dress.

Influence of individuals

Imitation is a form of social behavior that refers to copying another person's behaviors. Imitation occurs even in young infants, suggesting that people are born with an innate ability to imitate others. One area of research within this field concerns mirror neurons. *Mirror neurons* are neurons that are activated when an individual engages in a task and when an individual observes another person engaging in the same task. Theorists have suggested that these mirror neurons may be responsible for the human propensity to imitate others.

Identity formation is also influenced by the expectations of others. Individuals within a family or group of people tend to take on a specific role. The influence of this role-formation is closely related to social norms; we adapt to the expectations of others. Roles in one setting (e.g., family) can carry over into another (e.g., peer group). Individuals can then internalize these roles and view them as parts of themselves. For example, a girl who takes on a mothering role to her brother may also act in a nurturing manner within her friend group and subsequently view herself as a nurturer.

The *looking-glass self* is a social psychological concept that states that a person's identity grows out of the perceptions of others. According to this theory, people form their self-identity by combining how others view them. The three components to the looking-glass theory are that individuals imagine how they appear to others, they imagine others' judgments about how they appear and develop a sense of self through the judgments of others.

The looking-glass self is a social psychological concept that states that a person's identity grows out of the perceptions of others, imagining how others view and judge them.

Influence of groups

Social groups are collections of people who share similarities and interact with one another. Social groups can act as powerful influencers of behaviors. *Reference groups* are groups that the individual uses to compare themselves to. Three types of reference groups have been identified. The first type of reference group, the *aspirational reference group*, refers to a group of people that an individual wishes to be more like. *Associative reference groups* are groups that the individual belongs to and are made up of people who are similar to that individual. *Dissociative reference groups* are groups that an individual does not want to belong to. Dissociative reference groups can also be thought of as out-groups. People will typically adopt the social norms of their aspirational reference groups and associative reference groups, while actively disdaining the norms of dissociative reference groups.

Social groups can be further divided into primary groups and secondary groups. *Primary groups* are groups in which individuals intimately interact with one another. Primary groups typically exert a great deal of emphasis. Commonly found primary groups include families, fraternities, sororities, classmates, and friend groups. *Secondary groups* are groups individuals belong to but do not interact with often. Relationships within a secondary group are typically short in duration. Secondary groups do not exert as much influence on the individuals belonging to them as primary groups.

Influence of culture and socialization on identity formation

The way in which people view themselves is heavily influenced by the culture they grew up in and the socialization they received. This occurs through the social roles that individuals inherit through their socialization. When individuals internalize these roles, they become a part of their identity.

Individuals form their identities by comparing themselves to other individuals who they interact with. Individuals also compare themselves to the ideals and expectations of their culture. If individuals do not meet these cultural expectations, they may develop poor self-esteem. Culture has also been found to influence the locus of control of individuals. For example, individuals from the United States typically have a more internal locus of control than individuals from Japan. Within the United States, African Americans tend to have a more external locus of control than whites.

Self-Presentation and Interacting with Others

Expressing and detecting emotion

Individuals vary in how they express their emotions and detect the emotions of others. Researchers are increasingly concerned with the factors that influence these processes. The ability to express one's own emotions and detect the emotions of others is often referred to as emotional intelligence. People with high emotional intelligence are more likely to have better social support and avoid interpersonal conflicts. Individuals with high emotional intelligence are also less likely to abuse drugs and alcohol. Both gender and culture have been found to shape the way individuals express and detect emotions.

The role of gender in the expression and detection of emotion

Researchers have found differences between how men and women express their emotions and detect emotions in others. Women are typically able to read verbal and visual emotional reactions better than men. Women have also been found to experience emotions more intensely than men and are more likely to display these emotions. Women are more likely to experience disgust, shame, and guilt, while men are more likely to experience anger. Men are typically able to tolerate distressing emotions more than women. Research has found that women score higher on tests of emotional intelligence than men. However, men with high emotional intelligence are typically more successful than men with low emotional intelligence.

There is much debate on why these sex differences exist. Some researchers point to biological differences, like hormone levels, to explain these differences. Other researchers note that cultural stereotypes and socialization may be responsible for these gender differences. For example, the parents of a young boy might express disapproval when he cries, while the parents of a young girl might provide comfort to her. Likely, it is a combination of both biological factors and socialization that has led to these trends.

The role of culture in the expression and detection of emotion

While emotions are universal, how emotions are perceived and regulated differs across cultures. Research by Paul Ekman has found that different cultures share the same facial expressions of emotions. These expressions, however, occur at different frequencies depending on the culture. The cultural expectations of the expression of emotions are referred to as *display rules*. These norms dictate which emotions are acceptable for individuals of a culture to display in the presence of others. Display rules differ across cultures; for example, individuals in the Utku Eskimo population rarely express anger and face ostracism when they do.

In the United States, the expression of emotions is socially encouraged; repressing emotions is often considered as being insincere. Americans also tend to prefer excited smiles over calm smiles. In contrast, Japanese culture often discourages the expression of emotions; suppressing one's emotions is viewed as mature.

Presentation of self

Impression management

Impression management refers to the engagement in behaviors in an attempt to influence perceptions of others. Impression management can be either conscious or subconscious. Common strategies used in impression management include flattery, ingratiation, and intimidation. Impression management contributes to an individual's social identity, which refers to how individuals are regarded in social situations. Impression management is goal-directed, meaning that the individual engaging in impression management wants the person they are interacting with to perceive something in a specific way.

Individuals often engage in impression management to increase their own self-esteem. Thus, they may highlight their accomplishments and positives while downplaying their failures. People may also change their behavior to adapt to the person they are interacting with. For example, an individual might put on their "best self" when interacting with their boss but joke around with a coworker.

Impression management is not necessarily only used for self-presentation but can occur when an individual wants something or someone else to be perceived in a certain way. For example, a person might tell his parents all of the good things about his significant other, while leaving out information that puts his significant other in a negative light.

Front stage vs. back stage self

Dramaturgy is a sociological perspective on social interactions first proposed by Erving Goffman. Dramaturgy uses theater as a metaphor for the presentation of oneself in social situations; thus, the way an individual presents himself is considered their "performance." This approach emphasizes the context in which social behavior occurs. According to Goffman, the way in which people act is most influenced by the people that are around them.

Erving Goffman, Canadian-American sociologist and writer

Goffman identified three stages in which people "perform." The first is the *front stage*. On the front stage, the individual knows that they are being observed and behaves according to audience expectations. *Back stage* refers to situations where performers are present, but their usual audience is not. Thus, performers are able to act "out of character," but are still acting in order to fit in with their fellow performers.

Off-stage is the place where individuals are not involved in any performance. A waiter, for example, can be thought of as being front stage when waiting tables and interacting with customers. They can be thought of as back stage when they are in the kitchen with their fellow waiters, and off-stage on their way to the car after work.

Verbal and nonverbal communication

Interpersonal communication involves both verbal and nonverbal communication. Verbal communication is explicit communication, whereas nonverbal communication is implicit communication. Nonverbal communication consists of body movements, posture, eye contact, and facial expressions. Verbal and nonverbal communication interact in order to form a complete idea. It is therefore not typically helpful to isolate nonverbal communication and analyze individual gestures.

Posture is typically divided into open posture and closed posture. *Open posture* refers to a body position that conveys openness, typically sitting or standing with arms and legs uncrossed. In *closed posture*, the individual conveys disinterest or discomfort and typically has his arms and legs crossed. Another important aspect of posture is *mirroring*. Individuals who mirror one another reflect each other's body movements and position. Mirroring indicates interest in the other person.

Researchers typically categorize nonverbal communication by the functions that they serve. *Emblems* are gestures that can be roughly translated into words. For example, a handshake can be roughly translated into a greeting. *Illustrators* serve to emphasize spoken language. For example, an individual might point somewhere while giving directions to someone. *Affect displays* are gestures that show the person we are interacting with how we feel. For example, someone who is feeling sad might frown in order to let the person they are talking to know how they feel. *Regulators* are social gestures that are used to give feedback to another person during a conversation. For example, someone might nod their head to indicate that they are listening and to encourage the speaker to continue talking. *Adaptors* are gestures that satisfy a physical need. Adjusting a leg after it falls asleep is an example of an adaptor.

Chapter 10

Testing and Individual Differences

Understanding intelligence and assessments of individual differences in intelligence or personality is a key competency of psychology. Test construction and fair use issues must be understood. How an assessment is constructed and thoroughly mastering the concepts of standardization, reliability, and validity are critically important. These particular concepts can be challenging to grasp. Doing so requires familiarity with historical roots of intelligence testing, as well as consideration regarding the associated ethical issues, in particular , the test result uses.

Notes

Intelligence

Generally, intelligence is conceptualized as the ability to think rationally, to use resources to solve problems and capacity to understand the world. There is much ongoing debate about what exactly comprises intelligence and the best way to measure it. The following describes generally accepted theories of intelligence, as well as difficulties in trying to measure the construct.

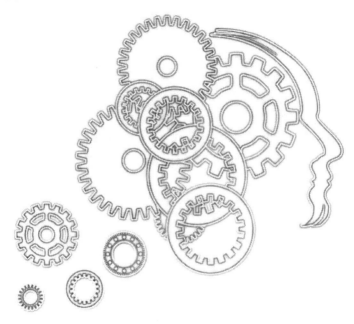

Historic and contemporary theories of intelligence

Sir Francis Galton is an important figure in modern intelligence testing. He hypothesized that intelligence is quantifiable and normally distributed. In other words, he proposed that a score could be assigned to intelligence, where the majority of people would fall in the average range, and the score of the individual would increase or decrease according to their variation from the average.

In the early 20th century, Charles Spearman developed a theory of general intelligence. Spearman was interested in examining correlations among the many measures of intelligence. He ultimately applied a statistical technique called factor analysis, which revealed that all of the different measures of intelligence were really measuring the same construct. Spearman hypothesized that the revealing of one construct was evidence for the existence of general intelligence.

Charles Spearman, English psychologist

General intelligence, or "g," is the basic, underlying trait responsible for all cognitive tasks including the ability to learn, reason and solve problems. Many studies have been conducted on "g" and it has been shown to correlate with income, success in long-term relationships and psychological well-being. However, other research has shown that people vary widely in their ability to socialize, to be artistic and to be physically active. These abilities are not well explained by "g."

In 1938, another researcher, L. L. Thurstone, utilized Spearman's techniques to examine general intelligence scores, finding seven different constructs that he named *Primary Mental Abilities*, which he believed more accurately described intelligence. Thurstone believed that these seven constructs (or factors) were independent, and individuals possessed them in varying degrees. Thurstone identified these seven factors as:

1) *Verbal comprehension* – the ability to define and understand words

2) *Verbal fluency* – the ability to produce words rapidly

3) *Number or arithmetic ability* – the ability to solve arithmetic problems

4) *Memory* – the ability to memorize and recall

5) *Perception* – the ability to see differences and similarities among objects

6) *Inductive reasoning* – the ability to find rules

7) *Spatial visualization* – the ability to visualize relationships.

After conducting subsequent research to test his theory, Thurstone found that his factors correlated with one another. This additional piece of information caused him to conclude that each factor is made up of a general factor that all factors share and an independent factor that makes each factor unique from the other factors.

Raymond Cattell and John Horn developed their own theory of intelligence in 1966. Cattell and Horn proposed that there were actually two types of intelligence: fluid intelligence and crystallized intelligence.

Fluid intelligence, which allows abstract reasoning, helps in adapting to new situations and solving problems without the need for previous knowledge. Cattell and Horn postulated that fluid intelligence is the biological aspect of intelligence.

Crystalized intelligence, on the contrary, is said to consist of knowledge (i.e., information, skills, and strategies) acquired through experience; essentially, it is skill expansion throughout life. This type of intelligence is thought to be the most stable because it relies on experience and knowledge, not on innate ability.

Raymond Cattell, psychologist

However, both types of intelligence are conceptualized to be important for everyday life. For example, when trying to stay within one's budget at the grocery store, one may use fluid intelligence to devise a strategy for prioritizing what needs to be purchased and crystallized intelligence to add the cost of groceries as they are being placed into the cart. Both fluid and crystallized intelligence increase through mid-adulthood. However, around the age of 30 or 40, fluid intelligence begins to decline, while crystallized intelligence continues to expand.

As medicine becomes more modern and research-focused, it has been documented that individuals can lose some abilities but not others from head injury, stroke or other brain damage. For example, an individual who has suffered a stroke may lose the ability to produce speech but not lose any other aspect of intelligence (e.g., ability to comprehend speech and understand what is being said), depending on where the damage is in the brain. Because of cases like this, more modern theories of intelligence continue to emphasize the belief that multiple abilities comprise the construct of intelligence. One of these theories is the triarchic theory of intelligence.

The triarchic theory of intelligence, created by Robert Sternberg, postulates that intelligence consists of three domains: creative intelligence, analytical intelligence, and practical intelligence. According to Sternberg, *creative intelligence* is the ability to solve problems in a new way; *analytical intelligence* is the problem-solving, mathematical and verbal types of intelligence (and most closely resembles "g"); *practical intelligence* is the ability to solve or address real-world problems (e.g., those that arise in work and family situations). While Sternberg hypothesized that these three domains are separate constructs, he acknowledged that they overlap and work together in day-to-day functioning.

Similar to Sternberg, Howard Gardner created a theory of intelligence that encompassed several different domains. However, Gardner's theory outlines nine domains (or spheres) of intelligence.

Gardner's *Multiple Intelligences Theory* identifies the following spheres of intelligence:

1) *Musical* – the ability to sense rhythm, tones, and sound

2) *Bodily kinesthetic* – the ability to use the body effectively

3) *Logical/mathematical* – the ability to reason and calculate

4) *Linguistic* – the ability to use words effectively

5) *Spatial* – the ability to think in terms of spatial judgment and visualize in the mind

6) *Interpersonal* – the ability to understand and interact with others

7) *Intrapersonal* – the ability to understand one's self

8) *Naturalist* – the ability to nurture and relate information to one's surroundings

9) *Existential* – the capacity for conceptualizing the larger questions about human existence.

Howard Gardner, American developmental psychologist

The latter two, naturalist and existential, were not part of Gardner's original theory; rather, he added them over 10 years later. Gardner also acknowledges that there may be many more spheres of intelligence that have yet to be identified. One key feature of this theory is that Gardner, unlike Sternberg, stated that these domains are independent of one another (rather than overlapping and working together). Thus, Gardner's theory accounts for the ability to lose some types of intelligence (e.g., due to a brain injury), but retain others. Gardner created his theory in the absence of any research. Subsequent research done to test the theory found that the nine intelligences correlate with "g." In other words, rather than supporting many separate spheres of intelligence, research now supports the idea of a single, underlying intelligence, as Spearman had theorized.

Abstract vs. verbal measures

Discussing theories of intelligence, the next question logically follows: How is intelligence measured? Similar to the debate over what intelligence encompasses, how to measure intelligence has also been debated. In 1904, Alfred Binet and Theodore Simon were commissioned by the French government to create a method to identify students who might need alternative education. Binet and Simon reasoned that because performance on certain tasks is expected to improve with chronological (or physical) age, performance on these tasks could be used to distinguish more intelligent people from less intelligent ones (those needing alternative education) within an age group. Binet and Simon created a series of tasks thought to represent children's abilities at given ages and coined the term "mental age," which was the child's score on the tasks children were tested on. It was thought that a marked gap between the chronological age of the child and the tested mental age of the child indicated a need for alternative education. These children could then receive additional assistance with the goal of bolstering their mental age to where it matched their chronological age.

Sample of the Binet-Simon Intelligence Scale from 1908. Children were asked to identify which faces were prettier.

In 1908, H.H. Goddard brought the Binet-Simon test to the United States after it was translated into English. In 1913, the United States Public Health Service began to administer the Binet-Simon test to immigrants. Several groups did not do well, but instead of examining the test and trying to identify why these groups might not do well, these immigrants were labeled "feebleminded." Lewis Terman at Stanford University modified the Binet-Simon test in order to identify high-achieving adults. Terman's test was published in 1916 and was called the Stanford-Binet Intelligence Scale. The scale, as used by the Public Health Service and Termon, was criticized for focusing too much on verbal abilities. It is now believed that many immigrants did not do well on the Binet-Simon test because it was administered in English, and many immigrants did not speak fluent English. Thus, their scores were more indicative of their ability to understand English than of their intelligence.

The Stanford-Binet Intelligence Scale in its present form tries to strike a balance between measuring verbal abilities and other abilities. It consists of a number of tasks that vary according to the age of the individual being tested and is thought to measure overall innate (general) intelligence. For example, a 4-year-old child should be able to define simple words (e.g., "ball") and discriminate between different shapes. A 12-year-old child should be able to do everything younger children are able to do and also define more difficult words (e.g., "muzzle") and repeat 5 digits in reverse order.

According to the Stanford-Binet Intelligence Scale, a 4-year-old child should be able to define simple words (e.g., ball) and discriminate between different shapes.

The Stanford-Binet Intelligence Scale also measures several sub-domains of intelligence, including fluid reasoning (i.e., ability to problem-solve), basic knowledge (i.e., knowledge acquired through education), quantitative reasoning (i.e., ability to think mathematically), visual-spatial processing (i.e., ability to see patterns and relationships in visual stimuli) and working memory (i.e., ability to temporarily store and process information in memory). Even so, the Stanford-Binet Intelligence Scale continues to be criticized for relying too much on verbal measures. Thus, the argument against this test is that it measures only verbal abilities, not intelligence itself (assuming that intelligence is more than just verbal abilities).

David Wechsler, who was labeled "feebleminded" at 9 years of age when his family immigrated to the United States from Romania, developed the major competitor to the Stanford-Binet Intelligence Scale. Wechsler developed this new intelligence scale because of his belief that the Stanford-Binet Intelligence Scale focused too much on verbal abilities. Wechsler sought to find a way to measure both verbal and nonverbal abilities.

The Wechsler Intelligence Scales consists of the Wechsler Preschool and Primary Scale of Intelligence (WPPSI; for children aged 2 years, 6 months to 7 years, 7 months); the Wechsler Intelligence Scale for Children (WISC; for children aged 6 years to 16 years, 11 months); and the Wechsler Adult Intelligence Scale (WAIS; for individuals aged 16 years to 90 years, 11 months). These scales seek to measure intelligence in terms of verbal abilities (known as the General Ability Index) and nonverbal abilities (known as the Cognitive Proficiency Index). Some of the verbal abilities include the ability to state similarities between two objects, define words and demonstrate general knowledge; the nonverbal abilities include spatial perception, abstract problem solving and spatial reasoning. For example, a test subject may be asked to examine a pattern of shapes and then predict the next shape in the sequence. This ability does not require any verbal abilities, only nonverbal reasoning abilities. Thus, it is possible for an individual to demonstrate intelligence even if their verbal ability is poor.

Speed of processing

While most people think of intelligence as the ability to problem-solve and demonstrate knowledge, other theories of intelligence emphasize the speed at which the problem is solved. It was hypothesized by Francis Galton that synaptic efficiency, or how quickly one can process information, accounted for why one individual is more intelligent than another. There are correlations between intelligence and inspection time (the amount of time it takes to perceive a stimulus), reaction time and evoked potentials (i.e., the brain wave response registered upon perceiving a stimulus).

Related to this is the Information-Processing Approach to intelligence. This approach emphasizes the way material is stored in memory and then used to solve problems. The processes used to solve a problem are examined in lieu of the structure or content of intelligence. It emphasizes the belief that the time it takes an individual to solve a problem (i.e., the speed at which it is processed) is a more accurate reflection of his or her overall intelligence. This approach draws a parallel between the human mind and a computer; both are information processors, and the important things to study are the processes that take place between the stimuli (in the environment) and the response made to it.

The Information-Processing Approach to intelligence focuses on the way material is stored in memory and then used to solve problems. It believes that the time it takes one to solve a problem is a more accurate reflection of overall intelligence, drawing a parallel between the human mind and a computer: both are information processors.

Influence of culture on the definition of intelligence

In the 1930's, John Raven recognized that existing intelligence tests may be biased against certain groups. He argued that intelligence tests should not be bound to a particular language or culture and sought to develop a culture-free test. Raven developed the Raven's Progressive Matrices, where individuals were asked to examine a pattern in shapes and colors and then determine which shape or color would complete the pattern. Raven argued that because the individual was looking at shapes and colors, no verbal abilities were needed, and therefore the test was a more culturally fair IQ test.

Raven was not the last person to talk about intelligence and the influences of culture. It has been frequently cited that some IQ tests consist of items that discriminate against minority groups. It is believed that because these groups have different experiences than the white majority, they cannot possibly do as well on these IQ tests.

There have been many attempts since Raven to create IQ test items that examine experiences common to all cultures and those that do not require language. However, because an individual's unique experiences, attitudes, and values nearly always have an impact on his or her answers, this is difficult to do. Many studies continue to detect differences in intelligence between members of different racial and ethnic groups. The debate remains: are the observed differences in intelligence among different ethnic and racial groups due to intelligence tests that are culturally unfair (or culture-free), due to differences in their environment or due to differences in innate ability?

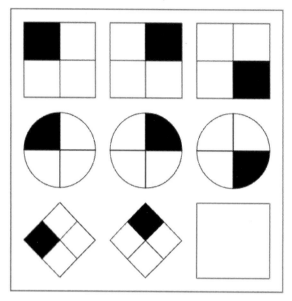

Example from Raven's Progressive Matrices

Research over the past several years has focused on intelligence in Africa, Asia, and other non-Western cultures. It has been found that ideas about intelligence (e.g., what intelligence is comprised of, how to measure intelligence) are conceptualized differently in non-Western cultures. For example, in Western cultures, people tend to see intelligence as a way to engage in debate and put people in categories. However, people in non-Western cultures see intelligence as a way to recognize complexity among individuals and to successfully play their social roles. Researchers believe that the differences in views of intelligence between Western and non-Western cultures are related to differences in the basic cognitive processes of the different cultures.

Some researchers say the focus of research should be on developing new intelligence tests that are sensitive to the unique aspects of intelligence and values of other cultures. It is argued that in this way intelligence can be accurately assessed based on cultural values and differences in viewpoints on what intelligence is. As described above, the Raven Progressive Matrices was designed to be a culture-free test. However, subsequent research has shown that even this test is culturally loaded. It is argued that even if a test is not a verbal test, nonverbal intelligence is still based on cultural constructs.

In Western societies, where formalized education and media technologies (e.g., television, video games) are common, individuals have an advantage in visual tests. Simply translating a Western intelligence test into a different language is not going to remedy this problem. Intelligence tests need to be created specifically for a culture.

Influence of heredity and environment on intelligence

The speed of mental processing is dependent on neurological efficiency and maturation, which are both controlled by genetic factors. Children who possess genetic defects, such as Down Syndrome, tend to have lower IQs than non-affected children.

However, the most convincing evidence comes from twin and adoption studies. Many research studies have utilized monozygotic (identical) twins and dizygotic (fraternal) twins to investigate the impact of heredity on IQ. Monozygotic twins are initially one fertilized egg that separates, so they are genetically identical. Dizygotic twins come from two separate fertilized eggs and share about 50% of their genetic makeup (like siblings). If identical twins have relatively the same genetic makeup, it is safe to conclude that heredity has a significant impact on intelligence and cognitive development.

Most twins tend to be raised by the same parent in the same home, sharing similar environments, and have a similar genetic makeup. However, sometimes twins are raised separately but still have the same IQ. Interestingly, these twins are more similar to each other than the fraternal twins who are raised in the same home.

Many research studies utilize identical and fraternal twins to investigate the impact of heredity on IQ.

Another way to portray this finding is through adoption studies. Researchers have found that while children's IQ scores are more highly related to the scores of their biological parents, their environment tends to be more closely aligned to that of their adopted parents.

In a group of people who placed their newborns up for adoption, the parents with the highest IQ had children who also had the highest IQ despite their being raised by other people. The IQ correlations between adopted children and their biological parents become stronger, and the correlations between the children and their adoptive parents become weaker as the child ages, especially during adolescence.

However, these studies are not able to completely distinguish the impact of heredity and the environment. The environment also makes an appreciable difference, which will be further discussed in the next section.

There is a great deal of research that has revealed that the environment has a significant impact on cognitive development. We find some of this evidence in twin studies and adoption studies. Studies of the effects of nutrition, toxic substances, home environment, early intervention, and formal schooling provide additional support for the influence of environment. Also, a steady increase in performance on intelligence tests over the past several decades (known as the *Flynn Effect*) is almost certainly attributable to environmental factors.

Serious malnutrition during the early years of life can cause a deterioration of neurological development and eventually have a lasting impact on intelligence and cognitive development. Attention, memory, abstract reasoning, and general school achievement are negatively affected due to improper levels of nutrition.

Toxic substances or teratogens in a child's prenatal or postnatal environments also affect neurological development. These toxic substances include alcohol, drugs, radiation, or lead-based paint. Fetal Alcohol Syndrome affects children who have a mother who consumed alcohol during her pregnancy resulting in poor motor coordination, delayed language, and overall cognitive delays in the child.

One of the benefits of adoption is that usually adoptive parents tend to be financially stable, educated, and provide a more stimulating home environment when compared to the environment their biological parents may have been able to offer. In a stimulating household, parents interact with their children frequently, have learning and reading materials readily available, encourage the development of new skills, and use complex language while communicating. All these factors are attributed to higher cognitive development and in turn higher IQ.

Also, when two biologically different children who are about the same age are raised by the same parents, their IQs are usually more similar than would be expected by chance alone. This suggests this similarity results from inhabiting the same environment.

The effect of going to school initiates small increases in IQ. Children who attend school at an early age regularly have higher IQ scores than children who do not attend school. If children start school later than normal, their IQs are usually five points lower for every year of delay. School has a great benefit for intellectual growth. The famous psychologist Vygotsky made a note that school provides a systemic means through which children can obtain many concepts and perspectives that previous generations have developed, which the child can then use to achieve day-to-day activities and solve problems.

In the last couple of years, there has been a slow but steady increase in individual performances on IQ tests. This increase has been identified as the *Flynn Effect.* This trend has also been observed in children's performance on traditional Piagetian tasks. These improvements cannot be caused by heredity because the same gene pool is passed along from one generation to the next, suggesting that the cause must be environmental. Better nutrition, smaller family size, higher quality home environments, better schooling, and more enriching and informative stimulation are all possibilities.

Variations in intellectual ability

Many argue that quantifying intelligence correctly is impossible, and that modern IQ tests can only test our knowledge and abilities. While it is true that a person can learn to improve his or her IQ score, this can only occur if correct responses are taught to the person, which is highly unethical. Research has also found that our individual IQ score remains consistent with age. Some argue, however, that modern IQ tests are prejudiced against certain ethnicities and cultures and tend to result in higher scores for other groups. Where this leaves us, however, is uncertain. As of today, IQ tests are the best available psychometric tool we have in our attempt to quantify the construct known as intelligence.

The Intelligence Quotient (IQ) score is calculated by considering the chronological age of the individual and the mental age (as measured by an intelligence test). The average IQ score is 100, with 95 percent of the population having an IQ score between 70 and 130. Those individuals with scores below 70 may be labeled as having an intellectual disability, and those with a score above 130 are labeled as intellectually gifted.

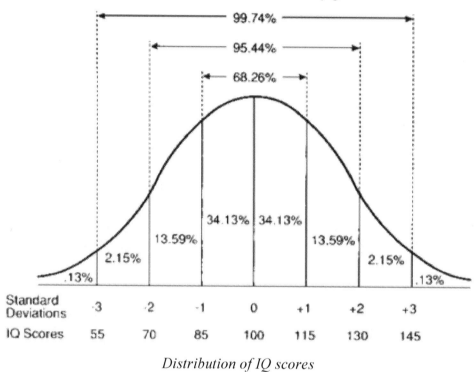

Distribution of IQ scores

Individuals with an IQ score below 70 are considered outside the norm with regard to intellectual ability. *Intellectual disability* refers to a person's level of cognitive ability or impairment presenting below the average level of intellectual functioning. People with intellectual disabilities are limited in two or more of the adaptive skill areas. When individuals score below 70 and also have difficulties with adaptive functioning, such as conceptual skills (e.g., ability to use money, ability to keep track of time), social skills (e.g., gullibility, naiveté) and/or practical skills (e.g., ability to engage in personal care, ability to provide own transportation), the individual may be diagnosed with intellectual developmental disorder. This disability affects approximately 3 to 5 percent of the United States population and has many different causes, including fetal alcohol syndrome, Trisomy 21 (i.e., Down syndrome), head injuries and meningitis.

This category is further divided into mild, moderate, severe and profound, depending on the IQ score of the individual. Mild intellectual disability is represented by an IQ score in the range of 50-70 and academic skills at the 3rd to 6th-grade levels. Moderate intellectual disability is represented by an IQ score in the range of 35-49, and academic skills at, or below the 2nd-grade level. Based on the severity of the disability, individuals may need additional help in one or more areas of life. In the United States, there are many programs in place to assist such individuals.

Severe intellectual disability is represented by an IQ score range of 20-34, with little ability to communicate, and requiring direct supervision. Profound intellectual disability is represented by an IQ score below 20, with little or no speech skills, and requiring constant supervision and care. A family history of intellectual disabilities is common in affected individuals. The integration of intellectually challenged individuals into a normal academic setting is one treatment option.

On the other end of the spectrum, intellectually gifted individuals have an IQ higher than 130 and represent 2-4% of the population. Many of the individuals in this category are very talented in one area but tend to be average in others. Also, frequently seen are large discrepancies between verbal and nonverbal abilities. Unlike Intellectual Developmental Disorder, programs for the gifted are rare. When they are in place, they are designed to provide a more enriching environment that allows the individual's talents to grow and flourish.

Notes

Test Design

Psychological testing is used in psychology for five basic purposes: classification (i.e., diagnosis), prediction (e.g., predicting behavior in a setting), description (e.g., to describe a person's strengths and weaknesses), choice of treatment, and to monitor a person over time (e.g., to determine if a treatment is effective). Psychometrics is the subfield of psychology that focuses on theory and technique as they relate to the measurement of psychological traits and abilities. This subfield attempts to create assessments that objectively measure personality, attitudes, intelligence, mood, and abilities for the purposes stated above. Items on tests designed to measure these constructs are carefully evaluated before the tests are administered to make sure they measure the trait they are intended to measure. Of importance when designing a test are standardization, norms, reliability, and validity.

Standardization and Norms

One important aspect of the test is standardization. Because so many variables can affect the way someone responds on psychological testing, it is important that the test is given exactly as it was intended to be given. Without this, it cannot be ensured that the construct that the test is intended to measure is actually what is being measured. For example, if a test of anger is given in a room that is incredibly hot, it is unclear if the responses actually measure the general level of anger in that individual or his irritation with the heat in the room.

Standardization in test administration helps to eliminate biases, whether conscious or unconscious. For example, without standardization in test administration, a researcher may give subtle hints about how he/she wants the test results to turn out. This may not be done intentionally but may still influence the test taker. By ensuring the test is administered in a standardized way, scores can be compared across different groups of people who may have been given the test at different times. In addition to ensuring the tests are administered uniformly, they must also be scored uniformly. If tests were scored haphazardly, the scores would not be able to be interpreted accurately and would not be able to be compared across individuals.

Norms are comparison scores that allow individuals to be compared or evaluated relative to a standard or typical score. Norms are created for a test by administering the test to hundreds of people and then calculating a mean and standard deviation for the test. The mean is the average of all scores, and the standard deviation is the variability around the mean. The standard deviation can be conceptualized as the average distance away from the mean. For example, most intelligence tests have an average score of 100 and a standard deviation of 15. (See *Meaning of scores and the normal curve* below for more details.) When the score an individual obtained is known, that score can be compared with the norms for the test and allow the researcher to make general statements about that individual. For example, if someone obtains a score of 102 on an intelligence test, this score is very close to average. Without norms, a test score only has meaning if it is put in rank with other test scores.

Reliability and Validity

Reliability and validity are necessary for the assessment of a construct. *Reliability* answers the question, "Does this test consistently measure what it says it measures?" There are several different types of reliability including test-retest and inter-observer. *Test-retest* reliability examines whether or not a test produces the same results consistently over time. For example, if an individual completes a test of intelligence in January and then again in June, the second score is expected to be about the same since intelligence is thought of as a construct that does not change over time. If both scores are about the same score, the test is considered to have good test-retest reliability. *Inter-observer* (or inter-rater) reliability is the degree to which two observers rate a behavior the same.

For example, if the test is a rating scale for aggressive behaviors in children, two individuals trained in administering the rating scale should score behaviors of the same child similarly if the scale has good inter-observer reliability.

Validity answers the question "Does this test measure what it says it measures?" For example, if a test says it measures depression, does it actually measure symptoms of depression, or is it measuring anxiety, psychosis or something else?

A researcher might purport that he or she is measuring intelligence by measuring the length of the ring finger on one's right hand. The length of this finger is not expected to change in an adult, so it could be measured over and over again with likely the same results. Thus, the measurement has reliability. However, is it valid? Does the length of the ring finger on the right hand have anything to do with intelligence? This question is getting at validity. Because the length of the ring finger on the right hand has nothing to do with intelligence, the measurement is not valid.

As described above, reliability may be present, but not the validity. In another example, a test may purport to measure anxiety. This test may be given over time and produce consistent results in individuals taking the test (i.e., it has reliability).

However, unless the measure correlates with other measures of anxiety, it cannot be said for certain that it is actually measuring anxiety. It may be consistently measuring another construct, such as depression. Reliability is necessary, but not sufficient for validity. Both reliability and validity are critical when constructing and evaluating tests.

Types of Tests

Historically, clinical psychology has been focused on testing, and even today, psychological testing is done primarily by a clinical psychologist. Tests provide one part of the picture of an individual; a clinical interview provides the other half. There are many different types of psychological tests to asses a variety of characteristics, depending on what type of information is sought.

Psychological tests can be categorized in several different ways. First, there are tests that are completed on an individual basis, and there are tests that can be completed in a group setting. It is essential to know how the test is administered before it is given. Recall that standardization is an important aspect of testing; giving a test in a group setting that was meant to be administered individually would be a violation of the standardization, and thus the results would be unreliable. Tests can also be performance-based (i.e., the person does something) or verbally based (i.e., the person uses language to convey something). Several tests looking for deficits after a brain injury are performance-based, while tests exploring different personality traits tend to be more verbal.

Psychological tests can also be categorized as structured (i.e., objective) or unstructured (i.e., projective). In structured tests, items tend to be clear and directed towards what is being measured. The individual has a limited number of responses to choose from and the scoring method tends to be simple. Unstructured tests, on the contrary, have test items that are ambiguous by design. These items are ambiguous because they measure how the individual interprets the questions and answers them. These types of tests tend to be more difficult to score because they have an infinite number of response options.

Finally, tests can be categorized based on the content area they attempt to measure. *Personality tests* attempt to measure traits that an individual possesses. Because it is generally believed that personality is stable over time, it is expected that measures of personality will remain stable over time and across tests, assuming the tests are measuring the same personality traits. *Neuropsychological tests* are tests used to examine functioning of the brain, such as speed of processing, language, memory, thinking patterns and executive functions. Finally, *psychology tests* can focus on effect and symptoms of disorders. These tests generally assess how a person is feeling and functioning based on their emotional well-being.

Meaning of scores and the normal curve

Test scores have no meaning without context. In other words, they have no meaning without something to compare them to. Recall that norms give a comparison group for test scores, so statements can be made about the score obtained.

If a test is given to a large group of individuals and the scores are plotted on a graph, the scores will form a normal curve (otherwise known as a *normal distribution*). The normal curve is a symmetrical, bell-shaped curve, where the right half mirrors the left half (see figure below). In the middle of the curve is the mean (or average) of all the scores. From this, the standard deviation (i.e., the average variability around the mean) can be calculated. Given a normal curve, 68% of individuals will have a score between one standard deviation below (34% of people) and one standard deviation above (34% of people) the mean.

For example, the mean of most intelligence tests is 100 and the standard deviation is 15. Based on these scores and the rules of a normal distribution, 68% of individuals who complete an intelligence test will obtain a score between 85 (i.e., 100 minus 15) and 115 (i.e., 100 plus 15). Likewise, scores between two standard deviations above and below the mean will capture 95% of the test-takers (i.e., 48% of the test-takers' scores will fall below the mean and 48% will fall above the mean). In the intelligence test example, that means that 95% of the people who take an intelligence test will obtain a score between 70 and 130.

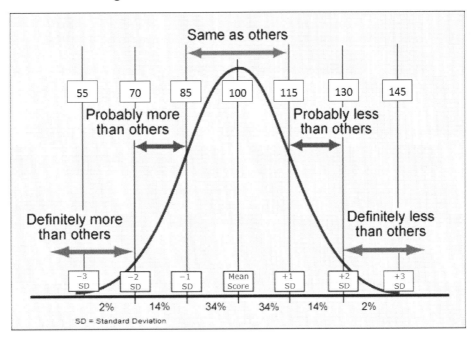

Normalized distribution of IQ with a mean of 100 and standard deviation of 15

With regards to interpretation, typically scores that are one standard deviation (or greater) above or below the mean are of interest because they indicate the individual's score is outside the expected norm for that group. What exactly this means depends on the test; however, for intelligence tests, someone with an IQ score of 70 or below (i.e., three standard deviations below the mean) may meet criteria for Intellectual Developmental Disability, whereas someone with an IQ score above 130 (i.e., three standard deviations above the mean), may be considered intellectually gifted.

Ethics and Standards in Testing

Outlined in the American Psychological Association (APA) Code of Ethics are general principles that govern the practice of psychology, including testing. First, psychologists must have competence in the area they intend to practice and know the limits of their expertise. In the realm of testing, this means a psychologist does not utilize a test that he/she is not trained in administering, scoring and interpreting. It is also important for psychologists to determine when psychological testing may and may not be useful. For example, when a psychologist can diagnose based on a clinical interview, testing may not be appropriate. Further, the psychologist must know if a test is appropriate for a particular individual (with regards to culture, language, etc.). Psychologists also have the responsibility to recognize when testing is being used inappropriately and make attempts to correct this.

In addition to the general principles from the APA Code of Ethics that can be applied to psychological testing, there are also specific standards governing psychological testing. First, a professional relationship should be established prior to conducting any psychological testing. For example, a psychologist would never score and interpret a psychological test without first meeting the individual. Psychologists must ensure that the tests are used appropriately and that the tests being used are developed with consideration for scientific procedures, including reliability and validity. Related to this, psychologists ensure that only the most up-to-date tests are used and when interpreting tests, the correct norms are utilized. Psychologists understand that tests have limitations and it is important to consider these limitations when scoring and interpreting tests. Finally, after scoring and interpreting tests, explanations of the results should be given to the tested individual in a way that he/she can understand.

Please, leave your Customer Review on Amazon

Chapter 11

Abnormal Behavior and Treatment

Psychological disorders can be brought on through a variety of causes and can be characterized by a wide range of symptoms. Psychologists utilize formal conventions to establish diagnosis and assess the severity. What hopefully results is the identification of the appropriate empirically-based treatment to pursue. Psychology professionals need to be competent in distinguishing between various approaches for differing mental illnesses; these can include behavioral, biological, cognitive, humanistic and psychodynamic approaches. Towards these ends, a foundational definition of abnormal behavior is important, and stereotypes can complicate diagnosis. In an environment of inadequate societal understanding of psychological disorders, controversy surrounding labeling has emerged.

Notes

Understanding Psychological Disorders

Psychological disorders can be a challenging subject to understand given the complexity of determining what separates a "healthy" mind from an "unhealthy" one. The word "abnormality" is used frequently in this topic of research, which generally gives the impression of something being *wrong* with an individual. However, abnormality can also be viewed in the opposite way. For example, a gifted genius like Albert Einstein is considered "abnormal," as opposed to "normal," because his intelligence far surpassed that of most of the people.

Abnormality is generally treated as a behavior that goes against what the general population considers "healthy" or "appropriate" from a social standpoint. It would be difficult to classify Einstein as "disordered" due to his intelligence. Researchers in the field have determined several definitions of abnormality in order to help elucidate the differences between normal and abnormal behavior.

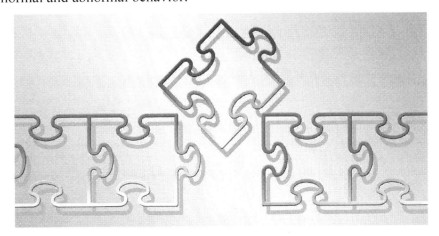

Definitions of Abnormality

Abnormal behavior can be defined in several ways, which include statistical infrequency, norm violation, and personal suffering. Before clinicians determine a diagnosis, they often consider whether a person's behavior, cognition or emotions deviate from the norm in any of the aforementioned ways. It is imperative to consider these different spectrums, as each definition of abnormality has merits and flaws.

Statistical infrequency suggests that any behavior that deviates from what is normal (or what the majority of people do, think or feel) is abnormal. While this provides some insight into the behavior of someone who is anxious (i.e., constantly seeking reassurance), it fails to account for the fact that some highly desirable traits are outside the spectrum of normal behavior. For example, Olympic athletes have abnormal athletic ability. Someone with a genius level IQ might also be considered abnormal according to this definition. This also implies that groups who hold minority opinions fall outside of the normal spectrum.

The problem with using statistics alone to classify "outliers" as *abnormal* neglects the fact that the traits the individual has could very well be positive. Researchers tend to avoid this way of defining abnormality. Instead, psychologists and other experts in the field say that abnormality MUST involve a behavior that negatively or pervasively impacts one's life – whether it is socially, at work, at home or in a relationship.

Personal suffering/distress is a required criterion for most psychiatric disorders. This means that there must be some impairment in one or more aspects of an individual's functioning (i.e., not attending school, failure to complete assignments at work, inability to get along with peers or family members, confusion with managing personal finances or medications, etc.). In addition, many individuals use personal suffering as a way to determine whether they should seek treatment for the symptoms that they are experiencing.

However, this definition of abnormal also has flaws. First, most people are likely to experience distress in some common life events, such as the loss of a close family member or being diagnosed with a new disability. This does not mean they are abnormal, rather that they are experiencing an acute stressor. In addition, some other individuals who exhibit abnormal behavior may not experience distress. This could be the case for someone who is experiencing mania and/or someone with antisocial personality disorder.

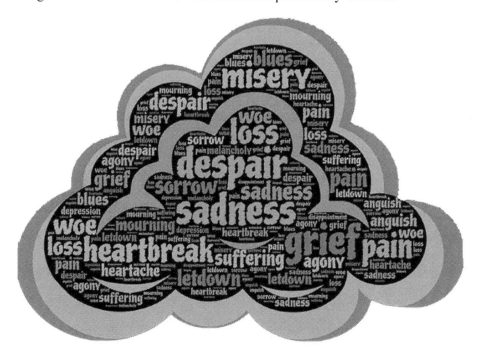

Norm violation can be used as another way to measure whether a behavior, thought or cognition is abnormal. It suggests that since cultural rules and norms dictate appropriate behaviors, if someone violates social norms, then their behavior is abnormal. Thus, if a behavior is bizarre or unusual enough, it would be considered abnormal. For example, someone who constantly fails to maintain eye contact or respond in social situations likely violates the norm for social behavior. However, one major flaw with this definition is that social norms vary by culture. Thus, what is acceptable in one culture may be unacceptable in another culture.

The 4 D's is a more recent model of abnormal behavior, which suggests that abnormal behavior can be conceptualized in the context of whether the behavior is *deviant*, *dysfunctional*, *distressing* or *dangerous*. The discussion above already touched upon deviance, distress, and dysfunction, but it is also important to consider whether a behavior is dangerous. Some abnormal behavior is illegal. Laws have been put into place to both protect and punish those who have psychological disorders.

As an example of protection, mentally ill patients are protected by law from having their information revealed to *anybody* other than their therapist, as this could affect their ability to gain employment or otherwise expose very personal subjects. This is known as "doctor-patient confidentiality," and it applies to the psychiatric field just as much as any other medical discipline.

On the other end, an example of punishment would be how the judicial system does not simply write off mentally ill people from the consequences of their actions if they understood right from wrong. "Pleading insanity" is often heard of but not well understood – if a serial killer "gets away" with an "insanity plea," they can be held for an *indefinite* amount of time at a psychiatric institution and may never be granted access back into society.

Biomedical vs. biopsychosocial approaches

Professionals in the field of psychology have divided themselves into two critical categories of treatment and conceptualizing mental illness. Here is a brief explanation of each.

Biomedical Therapy: The cause of the disorder is believed to be some sort of chemical imbalance in the brain, which must be neutralized in some way. Psychiatry is directly involved in this form of treatment. Certain drugs are prescribed to alter the brain's abnormal functioning (antidepressants, benzodiazepines, etc.) thereby allowing the individual the chance to function in society. This alone is a strictly short-term form of treatment. To stop taking the drug means returning to the abnormal behavior.

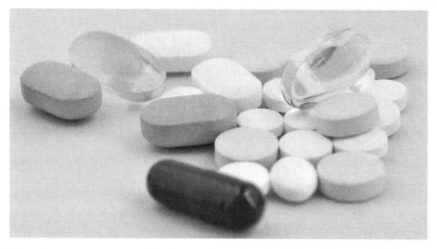

Certain drugs are prescribed to alter the brain's abnormal functioning (antidepressants, benzodiazepines, etc.) thereby allowing the individual the chance to function in society.

Biopsychosocial Therapy: To understand this form of treating mental disorders, it helps to break down the word "biopsychosocial" into its three parts:

Bio(logical) – the health professional may first look at one's physical state – are they maintaining a healthy lifestyle? Do their genetics play a role in the abnormality?

Psycho(logical) – to obtain insight into what is going on in the mind. How emotional are they on a regular basis? Do they have underlying beliefs about themselves or others that are causing them to behave abnormally?

Social – finally, the professional assesses the people in the individual's life. Did they grow up in an abusive environment? Were they the popular kid in elementary school, or were they unfortunately isolated from making real connections with others? This treatment may be considered more effective due to the increased focus on getting to the "root" of issues, but can often fail precisely because of the amount of effort and time required to "cure" the issue.

Classifying psychological disorders

The *Diagnostic and Statistical Manual of Mental Disorders, Fifth Edition (DSM-5)* was created to be used with a wide variety of populations, including inpatient, outpatient, and community mental health settings. The DSM-5 has three main parts: diagnostic classification, diagnostic criteria sets, and descriptive text. The diagnostic classification portion lists all official mental disorders. This allows clinicians to review the symptoms and signs that their patient is exhibiting and compare them with all existing disorders. Next to each psychological disorder, there is a diagnostic code, which serves to aid researchers and insurance companies.

The diagnostic criteria set for a disorder indicates how many symptoms must be present, which symptoms may not be present, the length of time that the symptoms must be present and what conditions may exclude the patient from receiving a certain diagnosis.

The descriptive text informs clinicians and researchers as to subtypes or specifiers that can be used with each disorder. It also provides additional information regarding how to make a differential diagnosis, such as what other disorders should be considered and/or excluded.

There has been controversy in the field of psychology regarding the usefulness of providing diagnostic labels. In many cases, applying these labels can lead to clients developing self-fulfilling prophecies and/or discrimination. However, the labels are often needed in order for insurance companies to bill for services and for researchers to understand how treatment works, how to improve treatment outcomes and what the prevalence rate of different disorders is.

One study, called the Rosenhan experiment, looked at the validity of psychiatric diagnoses. In this study, a total of eight healthy subjects feigned hallucinations in order to be admitted to psychiatric hospitals in different states. After admission, the patients acted normally and informed health care providers that they no longer were experiencing hallucinations. Despite being healthy and no longer "having hallucinations," all participants were diagnosed with a mental illness and were given antipsychotics as a condition of their release. This experiment highlights the challenges that psychiatric facilities face in distinguishing the sane from the insane.

Rates of psychological disorders

The exact rate of psychological disorders varies by country and by disorder. In the United States, about one in every five people suffers from a mental health condition at some point in their life. Some disorders, such as anxiety and depression, are more common than other disorders. Some disorders that are considered rare include: dissociative identity disorder, selective mutism, and factitious disorders. Recent prevalence rates for varying psychological disorders can be found in the DSM-5.

In the United States, about one in every five people suffers from a mental health condition at some point in their life.

Types of Psychological Disorders

The DSM-5 categorizes disorders into groupings based on shared symptoms or shared presentations. These groupings include: neurodevelopmental disorders, schizophrenia spectrum and other psychotic disorders, bipolar and related disorders, depressive disorders, anxiety disorders, obsessive-compulsive and related disorders, trauma and stressor-related disorders, dissociative disorders, somatic symptom and related disorders, feeding and eating disorders, elimination disorders, sleep-wake disorders, sexual dysfunctions, gender dysphoria, disruptive, impulse-control and conduct disorders, substance-related and addictive disorders, neurocognitive disorders, personality disorders, paraphilic disorders, other mental disorders, medication-induced movement disorders and other adverse effects of medication and other conditions that may be the focus of clinical attention. Some of these broad categories, such as depressive and anxiety disorders, occur more commonly in the population. The most common psychological disorders are discussed below in further detail.

Anxiety disorders

The DSM-5 includes twelve unique disorders as *anxiety disorders*. These twelve disorders include: separation anxiety disorder, selective mutism, specific phobia, social anxiety disorder (social phobia), panic disorder, panic attack specifier, agoraphobia, generalized anxiety disorder, substance/medication-induced anxiety disorder, anxiety disorder due to another medical condition, other specified anxiety disorder, and unspecified anxiety disorder.

The hallmark of all these anxiety disorders is excessive fear and/or anxiety to aversive stimuli. The fight-or-flight response is often seen across each of the aforementioned anxiety disorders. This means that when faced with a feared stimulus, a person's automatic response is either to fight or flee. For example, if someone is walking through the woods and encounters a lion, they will likely experience elevated levels of anxiety. In this situation, most people would either choose to run away from the lion or to fight the lion.

While all the anxiety disorders have common elements, they can be differentiated from each other by examining the circumstances (i.e., settings, situations, etc.) that produce the fear or avoidant response. Below, each disorder is described in more detail to better understand the differences among the anxiety disorders.

Research has indicated that there is high symptom overlap among the anxiety disorders, and most individuals diagnosed with an anxiety disorder will have at least one other comorbid anxiety disorder. Before a diagnosis can be made for each of the disorders below, it is imperative to verify that the symptoms cause significant distress in one or more areas of functioning (i.e., school, work, home, etc.) and that the symptoms are not better explained by another mental health or physical disorder.

Separation anxiety disorder is most common in children but can also occur in adults. It is characterized by excessive fear upon actual or anticipated separation from a parent or other caregiver. The fear must be inappropriate for the person's age. Children and adults with separation concerns may worry that something bad will happen to their caregiver when they are separated or that something bad may happen to them during the separation. This may include being in an accident, getting kidnapped or becoming sick. As a result, there is often a behavioral pattern in which the individual constantly refuses to leave home due to their worries about being separated from the caregiver. There is also a reluctance to go places alone unless accompanied by a caregiver.

Separation anxiety disorder in children is characterized by excessive fear of actual or anticipated separation from a parent or other caregiver.

For example, children may refuse to go to school or to a friend's house unless a parent goes with them. They may also need a caregiver in order to fall asleep at night or may experience frequent nightmares about being separated from their caregiver. These individuals may complain of various physical symptoms when separation occurs (e.g., upset stomach, headache, etc.). Only three of the aforementioned symptoms need to exist in order for an individual to qualify for a diagnosis of separation anxiety disorder. In addition, the excessive fear must have been persistent for a while (at least four weeks for children and six months for adults).

Selective mutism is a pattern of refraining from speech in one or more settings despite the ability to speak in other settings. This behavior of not speaking in some situations (e.g., school) negatively impacts achievement and/or social development. A child who is shy or who does not talk sometimes is not the same as a child who has selective mutism. The DSM-5 indicates that the pattern of not speaking in one or more settings must have been going on for at least one month (excluding the first month of school). Furthermore, if a child is not familiar with the language being spoken, then he or she cannot be diagnosed with selective mutism. Selective mutism can sometimes be confused with other childhood communication disorders, such as autism.

Selective mutism is a pattern of refraining from speech in one or more settings despite the ability to speak in other settings. This behavior of not speaking in some situations (e.g., school) negatively impacts achievement and/or social development.

Typically, children with selective mutism refuse to speak in school or social situations despite being overly talkative at home. They may refuse to answer questions in class, as well as initiate conversations or respond to peers. Some children may not speak in front of extended family members as well. These children may be more comfortable pointing, writing or using alternative methods of communication. This disorder is considered rare and can impede academic and social skill development in children. For example, it is difficult for teachers to evaluate whether the child meets reading milestones if the child refuses to speak.

Specific phobia is the most common psychological disorder. Often, individuals with specific phobia meet the criteria for more than one specific phobia. Phobias may include a variety of fears, such as a specific animal (e.g., dog) or a specific situation, such as flying or seeing blood. Children commonly express their excessive fear of an object or situation by crying, freezing, or having a temper tantrum. Adults can also meet the criteria for a specific phobia if they display excessive fear of a particular object or situation.

However, excessive fear is not the only criteria for a specific phobia. In addition, the feared stimuli must often produce immediate fear or anxiety (not just once in a while), the person tries to avoid the stimuli or experiences it only with extreme distress and the experienced fear/anxiety is unrealistic when compared to the actual danger that is posed by the situation. For example, an adult may refuse to drive over a bridge due to an excessive fear of the bridge collapsing. They may require that someone else first drive over the bridge or refuse to go over the bridge at all. Most people are able to drive over bridges every day without it collapsing, so this would be an unrealistic fear compared to the actual danger in driving over a bridge.

Furthermore, in specific phobias, the core fear is a persistent concern (lasting for at least six months or more), not a temporary fear of something. Many phobias develop in childhood, and other common phobias include animals (i.e., snakes, spiders), costumed characters, having an injection, clowns, heights, bodies of water, etc.

Social anxiety disorder refers to the excessive and unreasonable fearsome individuals experience in social situations where they may be judged or scrutinized by other people. There are numerous types of feared social situations. Some common examples include: eating in front of others in a restaurant or cafeteria, giving a presentation in front of an audience, meeting new people or sometimes simply having a conversation with a boss or coworker. This disorder can occur in both children and adults. However, for children, the anxiety must be present with peer interactions, not only when interacting with adults.

Regardless of age, there is a fear that other people will negatively judge or evaluate the individual. For example, an individual may worry that they will trip and embarrass themselves, or that they will say something that might offend other people. The social situations must often produce anxiety (not just once in a while), and the individuals must be actively avoiding the social situations or experiencing them with great distress. The excessive fear must be disproportional to the actual danger of the situation, must last for six months or more and the fear must be unrelated to other medical or mental health conditions. One type of social anxiety disorder is performance anxiety. This can only be diagnosed if the individual worries about performing in public.

Panic disorder occurs when there are repeated, intense surges of fear of discomfort that subside within minutes. During the intense fear, at least four of the following physical symptoms must occur: pounding heart, sweating, shaking, feeling short of breath, experiencing feelings of choking, having discomfort or pain in the chest, abdominal discomfort, feeling dizzy or faint, feeling very cold or hot, feeling numbness or tingling in parts of the body, feeling like things are not real, feeling out of control and/or fearing that one is dying. Furthermore, the first attack must be followed by at least one month of continual worry about having another panic attack and/or behavior changes, such as avoidance of the place of previous attack or of new places in an effort to prevent more attacks. The symptoms of panic disorder can mimic physical disorders, such as hyperthyroidism, so it is important to have a physical examination to rule out other causes for the symptoms endorsed prior to giving a diagnosis of panic disorder.

Panic disorder specifier allows for the diagnosis of panic attacks without a diagnosis of panic disorder. This means that panic attacks may occur within any of the other anxiety disorders as well as non-anxiety disorders, such as depression and post-traumatic stress disorder. Basically, it occurs when there are repeated, intense surges of fear of discomfort that subside within minutes. During the intense fear, at least four of the following physical symptoms must occur: pounding heart, sweating, shaking, feeling short of breath, experiencing feelings of choking, having discomfort or pain in the chest, abdominal discomfort, feeling dizzy or faint, feeling very cold or hot, feeling numbness or tingling in parts of the body, feeling like things are not real, feeling out of control and/or fearing that one is dying. Unlike panic disorder, there does not have to be a month where there are behavioral or cognitive changes due to the first attack.

Agoraphobia can be diagnosed when an individual demonstrates an extreme fear or anxiety in at least two of these situations: the utilization of public transportation like buses or trains, going to open spaces like a shopping mall or parking lot, fear of being in enclosed places such as a store or movie theater, waiting in line or standing in a large group of people, and/or being alone outside of the individual's home. Furthermore, the reason for the fear or avoidance of these situations must be due to concerns about not being able to get away or get help if panic symptoms occur. These situations must produce anxiety most of the time and must be actively avoided or experienced only with great distress. The fear must be unrealistic compared to the actual danger and must have lasted for at least six months.

Generalized anxiety disorder can be particularly difficult to diagnose because it basically occurs when an individual worries about several areas, which may overlap with other anxiety disorders (i.e., social anxiety disorder). The areas of worry may include school or work performance, finances, peer or family relationships, the health of the individual or their family members, current events or other domains. The worry must be excessive and occur on most days for at least six months. Furthermore, some of the following symptoms must be present (one symptom for children and at least three for adults): feeling restless or on edge, getting tired easily, having trouble focusing on things, feeling irritable, having tension in the muscles and/or having difficulties sleeping. Most importantly, the individual must find it very hard to be able to control the worries. As with the other anxiety disorders, it is important to rule out other mental and physical disorders before making this diagnosis.

Substance/medication-induced anxiety disorder occurs when the anxiety can be attributed to intoxication or withdrawal from some substance or to the use of a medication.

Anxiety disorder due to another medical condition is anxiety caused by another medical condition, as determined by a physical exam or laboratory findings.

Other specified anxiety disorder can be used when there is evidence of anxiety symptoms that do not meet the full diagnostic criteria of another anxiety disorder. For example, a person may have a lot of anxiety but not endorse enough of the required symptoms to be diagnosed with a disorder such as panic attacks. Alternatively, instead of not endorsing enough symptoms, a person may not endorse one of the required criteria of a disorder.

For example, they may endorse every other symptom of generalized anxiety disorder except that they do not worry more days than not, thereby ruling out the generalized anxiety disorder diagnosis. Several disorders that exist in other cultures (such as wind attacks and attack of nerves) may mimic anxiety symptoms but not meet the full criteria of other anxiety disorders. In those instances, clinicians may diagnose the other specified anxiety disorder.

Unspecified anxiety disorder is most often used by clinicians when there is not enough information to determine the exact anxiety disorder, for example in emergency situations or before completing an intake assessment. However, clinicians may use this diagnosis when there are symptoms that mimic an anxiety disorder but do not meet the full criteria for any specific anxiety disorder.

Obsessive-compulsive disorder

Obsessive–compulsive disorder (OCD) occurs when an individual experiences either obsessions or compulsions. Frequently, people experience both obsessions and compulsions. An obsession is a recurring thought, urge or mental picture that is unwanted and causes great distress. For example, a person with a contamination fear might have the recurring thought that their hands have a lot of germs on them. The person will likely try to alleviate this by frequent hand washing, which would be considered a compulsion if the individual felt compelled to wash his hands to counter the obsession.

A person with an OCD manifested in a contamination fear might have the recurring thought that their hands have a lot of germs on them.

These compulsions help to alleviate the person's anxiety or are used to prevent an unwanted event or situation from occurring, despite the fact that the unwanted outcome will most likely not occur regardless of the behavior. For example, a child may fear that unless he lines up his toys from largest to smallest, he will be kidnapped. OCD can be difficult to diagnose in children, since they may not have insight into what is causing the behavior.

Regardless of whether a child or adult is experiencing obsessions and/or compulsions, additional criteria must be met in order to meet the OCD diagnostic criteria. The person must dedicate a large amount of time to the endorsed obsessions or compulsions, and the behaviors or thoughts must interfere with daily functioning. Other medical and mental health conditions must be ruled out before giving this diagnosis. Individuals have varying levels of insight into whether the feared beliefs might or might not come true. As such, clinicians may specify whether the individual has good, fair, poor or no insight into their disorder.

Body dysmorphic disorder is present when a person is preoccupied with at least one perceived flaw in their body. These flaws are only minimally noticeable to others or are not apparent at all. For example, a person may spend hours staring in the mirror at a spot on their skin. The individual may feel compelled to engage in repetitive behaviors related to the perceived flaw (i.e., grooming, picking their skin, etc.) and it causes them great distress. It is important that other disorders, such as the weight concerns seen in eating disorders, be ruled out before assigning this diagnosis.

Hoarding disorder occurs when a person is unable to get rid of their material possessions and they accumulate. Furthermore, the person feels that the material items must be saved, and they experience great distress if they have to let go of items. As such, living areas often become cluttered and potentially unusable. Family members or other supporters may need to maintain the cluttered areas.

In extreme cases, authorities may become involved if the living area becomes a hazard. The need to keep items must cause great distress and interfere with daily functioning, which includes living in a safe environment. Other mental and physical conditions should be ruled out, and clinicians may specify the patient's level of insight related to their hoarding practices.

Trichotillomania (hair pulling disorder) occurs when an individual repeatedly pulls or plucks their hair and the hair loss is noticeable as a result. The person must have tried to stop pulling their hair, and this behavior must cause elevated levels of distress and interfere with daily functioning.

Excoriation (skin-picking) disorder occurs when the repeated behavior of picking at one's skin leads to lesions on the skin. The person must be unable to stop the skin-picking behavior, and it must cause distress and interfere with daily functioning.

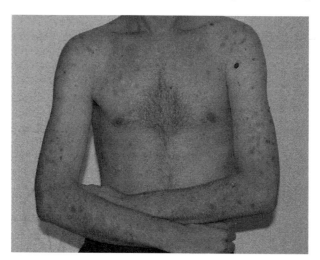

Excoriation (skin-picking) disorder

Substance/medication-induced obsessive-compulsive and related disorders may be diagnosed if there is evidence from a medical examination or lab result that indicates that an obsession, compulsion, skin picking or hair pulling has occurred soon after starting or stopping the use of a medication or substance.

Obsessive-compulsive and related disorders due to another medical condition may be diagnosed when an obsession, compulsion, hair-pulling or skin-picking behavior can be attributed to another medical condition. This must be evidenced by a physical examination or a lab result.

*Other specified obsessive-compulsive and related disorder*s refer to a number of presentations that mimic OCD, yet do not meet full criteria for one of the aforementioned OCD disorders. For example, a person may display body dysmorphic-like behaviors but have an actual flaw that is readily apparent to other people.

Unspecified obsessive-compulsive and related disorders may be diagnosed when symptoms of OCD appear to be present and cause distress and impairment in functioning, yet do not meet full criteria for another disorder.

Trauma and stressor-related disorders

Reactive attachment disorder occurs in children who are emotionally distant from their adult caregiver. When they become distressed, they do not seek out their caregiver for comfort and/or rarely respond to caregivers' attempts to offer comfort when they are upset. Additionally, at least two of the following criteria must be met: they rarely respond socially or emotionally to other individuals, they have minimal positive gestures (i.e., smiling) and/or become irritable, sad or fearful for no reason.

Furthermore, one or more of the following must also be true: the child must have experienced neglect or emotional deprivation at some point in his or her life, stable attachments could not form due to frequent changes in primary caregivers and/or the child was brought up in a setting that inhibited attachment (i.e., an orphanage). This pattern of insufficient attachment must first have appeared before the child's fifth birthday, and the child must be at least nine months of age. It is important to rule out other medical and mental health conditions, particularly autism, given the overlap in lack of social responsiveness.

Disinhibited social engagement disorder can be diagnosed in children who meet at least two of the following criteria when interacting with new adults: reluctance or refusal to approach new adults, treating a new adult as if they are very familiar with them, failure to look back toward their known caregiver (the child might even tend to venture away) and/or going off with a new adult without hesitation. These behaviors must not be limited to impulsive behaviors, as those seen in children with ADHD. Rather, there must be social deficits, which must be due to some form of neglect or deprivation. This often occurs due to abuse, being raised in a non-traditional setting such as an orphanage or being moved around to different foster care homes. A child must have a developmental age of at least nine months, and the symptoms must have been present for at least one year.

Post-traumatic stress disorder (PTSD) can be diagnosed in any individual who is at least six years of age, although the exact criteria needed for diagnosis vary depending on age. Basically, PTSD refers to a condition that occurs when a person was in a situation where the threat of bodily harm or even death was present (i.e., threat of rape, abuse, car accident, fighting, terrorist attack, war experiences, etc.). This may have happened to the person themselves or the person may have witnessed this event happen to someone else. For example, someone who escaped the terrorist attacks on 9/11 or even those who witnessed the attacks or the aftermath may qualify for a diagnosis of PTSD.

In order to determine whether the individual has PTSD, the individual must have either repeated and unwanted memories of the event, upsetting dreams about the violent event, "flashbacks" where the person feels as if the event is happening to them again or distress when hearing some cue that reminds them of the violent event (i.e., hearing screams, sirens, etc.). The person attempts to avoid these distressing memories or flashbacks, which may include behavioral avoidance of people, places, topics or any other thing that might remind them of the violent event.

The person must also have at least two of the following:

- experience worsening mood and/or thoughts related to the event, which may include the inability to recall important details of the traumatic event;

- have negative beliefs about oneself;

- blaming oneself or others (who bear no responsibility) for the event;

- have a constant negative emotional state (such as anger or horror);

- reduced interest in becoming involved in activities of interest;

- feel detached from others;

- be unable to feel positive emotions.

The person must also have changes in how they become aware and respond to things associated with the original event, such as: reckless behavior, being overly aware of surroundings, exaggerated responses to non-threatening stimuli, trouble concentrating or sleeping and irritable or angry outbursts. The above criteria must have been going on for at least one month, and these changes must cause distress and impairment nearly every day.

Service dogs provide aid to military veterans with PTSD

Acute stress disorder is very similar to PTSD, with the exception of the timeline. Acute stress disorder may only be diagnosed from three days after the event to one month after the event. After one month, the diagnosis would change to PTSD. This also involves exposure to a traumatic event in which death or physical harm to oneself or another person was likely. In addition, they must meet at least nine specific symptoms, which include several intrusive symptoms, negative mood, dissociative symptoms, behavioral avoidance and/or changes in arousal due to the event.

Adjustment disorder occurs when any stressor provokes either emotional or behavioral changes in an individual within three months of experiencing the stressor. These changes must be out of proportion with the actual danger posed by the stressor and must cause impairment with daily functioning. Other mental and physical disorders must be ruled out, including the possibility that the person is grieving normally for a person he or she lost. Once the stressor is removed, the symptoms must remit within six months.

One of the differences between adjustment disorder and PTSD is the severity of the stressor. For example, PTSD always includes the possibility that bodily harm or injury may befall someone. However, the stressor referred to in adjustment disorder may be something less severe but equally upsetting to the person. For example, the person may have lost their job, gotten divorced or lost custody of a child.

Other specified trauma and stressor-related disorder can be used as a diagnosis when symptoms mimic those that are hallmarks of a trauma or stressor-related disorder, yet do not meet the full criteria for one of the aforementioned disorders. This may occur due to not meeting the time criteria or having a presentation that may be culturally different (i.e., *ataque de nervios*, which occurs in some Latino cultures).

Unspecified trauma and stressor-related disorder is most often diagnosed when the clinician does not have enough information to determine which traumatic or related disorder best applies to the individual. For example, in a crisis situation like an emergency room, the clinician may not yet have enough information to determine whether the patient meets full criteria for another disorder. Thus, the clinician may choose to give this diagnosis if symptoms of a traumatic disorder are present.

Somatic symptom and related disorders

Somatic symptom disorder can be diagnosed when at least one physical symptom is distressing and causes excessive disruption in daily functioning, due to maladaptive thoughts, feelings or behavioral responses which occur due to the physical symptom. For example, the person may have elevated levels of worry or spend excessive time thinking about their physical symptoms. The person must also have had at least one somatic symptom (it could be different symptoms) for at least six months.

Illness anxiety disorder occurs when individuals become convinced that they have or will at some point in the future become seriously ill. Unlike somatic symptom disorder, symptoms are rarely present or only mildly present, yet the person is still convinced that they will develop an illness. The person becomes easily worried about their health and as a result, engages in excessive health-checking behaviors or avoids checking for fear of what they will find. For example, someone may completely avoid medical appointments or check his or her body daily for signs of bumps. The worry about illness must have been going on for at least six months, and other mental and physical disorders must be ruled out. Clinicians may specify whether the individual displays care-seeking or care-avoidant behaviors.

Conversion disorder (functional neurological symptom disorder) describes a condition in which a person has symptoms of being blind or paralyzed (or has altered motor or sensory skills), which cannot be explained by another medical or mental health condition. This condition may occur with seizures, weakness or paralysis, atypical movements, sensory loss, etc. In addition, the episodes may be acute if they last less than six months and persistent if they last longer than six months.

Psychological factors affecting other medical conditions is when a medical symptom or condition is negatively impacted by psychological factors in at least one of the following ways: development, worsening or delayed recovery from the disorder due to psychological causes, psychological factors inhibiting adequate treatment (i.e., the person refuses to take their medication), health risks and/or psychological factors that influence the cause or maintenance of the disorder need to be addressed. Other mental health conditions should first be ruled out prior to giving this diagnosis. The clinician may indicate whether the condition is mild, moderate, severe or extreme. In extreme cases, the patient may not report symptoms of a major health risk, such as heart attack or seizure symptoms.

Factitious disorder can either be imposed on the individual himself or imposed on another person. Individuals with this disorder make up or falsify information about symptoms of either a medical or mental health condition. The person either indicates that they themselves or another person is ill or injured. Their deceptive behavior continues when rewards are removed, and other mental health conditions must be ruled out (especially delusional disorder and psychotic disorder). Clinicians may specify whether this is a single episode or whether it is recurrent.

Other specified somatic symptom and related disorders may be diagnosed when symptoms that mimic those seen in somatic symptom and related disorders are evident, yet do not meet the full criteria for one of the previous disorders in this category. For example, this may occur during a brief somatic symptom disorder or illness anxiety which lasts less than six months.

Unspecified somatic symptom and related disorders occur when symptoms of a somatic disorder are present, but the clinician chooses not to specify which disorder. This most often occurs when there is not yet enough information to make this determination, such as in a hospital setting.

Bipolar and related disorders

Bipolar I disorder refers to the classic type of bipolar disorder, in which a person experiences a manic episode. The individual must have had at least one manic episode, which is usually a period of increased activity and productivity. Manic episodes are characterized by ideas of grandiosity, distractibility and excessive talkativeness. Hypomanic or depressive episodes may occur before or after the manic episode.

Bipolar II disorder differs from Bipolar I disorder because it requires that the person has experienced at least one episode of major depression and at least one hypomanic episode at some point in their life.

Cyclothymic disorder can be diagnosed in both children and adults when both hypomanic and depressive experiences have occurred (for at least two years for adults and one year for children). While these episodes occur, they do not meet the full criteria for hypomania, mania or major depressive disorder.

Substance/medication-induced bipolar and related disorders can be used when symptoms mimic bipolar I, bipolar II or cyclothymic disorders, but can be attributed to the use of a substance or medication. This must be evidenced from a physical examination or laboratory testing.

Bipolar and related disorders due to another medical condition are used when the elevated and/or irritable mood symptoms that mimic bipolar disorders are due to another medical condition, as evidenced by a physical examination or laboratory testing.

Other specified bipolar and related disorders are diagnosed when symptoms clearly mimic the symptoms of bipolar and related disorders but do not meet the full criteria. This could occur due to the short duration of the illness or not meeting enough of the criteria to qualify for a hypomanic, manic or depressive episode.

Unspecified bipolar and related disorders are most often used in emergency situations when symptoms of a bipolar or related disorder are apparent, but not enough information is available to determine which disorder best matches the individual's symptoms.

Depressive disorders

Disruptive mood dysregulation disorder is a new addition to the DSM-5. It was added to address growing concerns that children were being diagnosed with too many disorders, all of which had a component of dysregulation of mood. These children often display irritability and have episodes in which they are unable to control their behavior. In fact, they display severe temper or verbal outbursts and may even become physically aggressive for unknown reasons. These outbursts must happen about three times per week and be inappropriate for the child's age. In between these outbursts, the child must display an angry or irritable mood most of the time.

The symptoms must have been occurring for at least three months, but not more than twelve months. In addition, they must occur in more than one setting (for example, both at school and at home). The child must be between the ages of 6 and 18, and the symptoms must have been apparent in the child's history prior to his or her tenth birthday. Other physical and mental health conditions must be ruled out, as symptoms of this disorder may mimic those seen in bipolar disorder, oppositional defiant disorder, ADHD and other childhood disorders. Children who display these symptoms are often later diagnosed with either a depressive disorder or an anxiety disorder.

Major depressive disorder describes an episode of sadness that must last at least two weeks and involves observable changes in mood, thoughts and other bodily functions such as sleep and weight. In fact, at least five of the following symptoms must be present for most of the two-week time period: feeling sad most of the day, a loss of interest in previously enjoyed activities, weight loss or weight gain, sleeping more or less than usual, speaking a lot more slowly or quickly than normal, feeling tired or fatigued most of the day, experiencing feelings of worthlessness or guilt, having difficulty concentrating or making decisions and/or thinking frequently about death or dying. These symptoms must interfere with daily functioning and must cause distress. Clinicians may specify whether the episode is mild, moderate or severe. Only one episode is needed to make the diagnosis; however, clinicians must be careful to ensure that the level of sadness exceeds that usually seen during the course of normal bereavement.

Major depressive disorder describes an episode of sadness which must last at least two weeks and involves observable changes in mood, thoughts and other bodily functions such as sleep and weight.

Persistent depressive disorder (dysthymia) is a more enduring pattern of sadness than major depressive disorder, as it must last for at least one to two years instead of only two weeks. The sadness must last at least one year for children and two years for adults, during which time at least two of the following symptoms are also evident: eating more or less than usual, sleeping more or less, feeling easily tired or tired all the time, not feeling worthwhile, having difficulty concentrating or being indecisive and/or feeling like "things are never going to work out." Other medical and mental health conditions must be ruled out. Clinicians may specify whether the disorder is mild, moderate or severe as well as whether the individual had an early or late onset of the disorder.

Premenstrual dysphoric disorder is a condition in which women become extremely sad before the onset of their period; the symptoms improve a few days after the period begins. At least five symptoms characteristic of a major depressive disorder must be evident (i.e., changes in weight, sleeping patterns, etc.). In addition, at least one of the following symptoms must exist: extreme changes in mood (such as feeling sad quickly), feeling irritable or angry, feeling depressed, hopeless, or bad about oneself and/or feeling anxious or on edge.

Furthermore, at least one of the following symptoms must appear: having no interest in previously enjoyable activities, trouble concentrating, feeling tired easily, changes in eating patterns, sleeping more or less, feeling overwhelmed and/or feeling bloated or tender in areas of the body. The symptoms must cause distress and interfere with the woman's ability to perform school, work or home life tasks. Other medical and mental health conditions must be ruled out.

Substance/medication-induced depressive disorder occurs when an individual experiences a chronic low mood or lack of interest in activities that they previously enjoyed, and when there is evidence that these changes are due to the use or withdrawal from a substance or medication. Some substances that can cause these symptoms are alcohol, opioids, and cocaine. Other medical and mental health conditions must be ruled out.

Depressive disorder due to another medical condition occurs when the depressed mood that a person exhibits is the result of a medical condition, as evidenced by a medical examination or laboratory finding. Other mental health disorders, particularly adjustment disorder, should be ruled out. This causes distress and interferes with daily functioning.

Other specified depressive disorders refer to varied presentations of depressive disorders, in which the symptoms do not qualify for one of the aforementioned depressive disorders. Examples include recurrent brief depression and short-duration depressive episodes, in which the symptoms of depression last for less than 13 days, ruling out major depressive disorder. This category may also be used if the minimum number of depression symptoms is not met, yet the individual experiences sadness and at least one other symptom of a major depressive episode that causes distress and has been occurring for at least two weeks.

Unspecified depressive disorder may be diagnosed when an individual appears to have symptoms that mimic depression and cause distress and impairment, yet the individual does not meet the full diagnostic criteria for any of the previous depressive disorders. This most often occurs in an emergency room setting, when a clinician is uncertain or does not have enough information about the patient's symptoms.

Schizophrenia spectrum

Schizotypal (personality) disorder is considered to be on the schizophrenia spectrum but is discussed in more detail in the "Personality disorders" section further in this chapter.

Delusional disorder is present when there has been at least one month during which an individual was experiencing delusions without any other psychotic symptoms. In fact, the person's daily functioning is not really impaired. There are different types of delusions: erotomanic (false belief that another person is in love with the individual), grandiose (belief that the individual has some special talent or brilliant insight unrecognized by others), jealous (belief that a spouse or lover is cheating), persecutory (belief that someone is conspiring against, harassing or spying on the individual), somatic (delusions centered around feelings in the body), mixed (when there is no clearly identifiable delusion theme) and unspecified (when the prominent delusion is unable to be determined or does not fit into one type). Clinicians may specify whether the delusion contains bizarre content and whether it is the first such episode of delusional thinking.

Brief psychotic disorder must occur for more than one day but not longer than one month. During this time period, a person must experience delusions, hallucinations and/or disorganized speech. Other mental health conditions, especially major depressive disorder and bipolar disorder, must be ruled out before assigning this diagnosis. Clinicians may specify whether or not there is a marked stressor, meaning an event which would be stressful to almost anyone in that situation. Doctors may also specify whether the psychotic symptoms occurred during pregnancy or within the first four weeks after giving birth.

Schizophrenia must last for at least six months, during which there must be at least one month where symptoms are in the active phase (delusions, hallucinations, disorganized speech, behavior that is catatonic or disorganized and/or negative symptoms such as avolition). At least one area of functioning must be greatly impacted by the symptoms, and other mental health and medical conditions must be ruled out.

Schizophreniform disorder is very similar to schizophrenia except that it has a shorter duration, less than six months, during which symptoms occur. It also differs from schizophrenia in that there is no requirement that the person's daily functioning level has declined. In order to meet the criteria for schizophreniform disorder, an individual must display at least two of the following symptoms for a one-month period: delusions, hallucinations, disorganization during speech processes, behavior that is disorganized or catatonic and/or negative symptoms such as decreased emotional expressions. Other medical and mental health conditions must be ruled out, especially depressive and bipolar disorders.

Schizoaffective disorder may be diagnosed when there is a mood problem and the active-phase symptoms of schizophrenia co-occur (i.e., disorganized speech, negative symptoms, etc.). Additionally, these symptoms were preceded by either hallucinations or delusions which lasted for at least two weeks without the presence of mood symptoms. Clinicians may specify whether the specific symptoms are best described as bipolar or depressive and whether catatonia is present.

Substance/medication-induced psychotic disorder occurs when the psychotic symptoms that an individual exhibits are the result of drug abuse, medication use or another toxin, and the symptoms remit after exposure to the medication or substance has stopped. There must be evidence from a physical examination or laboratory work indicating that a substance or medication has caused the psychotic symptoms. Some medications and substances that may cause psychotic symptoms include: alcohol, inhalants, amphetamines, and cocaine. Other medical and mental health conditions must be ruled out.

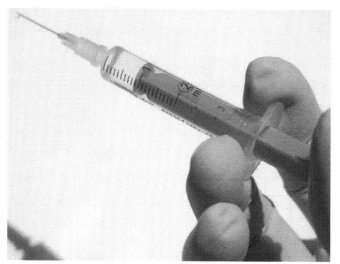

Substance/medication-induced psychotic disorder occurs when the psychotic symptoms that an individual exhibits are the result of drug abuse, medication use or another toxin.

Psychotic disorder due to another medical condition occurs when the psychotic symptoms that an individual experiences are the result of another medical condition, as evidenced by a physical examination or laboratory results.

Catatonia associated with another mental disorder can be diagnosed with at least three of the following symptoms present: stupor, copying another person's movements, copying another person's speech, facial grimacing, stereotypic behaviors, odd mannerisms, posturing, not responding or following directions, not speaking, waxy flexibility and/or catalepsy.

Catatonic disorder due to another medical condition occurs when a person meets three of the criteria for catatonia, but the catatonic state is due to another medical condition as evidenced by a physical examination or lab result. Other mental health conditions must be ruled out.

Unspecified catatonia may be diagnosed when symptoms that mimic catatonia are present and cause distress and impairment, but do not meet the full criteria for another diagnosis. Additionally, it can be used if the underlying medical or mental health disorder causing it is unclear or if there is not enough information to make a more accurate diagnosis.

Other specified schizophrenia spectrum and other psychotic disorder can be used to describe symptoms that are characteristic of schizophrenia and related disorders, yet do not meet the full criteria for another disorder. This may occur with repeated auditory hallucinations, delusions that overlap with mood episodes and in other unique cases.

Unspecified schizophrenia spectrum and other psychotic disorder is most often diagnosed when there is not enough information to determine the specific disorder that matches the patient's symptoms. There is evidence of symptoms that fall on the schizophrenia spectrum, but the clinician may be uncertain or not have enough information to make a more accurate diagnosis, such as when seen in an emergency room setting.

Dissociative disorder

Dissociative identity disorder occurs when two or more different personalities exist, and there are repeated episodes of amnesia. The symptoms may either be noticed by others or the individual may notice them. Individuals have gaps or holes in their memory and may have trouble recalling personal information about typical events. Other medical and mental health conditions must be ruled out, especially seizure disorders, personality disorders, PTSD, bipolar and major depressive disorders.

Dissociative identity disorder occurs when two or more different personalities exist and there are repeated episodes of amnesia.

Dissociative amnesia occurs when a person is unable to recall information about themselves, such as their name, where they live, or where they were born. Often, people are unable to recall some traumatic event that has occurred or some of the details surrounding the event. The exact type of amnesia may differ, depending on the individual; it can be localized, selective and/or generalized. Other medical and mental health conditions, such as PTSD and neurocognitive disorders, must be ruled out.

Depersonalization/derealization disorder occurs when there are repeated episodes of depersonalization and/or derealization. During the experiences, the person is aware of reality. Other medical and mental health conditions must be ruled out before giving this diagnosis.

Other specified dissociative disorder may be applied when symptoms of a dissociative disorder are present, but they do not meet full criteria for one of the disorders. This may occur, for example, when there is an identity disturbance due to outside coercive forces, as can sometimes be seen in prisoners of war.

Unspecified dissociative disorder occurs when there is evidence of a dissociative disorder, but not enough information to determine which disorder. This most often occurs in emergency room situations.

Personality disorders

Personality disorders fall into three main clusters:

- *Cluster A* (the "odd, eccentric" cluster: paranoid personality disorder, schizoid personality disorder, and schizotypal personality disorder),

- *Cluster B* (the "dramatic, emotional, erratic" cluster: antisocial personality disorder, borderline personality disorder, histrionic personality disorder, and narcissistic personality disorder), and

- *Cluster C* (the "anxious, fearful" cluster: avoidant personality disorder, dependent personality disorder, and obsessive-compulsive personality disorder).

Paranoid personality disorder involves a persistent distrust or suspicion of other people. Four of the following criteria must be evident, beginning before early adulthood (with other medical and mental health conditions being ruled out):

- worries that other people are going to harm, exploit or deceive them;

- being excessively worried about the trustworthiness or loyalty of peers;

- being hesitant to confide in others because they believe the other person will use the information to harm them;

- interpreting benign remarks as demeaning or threatening;

- holding grudges;

- believing falsely that others are attacking their character and responding quickly with anger;

- persistent suspicions about their spouse or lover being unfaithful.

Schizoid personality disorder is a consistent pattern of behaviors, beginning before early adulthood, in which there is restricted emotional expression and detachment from social relationships. These must occur in more than one setting. The individual must experience at least four of the following symptoms (with other mental health and medical conditions being ruled out):

- no desire for or enjoyment of interpersonal relationships;

- preference for solitary activities;

- little or no interest in sexual activities;

- experiencing no pleasure in activities;

- paucity of close relationships;

- indifference to praise and critiques from other people;

- detachment or flat affect.

Schizotypal personality disorder is a repeated pattern of social and interpersonal difficulties. This includes discomfort with close relationships and is marked by thought or perceptual changes and eccentric behavior which begin by early adulthood. The symptoms must be present in more than one setting, and at least five of the following criteria must be met, while other mental health and medical conditions are ruled out:

- endorsement of ideas of reference (i.e., believing that all events experienced in daily life are important signs of destiny);

- eccentric beliefs;

- strange perceptual experiences;

- oddities in thinking or speech;

- paranoia;

- inappropriate or restricted affect;

- odd behavior or appearance;

- few close friends;

- social anxiety that does not remit even after becoming familiar with a person.

Antisocial personality disorder is a consistent pattern in which an individual flagrantly disregards the rights of other people. The individual must be at least 18 years old and the behavior must have begun prior to their fifteenth birthday. At least three of the following criteria must be met with other mental health conditions ruled out:

- disregard for social norms which results in arrests;

- repeated lying or deceit;

- impulsive behaviors;

- violence or aggressiveness toward others;

- lack of caring for one's own safety and the safety of others;

- irresponsibility in areas of work and financial obligations;

- not feeling bad when one's actions are hurtful to others.

Borderline personality disorder describes a condition in which there is a chronic instability in self-image, close relationships and effect. It is typically marked by impulsive behaviors and must begin by early adulthood. At least five of the following behaviors must be present and other medical and mental health conditions ruled out:

- fear of real or imagined abandonment;

- interpersonal relationships that alter between idealization and hate;

- disturbance in self-image;

- impulsivity in two or more areas that are self-damaging (i.e., spending too much, risky sex, reckless driving, binge eating);

- repeated suicidal gestures, threats or self-harm;

- instability in moods;

- feeling "empty" most of the time;

- difficulty controlling anger and/or temporary paranoid ideation.

Histrionic personality disorder is a chronic pattern of excessive attention-seeking and emotional behaviors, which begins before early adulthood. At least five or more of the following symptoms must be present and other medical and mental health conditions ruled out:

- discomfort in situations where they are not the center of attention;

- inappropriate sexual or provocative behavior;

- changing and shallow emotional expression;

- using physical appearance to gain attention;

- speaking in an impressionistic manner or speech that lacks specificity;

- dramatic or exaggerated speech;

- being easily influenced by others and/or believing relationships are more close than they actually are.

Narcissistic personality disorder is a pattern of behavior in which a person displays grandiose ideas, wants admiration and lacks the ability to empathize with others. This pattern must have started at or before early adulthood and must meet at least five of the following criteria with other medical and mental health conditions ruled out:

- exaggeration of one's achievements or talents;

- thinking often about achieving unlimited wealth, power, success or love;

- the belief that one is "special" and should only associate with other "special" (i.e., wealthy, famous, etc.) people;

- needing a lot of admiration;

- displaying a sense of entitlement;

- taking advantage of other people to achieve one's own goals;

- not being able to empathize with other people;

- jealousy of others and arrogance.

Narcisstic personality disorder is a pattern of behavior in which a person displays grandiose ideas, wants admiration and lacks the ability to empathize with others.

Avoidant personality disorder occurs when there is a repeated pattern of social inhibition, feeling hypersensitive and/or feeling inadequate, which occurs in more than one context and began before early adulthood. At least four or more of the following criteria must be met with other medical and mental health conditions ruled out:

- avoidance of interpersonal contact even in the work setting due to fear of criticism or rejection;

- lack of involvement with others unless they are sure they will be liked;

- hesitation in intimate relationships because of fear or shame;

- worry about being criticized or rejected when around other people;

- feeling inadequate in new situations which leads to social concerns;

- believing oneself to be inept or inferior to others;

- reluctant to take personal risks or to become involved in novel activities because of fear of embarrassment.

Dependent personality disorder involves a repeated pattern where the person shows an excessive need to be cared for by others due to fear of separation. These behaviors must begin by early adulthood and must meet at least five of the following criteria with other medical and mental health conditions ruled out:

- trouble making everyday life decisions without advice from others;

- letting other people take responsibility for major areas of one's life;

- having difficulty expressing disagreement;

- lacking the self-confidence to do things on their own;

- going to great extremes to get support from other people;

- feeling uncomfortable when alone;

- needing a relationship as a source of care;

- frantically seeking a replacement relationship after one ends;

- excessive fears about caring for themselves alone.

Obsessive-compulsive disorder is a repeated pattern of behavior which overemphasizes neatness, perfection, and control over mental and personal issues. People with OCD have limited flexibility and openness. Symptoms must begin by early adulthood and include at least four or more of the following criteria with other medical and mental health conditions ruled out:

- excessive worry about details, rules, organization, schedules or order;

- perfectionism that interferes with finishing assignments;

- spending excessive time on work and being "productive" instead of doing recreational activities or spending time with friends;

- caring too much about morality, ethics, and values;

- having a hard time letting go of used or worthless objects that do not have sentimental meaning;

- having a hard time delegating tasks to others;

- spending very little money on oneself and others;

- being stubborn or rigid.

Personality change due to another medical condition occurs when there is an established change from the individual's previous personality pattern. There must be evidence from a physical examination or laboratory finding that indicates that such a change is due to another medical condition. Other medical and mental health conditions must be ruled out, and the symptoms must cause significant distress in one or more area of functioning. Clinicians may specify a number of subtypes, including being paranoid, aggressive or apathetic.

Other specified personality disorder may be used to designate symptoms which mimic those of a personality disorder and cause distress or impairment, yet do not meet the full diagnostic criteria of another mental health disorder.

Unspecified personality disorder may be diagnosed when symptoms of a personality disorder are present, yet it is unclear which personality disorder best matches the patient's present symptoms. It may also be used if there is not enough information to determine a more specific diagnosis.

Eating disorders

Pica occurs when food without nutrients or nonfood items are consistently eaten over a period of at least one month. For example, a child may eat a small toy, coin or pencil tip repeatedly. The items eaten must be items that are not typically eaten in that individual's culture and may only be diagnosed in the context of another mental health disorder (i.e., autism spectrum) if the behavior is severe enough to merit treatment.

1,440 items found in the stomach of a patient suffering from pica.

Rumination disorder occurs when food is repeatedly spat up for at least one month. This may include re-chewing food, re-swallowing food or spitting out chewed up food. The repeated spitting up of food may not be due to another medical disorder (i.e., acid reflux) and it must not occur only during the course of another eating disorder. If symptoms co-occur with another mental health disorder (i.e., autism) they must be severe enough to merit clinical attention.

Avoidant/restrictive food intake disorder is a repeated pattern of eating in which certain foods are avoided based on lack of interest in food, the food's appearance or taste, or concern about the negative consequences of eating the food. As a result, the individual fails to maintain adequate nutritional needs as evidenced by at least one of the following: weight loss or failure to achieve weight gain in children, nutritional deficiency, the need to be fed through tubes or through nutritional supplements and/or interference with daily functioning. Food must be available and culturally appropriate. Other medical and mental health conditions must be ruled out.

Anorexia nervosa occurs when an individual restricts his or her food intake due to a desire to lose weight. As a result, significantly low body weight, based on Body Mass Index (BMI), is reached. The person must fear gaining weight and demonstrate behaviors which interfere with weight gain. Furthermore, there is a distortion in the way in which the individual perceives his or her weight or shape. The two subtypes are the restricting type, in which food is not eaten or eaten in minimal quantities, and binge-eating/purging, in which there are repeated episodes of eating large quantities of food followed by some method to purge the food (i.e., vomiting, laxative use, etc.). The condition may be mild, moderate, severe or extreme based on the individual's BMI.

Anorexia nervosa occurs when an individual restricts his or her food intake due to a desire to lose weight. The person fears gaining weight. There is also a distortion in the way in which the individual perceives his or her weight or shape.

Bulimia nervosa occurs when there are repeated episodes of binge-eating, in which more food than most people would eat is consumed and the person may feel out of control when they are eating. The individual also engages in compensatory behaviors to make up for the quantity of food eaten, such as vomiting or fasting in order to thwart gaining weight. Both the eating and compensatory behaviors must occur for at least three months, approximately once per week. The person with bulimia overvalues their shape and weight. Other medical and mental health disorders should be ruled out.

Bulimia nervosa is repeated episodes of binge-eating, in which more food than most people would eat is consumed and the individual engages in compensatory behaviors, such as vomiting or fasting in order to thwart gaining weight.

Binge-eating disorder involves repeated episodes of eating more than most individuals would eat at one time, or an individual feeling out of control while eating. During the eating episodes, at least three of the following criteria must be met: eating more quickly than normal, feeling ill or full, eating even when not physically hungry, eating alone due to being embarrassed about the quantity of food that is being consumed and/or feeling disgusted, guilty or depressed after eating. There is distress, with no compensatory behaviors present. The disorder may be mild, moderate, severe or excessive depending on the number of weekly binges. Other medical and mental health conditions should be ruled out.

Other specified feeding or eating disorder may describe atypical presentations of eating disorders, including atypical anorexia (when the individual's weight is still within the normal limits despite weight loss), binge-eating or bulimia that is of low frequency or limited in time and/or night eating syndrome.

Unspecified feeding or eating disorder may be used to describe a disorder where symptoms of an eating disorder are present, yet do not meet the full criteria for the disorder. It may also be used if not enough information is available to make an accurate diagnosis.

Neurodevelopmental disorders

Intellectual disability (intellectual developmental disability) is marked by gaps in general cognitive abilities, such as reasoning, planning, abstract thinking or developing solutions to problems. It may also include trouble with academic learning or learning from one's experiences. As a result, there are deficits in adaptive functioning and the individual has trouble with typical tasks associated with daily life (i.e., school, peer relationships, communication, self-care, etc.).

Global development delay occurs when individuals do not meet their expected developmental milestones compared with peers of the same age. This disorder suggests that there are several areas of cognitive abilities which are impacted, and as a result, these individuals cannot be assessed using IQ tests. This may occur due to head trauma or a birth defect.

Unspecified intellectual disability (intellectual developmental disability) may be used for children over the age of 5 who are unable to be assessed due to physical or sensory issues. This disorder requires that children be reassessed after a reasonable amount of time.

Language disorder connotes chronic difficulties with learning or using language due to a lack of understanding or a lack of ability to produce language. As a result, the following criteria must be met: reduced vocabulary, inability to use a wide variety of sentence structures, having trouble using vocabulary and/or connecting sentences to each other. The language level must be significantly below same-age peers and other medical and mental health conditions must be ruled out.

Speech sound disorder is characterized by problems making sounds or not being able to make sounds at all. As a result, normal communication is limited. Other medical and mental health conditions must be ruled out.

Childhood-onset fluency disorder (stuttering) affects the normal flow and timing of speech and is considered abnormal given the child's age and language abilities. These symptoms persist for a long time and occur with at least one of the following: repeating sounds or syllables, prolonged sounds of consonants and vowels, pauses when saying a word, blocking, substituting words that are difficult to pronounce for other words that are easier to pronounce, physical tension when saying a word and/or whole word repetitions. Typically, this condition produces anxiety about having to speak and usually emerges in young childhood. Other medical and mental health conditions must be ruled out.

Social (pragmatic) communication disorder connotes difficulty using verbal and nonverbal communication in social settings. This may include greeting people, sharing information, changing the communication to match the needs of the listener, trouble following rules when conversing with other individuals and inability to make inferences from what is being said. This often begins in early childhood. Other medical and mental health conditions must be ruled out.

Unspecified communication disorder may be diagnosed when symptoms of a communication disorder are present, but more information is needed to determine the exact diagnosis.

Autism spectrum disorder represents chronic impairments in social realms across different contexts. These may include a lack of communication, not looking, not responding or lack of non-verbal cues. Children also display restricted or repetitive movements such as hand flipping, repeating words or lining up toys in the same way. These symptoms must begin in early childhood and cause significant impairment.

Attention deficit hyperactivity disorder may occur in both children and adults. A chronic pattern of trouble paying attention and/or impulsivity is present to the extent that it impairs the person's ability to perform daily tasks of living. Symptoms of inattention may include failure to follow directions or listen, trouble organizing tasks or forgetting materials needed for school or work. Symptoms of impulsivity include fidgeting, getting up frequently, trouble staying quiet and having trouble waiting for one's turn. Other medical and mental health conditions should be ruled out.

Other specified attention deficit hyperactivity disorder may be used when symptoms of ADHD are present, but the full criteria of ADHD are not met.

Unspecified attention deficit hyperactivity disorder may be used when symptoms of ADHD appear to be present, but there is not enough information to make a more accurate diagnosis.

Specific learning disability refers to problems either learning or applying different academic skills. At least one of the following symptoms must be present for at least six months: slow reading, trouble understanding what has been read, trouble spelling, difficulty expressing oneself in writing and/or trouble mastering math skills. The deficits must be significantly below those of same-age peers and other medical and mental health disorders must be ruled out.

Developmental coordination disorder is a problem in both acquiring and using motor skills. As a result, movement may be slowed or look clumsy.

Stereotypic movement disorder may be present when individuals exhibit repeated purposeless behaviors like hand flapping, rocking back and forth or banging their head. These repeated motions cause problems with peers, family, school and/or home life.

Tic disorders are marked by the presence of either motor or vocal tics that occur repeatedly. A tic is a sudden, repetitive, non-rhythmic movement or vocalization of discrete muscle groups. They may be unnoticeable to the observer (e.g., abdominal tensing, toe crunching). Eye blinking and throat clearing are common motor and phonic tics, respectively. As many as 1 in 100 people may experience some form of tic disorder, usually before the onset of puberty; tic disorders are more common among males than females. Tourette syndrome is the more severe form of tic disorder, and some researchers link it to genetic vulnerability.

Other specified tic disorders and unspecified tic disorders may also be used when symptoms of a tic disorder are present but do not meet the full criteria for a tic disorder.

Other specified neurodevelopmental disorders may be used when symptoms of a neurodevelopmental disorder are present, but the symptoms do not meet the full criteria.

Unspecified neurodevelopmental disorders may be used when symptoms mimic those of a neurodevelopmental disorder, but not enough information is available to make a diagnosis.

Notes

Biological Bases of Nervous System Disorders

Schizophrenia

Despite strong evidence for a biological basis of schizophrenia, the mechanisms underlying this disease remain unclear. Our current conceptualization might actually comprise multiple versions of the disorder; the "disorder" might be better conceptualized as a "syndrome" with multiple possible etiologies and outcomes.

Neuroanatomical studies have found evidence for enlarged ventricles (especially the third ventricle and the lateral ventricles) and enlarged cortical sulci in many patients with schizophrenia. Researchers have also found a subtle reduction in brain volume of about 3%. These reductions in volume have been found primarily in the gray matter versus the white matter of the brain, particularly in the front-temporal regions.

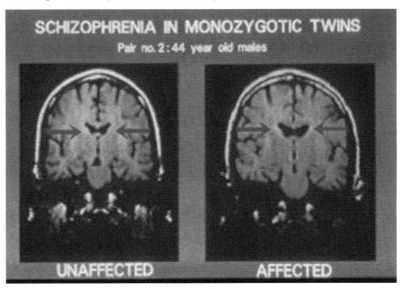

Enlarged lateral ventricles in schizophrenia

For many years the dopamine hypothesis of schizophrenia has been the most prominent theory regarding the neurochemical underpinnings of the disorder. Since its emergence, this theory has undergone multiple revisions, with the latest version stating that the symptoms of the disease are the result of increased activity in the dopaminergic system, specifically dopamine type 2 receptors (D2). The first version of this theory was derived from an early finding in 1950, which noted that the drug chlorpromazine alleviated symptoms in schizophrenic patients.

Later findings have provided further support for this hypothesis, as many effective anti-psychotic medications block dopamine brain receptors, and their potency is correlated to the strength of binding to D2 receptors in the brain. Moreover, the administration of drugs that increase dopamine can elicit symptoms that resemble the symptoms of schizophrenia. Post-mortem studies have also found an increased number of D2 receptors in the basal ganglia and the limbic system.

However, there are multiple limitations to the dopamine hypothesis of schizophrenia. One issue is that clozapine, one of the drugs effectively used to treat schizophrenia, in fact, has a low affinity to D2 receptors. Moreover, it is unlikely that dopaminergic dysfunction is the sole cause of schizophrenia; antipsychotics bring dopamine levels up to normal quickly but need to be taken for a while before alleviating symptoms. Current pharmacological treatment also fails to alleviate symptoms in all patients.

Other hypotheses conceptualize schizophrenia as caused during early neural development perinatally or intrauterinally. Another theory conceptualizes schizophrenia as progredient neurodegeneration and a result of abnormal or excessive synaptic pruning.

Depression

The search for the biological basis of depression has been largely guided by the knowledge about mechanisms involved in effective anti-depressive drug treatment. The most prominent theory about depression is the monoamine hypothesis, which postulates that the emergence of depression is linked to underactivity at the serotonergic and noradrenergic synapses. This theory has been supported by studies showing that the brains of depressed patients show increased amounts of serotonergic and noradrenergic synapses. These findings point to up-regulatory mechanisms to compensate for lack of monoamines.

The monoamine hypothesis has multiple limitations. First, it is unlikely that serotonin system dysfunction is the sole cause of depression, as antidepressants usually bring serotonin levels up to normal very quickly, but it often takes at least two to four weeks for depressive symptoms to improve significantly. Moreover, some effective antidepressants, such as Tianeptine and Opipramol, do not act through the monoamine system.

Consistent with the monoamine hypothesis, a longitudinal study examining the genetic basis of the disorder uncovered a moderating effect of a certain gene, the serotonin transporter (5-HTT) gene, on susceptibility to depression after stressful life events. This finding is consistent with the diathesis-stress model of depression, which postulates that depression is a result of both an innate vulnerability to depression (comprising genes, prenatal development, etc.) and later life events. An individual then develops depression if they have both the vulnerability and the experience of certain stressful life events. This model is supported by findings that depression seems especially likely to follow stressful life events, but even more so for people with one or two short alleles of the 5-HTT gene. Serotonin may help to regulate other neurotransmitter systems, and decreased serotonin interferes with this regulation. Different facets of depression may be emergent properties of this dysregulation.

Alzheimer's disease

Studies examining the biological basis of Alzheimer's disease have identified certain structural pathology characterized by neuritic plaques and neurofibrillary tangles. The mechanisms, however, remain unclear. Recent studies suggest that proteins ACT and ApoE4 might be related to fibrous clumps seen in Alzheimer's disease. Neurochemical abnormalities were also suggested, with a decrease in the enzyme choline acetyltransferase, suggesting a deficit in a specific neurotransmitter. Another theory points to a loss of subcortical neurons; however, signs of brain atrophy may or may not be present.

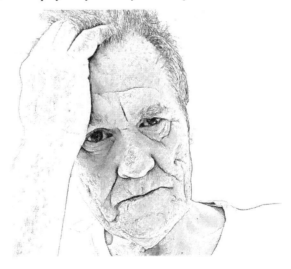

Parkinson's disease

The primary symptoms of Parkinson's disease have been associated with the degeneration of the substantia nigra, a part of the brain that controls motor functioning (NHGRI, 1998). This region is found deep within the brain stem and its neurons project via the nigrostriatal pathway to the striatum. The striatum is responsible for the control of movements and balance, as well as walking. The main neurotransmitter in the substantia nigra is dopamine, which is responsible for passing messages between the striatum and the substantia nigra.

Deterioration of the cells in the substantia nigra also corresponds with a decrease in the amount of dopamine produced between these cells. The decreased levels of dopamine then interfere with controlled motor function. Decreased levels of dopamine can also adversely affect the neurotransmitter acetylcholine. The motor function of the striatum is dependent on the balance between dopamine and acetylcholine. This disrupted balance between neurotransmitters may contribute to the progression of the disease.

Treatment of Psychological Disorders

Treatment Approaches

While differing treatments exist to address mental disorders, all treatments share some commonalities. All treatments include a patient, a therapist who is trained to assist the patient and the development of a patient-therapist relationship. All of the theories used to treat clients also have some hypotheses about what is causing the patient's symptoms.

Psychodynamic

This mode of treatment was made famous by Sigmund Freud. Through the use of psychoanalysis, Freud attempted to understand the conflict between the id, the ego, and the superego. Freud and his followers used a process called free association to help individuals get to the root of their problems. This process involves patients lying on a couch and saying whatever comes to mind without filtering their thoughts. The goal is to help individuals gain insight into their unconscious in an effort to see how those conflicts transfer to daily life. Psychodynamic therapy has often been criticized for the length of time needed to treat patients; it is often several years.

Humanistic

Humanistic psychologists believe that a patient's ailments stem from the way they are interpreting occurrences or situations in their life. As such, they believe that patients can choose to control their own actions and decisions. In this type of therapy, a patient's natural growth is promoted by therapists who enhance their awareness, expression, and acceptance of their feelings. Unlike psychodynamic therapy, humanistic therapists strive to promote an individual's insight into present situations, not childhood conflicts. Humanistic psychologists also emphasize the importance of acceptance in the therapist-patient relationship.

Behavioral

Behavioral therapists believe that maladaptive thoughts and behaviors are learned behaviors that can be changed by learning new adaptive behaviors. John Watson, Ivan Pavlov, and B.F. Skinner suggested the use of classical conditioning, operant conditioning and observational learning to change human behavior. The therapeutic relationship must be developed in order to be productive. Therapists must listen closely to the behaviors and thoughts that are to be targeted for change. The behavioral therapist tends to act as a teacher by assigning homework, offering home-based learning opportunities and helping the client take some type of defined action to handle the problem.

Behaviorists use various techniques to change behavior. These include systematic desensitization, modeling, positive reinforcement, extinction, aversion therapy, and punishment.

Cognitive

Cognitive therapy posits that negative feelings stem from how people think and feel about themselves and the world around them. Therefore, they try to change their client's maladaptive thought processes. For example, an individual may have a negative cognition such as "no one likes me." This leads to the behavior of avoiding people, and thus to a feeling of sadness. Clients are taught that these three constructs — cognition, behavior, feelings — are linked and that making a change in one often leads to changes in the other two. It is often easiest for the client to make a change in their behavior to influence how he or she feels and thinks.

Biological

Biological therapy most often involves the use of psychopharmacology to treat symptoms. That means that medication is given to the client to counteract the imbalances that may be occurring in his or her brain. However, biological therapy can also involve the use of more drastic treatments, such as electroconvulsive therapy, psychosurgery, and prefrontal lobotomy.

Stem cell-based therapy to regenerate neurons in the central nervous system

According to NIH, researchers have been investigating regenerative mechanisms of the central nervous system. Recently, stem cells (i.e., undifferentiated cells that resemble cells in a developing fetus) in the adult brain have been discovered to give rise to new neurons and neural support cells. This implies that some parts of the adult human brain can generate new neurons. They found that the new neurons arise from "neural stem cells" in the fetal, as well as the adult, brain.

Moreover, these researchers found that the neural stem cells could generate many different types of cells in the brain. This can include both neurons and oligodendrocytes and astrocytes (important neural-support cells). These findings have raised hopes that it may be possible to repair central nervous system damage by restoring lost functions through cell-replacement therapy.

Researchers are investigating two ways to make use of this discovery. One way is to grow differentiated cells in a laboratory dish, which can then be implanted into a patient, starting with undifferentiated neural cells. The idea is either to treat the cells in culture to nudge them toward the desired differentiated neuronal cell type before implantation, or to implant them directly and rely on signals inside the body to direct their maturation into the right kind of brain cell.

The second way relies on identifying growth hormones and other trophic factors that support a patient's own stem cells and endogenous repair mechanisms. This way the body is supported in coping with damage from disease or injury to itself.

Community and Preventative Approaches

Community approaches aim to screen and treat large populations for mental health disorders. In addition, they focus on providing psychoeducation regarding mental illness to community members. Preventative approaches to mental health are similar to yearly physical examinations. The goal is to prevent mental health problems from occurring. This can be done by helping people learn how to manage stress, increase social support and learn to recognize the symptoms of mental health disorders. Basically, an increase in coping skills can be effective in preventing mental health disorders. Community and preventative approaches are among the most cost-effective solutions to mental health issues.

Cultural and ethnic contexts influence the choice and acceptance of a treatment. For example, in the Latino culture, machismo is prevalent. As a result, if the male head of the household does not agree to seek treatment for a family member, it may be very difficult to convince other family members of the need for mental health treatment. Some cultures also find it very stigmatizing to seek mental health care. Factors such as high cost of treatment, distance and time may cause certain individuals to terminate treatment prematurely.

Modes of Therapy

Treatment can occur on an inpatient or outpatient basis. Inpatients are treated in a hospital or residential setting. They may either be admitted on a voluntary or involuntary basis. Admission occurs when symptoms are so severe that the patient is either a threat to themselves or others. Depending on the state rules and the patient's symptoms, an inpatient stay may range from a few days to several years. In most cases, psychotropic drugs are used to assist patients in achieving stability.

Outpatients are treated either with psychotherapy and/or medication while living in a community setting. They may visit a psychiatrist or psychologist, usually one to three times per week, depending on the level of severity. Group therapy may also be indicated for additional support.

Individual therapy occurs when a patient meets with only one therapist alone.

Group therapy is conducted with several unrelated patients. A leader of the group, or the therapist, encourages positive interactions among members of the group. Group themes can vary depending on the patients' problems, but the group is usually made up of people with similar problems. For example, alcoholism, depression, anxiety or personality disorders can be the theme of discussion. Group therapy enables therapists to gain insight into how clients interact with others. This modality also offers patients a support system and enables them to see that others share similar problems, thereby reducing their sense of isolation. Patients can also learn from one another and help each other boost their self-confidence.

Family and couples' therapy involves either one couple or members of the family. The family systems theory suggests that the identified patient (i.e., the patient who is displaying symptoms) is a reflection of problems in the family's functioning. The goal of family therapy is to create balance within the family.

Chapter 12

Social Psychology

In social situations, how people relate to one another is a topic of great interest among psychologists. In delving into it, they study social attitudes, influences, and phenomena. To undertake this task, competency in understanding how group and individual behavior is influenced is required. Particular attention on attribution theory, fundamental attribution error, and social cognition are expected. This gives perspectives on navigating the formation of attitudes and how they might be transformed. It is also important to recognize the power of stereotypes and how they affect attribution and prejudice development. The wide breadth of social influence, particularly conformity, compliance, obedience, and altruism, must also be considered.

Notes

How the Presence of Others Affects Individual Behavior

Social facilitation

Social facilitation refers to the tendency of individuals to perform better when in the presence of others. This phenomenon was identified in 1898 by Norman Triplett, who noticed that cyclists went faster when racing against one another than when racing alone against a clock. Many believe that social facilitation is caused by an arousal response based on apprehension about receiving negative evaluations by others.

Two types of social facilitation have been identified: co-action effects and audience effects. *Co-action effects* refer to social facilitation that occurs when individuals are all engaged in the same activity. Co-action effects have been observed in both humans and animals. Animals eating together tend to eat more than animals eating alone. Ants that work in view of one another have been found to work more than ants working independently.

Audience effects refer to social facilitation that occurs when an individual engages in a task and is observed by others who are not participating in the task. In experiments involving word output, the presence of an audience increased individuals' output but also increased the number of errors made. Research suggests that social facilitation via audience effects occurs when individuals engage in tasks that they have experience with; social inhibition occurs when individuals engage in a novel task under the same conditions.

Deindividuation

Deindividuation refers to the process of losing one's sense of self-awareness and self-restraint within a group. This often results in people engaging in behaviors in groups that they would not otherwise perform on their own. Deindividuation is closely linked with *diffusion of responsibility*. This phenomenon refers to individuals being less likely to take responsibility for their actions when others are present. Deindividuation can lead to a "mob mentality," resulting in riots and deviant behavior.

Philip Zimbardo studied deindividuation in his 1971 prison experiment at Stanford University. In this experiment, twenty-four men were randomly assigned either the role of a "guard" or a "prisoner." The guards were not given any instructions on how they should treat the prisoners. The experiment had to be cut short due to the guards' cruel treatment of the prisoners. Zimbardo believed that this behavior resulted from deindividuation of the guards.

Bystander effect

The *bystander effect* refers to the tendency of individuals to not help victims when in the presence of others. The term was popularized following the murder of Kitty Genovese in 1964. Many people saw Genovese being stabbed, but no one stepped in or called the police. Social psychologists who studied this murder determined that the onlookers saw others not helping and concluded that their personal help was not needed. Like deindividuation, the bystander effect is closely tied to diffusion of responsibility. People tend to believe that if there are others around, their help is not needed.

The bystander effect is the tendency of individuals to not help victims when in the presence of others. When onlookers see others not helping, they conclude that their help is not needed. The bystander effect is closely tied to diffusion of responsibility.

Further research into the bystander effect found that the more bystanders that are present, the less likely people are to help a victim. This may stem from individuals assuming that there are more qualified bystanders available to help, or that if help is needed someone else will step in.

Social loafing

Social loafing describes the loss of motivation that occurs when people exert less effort while performing a task in a group than when they work alone. It is believed that social loafing stems from individuals believing that their efforts will not matter to the group. Social loafing is more likely to occur in larger groups than in smaller ones; this tendency is referred to as the *Ringelmann effect*.

Social loafing refers to the loss of motivation when people performing a task in a group, as compared to working alone. It stems from individuals believing that their efforts will not matter to the group.

An early experiment on social loafing was conducted in 1913 by Maximilien Ringelmann when he was studying the relationship between performance effectiveness and group productivity. The experiments showed that individuals who pulled on a rope when in a group did not pull as hard as they did when they acted alone. Furthermore, Ringelmann discovered that the bigger the group, the more inefficient it becomes, which went against a common notion that group effort and teamwork results in increased effort by the group members and increased overall productivity.

Ringelmann concluded that groups fail to reach their full potential due to a variety of interpersonal processes, one of the main ones being loss of motivation (i.e., social loafing).

Peer pressure

Peer pressure refers to influence that is exerted on an individual in order to change the individual's behavior. Peer pressure is not necessarily negative, but it is often associated with misconduct in adolescence. Peer pressure has been found to contribute to the likelihood of substance abuse, unsafe sexual practices, and deviant behaviors. Research suggests that women, people from a collectivist culture, and people with low self-esteem are more susceptible to peer pressure.

The four possible responses to peer pressure are compliance, conversion, congruence, and non-conformity. *Compliance* occurs when an individual privately or publically disagrees with the group but goes along anyway. *Conversion* occurs when an individual changes their opinion to match the group's opinion. *Congruence* occurs when an individual's opinion already matches that of the group. *Non-conformity* occurs when individuals refuse to go along with the group.

Peer pressure is the influence exerted on an individual by their peers to change the individual's behavior. Peer pressure is not always negative, but it is often associated with misconduct in adolescence, such as substance abuse, unsafe sexual practices, and deviant behaviors.

Conformity

Conformity, or majority influence, refers to the changing of one's beliefs and behaviors in order to fit into a social group. Conformity is often adaptive; it allows individuals to benefit from the ideas and knowledge of others without exerting much energy.

In one of the first experiments examining conformity, Arthur Jenness asked individual participants to guess the number of beans in a bottle. The participants were then brought together into a group. Jenness found that the participants changed their answers to be closer to what other participants had guessed.

Researchers have identified six types of conformity. In *normative conformity*, individuals yield to group pressure out of fear of rejection. In *informational conformity*, individuals yield to group pressure due to their lack of knowledge and accept the views and behaviors of the group as their own. In *compliance*, individuals change their behavior to match the behavior of the group while disagreeing privately. In *internalization*, individuals publicly change their behavior and privately adopt the views of the group. In *ingratiational conformity*, individuals conform in order to gain acceptance from others. In *identification*, individuals conform to expectations stemming from a social role.

Conformity refers to the changing of one's beliefs and behaviors in order to fit into a social group.

Obedience

Obedience is a form of social influence involving compliance with someone else's authority. Obedience involves an order or demand from someone of a higher status, thus involving a hierarchy of power and prestige.

One of the most famous experiments concerning obedience is Stanley Milgram's shock experiment. In this experiment, participants were instructed to shock a person in another room in response to each wrong answer that they gave. The person in the other room was a confederate and was not actually being shocked. To Milgram's surprise, participants persisted in following instructions and continued to "shock" the person in the other room even when the person being "shocked" said they wanted it to stop. This experiment highlighted the powerful influence that authority figures can exert. The results of this experiment have been used to explain why ordinary people took part in the Holocaust, a concept which Milgram was fascinated by because much of his extended family were killed in the atrocities.

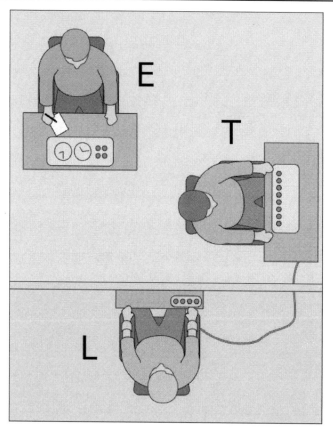

One of the most famous experiments concerning obedience is Stanley Milgram's shock experiment.

Group Decision-Making Processes

Group polarization

Group polarization refers to the phenomenon in which groups form more extreme opinions than those of the individuals within the group when they are alone. Individuals in a group will also advocate for riskier actions than they would advocate for when they are alone. The two theories that attempt to explain this phenomenon are the social comparison theory and informational influence theory.

According to the *social comparison theory*, individuals attempt to gain approval of their peers within a group by taking on the opinion most pervasive in the group but making it slightly more extreme. Social comparison theorists believe that this allows individuals to assert themselves as leaders of the group. According to the *informational influence theory*, individuals in a group become more convinced of their original position after hearing arguments in support of their position by others.

Groupthink

Groupthink was a term first coined by Irving Lester Janis, a Yale University psychologist. Groupthink refers to decision-making errors that result from homogenous groups making collective decisions. Janis identified eight symptoms of groupthink: an illusion of invulnerability, collective rationalization, belief in an inherent morality, stereotyped views of outgroups, pressure on dissenters, self-censorship, an illusion of unanimity and self-appointed "mindguards."

Groupthink occurs when groups are highly cohesive, isolated and under pressure to make a decision. This leads to failure of the group to consider alternative decisions. One famous example of groupthink involves the bombing of Pearl Harbor. American officers did not take action after warnings about the potential for a Japanese invasion due to their groupthink that the Japanese would never attack the United States.

Groupthink refers to decision-making errors that result from homogenous groups making collective decisions and occurs when groups are highly cohesive, isolated and under pressure to make a decision, leading to failure of the group to consider alternative decisions.

Normative and Non-Normative Behavior

Social norms

Social norms refer to behaviors, values, and beliefs that are deemed appropriate for a specific social group. These norms, though unwritten, establish expectations for the behavior of others. Social norms vary by social group and situation. Social norms can range from the religion of a group to how individuals in a group wear their hair. Typically, individuals who do not follow group norms suffer social consequences, such as rejection. Social norms influence the behavior of individuals within a social group through conformity. When an individual moves to a different social group, their behavior typically changes accordingly.

Social Control and Sanctions

Social control refers to the ways in which society influences human behavior. Social control is viewed as maintaining order and social norms. It is exerted by sanctions carried out by members of society.

Sanctions can be positive or negative to punish for undesired behavior and reinforce desired behavior. Negative sanctions follow when an individual has violated the group's social norms and can be informal (e.g., displays of shame, criticism, disapproval) or formal (e.g., fines, imprisonment). Positive sanctions are rewards for following the social norms of a group. Informal sanctions can cause the group's social values to become internalized in the individual, resulting in lasting behavioral change.

Folkways, mores, and taboos

Folkways, or customs, are social norms that are followed for the sake of tradition. Dressing in a culturally appropriate way is one example of a folkway. Violation of a folkway does not typically have lasting or serious consequences.

Mores are norms based on morality and ethics. People typically feel stronger about mores than they do about folkways. The belief that individuals should be clothed in public areas is one example of a commonly held more. Religious doctrines are also forms of mores. Violation of a more is more serious than a violation of a folkway and may result in informal (and in some case, formal) sanctions.

Taboos are strongly held social norms; their violation results in rejection and disgust. In most countries, cannibalism is considered taboo. Some taboos have formal sanctions against them.

Anomie

In sociology, *anomie* refers to the breakdown of social norms and ethical standards within a social group. In this state, common values are not understood, and new values have not yet developed. The term was popularized by Emile Durkheim in his book on the social influences of suicide. Durkheim viewed anomie as a mismatch of values and ideals within a society due to a rapid change that occurred. Major economic depressions are often the cause of anomie in societies. According to anomie theory, a lack of social norms and standards results in people feeling purposeless and worthless. Common reactions to anomie include delinquency, crime, and suicide.

Emile Durkheim, French psychologist

Socialization

Socialization refers to the process by which individuals acquire social norms and ideologies, enabling them to function within a society. Socialization is a lifelong process, but most researchers agree that the most important socialization occurs in childhood. *Primary socialization* refers to the socialization beginning at birth by caregivers. During primary socialization, children learn the values and attitudes held by their caregivers.

Agents of socialization

People become socialized through interaction with a variety of people and environments. The main agents of socialization are the family, the mass media, peers, and the workplace.

Family is typically the earliest unit of socialization for an individual. Parents, siblings, and extended family members provide basic needs and guidance to children. The family heavily influences the language, religion and social class of an individual.

Forms of *mass media* include television, movies, press and the internet. Mass media has been found to influence individuals' political views, as well as how they view women and people of color. Some theorists believe the depiction of violence in the mass media has an effect on violent behavior.

Research suggests that *peer groups* exert the most influence over a person's personality. Peer groups are social groups in which members of the same age influence each other. Exposure to peers allows individuals to decide what norms they will keep and reject.

The *workplace* also acts as an agent of socialization. The workplace environment and the employing organization as a whole have their own culture and sets of norms. The workplace is typically seen as an agent of mild *resocialization*, which is the learning of new norms when entering a new social group.

Deviance

Deviance refers to engagement in behaviors that violate social norms. These behaviors can be criminal or non-criminal. Alcoholism, for example, is a form of non-criminal deviance. Deviance is culturally bound because social norms vary by social group and culture. There are several theories, typically stemming from criminology and sociology, which seek to explain why individuals engage in deviant behaviors.

Perspectives on deviance

Differential association theory proposes that deviant behaviors are learned from an individual's environment, specifically intimate personal groups. According to this theory, deviant individuals have witnessed others acting in a deviant manner and, through exposure to their motives and attitudes, come to adopt those motives, attitudes, and behaviors themselves.

Labeling theory proposes that the attitudes and reactions of others to deviant acts, not the acts themselves, influence further engagement in deviant behaviors. According to this theory, behaviors are only deviant when society labels them as such. Labeling theorists are concerned with the negative effects of labeling individuals as "deviant," and believe that labels often create self-fulfilling prophecies.

According to *strain theory*, gaps between individuals' goals and the means that they have to achieve those goals leads individuals to engage in deviant behaviors. This social strain was originally viewed as resulting from the social structures in place within a society but has been expanded to include the individual difficulties experienced in a person's life.

Aspects of collective behavior

Collective behavior is a form of social behavior that typically opposes existing social norms. Collective behavior differs from group behavior because it is spontaneous and temporary. Two types of collective behavior have been identified: localized behaviors and dispersed behaviors. *Localized collective behavior* occurs when members are in a crowd or are close in proximity. *Dispersed collective behavior* occurs when members are not in close proximity but are still able to impact one another. The rise of social media use has increased the potential for dispersed collective behavior.

The three main types of collective behavior are fads, mass hysteria, and riots. *Fads* are behaviors that gain and lose popularity very quickly among a large number of people. *Mass hysteria* refers to fear reactions that are spread through rumors or incorrect information. In mass hysteria, people typically act in an irrational manner due to their unwarranted fear. Major storms, health scares, and terrorist acts often result in mass hysteria. *Riots* are large groups of people unified, for the moment, by their excited engagement in deviant behaviors. Riots are viewed as costly and damaging to society.

Riots occur when large groups of people unify for a short time to engagement in deviant behaviors. Riots are viewed as costly and damaging to society.

Attributing Behavior to Persons or Situations

Attributional processes

Attribution is the process by which individuals explain events. Specifically, attribution refers to the explanation of events through internal or external factors. People typically view events, often inaccurately, in terms of cause and effect relationships. The *fundamental attribution error* refers to people's tendency to view and explain the behavior of others through internal attributions while explaining their own behavior through external attributions. For example, an individual might believe that others are obese due to laziness or poor self-control while believing that their own obesity is a result of being poor. The first is an example of a *dispositional attribution*; obesity results from the person's disposition. The second attribution is an example of a *situational attribution*; obesity results from uncontrollable circumstances.

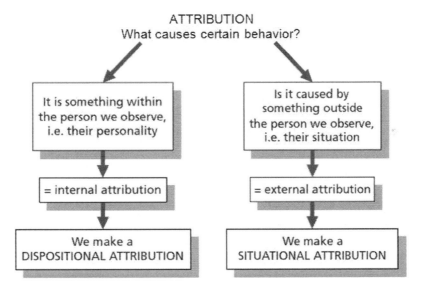

Research shows that culture plays an important role in how people form attributions. Most extensively studied are the differences in attribution by people from individualist cultures and collectivist cultures. People from individualistic cultures are more likely to engage in self-serving biases, meaning that they will attribute their successes to internal factors and their failures to external factors. People from collectivist cultures, however, are more likely to engage in *self-effacing* biases, meaning they are more likely to attribute their successes to external factors and their failures to internal factors.

How self-perceptions shape perceptions of others

The way individuals perceive themselves can shape how they perceive others. For example, people tend to assume that others share the same beliefs they do. However, differences tend to emerge and become apparent through interactions, rather than by being assumed.

People tend to also view others with respect to their goals. For example, someone looking for a dating relationship will view a person through this lens and pick up on different characteristics than they would if they were looking for a babysitter.

How perceptions of the environment shape perceptions of others

The way individuals perceive their environment influences how they perceive others. This idea is closely related to social norms; someone who swears when walking down the street will be perceived differently than someone who swears in an office setting, as a result of the social norms surrounding each setting.

In one experiment demonstrating the importance of the environment on the perception of others, eight healthy researchers were admitted into mental health hospitals after claiming to hear voices. Once admitted, the researchers acted normally and reported that the "voices" had stopped. Nevertheless, the staff at the mental health hospitals persisted in believing that all of the researchers had schizophrenia.

Processes Related to Stereotypes

Stereotypes

Stereotypes are widely held, oversimplified ideas about a group of people. Stereotypes allow people to simplify the world and make rapid judgments to situations. Stereotypes can be positive but are often negative. They lead to social categorization, or the formation of ingroups and outgroups, and can form the basis of prejudice.

Stereotypes neglect to acknowledge the individual variation that exists within groups of people. They are often exaggerated generalizations. Racial stereotypes typically favor the race of the stereotype holder and can be harmful to individuals in the group that is stereotyped (through stereotype threat and self-fulfilling prophecy).

Self-fulfilling prophecy

A *self-fulfilling prophecy* refers to a prediction that becomes true as a result of the prediction being made. For example, an employer who believes his employees will be lazy and incompetent will act in a way that will likely result in his employees acting in a lazy and incompetent manner. Self-fulfilling prophecies occur because behavior is influenced by beliefs and expectations.

Self-fulfilling prophecies have typically been studied in classroom settings and have been found to have more of an effect on students who are ethnic minorities. Negative stereotypes of ethnic and racial groups have been theorized to create self-fulfilling prophecies for individuals within these groups.

Stereotype threat

Stereotype threat refers to a situation in which an individual feels at risk of confirming a negative stereotype about their social group. Stereotype threat causes anxiety and decreases the performance of individuals within a stereotyped group across a variety of domains. Individuals do not need to believe the stereotypes surrounding their social group in order for stereotype threat to affect them.

Studies have shown that stereotype threat can result in decreased performance on the SAT by students from low-income families, due to the stereotype that low-income students are less intelligent than other groups.

Stereotype boost refers to situations in which people perform a task better following exposure to positive stereotypes about a social group that they belong to. Similarly, *stereotype lift* refers to the phenomenon where individuals perform better at a task after exposure to negative stereotypes about a different social group. Stereotype boost and stereotype lift are hypothesized to result from decreased anxiety, while stereotype threat is hypothesized to result from increased anxiety.

Prejudice and Bias

In sociology, *prejudice* refers to adverse judgments made about an individual or group of individuals that are not based on reason or actual experience. Prejudice often leads to *discrimination*, treating a person differently based on the group that they belong to. Prejudice typically stems from a difference in physical or cultural characteristics, which then become socially significant.

Processes that contribute to prejudice

Power, prestige, and class

When examining prejudice, power typically refers to economic and political power. Groups that hold this power are able to keep laws in place to benefit them and maintain their power, often putting those without economic or political power at a disadvantage.

The existence of social classes contributes to prejudice by creating a hierarchy in which some individuals are better off than others. The *just world phenomenon* also contributes to prejudice. This phenomenon refers to people's belief that when bad things happen to other people, they have usually done something to deserve it.

Prestige refers to the respect and admiration of an individual and is typically based on occupation. Those in prestigious positions may look down on those who are not, and prevent them from achieving a higher status.

The role of emotion in prejudice

Research suggests that emotions also play a role in prejudice and prejudicial behavior through the behaviors associated with them. Specifically, fear, disgust, anger, contempt, and jealousy have been indicated as contributing to prejudicial behavior. Note that these emotions do not cause prejudicial behavior per se but increase the likelihood that it will occur. For example, fear and disgust act as social emotions that contribute to prejudice by making individuals more likely to avoid members of a different group. Anger and contempt can contribute to an individual acting out against members of the outgroup. Jealousy can alert individuals to the benefits that others are receiving and cause them to demand similar benefits for themselves, sometimes acting in a resentful manner.

The role of cognition in prejudice

Research suggests that *cognitive appraisals* can lead to the aforementioned emotions of fear, disgust, contempt, anger, and jealousy. For example, individuals from one group may think that individuals in another group will take their power, resulting in fear and possibly discrimination against that group.

Individuals can learn to reappraise their cognitions in order to reduce their effects on prejudicial behavior. For example, those who believe that individuals from a minority group receive unfair treatment by having more scholarship opportunities might also consider the ways when those individuals have received unfair treatment based on their minority status.

Stereotypical beliefs about outgroup members can also contribute to prejudice and discrimination. For example, a teacher who holds the stereotype that Asians are good at math might overlook an Asian student who needs additional help with the subject.

Stigma

Stigma refers to the disapproval of a group based on perceived characteristics that distinguish them from other members of society. Note that the perception of these characteristics is what matters, not their actual existence. Erving Goffman, an American sociologist, interprets stigma as "spoiling" identity. According to Goffman, three types of stigma can be identified: character, physical and group association. *Character stigma* refers to the stigma that occurs from characteristics that become apparent through interaction with another person. *Physical stigma* results from visible deformities or an atypical appearance. Stigma from *group association* results from negative stereotypes surrounding the social group of the individual.

Ethnocentrism

Ethnocentrism refers to judging another culture based on the standards and values of one's own culture. Ethnocentrism typically implies the belief that one's culture is superior to other cultures. Ethnocentrism often occurs outside of one's conscious awareness.

Ethnocentrism vs. cultural relativism

Cultural relativism asserts that all cultures are of equal value; there is, therefore, no "superior culture." Cultural relativism also takes the position that whether something is "good" or "bad" is relative to its cultural context. Cultural relativists accept that people's perspectives are heavily influenced by their cultural background, acknowledging that it is impossible to study cultures from a neutral position.

Social Behavior

Social behavior broadly refers to behavior that occurs between members of the same species. Social behaviors include forms of communication and social actions designed to induce a response in another individual. Specific social behaviors include attraction, aggression, attachment, and altruism.

Attraction

Attraction is related to how much we like or dislike another person. Attraction often leads to friendships and romantic relationships. Well-studied factors that lead to interpersonal attraction between two people include: proximity, familiarity, similarity, physical attractiveness, and reinforcement. Attraction is influenced by physical proximity; long-distance relationships are often difficult to form. Similarly, people who are familiar with each other are more likely to experience interpersonal attraction, a concept known as the *propinquity effect,* or exposure effect.

Attraction is related to how much individuals like or dislike another person. Attraction often leads to friendships and romantic relationships.

Another factor that influences attraction is similarity. The more similar two people are in terms of attitudes, interests, personality, and communication skills, the more likely that they will be attracted to each other. Researchers have also found that individuals who are similar in terms of their physical attractiveness tend to form relationships; this is known as the *matching hypothesis*. Studies have also found that people will rate those who are physically attractive as having more desirable internal qualities, such as kindness and sociability.

Some social psychology theories point to reinforcement to explain attraction. According to these theories, individuals form and stay in relationships due to receiving reinforcement from being with the other person. One well-known reinforcement model of attraction is the *reinforcement-affect model of attraction*. This theory focuses on positive affect as a reinforcer for engaging in social behavior with another person. Studies have found that couples stay together longer if they are continuously exchanging resources and rewards.

Aggression

Aggression refers to social behaviors that are intended to hurt or damage another individual of the same species. Two subtypes of human aggression have been identified: controlled-instrumental aggression and reactive-impulsive aggression. *Controlled-instrumental aggression* refers to aggression that is used as a means to a goal. *Reactive-impulsive aggression*, also called hostile aggression, stems from anger and is intended to cause pain to another person.

Aggression refers to social behaviors that are intended to hurt or damage another individual of the same species. Physiologically, aggression is linked to higher levels of testosterone.

Physiologically, aggression is linked to higher levels of testosterone. One study found that testosterone levels are higher among prisoners convicted of violent crimes than those convicted of nonviolent crimes. There appears to be a bidirectional relationship between aggression and testosterone. While injecting animals with testosterone increases aggressive behaviors, behaving aggressively increases the levels of testosterone in an animal's blood.

Social learning has also been identified as an influential factor for whether or not an individual will engage in aggressive behaviors. In Bandura's famous bobo doll experiment, children were much more likely to play aggressively with a bobo doll if they had watched an adult do the same earlier. Some theorists argue that violence in the media can contribute to the perpetration of aggressive behaviors through the mechanism of social learning.

Though aggression is thought of typically as physical aggression, researchers have recently identified another form of aggression, known as relational aggression. *Relational aggression* causes harm to another person by damaging their relationships or social status. While physical aggression has been found to occur more in males than females, relationally aggressive behaviors seem to be carried out more by females. Relational aggression has typically been studied in adolescents and has been associated with bullying. Common forms of relational aggression are: excluding the individual, spreading malicious rumors about the individual and humiliating the individual in front of other people.

While physical aggression has been found to occur more in males than females, relationally aggressive behaviors seem to be carried out more by females. Relational aggression causes harm to another person by damaging their relationships or social status.

Alcohol has also been associated with engagement in aggressive behaviors. It is believed that the use of alcohol increases aggressive behaviors by lowering inhibition. Violence may also contribute to alcohol consumption; for example, violent individuals may be more likely to seek out social situations that encourage heavy drinking.

Attachment

Attachment is a deep emotional bond connecting two individuals. Work on attachment and the attachment theory was first conducted by John Bowlby and Mary Ainsworth. Bowlby theorized that individuals develop a particular attachment style based on their past interactions with their caregivers. Attachment styles develop based on an infant's ability to trust his or her caregivers. The main purpose of attachment is to develop and sustain a sense of security. These attachment styles are theorized to persist into adulthood and shape the romantic relationships that an individual will have. Elements leading to attachment in both infancy and adulthood include holding, touching, smiling, a desire to be comforted when distressed, anxiety following separation and happiness upon return.

The three attachment styles proposed by this theory are secure, anxious and avoidant. Anxious and avoidant styles are often grouped together and considered *insecure attachment*. According to attachment theory, having a sensitive, caring and responsible caregiver would lead to the formation of a *secure attachment*, a type of attachment where children show some distress when their caregiver leaves, but are able to eventually comfort themselves knowing that their caregiver will return. Upon the return of caregiver, a child exhibits joy. Secure attachment is considered the best form of attachment, as within this style infants feel comfortable with their caregivers, and later in life, it is easier for them to become emotionally close to others as adults. Similarly, adults who are securely attached are more likely to have positive views of their relationships.

Children with caregivers who are unpredictably responsive are believed to form an *anxious attachment* style. Infants with unpredictable caregivers are unable to predict whether or not their needs will be met at any given time. Adults who are anxiously attached tend to look for and find signs that their relationships are ending, often without basis. They tend to have low self-esteem and seek constant reassurance from their partners; they are often characterized as being needy or clingy.

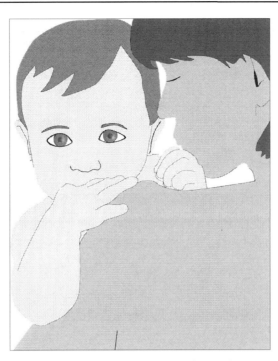

Secure attachment is considered the best form of attachment, as within this style infants feel comfortable with their caregivers, and later in life, it is easier for them to become emotionally close to others as adults.

Children with caregivers who are unresponsive to their needs and attempts at communication are believed to form an *avoidant attachment*. Children with an avoidant attachment tend to ignore their caregivers. Adults with an avoidant attachment style have trouble forming meaningful relationships and are uncomfortable with close emotional bonds. Research has found that adults who have an anxious or avoidant attachment style are more likely to identify their romantic partners as safe havens, or secure bases. Both insecure attachment styles are also associated with low self-esteem.

The avoidant attachment style can be further divided into dismissive-avoidant and fearful-avoidant. People with a *dismissive-avoidant* attachment style report that they are more comfortable without close emotional bonds and highly value their independence. Also, individuals with this attachment style tend to suppress their feelings. Individuals with a *fearful-avoidant* (or anxious-avoidant) attachment style differ from dismissive-avoidant individuals because they want emotionally close relationships but find it difficult to trust others enough to actually form them. This attachment style is characterized by a strong desire to be in a relationship, while at the same time wanting to protect oneself from getting hurt by the other person. Individuals with an anxious-avoidant attachment style can be mistrusting of their partners and uncomfortable expressing affection.

Altruism

Altruism refers to the engagement in behaviors out of concern for the well-being of others. Altruism is often referred to as selflessness. Altruism is characterized by costing the individual engaging in it while benefiting another party.

Social exchange theory posits that altruism only occurs when the benefits of engaging in an altruistic act outweigh the costs, suggesting that true altruism does not exist. The *empathy-altruism hypothesis* proposes that altruistic behaviors are evoked by the desire to help someone who is suffering, suggesting that altruism does exist. According to this hypothesis, altruistic behaviors stem from empathy.

The *reciprocity norm theory* suggests that people are most likely to engage in altruistic behaviors when others are likely to reciprocate. Research supporting this theory has also found that individuals who have received help from someone tend to become more helpful toward others.

Social support

Social support is the perception that one is cared for by others. Social support also refers to the social resources that an individual has available to them. These resources are typically categorized into four types: emotional, instrumental, informational and appraisal support. *Emotional* social support includes expressions of empathy and love. *Instrumental* social support refers to tangible aid; loaning money to a friend, for example, is a type of instrumental social support. *Informational* social support refers to advice giving. Individuals who provide social support in the form of *appraisal* help others reframe their thoughts about a given situation.

Social support has been found to be strongly linked with mental and physical health. Individuals with strong social support networks are at lower risks of depression and anxiety and experience less overall psychological distress than individuals with poor social support. Individuals with poor social support also show higher rates of post-traumatic stress disorder, panic disorder, social anxiety disorder, and suicidal ideation. Individuals with strong social support networks have been found to have lower mortality rates following a heart attack, and also have less cardiovascular diseases and better immune systems functioning than their low-social-support counterparts.

Social support has been found to be strongly linked with mental and physical health. Individuals with strong social support networks are at lower risks of depression and anxiety and experience less overall psychological distress than individuals with poor social support.

The two main theories that aim to explain the role of social support in health and stress management are the buffering hypothesis and the direct effects hypothesis. The *buffering hypothesis* proposes that individuals need social support only during stressful times since this type of social support protects the individual from the detrimental effects of stress. The *direct effects (or main effects) hypothesis* states that individuals with high levels of social support will have an overall better quality of life, regardless of stress levels.

Biological explanations of social behavior in animals

Social behavior is directed towards members of the same species. Social behaviors have evolved over time because they are often beneficial to those who engage in them. The study of social behaviors through a biological lens is known as sociobiology. Social behavior serves many purposes, including aiding in the acquisition of food, defense against predators, grooming and raising young animals.

Foraging behavior

Foraging is the process of searching for wild food resources within an animal's environment. Common foraging strategies used by animals include searching for food, stalking prey and lying in wait for prey. Different species typically engage in one of two types of foraging: solitary foraging or group foraging. *Solitary foraging* refers to foraging that is done by an animal alone. Solitary foraging reduces the competition between other foragers. *Group foraging* occurs when animals find and capture prey in the presence of other foragers. Group foraging does not imply that the animals present are aiding one another in the capture of prey. For example, birds being fed by humans usually feed in the presence of one another but do not help each other get the food. Group foraging allows animals to take down larger or more aggressive prey. Group foraging, however, can increase competition between group members when resources are scarce.

Foraging is crucial to survival; however, foraging comes with a cost to the animal in the form of lost energy. Thus, the goal of foraging is to gain a large amount of energy (in the form of food) while exerting as little energy as possible. Foraging success is then best measured by the net rate of energy gain for an animal. *Optimal foraging theory* uses a cost and benefit analysis to explain the foraging behaviors of animals. According to optimal foraging theory, animals who engage in optimal foraging behaviors are more likely to survive and reproduce than members of the same species who do not.

Foraging is made up of a series of behavioral acts culminating in the consumption of food. Foraging behaviors are believed to be primarily the result of genetics. The genes of honeybees have been found to be responsible for their foraging behaviors. In some species, however, learning is the main way through which animals acquire foraging behavior. Young primates, for example, learn to forage by watching older animals within the group and imitating their behavior.

Mating behavior and mate choice

Mate selection is an evolutionary process by which an organism's mate is chosen based on his or her traits. In most species of animals, males seek to reproduce with as many females as possible, while females are more selective about their mates. Females typically choose males who have adaptive traits, because females typically have a greater parental investment, and are often the *limiting sex*. Being selective increases the female's offspring's fitness. Males get to reproduce with females either by making themselves attractive or by defeating same-sex rivals.

Some theories of mating selection propose that organisms tend to select mates with dissimilar genetic structures. Supporting this idea, one experiment with humans found that females are more likely to rate the body odor of males who have dissimilar genes as more attractive than that of males who have similar genes. Similarly, mice have been found to use the urine odor of other mice in order to assess their genetic compatibility.

In most species of animals, males seek to reproduce with as many females as possible, while females are more selective about their mates. Being selective increases the female's offspring's fitness. Males get to reproduce with females either by making themselves attractive or by defeating rivals.

Applying game theory

Game theory is a branch of mathematics concerned with the study of strategic decision making. Game theory takes benefits, costs, and interactions between organisms into consideration. Game theory that has been applied to evolving organisms is called *evolutionary game theory*. Evolutionary game theory focuses on the interaction between multiple organisms, and how their behaviors impact each other.

Common animal conflicts, such as territory disputes, the defense of food sources and competition over potential mates, can be modeled after games. One classic example of the application of game theory to animal behavior is the *hawk-dove game*. In this model, two animals are capable of choosing from one of two strategies when in conflict. The animals can choose to fight the other animal (hawk) or can choose to back down (dove). Hawks will always receive either a benefit or a cost, while there is no cost and no reward for being a dove. Whether or not an organism should act as a dove or hawk depends on whether the benefit of winning a fight is greater than the cost of losing a fight.

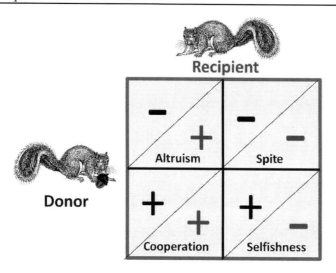

Example of evolutionary game theory

Altruistic behavior in animals can be understood as a form of the *prisoner's dilemma game*. In this game, two partners in crime are arrested and separated. They are given the chance to expose each other. If both remain silent, they will only serve one year in prison. If they both give each other up, they will both serve two years in prison. If one gives the other up and one remains silent, the one that betrayed his partner will be set free, and the one that remained silent will serve three years in prison. Reciprocal food exchange and other cooperative behaviors can be understood through this game.

Altruism

Altruism refers to the behavior of one organism that increases the chances of survival of another organism. Altruistic behaviors occur most frequently within parenting and familial relationships.

Reciprocal altruism theory suggests that individuals help others in the expectation of receiving a benefit at a later date. Male blackbirds often help defend the nests of other blackbirds living close to them. Researchers studying this phenomenon found that birds were more likely to help those who had helped them before, providing support for the reciprocal altruism theory. In humans, research has found that acting in an altruistic manner often has a long-term payoff.

Other theorists have proposed that inclusive fitness is responsible for organisms engaging in altruistic behaviors. Since relatives are likely to share genes, if individuals die as a result of coming to the aid of their relatives, their genes will still be passed on to later generations.

Inclusive fitness

The concept of *inclusive fitness* was popularized by William Hamilton, an English biologist. This theory states that each gene that an organism possesses can be passed down into the next generation either by that organism surviving and reproducing, or other organisms with similar genetic structure surviving and reproducing. This theory explains why some animals engage in altruistic behaviors. *Hamilton's rule* states that genes should increase in frequency when the genetic relatedness of the organism engaging in the altruistic behavior and the organism benefitting from it, multiplied by the benefit gained by the recipient of the altruistic act, is greater than the reproductive cost to the organism engaging in the altruistic behavior.

Kin selection is a more specific type of inclusive fitness. Since relatives share many of the same genes, organisms often act in altruistic ways to increase their relatives' chances of survival, even when it comes at a cost to them.

Notes

Discrimination

Individual vs. institutional discrimination

Discrimination is the prejudicial treatment of an individual or group of individuals based on their perceived membership in a certain group. Discrimination is always an action and can be based on a variety of factors. Common areas of discrimination include age, gender, weight, race, and sexual orientation, among others.

Discrimination can be divided into institutional and individual discrimination. *Institutional discrimination* occurs on a macro scale and refers to the mistreatment of individuals by organizations, including government organizations, public institutions, and corporations. More specifically, law enforcement, housing, employment, and educational institutions are often cited as contributing to discrimination. Many studies have found that African Americans are more likely to have their mortgage applications declined than white people, even when income and credit history is controlled for. Institutionalized discrimination stems from widely held and systemic stereotypical beliefs that may be conscious or unconscious. Institutional discrimination is believed to contribute heavily to the racial wealth gap.

Individual discrimination occurs at the micro, or individual level. Individual discrimination can stem from conscious or subconscious prejudice and bias. Individual discrimination can include derogatory remarks, excluding an individual from a group or limiting the opportunities of another individual solely based on their group membership.

The relationship between prejudice and discrimination

Prejudice refers to unjustified attitudes towards an individual or group of individuals based on their membership in a social group. Prejudice does not imply an action, but rather refers to holding certain beliefs. That is, someone may be prejudiced, but not act upon their prejudice. Prejudice typically precedes discrimination. However, prejudice is influenced by the prevailing social norms within a society; if someone's peer group is prejudiced against a certain group of individuals, it is likely that the person will also come to share the prejudicial beliefs of the group. Other social factors that have been identified as contributing to prejudice and discrimination include conflict theory, group closure, and an authoritarian personality.

According to *conflict theory*, privileged groups and individuals who wish to keep their power may act in specific ways to prevent members of minority groups from gaining power. Other theorists feel that *group closure* best explains prejudicial beliefs; according to this theory, group members tend to maintain clear boundaries between themselves and others. People with an *authoritarian personality* are rigid in their thinking and reject those whom they consider to be inferior.

Discrimination is the prejudicial treatment of an individual or group of individuals based on their perceived membership in a certain group. Individual discrimination can include derogatory remarks, excluding an individual from a group or limiting the opportunities of another individual solely based on their group membership.

How power, prestige, and class facilitate discrimination

Power typically refers to economic power or political power. Individuals with economic and political power are able to put individuals like themselves into political office. Similarly, these individuals will be more likely to protect the interests of the people who put them in office and the interests of those most similar to them. Minority groups are therefore often underrepresented in political positions. Individuals who hold economic power may be more likely to share this power with individuals similar to them through the hiring process. This can prevent individuals from minority groups from gaining economic power.

People may also discriminate against others based on their social class. Social classes form hierarchical structures, enabling individuals in higher social classes to discriminate against those who are beneath them in the social class hierarchy.

Prestige refers to how an individual is viewed within society. Prestige is typically based on occupation and income. Jobs associated with high prestige often go to members of the majority group, while jobs associated with low prestige tend to go to individuals belonging to a minority group.

Elements of Social Interaction

Status

Social status refers to one's position in the social hierarchy and standing within the community. Social status reflects a variety of factors, including occupation, income, moral values, and perceived influence.

Social mobility refers to an individual's movement either up or down the social hierarchy. Social status is therefore malleable. Social status can also be used as a synonym for prestige, which refers to an individual's reputation as perceived by their peers. Some theories of social mobility define social status by the social "tastes" that divide classes.

Ultimately, an individual's social status is determined by others. Usually, this is done by grouping the individual into a specific social class. This process is known as *social stratification* and occurs within all societies.

Types of status

Social status that has been inherited is known as *ascribed* social status. Individuals acquire an ascribed status when they are born into a particular social class. Individuals can also acquire an ascribed status by marrying into a particular social class. Individuals raised in different social classes tend to be treated differently by others and may have different opportunities available to them. Race, gender, religion, and age also affect an individual's ascribed status. The caste system in India is an example of stratification based on ascribed status. Each level of social status is known as a *caste*. Individuals are born into their caste and are generally unable to move up or down within the system.

Social status that has been earned through an individual's own achievements is known as *achieved* social status. Individuals can achieve a higher social status by getting a prestigious job or earning a substantial amount of money. Similarly, individuals can move into a lower social status by getting a job that is not at all prestigious or by losing all of their money. Overall, social status is the combination of ascribed status and achieved status.

Role

According to *role theory*, behavior is influenced by expectations held by individuals and other community members. *Roles* therefore act as social categories with a set of norms that guide the behavior of individuals. Role theory emphasizes the social context in which behaviors occur. Typical roles include gender roles, occupational roles, situation-specific roles, and familial roles. Therefore, people have a variety of roles that change depending on social context.

People have a variety of roles that change depending on social context, such as gender roles, occupational roles, situation-specific roles, and familial roles.

Role conflict and role strain

Role conflict occurs when an individual is expected to carry out roles that have differing norms and expectations associated with them. For example, the CEO of a large company might find that her expectations as a mother sometimes conflict with the expectations of her as the head of the company. Role conflict is also distressing, as one role must always be compromised for another.

Role strain occurs when an individual cannot meet all of the demands and expectations of a single role. For example, a mother may feel that she is unable to get her kids ready in the morning, help them with their homework, and make breakfast for them, all within an hour. In this example, role strain results from the inability to meet all of the expectations set by her role as a mother. Similar to role conflict, role strain is usually distressing for the individual experiencing it.

Role exit

Role exit refers to the process of disengaging from a particular role in order to establish a new role or roles. Individuals usually exit a role if role conflict or role strain becomes too distressing for them. Individuals can also undergo role exit as a result of changing circumstances, such as moving to a new city or having a child. Role exit is usually discussed in terms of leaving a place of employment.

Role exits can have a large impact on an individual's self-identity, particularly if the role that a person is leaving was one that they highly identified with. Role exiting is not always planned and can sometimes be distressing.

Helen Ebaugh identified four stages of the role exit process. In the first stage, the individual has doubts about and becomes frustrated with their current role. In the second stage, the individual searches for alternatives to their current role. In the third stage, the individual exits their current role. The final stage identified by Ebaugh involves the individual assuming a new role and a new identity for themselves.

Groups

Social groups are made up of two or more people who regularly interact with one another. Members of a social group share a sense of unity and consider themselves a part of the group. People can, and often do, belong to many different types of social groups at once. Social groups are a significant source of identity for many individuals but can also play a role in discrimination and prejudice against these individuals.

Primary and secondary groups

The concepts of primary and secondary groups were first proposed by sociologist Charles Cooley. A *primary group* is a small social group that is close-knit. These groups are called primary groups because they are a primary source of socialization. Primary social groups are long-lasting. Members of primary groups typically have intimate relationships with one another. Primary groups are important influencers of an individual's identity; the members within the group typically feel a strong connection between their personal identity and the group. Nuclear families, close friend groups and sports teams are all examples of primary social groups.

Examples of primary social groups are: nuclear families, close friend groups and sports teams. Primary groups are important influencers of an individual's identity; the members within the group typically feel a strong connection between their personal identity and the group.

Secondary groups are larger, temporary groups. The relationships within secondary groups are weaker than those in primary groups. The relationships in secondary groups are goal-oriented and typically less meaningful to the individuals within them. Secondary groups are often found at work and in school, but can also refer to groups exchanging commodities, such as doctor-patient dyads.

Secondary groups are often found at work and in school. Secondary groups are larger and have a temporary nature. The relationships within secondary groups are weaker than in primary groups; they are goal-oriented and less meaningful to the individuals within them.

Ingroup vs. outgroup

In sociology, *ingroups* are social groups that an individual feels he or she belongs to. *Outgroups* refer to social groups that an individual does not identify with. Individuals tend to hold positive beliefs about members of their own group while feeling contempt for those in an outgroup. This is referred to as *ingroup bias* or *outgroup derogation*. Ingroup bias often results when members of the ingroup help one another with resources and make a point of excluding those in the outgroup. This is referred to as *ingroup favoritism*.

Ingroup bias can sometimes result in intergroup aggression. *Intergroup aggression* refers to any behavior that is intended to harm an individual solely because the individual is a member of an outgroup. Intergroup aggression is more likely to occur when there is a perception of intergroup conflicts of interest. Common social groups that form ingroups and outgroups are divided by racial and ethnic characteristics, as well as by age, gender, and political affiliation.

People also tend to perceive outgroup members as more similar to one another than ingroup members. This is known as *the outgroup homogeneity effect*. This leads to the *cross-race effect*, or the ingroup advantage, which is the tendency of individuals to better recognize others of their own racial group.

Group size

Social groups are often categorized by their size. The size of a social group can influence the strength, organization, and attitudes of the group.

Dyads are social groups consisting of two people. Both members of a dyad must cooperate in order for the relationship between the two to continue. Thus, social interaction in a dyad is typically more intense than in triads or larger groups. Dyads can be formed through romantic relationships, family relationships, school relationships, and work relationships.

Triads are social groups made up of three individuals. Triads can still be intense but are usually less so than dyads; members of a triad do not have to be as engaged as members of a dyad because there are more people responsible for keeping the group integrated. Triads are also more stable than dyads because one member can act as a mediator between the other two members.

Dyads can be formed through romantic relationships, family relationships, school relationships, and work relationships. Both members of a dyad must cooperate in order for the relationship between the two to continue.

As group size increases beyond dyads and triads, intimacy between the members decreases. If a group becomes very large, leadership may be needed in order to make sure that the group functions properly. As a group increases in size, individual members can become more isolated; when this happens, the creation of smaller subgroups within the main group tends to take place.

Networks

Social networks are social structures made up of social relationships. Social networks are self-organizing, meaning that they are spontaneous and not directed by any agent. The individuals within a social network are often referred to as *social actors*. Social actors are the smallest units of analysis in a social setting.

The study of social networks is called *social network theory*. Within the social network theory, social relationships are discussed in terms of nodes and ties. *Nodes* are the individual social actors, and *ties* are the relationships between the actors. According to social network theory, an individual's ties with other actors are more important than their individual attributes.

In the social network theory, social relationships are discussed in terms of nodes (the individual social actors) and ties (the relationships between the actors). According to the theory, an individual's ties with other actors are more important than their individual attributes.

Two ideas that have emerged from the social network theory are six degrees of separation and the rule of 150. The *six degrees of separation theory* proposes that everyone is six or fewer individuals away from any other person in the world. Recent research of online social networking sites (e.g., Facebook and Twitter) has supported this idea. The *rule of 150* was proposed by anthropologist Robin Dunbar and states that humans can comfortably maintain no more than 150 stable relationships.

Organizations

Organizations are institutions that exist for a specific purpose or collective goal. Organizations are divided into three types: utilitarian, normative and coercive. In *utilitarian organizations*, individuals are paid for their membership in the organization. This payment is not necessarily monetary; students at a university, for example, are paid for their attendance with a diploma. Thus, the goal of the members within a utilitarian organization is to receive remuneration.

Normative organizations are characterized by a shared commitment to a moral goal. Membership in normative organizations is voluntary and members do not receive compensation. Normative organizations are also called *voluntary organizations*. Individuals join normative organizations to promote a social cause. Typically, all members of a normative organization have an equal opportunity to make decisions regarding the direction of the organization. Examples of normative organizations include: Mothers Against Drunk Driving (MADD), religious institutions and so on.

Coercive organizations are characterized by involuntary membership. Coercive organizations use force to keep members within the organization, and members are usually not allowed to leave the organization. Rules and regulations are very important within these organizations. Members within a coercive organization are expected to conform and to lose parts of their individual identity. Prison and the military are two examples of coercive organizations.

Organizations often do not fit neatly into one of these three categories but may be a combination of two or all three. For example, while the military is typically considered a coercive organization, members are compensated for their time and may have joined to fulfill a moral goal.

The military is an example of an organization that combines features of utilitarian, normative and coercive organization.

Formal organizations

Formal organizations are a type of secondary group. These organizations are typically large corporations. Formal organizations are deliberately constructed to have a shared goal. In corporations, this shared goal is usually to increase profits.

Formal organizations are characterized by three things. First is a deliberate division of labor and power. Within a hospital, for example, doctors, nurses, and technicians all have specific roles. The goals and responsibilities of the individuals within the organization are in line with the goals of the organization itself. Second, formal organizations have a written set of rules, policies, and procedures. Most places of employment have an employee handbook that serves this function. The third characteristic is a system for replacing members. Large organizations often have a human resources department dedicated to this function.

Bureaucracy

Bureaucracy refers to a way of organizing large amounts of people in both public and private sectors. When used in everyday speech, bureaucracies typically have a negative connotation. Traditionally, bureaucracies refer to a body of non-elected government officials. Three well-known models of bureaucracy are the Weberian model, the acquisitive model, and the monopolistic model. According to the *Weberian model*, bureaucracies are set up with a clear hierarchy, have an area of specialization, divide work into smaller tasks and have standard rules for operating.

According to the *acquisitive model*, bureaucracies are characterized by expansion and turf wars. *Turf wars* refer to disagreements over the duties and responsibilities of a particular agency. The *monopolistic model* takes a more negative view of bureaucracies than the first two and proposes that bureaucracies are characterized by monopoly and inefficiency.

Max Weber proposed a model for an ideal bureaucracy, dividing the defining characteristics of this ideal bureaucracy into six major principles. The first principle is defined as a hierarchical organization. In a hierarchical organization, subordinates follow the orders of their superiors. That is, each level of workers controls the level below it and is controlled by the level above it.

Max Weber, sociologist and political economist

The second characteristic is defined by the existence of rules and files. These rules are consistent across all levels of the bureaucracy. The third characteristic is defined by fixed areas of activity. People are organized by the type of work that they do. The fourth characteristic states that positions require specialized skills and training.

The fifth characteristic consists of task-oriented activities, meaning that a worker within a bureaucracy must always complete an assigned task rather than simply work for their allotted time. The final characteristic of an ideal bureaucracy states that individuals in management positions have exhaustive written rules that can be learned.

The *iron law of oligarchy* is a political theory that claims that rule by an elite is inevitable. This theory was first developed by Robert Michels, who believed that it is impossible to eliminate elite rule through a representative democracy. The common saying associated with this theory is "Who says organization, says oligarchy." Michels believed that any large organization must create a bureaucracy. In order for this bureaucracy to be effective, centralization of power must occur, resulting in a small elite who will hold all of the power.

Robert Michels, sociologist

McDonaldization was first proposed by George Ritzer in 1993. He referred to McDonaldization as the process in which a culture adopts the characteristics of a fast-food restaurant. The four components of McDonaldization emphasized by Ritzer are efficiency, calculability, predictability, and control.

Society and Social Culture

Culture is generally understood as the variety of codes used by a society. The sociology of culture examines culture and the codes that comprise it, as manifested in society. *Cultural sociology* focuses on aspects of a society's culture, such as ways of thinking, ways of acting and the material objects that collectively build a society's life.

Cultural sociology as a discipline was first explored in Weimar Germany in the 1920s and had a reemergence in the English-speaking world during the cultural upheaval of the 1960s. This decade saw the development of structuralist and postmodern approaches to social science, which largely incorporated aspects of cultural analysis and critical theory. Cultural sociology typically relies more heavily on words, artifacts, and symbols rather than the scientific method. The ascent of cultural sociology to a mainstream discipline has infused the concept of culture into strains of the "harder" sciences and, as a result, there are increasing amounts of quantitative cultural research as well.

Researchers who pioneered ethnographic strategies for analyzing and describing varied, global cultures were the originators of an intersection between sociology and anthropology that became cultural sociology. The essence of the organic, early development of the field can be seen in the methods (a tendency toward qualitative research), in the theories (many, varied critical approaches to sociology are central to current research communities) and in the substantive focus of the field. For instance, relationships between popular culture, political control, and social class were early and lasting concerns in the field.

Now, there are three main theoretical perspectives in the study of cultural sociology: functionalism, conflict theory, and symbolic interactionism. Social constructionism, social exchange theory, and feminist theory are also very important in cultural sociology and are considered main theoretical perspectives by some.

Microsociology vs. macrosociology

The study of *microsociology* is a subsection of sociology concerned with every day, small-scale human social interactions and agency. Microsociology, in many ways associated with phenomenology, rarely works with statistical or empirical observation. Microsociology relies more heavily on interpretative analysis. The methods of this interpretative analysis may include symbolic interactionism and ethnomethodology. The latter has opened up fields of academic subdivisions and studies, such as microlinguistical research.

Conversely, *macrosociology* examines populations and social systems on a broad scale, often drawing conclusions and analyzing research using necessarily high levels of theoretical abstraction. Macrosociology also examines individuals, families and other constituent aspects of larger society, but always with a focus on relationships to a larger social system. Large collectivities, such as the church or education system, are also studied in macrosociology.

Human populations are considered societies to the degree in which they are politically autonomous, and their members engage in a broad range of cooperative activities. To clarify, French people would be considered a society, but every person around the world who speaks French is not a member of that a society. Macrosociology deals with broad societal and global trends, including issues such as war, poverty, and environmental deprivation. Oftentimes, microsociology looks at certain outcomes of those trends, such as the role of women, the nature of the family and immigration.

Functionalism

Structural functionalism, or simply *functionalism*, is one of the main theoretical perspectives in sociology. It is a macrosociological analysis and focuses on the role of society in promoting solidarity, functionality, and stability as a complex system of working parts. Functionalism approaches society from a macro-level orientation, looking broadly at social structures and social functions that shape society as a whole. Elements within society that functionalism focuses on are norms, customs, traditions, and institutions. English sociologist Herbert Spencer (1820-1903), in a popular analogy, represented society as being similar to the human body. Constituent parts of society are "organs" that work toward the proper functioning of the "body" as a whole. Talcott Parsons (1927-1973), an American sociologist, distinguished structural functionalism as less of a specific school of thought, and more a particular stage in the methodological development of social science.

General diagram of structural functionalism

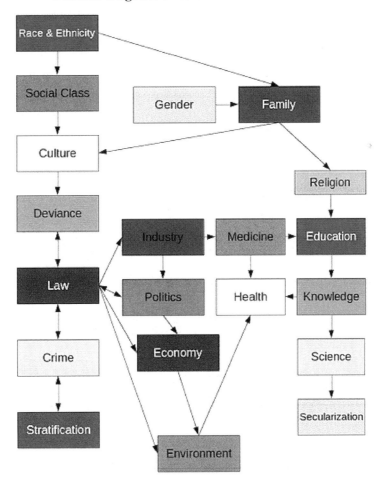

Herbert Spencer, English sociologist

Conflict theory

Another main perspective of sociology, and a macrosociological theory used to examine society, is *conflict theory*. Conflict theory provides emphasis on and deconstruction of the social, political or material inequality of a social group and critiques the broad socio-political system. It is a theory fundamentally at odds with structural functionalism and ideological conservativism.

Generally, conflict theory contrasts historically-dominant ideologies by specifically drawing attention to power differentials. Social conflict theory stresses the role of coercion and power in producing social order and operates on the notion that social order is established by the exerted dominance of those in the society with the greatest political, economic or social resources. Often an approach of conflict theory is to highlight ideological aspects inherent in traditional thought. There are varied types of conflict theories and many of them may be similar in certain aspects, but conflict theory cannot be considered a single, cohesive school of thought.

Karl Marx (1818-1883) was a revolutionary German philosopher and sociologist and is the father of social conflict theory. One of the tenets of Marxism asserts that the various institutions of society, such as the legal and political systems, serve to further the domination and interests of the ruling class. Western society, according to Marx, evolved through four principal epochs: primitive communism, ancient society, feudal society, and capitalist society. Prehistoric societies constituted classless societies with a primitive kind of communism. From that point in history, all societies have been divided into one of two major classes. In ancient societies there were masters and slaves, in feudal societies there were lords and serfs, and in capitalist societies there are capitalists and wage laborers.

Karl Marx, German philosopher and socialist

Max Weber (1864-1920), another German sociologist widely cited as one of the founders of sociology, disagreed slightly with Marx in his categorization of class in economic terms. Weber believed that classes develop in market economies in which individuals compete for economic gain. To Weber, a class or a group of individuals was determined by the similar position of those individuals in a market economy. Because of a common place in the market, these individuals received similar economic rewards. An individual's class could also be thought of as his or her market situation. The number of opportunities available to an individual was shared with other individuals in a similar class. Within each class, a corresponding economic position directly affected the likelihood of the individuals in that class obtaining the things which are deemed "desirable" by their society.

Symbolic interactionism

Symbolic interactionism, one of the main theoretical perspectives of sociology, is a particularly influential perspective in regards to microsociology and social psychology. Symbolic interactionism draws strongly on American pragmatism (an assertion that the meaning of any idea is the function of its practical outcome) and specifically on the work of American pragmatist philosopher George Herbert Mead (1863-1931). Mead's work was closely studied and interpreted by his student, Herbert Blumer (1900-1987), who actually coined the term "symbolic interactionism" and wrote what is still considered the clearest theoretical summary of symbolic interactionism. The interactionist perspective operates from the essential idea that people act toward objects based on the meaning they ascribe to those objects, which are first derived from social interaction and then modified through interpretation.

George Herbert Mead, American philosopher

Sociologists working in the tradition of social interactionism have conducted wide-ranging research using a variety of research methods. The most common are qualitative research methods, such as participant observation, in which an investigator attains entrance and acceptance into a foreign society to understand its internal structure. These type of research methods focus on studying aspects of social interaction and/or people's relationship with themselves.

In Blumer's summary, he established three core principles of interactionism: that people act toward things, including each other, on the basis of the meanings they have for them; that these meanings are derived through social interaction with others; and that these meanings are managed and transformed through an interpretive process that people use to make sense of and handle the objects that constitute their social worlds. David A. Snow, professor of Sociology at the University of California, in a continuation and broadening of Blumer's principles, developed a "framing perspective" which contains four basic orienting principles. Snow uses human agency, interactive determination, symbolization and emergence as the bases for discussing the study of social movements.

Human agency, the ability to act independently and of one's own free will, emphasizes the active, willful, goal-oriented character of humans. The emphasis on agency focuses observation on actions, events and moments in social life which require the assertion of agency. The concept of *interactive determination* means that individuals, society, and groups of people do not exist only in relation to each other, and therefore can be fully understood only in terms of their interactions. This specifies the necessary understanding of certain objects of analysis, whether they are identities, roles, practices or social movements.

Symbolization is when any aspect of an environment, including events, conditions, objects or people, becomes meaningful based upon a prescribed orientation. Symbolization is important to the extent that human behavior is contingent upon what this prescribed orientation symbolizes or means to an individual, group or society. *Emergence* deals with the processual, routinized and habitual side of social life. It does not purely look at the organization of societies, but at the meaning behind various practices and the feelings of individuals engaged in the practices. Within this principle is space to discuss shifts and developments in functioning social systems, and the possibility of new forms of social existence and organization.

Social constructionism

Social constructionism is a sociological perspective operating on the premise that ideas about the world are constructed in coordination with other human beings. In other words, an individual's perception of aspects of his or her environment does not develop significance or meaning separately within the individual; an individual's perception is developed in contingency with other humans. This theory is based on the assumptions that humans process experiences by creating a perception of the social world and how it functions, and that language is the most essential system through which humans construct reality. It also approaches social constructs as the cumulative, organic and amorphous result of countless human choices, rather than strict codes designated by human reason. Social constructionism can be viewed as at odds with *essentialism*, which sees phenomena (cultural occurrences) in terms of inherent, timeless essences, or truths, independent of human reason.

An important focus of social constructionism is to decipher the ways in which individuals and groups participate in the construction of their perceived social reality. Analysis of this involves looking at the ways social phenomena and behaviors are created, accepted, routinized and made into customs by humans. The social construction of reality is an ongoing, dynamic process that is (and must be) reproduced by people acting on their unique, individual interpretations and knowledge of it. Societies and the individuals that comprise them must constantly maintain and re-affirm perceived social constructs in order for them to persist because social constructs do not inherently exist in nature. This process of participation allows for the possibility of change. The answers to the questions what are human rights and who deserves them, as well as other questions, shape the reality of a social construct and have evolved immensely over time due to a change in human perception and resulting social phenomena.

Social exchange theory and rational choice theory

Social exchange theory was pioneered by sociologist George Homas in 1961 and posits that human relationships are formed and broken by use of a subjective cost-benefit analysis and the comparison of alternatives. This theory draws on economic principles employed in the business world and assumptions which are founded in rational choice theory and structuralism. Development of social stability between two parties engaged in a mutually beneficial relationship forms the basis of social exchange theory.

During the 1960s and 1970s, other researchers Peter Blau, James Coleman, and Karen Cook expanded Homas' original framework and developed it into a more formal modern model of *rational choice*, which over the years became increasingly mathematical. The basic premise of rational choice theory is that aggregate social behavior is the result of the behavior of individual actors, each of whom is making their individual decisions.

Rational choice theory assumes that an individual has preferences among the available choices, which allows them to state which is preferable to them. The concept of rationality used in the theory is different from the common usage of the word "rational," which typically means "sensible," "predictable" or "thoughtful." Rational choice theory uses a narrower definition of rationality, whereby at its most basic level, behavior is considered rational if it is goal-oriented, reflective (evaluative) and consistent (across time and situations). In this meaning, rational behavior is different from random, impulsive, conditioned or adopted by blind imitation.

Elements of culture

Culture, an integral component of being human, is a set of general codes followed by a specific group of people which were developed through history. "A culture" refers to the set of customs, traditions, and values of a society or community, such as an ethnic group or nation. *Multiculturalism* can be defined as the peaceful and mutually respectful coexistence between two or more different cultures within the same area. Specific practices or customs of a subgroup, subculture or counterculture of a society may also be referred to as culture. *Cultural relativism* is an important ideology and analysis of culture. It asserts that cultures are unable to be held to any objective evaluation system because any evaluation is necessarily situated within the value system of the evaluating culture and is therefore inherently subjective.

Culture is composed of numerous elements which can be divided into the general categories of: material, expression, human behavior, beliefs, and values. The material encompasses food preparation and shelter, as well as architecture and technologies. Expression can be the art, writing, dance or music of a culture. Human behavior accounts for specific practices of a culture, such as language, kinship, gender norms, and marriage. Beliefs and values stem from principles of social organization (including political organization and social institutions), written and oral history, literature, mythology, and philosophy.

A hierarchical perspective of culture, focusing on the degree to which sophistication in the area of the arts, sciences, education or manners has been achieved, has been employed on larger scales, distinguishing civilizations from less complex societies. It has also been applied to class-based distinctions between the high, elite culture of the upper class, and the low or popular culture of the lower or middle class. Hierarchical culture is associated with mass culture, or mass-produced and mediated consumer culture, which has become extremely prevalent in the twentieth century.

The physical evidence of a culture, such as objects and architecture, make up *material culture*. The interdisciplinary study of relationships between people and their things is called material culture studies. This field focuses on aspects including the making, history, preservation and interpretation of objects. Material culture encompasses anything from buildings to toothbrushes to jewelry.

Symbolic culture is the culmination of learned and transmitted behavioral traditions that emerge and habituate generationally and are based on belief and value systems situated entirely in the symbolic realm. Symbolic culture can include concepts such as good and evil, religion and mythology, and constructs of a purely social nature—like promises or sporting events. The ability of symbolic culture to exist is based on collective belief in its existence. As a domain of objective facts, symbolic culture only exists as long as those subscribing to the culture maintain belief in those facts. Symbolic culture interacts frequently with *semiotics*, or the mediation of human culture through signs and concepts.

Culture lag refers to the phenomena of a society's culture taking time to catch up with the society's technological advances and other social changes. It also addresses, through theory and explanations of these occurrences, the social problems and conflicts that tend to arise in a society when progress and social practices are moving at different speeds.

American sociologist William F. Ogburn (1886-1959) coined the term "culture lag." He focused his reasoning on material and non-material aspects of culture and concluded that this period of conflict occurs in a society when the non-material culture is struggling to adapt to material changes or advances. The idea of technological determinism_resonates with the concept of culture lag in the sense that both assume technology affects the broader society.

Culture lag does not necessarily label technology as the major causative element of societal conflict but examines a society's adjustment to new technologies.

Ogburn designated the differences between material and non-material. He believed that while material culture tends to evolve and change rapidly, voluminously and exponentially, non-material culture usually resists changes and likes to remain fixed. Culture lag manifests itself in many ways and is prevalent in most modern societies.

Culture shock is the disorientation an individual may feel when exposed to an unfamiliar location, way of living or social situation. This happens frequently to people visiting foreign countries and can also occur upon immigration. The way culture shock occurs can be described in at least four distinct phases: honeymoon, frustration, adjustment, and mastery. Common problems an individual may need to grapple with during (or which contribute to) culture shock include: information overload, language barrier, generation gap, technology gap, skill interdependence, formulation dependency, homesickness (cultural), infinite regress (homesickness), boredom (job dependency) and response ability (cultural skill set). There is no true solution for culture shock; it can happen to any individual experiencing a new culture.

During *cultural assimilation*, one group's culture transforms to resemble the culture of a different group. A person can go through the process of assimilation individually or in a group, such as immigrants or a native population dominated by a different population. Assimilation may occur quickly or happen gradually. Only when there is no distinguishing between a new and an original member of the society, it can be said that full assimilation has occurred. There is much controversy over whether it is positive or negative for a minority culture to assimilate into a dominant culture.

Within sociology, *multiculturalism* is the view that cultural differences should be accepted, promoted and even encouraged. Multiculturalism speaks to an idea of multicultural coexistence in which multiple cultures can live together peacefully in a single society without assimilating. Multiculturalism has been described as a "melting pot," a "salad bowl" and a "cultural mosaic" and the idea of multiculturalism has a few different interpretations. Multiculturalism can advocate for cultures to retain aspects of their native culture, and that a loss of diverse culture is detrimental and undesirable. It can take the form of promoting equal rights and representation for various cultures in a society and promoting policies which maintain cultural diversity. Multiculturalism, interested in retaining the distinctiveness of multiple cultures, is often at odds with proponents of social integration and cultural assimilation.

Two different, seemingly incompatible, government strategies for policy-making in regards to multiculturalism have developed. One is intent on interaction and communication between different cultures and promotes interculturalism. The second strategy is focused on intercultural competition which can result from diversity and cultural uniqueness. Cultural isolation can maintain the individuality of a nation or area's local culture, and also adds to global cultural diversity. A commonality of many of the policies following the second approach is that they do not present any specific ethnic, religious or cultural community values as central.

Evolution and human culture

Evolution is a successive change of biological populations' heritable traits. Processes of evolution have created a diversity of species, individual organisms, and molecules. The early twentieth century saw the integration of classical genetics with Darwin's theory of evolution by natural selection.

The discipline of *sociocultural evolutionism* formed to address a need for formal social theorizing and research along scientific lines. This study was undertaken with the assumption that if organisms could develop over time according to discernible, deterministic laws, then it seemed reasonable that societies could as well. Human society was compared to a biological organism and concepts like variation, natural selection and inheritance were introduced, from a sociological perspective, as factors resulting in the progress of societies. The stages through which human societies progress are usually numbered as three – savagery, barbarism, and civilization – but sometimes many more were developed.

Today, most social scientists have adopted a general systems approach, examining cultures as emergent systems and as constituent parts of a whole social environment, which can also include political and economic relations among cultures. More simplistically, humanistic notions of progressive evolution leave little room in discourse and research for more modern, complex cultural evolution theories. These humanistic approaches prefer to focus on historical contingencies, contacts with other cultures and the operation of cultural symbol systems.

Cultural transmission, oftentimes called cultural learning, is how the population of a society primarily learns and relays information. The way young people are socialized by their cultures greatly affects their learning style. Unlike a child's physical traits, a person does not attain all of his or her experiences and knowledge from his or her parents. The process of a child understanding his or her culture is called *enculturation*, and the skills and knowledge that children learn from this process are more than they would ever pick up alone.

Humans, as opposed to other species, are dependent on caretakers for a relatively long time once they are born before they are ready to take care of themselves, which also allows time for an understanding of culture to form. The basis of cultural learning allows people to create, remember, understand and deal with ideas, and understand and apply systems of symbolic meaning. Cultural learning is reliant on the ability to communicate or imitate the behavior of others and create new responses to the environment based on processed knowledge. Successful communication between people of other cultures is called *intercultural competence*.

Diffusion, in its basic definition, means the spreading of something from a point of high concentration to a point of low concentration. From a sociological perspective, culture is being diffused (or elements of which a culture is composed are being spread) to places where those elements did not previously exist. This can include the spread of ideas, religions, technologies, languages or fashions, and can occur between individuals within a single culture or between individuals in different cultures. Diffusion is largely seen as positive. For example, new and different ideas of agriculture and technologies have spread from nation to nation, ultimately allowing for higher levels of productivity and efficiency.

Demographic Structure of Society

Demography is the statistical study of various indicators to capture and report the evolving composition of human populations. Demographers gather and report various statistics, such as the number of deaths and births, to describe how the structures of societies change over the course of time and space. Demographers may choose to sample entire societies or smaller sections of a society. For example, if the question of interest focuses on a specific indicator, such as the level of education of people in a society, a demographer may choose to sample only a subsection of the population (i.e., adults) or the entire population.

Every ten years, the United States Census Bureau attempts to gather a wide array of demographics about every person living in the United States. This data offers demographers the most complete picture of the contemporary composition of U.S. society, including indicators such as race, age, education level, and gender.

Demographers use two main methods to collect data: direct and indirect methods. Direct methods of data collection include: birth certificate registries, death certificates, marriage and divorce registries, and censuses. Indirect methods provide an alternate way to collect data when direct methods are not possible, such as in developing countries where registries are lacking or when polling an entire population is not feasible (e.g., too expensive, lack of access to the entire population). One indirect method used in Africa, where it is hard to poll every person due to the heavily rural areas and the lack of regularly-updated registries, involves asking participants how many of their sisters are alive or dead. This data is then used to estimate population birth and death ratios for that society.

It is imperative to gather statistics on the people who comprise a society and how a society's composition may change over time in order to form an understanding of social interactions and other important aspects of societies. Generally, the main categories of demographics studied include age, gender, race and ethnicity, immigration status and sexual orientation in the society or one of its subgroups.

Age

Age is an important indicator within society and can be divided into qualitative categories, such as young and old, or it can be categorized by the number of years since a person was born. Regardless of how the data is categorized, the age spread of a population is important in making policy-level decisions, such as which age groups need the most resources.

An example of this is the high number of "baby boomers" in the United States, who represent a large portion of America's aging population, and are beginning to retire. They are placing more strain on medical and government resources than previous generations. The "baby boomers" were the highest earning generation and their decisions have a large impact on economic factors. The Baby Boomers generation controls more than fifty percent of consumer spending in the United States, and they purchase over three-quarters of prescription drugs sold in the United States.

Aging and the life course

Aging is much more than simply becoming older. Aging over the life course combines biological and sociological processes through which a person develops and matures.

Populations are increasing worldwide, which means more people are aging than ever before. People are also living longer than ever before, which poses both challenges and benefits to society. Because more people are living well into old age, healthcare systems, social security systems, and pension plans are experiencing increased strain. For example, more elderly patients are being diagnosed with dementia and Alzheimer's disease. This has led to an increased demand for long-term care facilities able to handle the unique challenges that people with these diseases face. Pension plans and social security systems were never designed to last as long as people are now living.

While there are certainly a number of economic and healthcare challenges associated with an aging population, society as a whole benefits in certain ways from the growing population of elderly people. The elderly contribute wisdom and life experience to benefit their families and communities. In fact, recent statistics suggest that more elderly people than ever are now helping raise their grandchildren. They are actively involved in families and help out with domestic responsibilities. Many retirees also contribute to society by obtaining part-time jobs. Social gerontology, which is a subfield of gerontology, examines the social aspect of aging and asserts that aging is more than just a physical and biological process.

Age cohorts

Generally, demographers look at aging through generations or age cohorts. *Age cohorts* refer to a group of individuals who have lived through similar experiences in the same time period. Most age cohorts are determined by year of birth and are constructed based on defining historical events or changes in the social structure that occurred during their lives. An age cohort implies that all the members of a cohort have aged similarly to each other and distinctly from a different age cohort. Typically, cross-sectional research studies are used to examine behavior and attitude differences among age cohorts. This research draws from both qualitative and quantitative studies, including field interviews, survey data, oral histories, and other methods.

Common age cohorts within the United States include the Greatest Generation (children born between 1901-1924), the Silent Generation (children born between 1925-1942), the Baby Boomers (children born between the mid-1940s and the early 1960s), Generation X (children born from the early 1960s to the early 1980s), Millennials or

Generation Y (children born from the early 1980s to the early 2000s) and Generation Z (children born around the mid-2000s to present day).

For example, the Greatest Generation in their adult years lived through the Great Depression and WWII. The Baby Boomers cohort shared important historical milestones, such as the Cuban Missile Crisis, the Vietnam War and the first person to walk on the Moon, which are seen as culturally significant events.

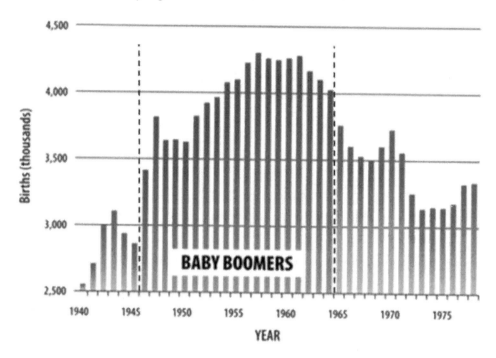

Other countries have developed their own cohorts, often based on important political or human rights changes (e.g., Armenia's Independence Generation). However, cohorts may also form based on other criteria or events, such as survivors of the terrorist attack on the World Trade Center or tsunami survivors.

Social significance of aging

Aging is not simply the biological process through which human beings mature. Human beings are social creatures, and it is important to consider how humans understand and maneuver through the process of aging, as well as what age means on a level of social significance. For example, some cultures tend to value youth more than age. These cultures tend to put older family members in nursing or assisted living homes and often consider the elderly a burden, both socially and economically. In other cultures, aging is valued and respected; the elderly are often the heads of their families and revered for their knowledge. They are taken into a family's home and cared for as they become more dependent with age.

The actual labels of "young" and "old" are socially constructed and have various meanings in different societies. For example, countries like Japan and the United States have long life expectancies. It is common for Japanese and American people to live well into their eighties or beyond, which necessitates a different view of the roles of "the young" and "the old," compared to a society with a relatively low life expectancy.

Ageism refers to the discrimination or stereotyping of a person based on his or her age. While examples of ageism directed toward the elderly are abundant, it is important to remember that ageism can happen to anyone throughout his or her lifespan. Ageism shows itself when children's ideas are considered worthless or in the treatment of recent graduates struggling to be taken seriously as they enter the workforce.

Gender

Gender is a socially constructed identity based on a person's biological sex traits. In other words, gender is the ideas a society holds about the appropriate behavior, actions, and roles of a particular sex. Cultural norms and values play a large part in shaping gender roles and gender differences. Societal ideas of gender are imposed upon every individual, regardless of the personal gender identity of the individual.

Most people are *cisgender*, meaning they ultimately identify with the gender identity of the sex assignment they received at birth. In other words, a baby who is pronounced a girl at birth and grows up to ultimately identify as female, is cisgender. Though most societies in the world adhere to a strict gender binary (classification of sex and gender into two distinct, disconnected and opposite forms, feminine and masculine), many people, though born with a certain biological makeup (either female or male), identify somewhere between female and male when it comes to gender.

The language of gender identity is constantly developing and changing and can mean different things to different individuals. Beyond the established genders of male and female, an individual can also identify as genderqueer. *Genderqueer* is a broad term for people who do not identify with binary gender categories, but who may identify as bi-gender (identifying with two genders), genderless (not identifying with any gender) or genderfluid (gender identity varies with time, fluctuating back and forth between genders). A *genderbender* is one who purposefully "bends" expected or normalized gender roles. This can be undertaken as a form of personal expression, awareness raising or political activism. Some people who are genderqueer undergo physical alterations to better fit their gender expression.

Transgender refers to individuals who feel there is a discrepancy between their sexual assignment and their gender identity. Transgender is an umbrella term and can refer to people in any stage of transition from one sex to another, and genderqueer individuals. The easiest and clearest way to know how a person gender-identifies and what that means is to ask them.

Gender and sexuality are not necessarily linked; a person of any gender identity may have any sexual orientation.

There is often confusion between sex and gender, but it is important to remember that sex and gender do not mean the same thing. Gender is a socially constructed identity, while sex is a biological assignment. The *sex* of an individual refers to their biological chromosomes; an individual with an XY genotype is a male, an XX genotype a female. Gender, on the other hand, encompasses psychological, behavioral and cultural traits rather than relying solely on biological traits.

Transgender people, individuals who believe there is a mismatch between their biological sex and their gender identity, will often undergo sexual reassignment surgery. Sexual reassignment surgery is only one part of an individual's entire transition process, which may include physical, social, psychological and legal processes and therapies.

Hermaphroditism, or intersex, is the uncommon condition of an individual being born with both male and female anatomy.

The social construction of gender

The prescribed roles, attitudes and beliefs of each gender are largely influenced by the culture of a society. Society influences how individuals speak, dress, think and act based on whether they are male or female. *Gender schemas* are cognitive frameworks which are deeply rooted both within society and individuals, and they influence what differentiates males and females. However, these gender schemas are reinforced by socializing agents, such as teachers, peers, caregivers, media and religion. Society exerts pressure for children to conform to gender roles and research indicates that parents have different expectations and treatment for boys and girls.

Gender stereotypes continue to be problematic in today's society. Stereotypes occur when generalizations are made about a certain gender or the role of a certain gender. These are most often inaccurate but can have either a positive or negative connotation. One female stereotype is that a woman should marry and start a family. Furthermore, a woman should feel compelled to put others' needs before her own, while still finding time to pay attention to her husband. This contradicts the reality of many working mothers who have to balance a career, a family and self-care. A stereotypical male role is that a man should be the protector and provide financial stability for his family. In addition to this, he should control his emotions and be dominant in both career and personal relationships.

Race and ethnicity

Race refers to the shared genetic or physical characteristics that differentiate members of one group from members of other racial groups. More simply, race refers to observable differences in phenotypes between groups of individuals. These may be biological differences but can also be differences based on skin color or other visible characteristics. It is important to note that race is socially constructed, and some researchers feel that race is an invalid classification type given the high genetic variations that exist within racial groups.

Ethnicity is the classification of human beings based on their common religious, cultural, ancestral or linguistic features. While it can appear that race and ethnicity are highly related, there is one important difference to keep in mind. People can choose whether or not to reveal their ethnic identity, but racial identity is visible to everyone and cannot be masked. A person may look Caucasian based on observable physical characteristics, but their ethnic identity may be African or Latino.

The social construction of race

The social constructions of race have changed over time but, presently, designated categories of race in the United States include African Americans, Native Americans, Hispanic Americans (or Latinos), Asian Americans and European Americans. Racial minorities in the United States are people of any race that do not hold the majority of power (meaning non-European Whites).

Numerous historical, geographical, socioeconomic and political factors contribute to and determine the racial makeup of a society and the interaction between racial majorities and minorities. Social constructions have led to various levels of discrimination and prejudice against certain racial groups throughout history.

A person's race has implications for a number of reasons. Generally, research suggests that racial minorities receive fewer resources than members of racial majorities do. This leads to differences in intelligence, education, employment and standards of living. Minorities also tend to have decreased access to health care, preventative care, and health insurance.

Racialization

The concept of racialization was an important stepping-stone to ideas of race being a process and a social construction. *Racialization* refers to the process of giving a new ethnic or racial identity to a social practice, a group of people or a relationship that did not heretofore identify itself as such. In other words, racialization is the process by which certain people are singled out for unique (often negative or detrimental) treatment because of their real or imagined characteristics.

Historically, the term "race" referred to a group of people who shared similar aspects of culture, such as language or religion, e.g., the French race or the Jewish race. However, racialization morphed the meaning of race. Racialization is a process and a perspective which turns a biological characteristic into a determination of status. Racialized objects and subjects are people who are observed to display the somatic and cultural characteristics that others attribute to the idea of race. Since race is socially constructed, these characteristics may not even be real. For example, Tiger Woods is Chinese, Thai, White, Native American and African American, but because he looks black, his treatment is based on society's racial connotations of "blackness." Racialization often targets the common physical characteristics of a group of people, resulting in a racialized group continuing itself biologically.

Tiger Woods is Chinese, Thai, White, Native American and African American, but because he looks black, his treatment is based on society's racial connotations of "blackness."

The process of racialization is typically initiated by a group exerting dominance over a particular population of people. The ascribed racial or ethnic identity by the dominant group is used as a means of continued dominance over the dominated population. This can be seen in early European colonists' failure to recognize African culture, instead ascribing to Africans a culture based on their own ignorant prejudices and agenda of exploitation. Racialization is commonly associated with colonialism, imperialism and the occupation of one country by another.

Some argue that the process of racialization includes, over time, a racialized population which slowly begins to accept and then embody and embrace ascribed attributes and identity. Ultimately, the racialized population becomes a self-proclaimed and self-ascribed race or ethnicity.

Please, leave your Customer Review on Amazon

Notes

Appendix

Important Figures in Psychology and Sociology (in alphabetical order)

Alfred Adler (1870-1937) was an Austrian physician and psychotherapist. He is known for his work establishing the school of individual psychology and for his development of personality theory. He is most famous for his attentive focus on the inferiority complex, an element in personality development that can have an isolating effect on individuals. Adler collaborated with Sigmund Freud to promote the emergent psychoanalytic movement.

Alfred Adler (1870-1937) Austrian psychiatrist. Ann Ronan Picture Library. 2015. Wikimedia Commons

Mary Ainsworth (1913-1999) was an American-Canadian developmental psychologist best known for her work on *attachment theory*. Ainsworth devised a particular situation design in order to study the emotional attachment of infants to their caregivers. In these experiments, a child would play in a room for twenty-four minutes while caregivers and strangers entered and exited. Children were observed based on the amount of exploration they engaged in, their reactions to the departure and return of their caregiver and their level of stranger anxiety. The children were then categorized based on their behaviors as either secure, anxious-avoidant or anxious-ambivalent/resistant.

Elliot Aronson (born 1932) is an American psychologist best known for his "jigsaw classroom." In this classroom model, classmates are divided into small groups to work together on a task. These groups are made up of a mix of race and academic ability. The use of this model was found to have positive effects on performance, self-esteem and racial attitudes.

Elliot Aronson. Vera Aronson. 2001. Wikimedia Commons

Solomon Asch (1907-1996) was a Polish-American social psychologist. Asch was a member of the Berlin School of experimental psychology and emphasized the role of the "whole" in his research. Asch is best known for his research on conformity. He found that group pressure can change the opinions of individuals.

Albert Bandura (born 1925) is a Canadian-American psychologist. He is best known for his development of the *social learning theory* and his Bobo doll experiment. In this experiment, Bandura found that children who had seen an adult playing aggressively with a Bobo doll were more likely to play aggressively with the same doll than children who had seen an adult playing gently with the doll.

Albert Bandura Psychologist. Albert Bandura. 2005. Wikimedia Commons

Philip Bard (1898-1977) was an American physiologist especially known for his work on the nervous system. He was particularly interested in the role of the vestibular system in emotions. In conjunction with Walter Cannon, Bard developed the *Cannon-Bard theory* of emotions, which posits that emotions occur independently of physiological changes.

Diana Baumrind (born 1927) is an American clinical and developmental psychologist. She is best known for her work categorizing parenting styles as authoritarian, permissive and authoritative and for her criticism of the use of deception in psychological research.

Aaron T. Beck (born 1921) is an American professor of psychiatry and is regarded as the founder of cognitive therapy. Additionally, Beck has developed theories relevant to clinical depression and created anxiety self-reporting measures.

Aaron T. Beck. Bealivefr. 2015. Wikimedia Commons

Alfred Binet (1857-1911) was a French psychologist and the inventor of the first intelligence test (the Binet-Simon Scale). His intelligence test was intended to gauge children's cognitive abilities at a variety of ages by use of thirty tasks of increasing difficulty. The number of tasks completed corresponded to the child's mental age.

Alfred Binet. United States National Library of Medicine. 2006.

Pierre Bourdieu (1930-2002) was a French sociologist, anthropologist, and philosopher best known for his work on social stratification based on aesthetic taste. Bourdieu theorized that social classes pass down their aesthetic preferences to the younger generation. These passed-down aesthetic dispositions are intended to distance oneself from other social groups.

John Bowlby (1907-1990) was a British psychologist, psychiatrist, and psychoanalyst best known for his theories on child development and his work on *attachment theory*. Bowlby's work emphasized the importance of having a warm and nurturing mother or mother-figure. He theorized that children and infants who had the presence of a warm caregiver in their lives would develop a secure base from which to learn and explore. He called this a secure attachment.

Paul Broca (1824-1880) was a French anatomist, anthropologist, physician and surgeon who is best known for his work on the frontal lobe of the human brain. His research revealed that the presence of lesions on the cortex of patients typically corresponds to the diagnosis of aphasia, providing the first anatomical proof of the brain's localization of function.

Paul Broca, scientist. Materialscientist. 2012. Wikimedia Commons

Mary Whiton Calkins (1863-1930) was an American philosopher and psychologist best known for her research on dream content and its general reproduction of persons, places, and events recently experienced by sense perception but rarely directly connected with what is deemed of utmost importance in the dreamer's real life. Calkins is also known for her work on memory and self-psychology, where she advocated practicing introspection on one's own mental experience.

Walter Bradford Cannon (1871-1945) was an American physiologist. He is best known for his identification of the fight-or-flight response, a term first coined to describe animals' physical responses to threats and subsequently expanded to include humans. Additionally, he developed the *Cannon-Bard theory* with Philip Bard.

Walter Bradford Cannon. Wellcome Library. 2014.

Noam Chomsky (born 1928) is an American cognitive scientist, historian, linguist, logician, (analytical) philosopher, political activist, and social critic. Academically, he is most renowned for contributing to the development of a new cognitivistic framework for the study of language and the mind, creating the *universal grammar theory*, the *generative grammar theory*, the Chomsky hierarchy, and the minimalist program.

Noam Chomsky. Andrew Rusk. 2011. Flickr

Charles Cooley (1864-1929) was an American sociologist best known for his concepts of the looking-glass self, primary groups, and secondary groups. According to his *looking-glass self theory*, individuals' identities are formed through the perceptions that others have of them. Cooley identified primary groups as closely-knit groups that exert a great amount of influence on their members, with secondary groups being less influential and more temporary social groups.

Charles Cooley. *Michiganensian*. 1902. Wikimedia Commons

Paul Costa, Jr. (born 1949) is an American psychologist renowned for his development of the Revised NEO Personality Inventory, a 240-item measure of a subject's extraversion, agreeableness, conscientiousness, neuroticism, and openness to experience (collectively called the Five-Factor Model). He also worked with Robert McCrae in developing six subordinate dimensions for the Five-Factor Model's partitions.

Paul Costa, Jr. United States Department of Health and Human Services, National Institutes of Health. 2011.

William E. Cross, Jr. (born 1940) is a psychologist and theorist best known for his work on ethnic and racial identity development, particularly his *Nigrescence model*. This model proposes that there are five stages that people of color go through when forming their racial identity. The first stage is the pre-encounter stage. In this stage, the individual is unaware of their race. The second stage is the encounter stage, when individuals have some experience which makes them conscious of their race. In the third stage, the immersion/emersion stage, individuals strongly identify with their racial identity and disparage the dominant racial culture. The fourth stage is the internalization stage. Individuals at this stage stop disparaging the dominant racial culture and are able to establish relationships with whites. The fifth stage is the Internalization/Commitment stage. Individuals in this stage advocate for the concerns of people of color as a whole and have a positive sense of their racial identity.

Charles Darwin (1809-1882) was an English naturalist and geologist. By far, Darwin is best known for his *theory of evolution* that claims all of Earth's species (both current and extinct) are connected, over the eons of time, to shared common ancestors. The branching pattern of species from these common ancestors is the product of natural selection, the condition by which only the most successful members of a species are the ones to survive and successfully reproduce, passing on their particular phenotype.

Charles Darwin. J. Cameron. 2007. Wikimedia Commons

Dorothea Lynde Dix (1802-1887) was an American activist for the more humane treatment of and provision for poverty-stricken mentally ill people. The United States' first mental asylums were created in large part due to her vigorous and successful lobbying of state legislatures and the Congress, actions inspired by her abhorrence to the situation of the mentally ill being largely confined in cruel, makeshift fashion around the country.

Dorothea Lynde Dix. Samuel Broadbent. c. 1850-1855.
The Boston Athenaeum

Hermann Ebbinghaus (1850-1909) was a German psychologist whose renowned pioneering study of memory led to the discovery of the forgetting curve, the learning curve and the spacing effect. He is also credited with having drafted and standardized the first research report.

Hermann Ebbinghaus. Marie Müller. 1850.
Wissenschaftliche Sammlungen an der Humboldt-Universität zu Berlin

Albert Ellis (1913-2007) was an American psychologist famous for his 1955 development of Rational Emotive Behavior Therapy (REBT) and being a guiding force in psychotherapy's cognitive revolutionary paradigm shift. This shift emphasized the importance of enabling people to understand their self-defeating behavior through rational analysis and cognitive reconstruction processes, allowing the development of more rational constructs to supersede core irrational beliefs.

Erik Erikson (1902-1994) is a German-American psychologist best known for his theory of psychosocial development (called *Erikson's stages of psychosocial development*). He proposed eight stages of development that are each characterized by a psychological conflict between the one favorable and the one unfavorable. These stages are: trust vs. mistrust, autonomy vs. shame and doubt, initiative vs. guilt, industry vs. inferiority, identity vs. role confusion, intimacy vs. isolation, generativity vs. stagnation and ego integrity vs. despair.

Erik Erikson. Q4233718. 2007. Wikimedia Commons

Gustav Fechner (1801-1887) was a German philosopher, physicist, and experimental psychologist best known for the inspiration he gave to subsequent scientists and philosophers through his pioneering in experimental psychology and founding of psychophysics. Gustav is also renowned for noticing that psychological sensations and the physical intensity of a stimulus had a non-linear relationship. Collaborating with Ernst Heinrich Weber, this became the *Weber-Fechner law*.

Gustav Fechner. Gdr. 2005. Wikimedia Commons

Leon Festinger (1919-1989) was an American social psychologist best known for his work on cognitive dissonance and *social comparison theory*. *Social comparison theory* proposes that humans evaluate their opinions by comparing them to the opinions of others who are close to them. Festinger's research on cognitive dissonance revealed that inconsistency is psychologically uncomfortable, and individuals experiencing dissonance will try to reduce it by changing their behaviors or their cognitions.

Sigmund Freud (1856-1939) was an Austrian neurologist best known for his theories of psychoanalysis and psychosexual development. Freud proposed a libido (or energy) exists that drives human behavior. Freud argued that libido is expressed in different ways depending on what stage of psychosexual development a person is in. The five stages that Freud identified are the oral, anal, phallic, latent and genital stages. Freud is also known for his conceptualization and articulation of important mental functions of the mind as comprising the entities the id, the ego, and the superego.

Sigmund Freud. Max Halberstadt. c. 1921. Bonham's

Francis Galton (1822-1911) was an English anthropologist, explorer, geneticist, geographer, inventor, meteorologist, polymath, progressive, proto-geneticist, psychologist, psychometrician, sociologist, and statistician. Academically, he is most renowned for his articulation of the concept of statistical correlation and advocating the practice of recognizing the regression toward the mean phenomenon. This statistical phenomenon holds that if a first measurement's variable is extreme, a second measurement will place it closer to the average. Reciprocally, if the second measurement's variable is extreme, then its first measurement will tend to have been closer to the average.

Francis Galton. *The Life, Letters, and Labors of Francis Galton*, (Ed.) Karl Pearson. n.d.

John Garcia (1917-2012) was an American cartoonist, educator, farmer and psychologist who is most famous for his taste aversion research. His work discovered the survival mechanism nature of conditioned taste aversion, a response intended to allow an organism to recognize poisonous foods to be avoided.

Howard Gardner (born 1943) is an American developmental psychologist acclaimed for his development of the *theory of multiple intelligences*, a claim that intelligence can be differentiated into nine categories: musical-rhythmic and harmonic, visual-spatial, verbal-linguistic, logical-mathematical, bodily-kinesthetic, interpersonal, intrapersonal, naturalistic and existential.

Good work team. Ehirsh. 2010. Wikimedia Commons

Michael Gazzaniga (born 1939) is an American psychologist and cognitive neuroscience researcher. He is academically praised for his pioneering studies on how split-brained patients' learning and understanding abilities work. Specifically, he studied how people with this rare condition function, with attention given to which halves of the brain control each bodily function.

Carol Gilligan (born 1936) is an American ethicist, feminist and psychologist academically praised for her endeavors on ethical communities and ethical relationships. She is also renowned for her collaboration with—and male-oriented criticism of—Lawrence Kohlberg and his stages of moral development. Gilligan advocates the recognition of two moral voices: the masculine (logical and individualistic) and the feminine (interpersonal and utilitarian).

Erving Goffman (1922-1982) was an American sociologist best known for his study of symbolic interaction and dramaturgical analysis. According to Goffman, individuals vary their behavior based on the "stage" that they are currently on. The front stage refers to the parts of our lives where we engage with people and put on a performance tailored for them. The back stage refers to times where we do not need to put on a show and can act like ourselves. Goffman is also known for his work on impression management. According to Goffman, individuals engage in strategies to portray themselves to others in a certain way.

G. Stanley Hall (1846-1924) was an American psychologist and educator who focused his research on childhood development and evolutionary theory. Pertaining to childhood development, Hall was particularly interested in discovering the effects adolescence has on education (educational psychology) and the inheritance of behavior. Hall is also famous for his interest in debunking psychic mediums by conducting rigorous psychological and physiological tests.

Photograph of Jung, Freud, and others at a 1909 celebration of the founding of Clark University. Library of Congress. 2014. Wikimedia Commons

Harry Harlow (1905-1981) was an American psychologist best known for his research on caregiving and compassion in social and cognitive development. To these ends, Harlow conducted maternal-separation, dependency needs and social isolation experiments on rhesus monkeys. While his research was successful in developing critical insights, its sometimes cruel methodology greatly helped to inspire the emergent animal liberation movement.

Picture of Harry Harlow. Achen1997. 2016. Wikimedia Commons

Ernest Hilgard (1904-2011) was an American psychologist famous for his hypnosis research. Specifically, Hilgard was interested in the applicability of hypnosis as a means to control pain. Controversially, Hilgard promoted the idea of the "hidden observer," an entity that was a part of human consciousness created during hypnosis that allows the subject to be aware of physical sensation but not to feel or experience them directly (such as suffering).

David Hubel (1926-2013) was a Canadian neurophysiologist renowned for his research on the structure and function of the visual cortex (the portion of the brain responsible for processing visual information). In one famous experiment, Hubel and his collaborator Torsten Wiesel surgically inserted a microelectrode into the primary visual cortex of a domestic cat. By projecting light and dark patterns on a screen in front of the animal and observing neuron behavior, they observed how simple stimulus features provide the basis for visual systems to construct complex representation.

William James (1842-1910) was an American psychologist and philosopher. He is known as the "father of American psychology" due to his contributions to the field. James is considered the founder of functional psychology, a school of psychology that considers thoughts and behaviors as adaptive responses to the environment.

William James. Houghton Library at Harvard University. 1903. Wikimedia Commons

Mary Cover Jones (1897-1987) was an American psychologist who helped pioneer behavior therapy. She is praised most for her development of desensitization techniques to cure phobias, notably through her "Little Peter" experiment, in which she treated a three-year-old boy's irrational fear of white rabbits (and any objects approximating one in appearance) by direct conditioning (through which a positive stimulus comes to be associated with the phobia trigger).

Carl Jung (1875-1961) was a Swiss psychiatrist, psychotherapist and founder of analytical psychology (of which the central concept is individuation, the process of integrating opposites while maintaining their relative autonomy). He is most famous for his creation of the psychological concepts of the archetype, the collective unconscious, the complex, extraversion, and introversion. His work has had a broad, lasting effect on anthropology, archaeology, literature, philosophy, psychiatry and religious studies.

Carl Gustav Jung. Ortmuseum Zollikon. 2014. Wikimedia Commons

Alfred Kinsey (1894-1956) was an American biologist, entomologist, sexologist and zoologist best known for his contributions to the field of sexology. In 1948, he published *The Kinsey Reports on Human Sexual Behavior*, two widely cited volumes discussing sexual behaviors of males and females. Kinsey primarily gathered information through face-to-face interviews, believing they were the best way to get accurate data. Kinsey was also known for his heterosexual/homosexual rating scale, a measure still sometimes used today.

Alfred Charles Kinsey. Proyecto Historiador 2. 2012. Wikimedia Commons

Lawrence Kohlberg (1927-1987) was an American psychologist and educator. Kohlberg is best known for his theory on the stages of moral development. According to Kohlberg, individuals go through six stages of moral development. In the earlier stages, individuals engage in moral behaviors by doing what will allow them to avoid punishment and receive benefits. As they develop to later stages, individuals come to engage in moral behavior out of a sense of universal ethical principles.

Wolfgang Köhler (1887-1967) was a German-American psychologist critical in the creation of Gestalt psychology (a holistic attitude toward psychology). His professional perspective is best embodied by his famous quote, "The whole is different from the sum of its parts" (often misquoted as "greater than"). He also played an important role in the study of problem solving and introspection.

Carl Lange (1834-1900) was a Danish physician known for his work *On Emotions: A Psycho-Physiological Study*, which gave rise to the *James-Lange theory* of emotion. This theory states that emotions result from physiological responses to stimuli.

Elizabeth Loftus (born 1944) is an American cognitive psychologist and human memory expert best known for her work pertaining to the misinformation effect, eyewitness memory, false memories, and recovered memories.

Konrad Lorenz (1903-1989) was an Austrian ethologist, ornithologist, and zoologist. He is most renowned for his study of birds, which revealed the imprinting principle (newborn nidifugous birds' bonding with the first moving object they see), and the innate releasing mechanism (a fixed action pattern, by which certain external sensory stimuli result in instinctive behavior). Collaborating with biologist Nikolaas Tinbergen, Lorenz helped establish ethology as a biology sub-discipline.

Lorenz and Tinbergen. Max Planck Gesellschaft. 1978.
Wikimedia Commons

Abraham Maslow (1908-1970) was an American psychologist best known for his "hierarchy of needs" diagram. This model states that individuals need to fulfill their most pressing needs before moving on to higher needs. According to Maslow, physiological needs are the most pressing, followed by safety, belonging, esteem and self-actualization. Maslow was also known for his work on "peak experiences." He believed that individuals who were self-actualized would experience profound moments of happiness, termed *peak experiences.*

Abraham Maslow. El Tao de la Transhumanidad. 2015.
Wikimedia Commons

Robert R. McCrae (born 1949) is an American personality psychologist best known for his cross-age and cross-culture study of the stability of personality. Further, he is known for his belief that personality is a biological trait and his findings that upon reaching the age of about 30, the Five-Factor Theory's traits of agreeableness and conscientiousness tend to increase, while neuroticism and extroversion decline. A curve shape peaking near age 19 marks openness to experience.

Robert R. McCrae. National Institute on Aging,
National Institutes of Health. 2012.

Robert Michels (1876-1936) was a German sociologist and student of Max Weber. He is best known for his theories contributing to *elite theory*. Michels also proposed the *iron law of oligarchy*, which is a political theory that claims rule by an elite is inevitable within any democratic organization.

Robert Michels. Ssociólogos. 2014. Wikimedia Commons

Stanley Milgram (1933-1984) was an American social psychologist and educator best known for his research on obedience. In his most famous experiment, volunteer participants were told that they were partaking in a study examining memory. Participants were instructed to administer shocks to Milgram's confederate (pretending to be a volunteer) whenever he answered a question incorrectly. In reality, the confederate was not actually receiving shocks. Whenever participants seemed disturbed by the confederate's acted "pain" and wanted to stop, the experimenter provided strong verbal encouragement to continue. Milgram found that 65% of participants would persist until they had administered the final "shock" of 450 volts. Milgram concluded that most individuals lack the cognitive resources to resist authority.

George Armitage Miller (1920-2012) was an American psychologist best remembered as one of the founding minds behind both psycholinguistics and cognitive science. Miller is also praised for discoveries he made on the limitations of human short-term memory capacity.

Ivan Pavlov (1849-1936) was a Russian physiologist renowned for his breakthrough discoveries in classical conditioning experiments. His most famous experiment, inspired by his observation that dogs salivate before food is actually given to them, was the first to demonstrate the relationship between environmental stimuli and behavioral responses. Out of this experiment came the well-known term "conditioned reflex," which describes an innate response resulting from a previously neutral stimulus that, over time, had been inculcated (where before a potent stimulus was required).

Ivan Pavlov. U.S. National Library of Medicine.

Jean Piaget (1896-1980) was a Swiss psychologist best known for his theory of cognitive development. He proposed that the cognitive processes of children are inherently different from those of adults. Piaget identified four stages of cognitive development: a sensorimotor stage, a preoperational stage, a concrete operational stage, and a formal operational stage.

Jean Piaget in Ann Arbor. *Michiganensian.* 1968.
Wikimedia Commons

Robert A. Rescorla (born 1940) is an American psychologist whose research is primarily concerned with cognitive processes and classical conditioning. He is most famous for his involvement in developing the Rescorla-Wagner Model of conditioning with Allan R. Wagner, which has deeply enriched knowledge of learning processes.

George Ritzer (born 1940) is an American sociologist best known for the concept of "McDonaldization." Ritzer identified four dimensions of McDonald's that have influenced society as a whole. These characteristics are efficiency, calculability, predictability, and control.

George Ritzer. 2010. Wikimedia Commons

Carl Rogers (1902-1987) was an American psychologist. He is still praised for his helping to establish the humanistic approach and psychotherapy research. Roger called his own particular brand of humanistic approach person-centered therapy (PCT), the goal of which is to provide clients with the opportunity to develop a sense of self, allowing them to become perceptive about how their attitudes, feelings, and behavior are being negatively affected.

Julian Rotter (1916-2014) was an American psychologist. Rotter is best known for his development of the locus of control concept and for his contributions to *social learning* *theory*. Rotter identified that some individuals believe that they can control events affecting them and some believe that these events are caused by outside forces. Individuals who believe they can control events affecting them are said to have an internal locus of control, while those who don't believe they have any control over them are said to have an external locus of control.

Stanley Schachter (1922-1997) was an American psychologist best known for his development of the Schachter-Singer model of emotion. This model proposes that emotions result from physiological arousal and the cognitive label assigned to this reaction.

Hans Selye (1907-1982) was an Austrian-Canadian endocrinologist best known for his work on stress and the stress response. He coined the term "stress" and found that the physical stress response was the same for both positive and negative stressors.

Muzafer Sherif (1906-1988) was a Turkish-American psychologist who is considered the founder of modern social psychology. He is best known for his *social judgment theory* and *realistic conflict theory*. *Social judgment theory* is a framework for studying human judgment that proposes that people weigh new ideas at the instant of perception. They then categorize these ideas based on their preferred position, the alternatives and their level of ego-involvement with the issue. *Realistic conflict theory* proposes that deviance and hostility result from competition over resources.

B. F. Skinner (1904-1990) was an American behaviorist, inventor, social philosopher, psychologist and innovator of radical behaviorism. Skinner is best remembered for his developing the principle of reinforcement and the term operant conditioning.

B. F. Skinner. Msanders nti. 2015. Wikimedia Commons

Charles Spearman (1863-1945) was an English statistician and psychologist known for his critical role in promoting factor analysis, developing Spearman's rank correlation coefficient and researching models for human intelligence.

Exposition universelle e 1900 - portraits des commissaires généraux-Charles Spearman. Bibliothèque nationale de France. 2012. Wikimedia Commons

Roger Wolcott Sperry (1913-1994) was an American neurobiologist and neuropsychologist. His early research focused on efforts to rearrange motor and sensory nerves. Later and more famously, he conducted research with Torsten Wiesel on the split-brain condition. This led to the discovery that cutting the corpus callosum portion of the brain prevents epileptic seizures from migrating from one hemisphere of the brain to the other.

Robert Sternberg (born 1949) is an American psychologist and psychometrician. He is praised for developing the *triarchic theory of intelligence* and his work related to creativity, love and hate, thinking styles and wisdom. Sternberg's triarchic theory of intelligence consists of a componential, experiential and practical part.

Lewis Terman (1877-1956) was an American psychologist noted for his early commitment to the emergent educational psychology movement. He is best known for work concerning the study of intelligence, including his Stanford-Binet IQ test revision and development of the Genetic Studies of Genius.

Lewis Madison Terman. ADR Formacion. 2016. Wikimedia Commons

Edward Thorndike (1874-1949) was an American psychologist renowned for his development of connectionism and inspiring educational psychology's emergence. He is also noted for his influence on reinforcement theory and behavior analysis through his law of effect principle. This principle holds that "responses that produce a satisfying effect in a particular situation become more likely to occur again in that situation, and responses that produce a discomforting effect become less likely to occur again in that situation."

Edward Lee Thorndike. *Popular Science*, 80. 1912.
Wikimedia Commons

Edward C. Tolman (1886-1959) was an American behaviorist and psychologist renowned for founding purposive behaviorism and promoting Hugh Blodgett's concept of latent learning. His best-remembered experiments involved rats placed in mazes to prove that animals are capable of learning facts that they subsequently can use in a flexible manner (as opposed to simply acquiring automatic responses triggered by environmental stimuli).

E.C. Tolman portrait. Frostburg State University. 2011.
Wikimedia Commons

Lev Vygotsky (1896-1934) was a Russian Jewish psychologist renowned for his work on cognitive development, emphasizing the importance of sociocultural factors. Vygotsky is also known for his concept of a zone of proximal development. According to Vygotsky, individuals best learn tasks that they are unable to do on their own but can complete with guidance.

Lev Vygotsky. The Vygotsky Project. 2001.

Margaret Floy Washburn (1871-1939) was an American psychologist whose research focused on animal behavior and cognition. She is best known for having developed the *motor theory of speech perception* and for legitimizing the study of mental events (the unseen) with the belief that they are just as important as behavioral events (the seen).

John B. Watson (1878-1958) was an American psychologist best known for establishing behaviorism, which intended to shift analysis emphasis from the internal mental state of people to their external behavior because it promotes an objective method. He is also known for his study of emotions, language, speech, and memory. In his controversial "Little Albert" experiment, Watson was able to condition a child who was initially unafraid of a white rat to demonstrate fear of the animal by clanging a metal rod every time the creature was presented. Eventually, no accompanying loud noise was needed to induce fear.

Ernst Heinrich Weber (1795-1878) was a German physician best remembered for his role in helping to found experimental psychology. His research primarily centered on sensation and touch. Some of his more praised contributions include just-noticeable difference, Weber's Law, *experimental wave theory*, hydrodynamics, the two-point threshold technique, and Weber's illusion.

Portrait of Ernst Heinrich Weber. Wellcome Library. 2014. Wikimedia Commons

Max Weber (1864-1920) was a German sociologist and is considered to be one of the founders of sociology. He is best known for his thesis on the Protestant ethic and for his model of bureaucracy. Weber identified six characteristics of an ideal bureaucracy and believed that bureaucracies were the ideal model for government agencies.

Max Weber. Elitenetzwerk Bayern. 2014. Wikimedia Commons

David Wechsler (1896-1981) was an American psychologist renowned for his research on intelligence and his development of intelligence scales (e.g., the Wechsler Adult Intelligence Scale (WAIS) and the Wechsler Intelligence Scale for Children (WISC)).

Carl Wernicke (1848-1905) was a German anatomist, physician, and psychiatrist. He is academically praised for his research on aphasia. This work revealed areas of the brain besides the Broca's area where damage can result in speech and language being affected.

Carl Wernicke. J. F. Lehmann. c. 1905. Wikimedia Commons

Torsten Wiesel (born 1924) is a Swedish neurophysiologist. He is best known for his contribution to the study of sensory processing and his collaborations with David Hubel on ocular dominance columns.

Torsten Wiesel. Festival della Scienza. 2006. Flickr

Joseph Wolpe (1915-1997) was a South African psychiatrist. He is well known for having been a critical advocate for behavior therapy and his innovative approach to treating soldiers experiencing post-traumatic stress disorder. Seeing there were few successful treatment outcomes using the then-predominant approach of administrating drugs to encourage discussion of traumatizing events, Wolpe developed his alternative Reciprocal Inhibition techniques.

Wilhelm Wundt (1832-1920) was a German philosopher, physician, physiologist, and professor. Regarded as one of modern psychology's founding figures, Wundt established the first laboratory dedicated to psychological research. Subjects he studied included the nature of religious beliefs, mental disorders, abnormal behavior, brain damage and the three areas of mental functioning (thoughts, perception, and feelings).

Wilhelm Wundt. Weltrundschau zu Reclams Universum. 1902. Wikimedia Commons

Philip Zimbardo (born 1933) is an American psychologist and professor best known for his Stanford "prison" experiment. In this experiment, 24 students that had been declared sane were randomly assigned to the roles of prisoner or guard. The guards were not provided with any instructions for how they should treat the prisoners. After only six days, the experiment was stopped due to the guards' cruel behavior. Zimbardo concluded that situational influences can make people act in cruel ways.

Zimbardo in Warsaw. Jdec. 2009. Wikimedia Commons

Notes

Glossary of Terms

A

A-B-A design — an experimental design in which participants first experience the baseline condition (A), then experience the experimental treatment (B) and then return to the baseline (A).

Abnormal psychology — the area of psychological investigation concerned with understanding the nature of individual pathologies of mind, mood, and behavior.

Absolute poverty — a deprivation of resources that is life-threatening; living on, or just above, the margin of survival (i.e., not having enough money to afford the most basic necessities of life).

Absolute threshold — the minimum amount of physical energy needed to produce a reliable sensory experience; operationally defined as the stimulus level at which a sensory signal is detected half the time.

Accommodation — 1) the process by which the ciliary muscles change the thickness of the lens of the eye to permit variable focusing on near and distant objects; 2) according to Piaget, the process of restructuring or modifying cognitive structures so that new information can fit into them more easily; this process works in tandem with assimilation.

Acquisition — the stage in a classical conditioning experiment during which the conditioned response is first elicited by the conditioned stimulus.

Action potential — the nerve impulse activated in a neuron that travels down the axon and causes neurotransmitters to be released into a synapse.

Acute stress — a transient state of tension-arousal with typically clear onset and offset patterns.

Addiction — a condition in which the body requires a drug in order to function without physical and psychological reactions to its absence; often the outcome of having developed tolerance and dependence.

Ageism — prejudice against older people, similar to racism and sexism in its use of negative stereotypes.

Aggression — behaviors that cause psychological or physical harm to another individual.

Agoraphobia — an extreme fear of being in public places or open spaces from which escape may be difficult or impossible.

AIDS — acronym for acquired immune deficiency syndrome; a syndrome caused by a virus that damages the immune system and weakens the body's ability to fight infection; see *HIV*.

Algorithm — a step-by-step procedure that always provides the right answer for a particular type of problem.

All-or-none law — the rule that the size of the action potential is unaffected by increases in the intensity of stimulation beyond the threshold level.

Altruism — prosocial behaviors a person carries out without considering their own safety or interests.

Alzheimer's disease — a chronic organic brain syndrome characterized by a gradual loss of memory, decline in intellectual ability and deterioration of personality.

Amacrine cells — cells that integrate information across the retina; rather than sending signals toward the brain, amacrine cells link bipolar cells to other bipolar cells and ganglion cells to other ganglion cells.

Ambiguity — a perceptual object that may have more than one interpretation.

Amnesia — a failure of memory caused by physical injury, disease, drug use or psychological trauma.

Amygdala — the part of the limbic system that controls emotion, aggression and the formation of emotional memory.

Analytic psychology — a branch of psychology that views the person as a constellation of compensatory internal forces in a dynamic balance.

Anchoring heuristic — an insufficient adjustment up or down from an original starting value when judging the probable value of some event or outcome.

Animal cognition — the cognitive capabilities of nonhuman animals; researchers trace the development of cognitive capabilities across species and the continuity of capabilities from nonhuman to human animals.

Anorexia nervosa — an eating disorder in which an individual weighs less than 85% of their expected weight but persists in controlling eating because of a self-perception of obesity.

Anticipatory coping — efforts made in advance of a potentially stressful event to overcome, reduce or tolerate the imbalance between perceived demands and available resources.

Anticipatory socialization — the process of learning how to perform a role one doesn't yet occupy.

Anxiety — an intense emotional response caused by the preconscious recognition that a repressed conflict is about to emerge into consciousness.

Anxiety disorders — mental disorders marked by physiological arousal, feelings of tension and intense apprehension without apparent reason.

Apparent motion — a movement illusion in which one or more stationary lights going on and off in succession are perceived as a single moving light; the simplest form of apparent motion is the phi phenomenon.

Archetype — a universal, inherited, primitive and symbolic representation of a particular experience or object.

Ascribed status — a social position that a person is born into.

Assimilation — 1) bringing ethnic and racial diversity within a society into a common cultural fold; making them more alike, or more like the dominant ethnic or racial group (i.e., "the melting-pot");

2) according to Piaget, the process whereby new cognitive elements are fitted in with old elements or modified to fit more easily; this process works in tandem with accommodation.

Association cortex — the parts of the cerebral cortex in which many high-level brain processes occur.

Attachment — the emotional relationship between a child and the caregiver.

Attention — a state of focused awareness on a subset of the available perceptual information.

Attitude — the learned, relatively stable tendency to respond to people, concepts and events in an evaluative way.

Attribution theory — a social-cognitive approach to describing the ways the social perceiver uses information to generate causal explanations.

Attributions — judgments about the causes of outcomes.

Audience design — the process of shaping a message depending on the audience for which it is intended.

Auditory cortex — the area of the temporal lobes that receives and processes auditory information.

Auditory nerve — the nerve that carries impulses from the cochlea to the cochlear nucleus of the brain.

Automatic processes — processes that do not require attention; they can often be performed along with other tasks without interference.

Autonomic nervous system (ANS) — the subdivision of the peripheral nervous system that controls the body's involuntary motor responses by connecting the sensory receptors to the *Central nervous system (CNS)* and the CNS to the smooth muscle, the cardiac muscle, and glands.

Availability heuristic — a judgment based on the information readily available in memory.

Aversion therapy — a type of behavioral therapy used to treat individuals attracted to harmful stimuli; the stimulus they find attractive is paired with a noxious stimulus in order to evoke a negative reaction to the target stimulus.

Axon — the extended fiber of a neuron through which nerve impulses travel from the soma to the terminal buttons.

B

Basic level — the level of categorization that can be retrieved from memory most quickly and used most efficiently.

Basilar membrane — a membrane in the cochlea that, when set into motion, stimulates hair cells that produce the neural effects of auditory stimulation.

Behavior — the actions by which an organism adjusts to its environment.

Behavior analysis — the area of psychology that focuses on the environmental determinants of learning and behavior.

Behavior modification — the systematic use of principles of learning to increase the frequency of desired behaviors and/or decrease the frequency of problem behaviors.

Behavior therapy — see *Behavior modification*.

Behavioral confirmation — the process by which people behave in ways that elicit from others specific expected reactions and then use those reactions to confirm their beliefs.

Behavioral data — observational reports about the behavior of organisms and the conditions under which the behavior occurs or changes.

Behavioral measures — overt actions and reactions that are observed and recorded, exclusive of self-reported behavior.

Behavioral rehearsal — procedures used to establish and strengthen basic skills; as used in social-skills training programs, requiring the client to rehearse a desirable behavior sequence mentally.

Behaviorism — a scientific approach that limits the study of psychology to measurable or observable behavior.

Behaviorist perspective — the psychological perspective primarily concerned with observable behavior that can be objectively recorded and with the relationships of observable behavior to environmental stimuli.

Belief-bias effect — a situation that occurs when a person's prior knowledge, attitudes or values distort the reasoning process by influencing the person to accept invalid arguments.

Between-subjects design — a research design in which different groups of participants are randomly assigned to experimental conditions or to control conditions.

Beyond Black and White — a book about interracial friendships which says that Asians and Hispanics are more likely to be friends with other races.

Biofeedback — a self-regulatory technique by which an individual acquires voluntary control over nonconscious biological processes.

Biological constraints on learning — any limitations on an organism's capacity to learn that are caused by the inherited sensory, response or cognitive capabilities of members of a given species.

Biological perspective — the approach to identifying causes of behavior that focuses on the functioning of the genes, the brain, the nervous system, and the endocrine system.

Biomedical therapies — treatments for psychological disorders that alter brain functioning with chemical or physical interventions such as drug therapy, surgery or electroconvulsive therapy.

Biopsychosocial model — a model of health and illness that suggests that links between the nervous system, the immune system, behavioral styles, cognitive processing, and environmental factors can put people at risk for illness.

Bipolar cells — nerve cells in the visual system that combine impulses from many receptors and transmit the results to ganglion cells.

Bipolar disorder — a mood disorder characterized by alternating periods of depression and mania.

Blocking — a phenomenon in which an organism does not learn a new stimulus that signals an unconditioned stimulus because the new stimulus is presented simultaneously with a stimulus that is already effective as a signal.

Body image — the subjective experience of the appearance of one's body.

Boomerang generation — young adults who move back into their parents' home after living independently for a while or who never leave it in the first place.

Bottom-up processing — perceptual analyses based on the sensory data available in the environment; results of analyses are passed upward, forming more abstract representations.

Brain stem — the brain structure that regulates the body's basic life processes.

Brightness — the dimension of color space that captures the intensity of light.

Broca's area — the region of the brain that translates thoughts into speech or sign.

Bulimia nervosa — an eating disorder characterized by binge eating followed by measures to purge the body of the excess calories.

Bureaucracy — an organizational model based on rational thought that seeks to accomplish tasks in a specialized and efficient manner (large businesses, governments, schools, etc.).

Bystander intervention — willingness to assist a person in need of help.

C

Cannon-Bard theory of emotion — a theory stating that an "emotional stimulus produces two co-occurring reactions (arousal and experience of emotion) that do not cause each other."

Case study — intensive observation of a particular individual or small group of individuals.

Catharsis — the process of expressing strongly felt but usually repressed emotions.

Central nervous system (CNS) — the part of the nervous system consisting of the brain and spinal cord.

Centration — a thought pattern common during the beginning of the preoperational stage of cognitive development; characterized by the child's inability to take more than one perceptual factor into account at the same time.

Cerebellum — the region of the brain attached to the brain stem that controls motor coordination, posture and balance, as well as the ability to learn control of body movements.

Cerebral cortex — the outer surface of the cerebrum.

Cerebral hemispheres — the two halves of the *Cerebrum*, connected by the corpus callosum.

Cerebrum — the region of the brain that regulates higher cognitive and emotional functions.

Child-directed speech — a special form of speech with an exaggerated and high-pitched intonation that adults adopt when speaking to infants and young children.

Chronic stress — a continuous state of tension-arousal in which an individual perceives demands as greater than the inner and outer resources available for dealing with them.

Chronological age — the number of months or years since an individual's birth.

Chunking — the process of taking single items of information and recoding them on the basis of similarity or some other organizing principle.

Circadian rhythm — a consistent pattern of cyclical body activities, usually lasting 24 to 25 hours and determined by an internal biological clock.

Civil religion — a quasi-religious loyalty binding individuals in a basically secular society that creates a sense of solidarity (e.g., patriotism, socialism or any social or political movement or program that people have strong feelings about).

Class system — a stratification system supposedly based on individual merit or distinction but often includes some structure of inequality like inheritance, sexism, racism, and ethnocentrism.

Classical conditioning — a type of learning in which a behavior (conditioned response) comes to be elicited by a stimulus (conditioned stimulus) that has acquired its power through an association with a biologically significant stimulus (unconditioned stimulus).

Client — the term used by clinicians who think of psychological disorders as problems in living, not as mental illnesses, to describe those being treated.

Client-centered therapy — a humanistic approach to treatment that emphasizes the healthy psychological growth of the individual; based on the assumption that all people share the basic tendency of human nature toward self-actualization.

Clinical ecology — a field of psychology that relates disorders such as anxiety and depression to environmental irritants and sources of trauma.

Clinical psychologist — an individual who has earned a doctorate in psychology and whose training is in the assessment and treatment of psychological problems.

Clinical social worker — a mental health professional whose specialized training prepares them to consider the social context of people's problems.

Closure — a perceptual organizing process that leads individuals to see incomplete figures as complete.

Cochlea — the primary organ of hearing; a fluid-filled coiled tube located in the inner ear.

Cognition — processes of knowing, including attending, remembering and reasoning; also the content of the processes, such as concepts and memories.

Cognitive appraisal — in regard to emotions, the process through which physiological arousal is interpreted with respect to circumstances in the particular setting in which it is being experienced; also, the recognition and evaluation of a stressor to assess the demand, the size of the threat, the resources available for dealing with it and appropriate coping strategies.

Cognitive appraisal theory of emotion — a theory stating that the experience of emotion is the joint effect of physiological arousal and cognitive appraisal, which together determine how an ambiguous inner state of arousal will be labeled.

Cognitive behavior modification — a therapeutic approach that combines cognitive emphasis on the role of thoughts and attitudes influencing motivations and response with behavioral emphasis on changing the client's performance through modification of reinforcement contingencies.

Cognitive development — the development of processes of knowing, including imagining, perceiving, reasoning and problem-solving.

Cognitive dissonance — the theory that the tension-producing effects of incongruous cognitions motivate individuals to reduce such tension, usually by refusing to recognize the incongruity.

Cognitive map — a mental representation of physical space.

Cognitive perspective — the perspective on psychology that stresses human thought and the processes of knowing, such as attending, thinking, remembering, expecting, solving problems, fantasizing and consciousness.

Cognitive processes — higher mental processes, such as perception, memory, language, problem-solving and abstract thinking.

Cognitive psychology — the study of higher mental processes such as attention, language use, memory, perception, problem-solving and thinking.

Cognitive science — the interdisciplinary field of study of the approach systems and processes that manipulate information.

Cognitive therapy — a type of psychotherapeutic treatment that attempts to change feelings and behaviors by changing the way a client thinks about or perceives significant life experiences.

Cohabitation — an arrangement in which two unrelated people are not married but live together and have a sexual relationship.

Collective unconscious — the part of an individual's unconscious that is inherited, evolutionarily developed and common to all members of the species.

Colonialism — the process by which some nations enrich themselves through political and economic control of other countries (e.g., European colonists in the Americas or in Africa in the 18th and 19th centuries).

Comorbidity — the experience of more than one disorder at the same time.

Complementary colors — colors opposite each other on the color circle; when additively mixed, they create the sensation of white light.

Compliance — a change in behavior consistent with a communication source's direct requests.

Concepts — mental representations of kinds or categories of items or ideas.

Conditioned reinforcers — in classical conditioning, formerly neutral stimuli that have become reinforcers.

Conditioned response (CR) — in classical conditioning, a response elicited by some previously neutral stimulus that occurs as a result of pairing the neutral stimulus with an unconditioned stimulus.

Conditioned stimulus (CS) — in classical conditioning, a previously neutral stimulus that comes to elicit a conditioned response.

Conditioning — the ways in which events, stimuli, and behavior become associated with one another.

Cones — photoreceptors concentrated in the center of the retina that are responsible for visual experience under normal viewing conditions and for all experiences of color.

Conflict theory — the idea that conflict between competing interests is the basic animating force of social change and society in general; named and promulgated by Karl Marx.

Conformity — the tendency for people to adopt the behaviors, attitudes, and values of other members of a reference group.

Confounding variable — a stimulus other than the variable that an experimenter explicitly introduces into a research setting that affects a participant's behavior.

Consciousness — a state of awareness of internal events and of the external environment.

Consensual validation — the mutual affirmation of conscious views of reality.

Conservation — according to Piaget, the understanding that physical properties do not change when nothing is added or taken away, even though their appearance may change.

Consistency paradox — the observation that personality ratings across time and among different observers are consistent, while behavior ratings across situations are not consistent.

Contact comfort — comfort derived from an infant's physical contact with the mother or caregiver.

Contact hypothesis — the idea that direct contact between hostile groups alone will reduce prejudice.

Content analysis — data collection method that systematically examines some form of communication.

Context of discovery — the initial phase of research in which observations, beliefs, information, and general knowledge lead to a new idea or a different way of thinking about some phenomenon.

Context of justification — the research phase in which evidence is brought to bear on hypotheses.

Contextual distinctiveness — the assumption that the serial position effect can be altered by the context and the distinctiveness of the experience being recalled.

Contingency management — a general treatment strategy involving changing behavior by modifying its consequences.

Control group — the group of subjects in an experiment who are not exposed to the independent variable.

Control procedures — consistent procedures for giving instructions, scoring responses and holding all other variables constant except those being systematically varied.

Controlled processes — processes that require attention; it is often difficult to carry out more than one controlled process at a time.

Convergence — the degree to which the eyes turn inward to fixate on an object.

Coping — the process of dealing with internal or external demands that are perceived to be threatening or overwhelming.

Corpus callosum — the mass of nerve fibers connecting the two hemispheres of the cerebrum.

Correlation — the association between two variables.

Correlation coefficient (r) — a statistic that indicates the degree of relationship between two variables.

Correlational methods — research methodologies that determine to what extent two variables, traits or attributes are related.

Counseling psychologist — psychologist who specializes in providing guidance in areas such as vocational selection, school problems, drug abuse, and marital conflict.

Counterconditioning — a technique used in therapy to substitute a new response for a maladaptive one by means of conditioning procedures.

Countertransference — circumstances in which a psychoanalyst develops personal feelings about a client because of the perceived similarity of the client to significant people in the therapist's life.

Covariation principle — a theory that suggests that people attribute a behavior to a causal factor if that factor was present whenever the behavior occurred but was absent whenever it did not occur.

Creativity — the ability to generate ideas or products that are both novel and appropriate to the circumstances.

Criterion validity — the degree to which test scores indicate a result on a specific measure that is consistent with some other criterion of the characteristic being assessed; see *Predictive validity*.

Cross-sectional design — a research method in which groups of participants of different chronological ages are observed and compared at a given time.

Crystallized intelligence — the facet of intelligence involving the knowledge a person has already acquired and their ability to access that knowledge; measured by vocabulary, arithmetic, and general information tests.

Culture — the set of beliefs, values, behaviors, traditions, practices and material objects that are learned, taught or shared and define a people's way of life; everything that a particular group of people can and do share in common (e.g., social norms, worldview).

Cultural imperialism — the influence or domination of the cultural values and products of one society over those of another.

Cultural integration — the consistency of various aspects of society that promotes order and stability.

Cultural lag — the fact that cultural elements change at different rates (nonmaterial changes faster than material), which may disrupt a cultural system (e.g., religion lagging behind the changes happening in science or technology, old traditions of gender roles that persist in an egalitarian, modern society).

Cultural perspective — the psychological perspective that focuses on cross-cultural differences in the causes and consequences of behavior.

Cultural relativism — the practice of judging a culture by its own standards; all culture groups are valid and functional to those who function within those cultures (i.e., there are no good or bad, inferior or superior cultures, just differences based on each group's own cultural evolution).

Culture shock — personal disorientation that accompanies exposure to foreign cultures or unfamiliar ways of life different from one's own.

Cultural universals — customs and practices that are common to all societies.

Cutaneous senses — the skin senses that register sensations of pressure, warmth and cold.

D

Dark adaptation — the gradual improvement of the eyes' sensitivity after a shift in illumination from light to near darkness.

Date rape — unwanted sexual violation by a social acquaintance in the context of a dating situation.

Davis-Moore Thesis — the assertion that social stratification is a universal pattern because it has beneficial consequences for the operation of a society; justifies the inequality in a class system (functionalist theory).

Daytime sleepiness — the experience of excessive sleepiness during daytime activities; the major complaint of patients evaluated at sleep disorder centers.

Debriefing — a procedure conducted at the end of an experiment in which the researcher provides the participant with as much information about the study as possible and makes sure that no participant leaves feeling confused, upset or embarrassed.

Decision aversion — the tendency to avoid decision making; the tougher the decision, the greater the likelihood of decision aversion.

Decision making — the process of choosing between alternatives; selecting or rejecting available options.

Declarative memory — memory for information such as facts and events.

Deductive reasoning — a form of thinking in which one draws a conclusion that is intended to follow logically from two or more statements or premises which is then tested through data collection.

Delusions — false or irrational beliefs maintained despite clear evidence to the contrary.

Demand characteristics — cues in an experimental setting that influence the participants' perception of what is expected of them and that systematically influence their behavior within that setting.

Dendrites — the branched fibers of neurons that receive incoming signals.

Dependent variable — in an experimental setting, any variable whose values are the result of changes in one or more independent variables.

Descriptive statistics — statistical procedures that are used to summarize sets of scores with respect to central tendencies, variability, and correlations.

Determinism — the doctrine that all events, whether physical, behavioral or mental, are determined by specific causal factors that are potentially knowable.

Developmental age — the chronological age at which most children show a particular level of physical or mental development.

Developmental psychology — the branch of psychology concerned with the interaction between physical and psychological processes and with stages of growth from conception throughout the entire lifespan.

Diathesis-stress hypothesis — a hypothesis about the cause of certain disorders, such as schizophrenia; suggests that genetic factors predispose an individual to a certain disorder, but environmental stress factors must impinge in order for the disorder to manifest itself.

Dichotic listening — an experimental technique in which a different auditory stimulus is simultaneously presented to each ear.

Difference threshold — the smallest physical difference between two stimuli that can still be recognized as a difference; operationally defined as the point at which the stimuli are recognized as different half of the time.

Diffusion of responsibility — in emergency situations, the larger the number of bystanders, the less responsibility any one bystander feels to help.

Discriminative stimuli — stimuli that act as predictors of reinforcement, signaling when particular behaviors will result in positive reinforcement.

Dispositional variables — the organismic variables, or inner determinants of behavior, that occur within human and nonhuman animals.

Dissociative amnesia — the inability to remember important personal experiences; caused by psychological factors in the absence of any organic dysfunction.

Dissociative disorder — a personality disorder marked by a disturbance in the integration of identity, memory or consciousness.

Dissociative identity disorder (DID) — a dissociative mental disorder in which two or more distinct personalities exist within the same individual; formerly known as multiple personality disorder.

Distal stimulus — in the processes of perception, the physical object in the world, as contrasted with the proximal stimulus (the optical image of it on the retina).

Divergent thinking — an aspect of creativity characterized by an ability to produce unusual but appropriate responses to problems.

Divorce — the legal dissolution of a marriage.

DNA (deoxyribonucleic acid) — the physical basis for the transmission of genetic information.

Double-blind control — an experimental technique in which biased expectations of experimenters are eliminated by keeping both the participants and the experimental assistants unaware of which participants have received which treatment.

Dramaturgical analysis — Erving Goffman's term for the investigation of social interaction in terms of theatrical performance (i.e., people are all actors in society playing different roles on different "sets" or "stages," adapting through the use of role-appropriate "scripts").

Dream analysis — the psychoanalytic interpretation of dreams used to gain insight into a person's unconscious motives or conflicts.

Dream work — in Freudian dream analysis, the process by which the internal censor transforms the latent content of a dream into manifest content.

Drives — internal states that arise in response to disequilibrium in an animal's physiological needs.

DSM — the *Diagnostic and Statistical Manual* of the American Psychiatric Association that classifies, defines and describes mental disorders; the most current edition is the DSM-V, published in 2013.

Dual-earner couples — an arrangement in which both partners are employed outside the home; also known as dual income, two-income, two-earner or dual-worker couples.

E

Echoic memory — sensory memory that allows auditory information to be stored for brief durations.

Egalitarian family system — when both partners share power and authority fairly and equally.

Ego — the aspect of personality involved in self-preservation activities and in directing instinctual drives and urges into appropriate channels.

Ego defense mechanisms — mental strategies (conscious or unconscious) used by the ego to defend itself against conflicts experienced in the normal course of life.

Egocentrism — in cognitive development, the inability of a young child at the preoperational stage to assume the perspective of another person.

Elaboration likelihood model — a theory of persuasion that defines how likely it is that people will focus their cognitive processes to elaborate upon a message and therefore follow the central and peripheral routes to persuasion.

Elaborative rehearsal — a technique for improving memory by enriching the encoding of information.

Electroconvulsive therapy (ECT) — the use of electroconvulsive shock as an effective treatment for severe depression.

Electroencephalogram (EEG) — a recording of the electrical activity of the brain.

Emotion — a complex pattern of changes, including physiological arousal, feelings, cognitive processes and behavioral reactions in response to a situation perceived to be personally significant.

Empirical — information that is based on observations, experiments or experiences, rather than on ideology, religious beliefs or intuition.

Emotional intelligence — a type of intelligence defined as the ability to perceive, appraise and express emotions accurately and appropriately, to use emotions to facilitate thinking, to understand and analyze emotions, to use emotional knowledge effectively and to regulate emotions to promote both emotional and intellectual growth.

Encoding — the process by which a mental representation is formed in memory.

Encoding specificity — the principle that subsequent retrieval of information is enhanced if cues received at the time of recall are consistent with those present at the time of encoding.

Endocrine system — the network of glands that manufacture and secrete hormones into the bloodstream.

Endogamy — the practice of selecting mates between people of the same social category or group (e.g., same religion, race, social class/caste, tribal group, ethnicity, etc.); see *Homogamy*.

Engram — the physical memory trace for information in the brain.

Environmental variables — external influences on behavior.

Episodic memories — long-term memories for autobiographical events and the contexts in which they occurred.

EQ — the emotional intelligence counterpart of IQ.

Equity theory — 1) a cognitive theory of work motivation that proposes that workers are motivated to maintain fair and equitable relationships with other relevant persons; 2) a model that postulates that equitable relationships are those in which the participants' outcomes are proportional to their inputs.

Erogenous zones — areas of the skin surface that are especially sensitive to stimulation and that give rise to erotic or sexual sensations.

Estrogen — the female sex hormone, produced by the ovaries, that is responsible for the release of eggs from the ovaries as well as for the development and maintenance of female reproductive structures and secondary sex characteristics.

Ethnicity — a shared cultural heritage; a group usually sharing a common language, religion, history, homeland, ancestry, and some remaining customs and traditions; today's ethnic groups often represent watered-down culture groups due to the assimilation pressures around them.

Ethnocentrism — the practice of judging another culture by the standards of one's own culture; an attitude of superiority about one's own culture or society.

Ethnomethodology — a term coined by Harold Garfinkel which is the study of how people construct and deal with reality; everyone learns shared definitions of reality to make everyday interactions possible.

Etiology — the causes of, or factors related to, the development of a disorder.

Evaluation research — research that relies on all of the standard data collection techniques to assess the effectiveness of social programs in both the public and the private sectors.

Evolutionary perspective — the approach to psychology that stresses the importance of behavioral and mental adaptiveness, based on the assumption that mental capabilities evolved over millions of years to serve particular adaptive purposes.

Excitatory inputs — information entering a neuron that signals it to fire.

Exogamy — the practice of selecting a mate from outside one's social group; marriage between people of different social categories; also known as *Heterogamy*.

Expectancy effects — results that occur when a researcher or observer subtly communicates to participants the kind of behavior they expect to find, thereby creating that expected reaction.

Expectancy theory — a cognitive theory of work motivation that proposes that workers are motivated when they expect their efforts and job performance to result in desired outcomes.

Experience-sampling method — an experimental method that assists researchers in describing the typical contents of consciousness; participants are asked to record what they are feeling and thinking whenever signaled to do so.

Experimental methods — research methodologies that involve the manipulation of independent variables in order to determine their effects on the dependent variables.

Explicit uses of memory — conscious efforts to recover information through memory processes.

Extended family — a family consisting of parents and children, as well as other kin, such as uncles and aunts, nieces and nephews, cousins and grandparents.

Extinction — in conditioning, the weakening of a conditioned association in the absence of a reinforcer or unconditioned stimulus.

F

Face validity — the degree to which test items appear to be directly related to the attribute the researcher wishes to measure.

Family — an intimate group of two or more people who are typically related, live together, care for the needs of each other and share close emotional ties and functions.

Fear — a rational reaction to an objectively identified external danger that may induce a person to flee or attack in self-defense.

Feminine traits — tactful, quiet, aware of feelings, connection, empathy, caring.

Feminism — the theory that proposes that women and men often experience culture differently and cultural values and norms can increase inequality due to gender.

Feminist theory — approaches that try to explain the social, economic and political positions of women in society with a view to freeing women from traditional expectations, constraints, roles, and behaviors, both micro and macrosociological.

Fictive kin — nonrelatives who are accepted as part of an African American family.

Field research — data collected by systematically observing people in their natural surroundings.

Fight-or-flight response — a sequence of internal activities triggered when an organism is faced with a threat; prepares the body for combat and struggle or for running away to safety; recent evidence suggests that the response is characteristic only of males.

Figure — object-like regions of the visual field that are distinguished from the background.

Five-factor model — a comprehensive descriptive personality system that maps out the relationships among common traits, theoretical concepts and personality scales (informally called the Big Five).

Fixation — a state in which a person remains attached to objects or activities more appropriate for an earlier stage of psychosexual development.

Fixed-interval schedule — a schedule of reinforcement in which a reinforcer is delivered for the first response made after a fixed period of time.

Fixed-ratio schedule — a schedule of reinforcement in which a reinforcer is delivered for the first response made after a fixed number of responses.

Flooding — a therapy for phobias in which clients are exposed, with their permission, to the stimuli most frightening to them.

Fluid intelligence — the aspect of intelligence that involves the ability to see complex relationships and solve problems.

Folkways — norms that members of a society (or a group within society) look upon as not being critical and that can be transgressed without severe punishment.

Formal assessment — the systematic procedures and measurement instruments used by trained professionals to assess an individual's functioning, aptitudes, abilities or mental state.

Foundational theories — frameworks for initial understanding formulated by children to explain their experiences of the world.

Fovea — the area of the retina that contains densely packed cones and forms the point of sharpest vision.

Frame — a particular description of a choice; the perspective from which a choice is described or framed affects how a decision is made and which option is ultimately exercised.

Free association — the therapeutic method in which a client gives a running account of their thoughts, wishes, physical sensations, and mental images as they occur.

Frequency distribution — a summary of how frequently each score appears in a set of observations.

Frequency theory — the theory that a tone produces a rate of vibration in the basilar membrane equal to its frequency, with the result that pitch can be coded by the frequency of the neural response.

Frontal lobe — region of the brain located above the lateral fissure and in front of the central sulcus; involved in motor control and cognitive activities.

Frustration-aggression hypothesis — according to this hypothesis, frustration occurs in situations in which people are prevented or blocked from attaining their goals; heightened frustration leads to a greater probability of aggression.

Functional fixedness — an inability to perceive a new use for an object previously associated with some other purpose; adversely affects problem solving and creativity.

Functional MRI (fMRI) — a brain imaging technique that combines the benefits of both MRI and PET scans by detecting magnetic changes in the flow of blood to cells in the brain.

Functionalism — the perspective on mind and behavior that focuses on the examination of their functions in an organism's interactions with the environment.

Functionalist theory — the theory stating that various social institutions and processes in society exist to serve some important/necessary function and work together in harmony to maintain society as a whole in a state of balance; also, a macrosociological theory which states that similar beliefs bind people together and create stability and that sharing core values unifies a society and promotes cultural solidarity.

Fundamental attribution error (FAE) — the tendency of observers both to underestimate the impact of situational factors and to overestimate the influence of dispositional factors on a person's behavior.

G

G factor — the factor of general intelligence underlying all intelligent performance (i.e., general intelligence or general mental ability factor).

Ganglion cells — cells in the visual system that integrate impulses from many bipolar cells in a single firing rate.

Gate-control theory — a theory about pain modulation that proposes that certain cells in the spinal cord act as gates to interrupt and block some pain signals while allowing others to travel on to the brain.

Gender — a psychological phenomenon that refers to learned sex-related behaviors and attitudes of males and females.

Gender identity — one's sense of maleness or femaleness; can include awareness and acceptance of one's biological sex or awareness that one's biological sex does not match their sense of maleness/femaleness.

Gender roles — sets of behaviors and attitudes associated by society with being male or female and expressed publicly by the individual.

Generalized other — George Herbert Mead's term for widespread cultural norms and values used as references in evaluating oneself; the roles society lays out becomes a part of one's individual identity and the identity superimposed upon others; used to refer to people who do not have close ties to a child but who will influence the child's internalization of society's norms and values (e.g., librarian, policeman, drill sergeant).

General adaption syndrome (GAS) — the pattern of nonspecific, adaptational physiological mechanisms that occur in response to a continuing threat by almost any serious stressor.

Generalized anxiety disorder — an anxiety disorder in which an individual feels anxious and worried most of the time for at least six months when not threatened by any specific danger or object.

Generativity — a commitment beyond one's self and one's partner to family, work, society and future generations; typically, a crucial step in development in one's thirties and forties.

Genes — the biological units of heredity; discrete sections of chromosomes responsible for transmission of traits.

Genetics — the study of the inheritance of physical and psychological traits from ancestors.

Genocide — the systematic destruction of one group of people, often an ethnic or racial group, by another.

Genotype — the genetic structure an organism inherits from its parents.

Gestalt psychology — a school of psychology that maintains that psychological phenomena can be understood only when viewed as organized, structured wholes, not when broken down into primitive perceptual elements.

Gestalt therapy — therapy that focuses on ways to unite mind and body to make a person whole.

Glia — the cells that hold neurons together and facilitate neural transmission, remove damaged and dead neurons and prevent poisonous substances in the blood from reaching the brain.

Globalization — the growth and spread of investment, trade, communication, production and new technology around the world.

Global perspective — the study of the larger world and society's place in it; comparing one's thinking and behavior to that of other cultures around the world.

Goal-directed selection — a determinant of why people select some parts of sensory input for further processing; reflects the choices made as a function of one's own goals.

Ground — the background areas of the visual field against which figures stand out.

Group dynamics — the study of how group processes change individual functioning.

Group polarization — the tendency for groups to make decisions that are more extreme than the decisions that would be made by any of its members acting alone.

Groupthink — the tendency of group members to conform by adopting a narrow view of some issue so that a consensus may be reached; in groupthink, individual members tend not to challenge the opinions or prejudices held by the group because of its solidarity and/or the charisma of its leader.

Guided search — in visual perception, a parallel search of the environment for single, basic attributes to guide attention to the likely locations of objects with more complex combinations of attributes.

H

Hallucinations — false perceptions that occur in the absence of objective stimulation.

Health — a general condition of soundness and vigor of body and mind; not simply the absence of illness or injury.

Health promotion — the development and implementation of general strategies and specific tactics to eliminate or reduce the risk that people will become ill.

Health psychology — the field of psychology devoted to understanding the ways people stay healthy, the reasons they become ill and the ways they respond when ill.

Hegemonic masculinity — societal practices that encourage men to place themselves in a higher standing, while keeping women in subordinate positions.

Heredity — the biological transmission of traits from parents to offspring.

Heritability estimate — a statistical estimate of the degree of inheritance of a given trait or behavior, assessed by the degree of similarity between individuals who vary in the extent of their genetic similarity.

Heterogamy — see *Exogamy*.

Heterosexism — the belief that heterosexuality is superior.

Heuristics — cognitive strategies or "rules of thumb," often used as shortcuts in solving a complex inferential task.

Hierarchy of needs — Maslow's view that basic human motives form a hierarchy and that the needs at each level of the hierarchy must be satisfied before the next level can be achieved; these needs progress from basic biological needs to the need for transcendence.

Hippocampus — the part of the limbic system that is involved in the acquisition of explicit memory.

HIV — human immunodeficiency virus; a virus that attacks white blood cells (T lymphocytes) in human blood, thereby weakening the functioning of the immune system; HIV causes *AIDS*.

Homeostasis — a state of equilibrium of the internal conditions of the body.

Horizontal cells — the cells that integrate information across the retina; rather than sending signals toward the brain, horizontal cells connect receptors to each other.

Homogamy — marriage between people with the same social/cultural characteristics; see *Endogamy*.

Horizontal mobility — 1) the movement from one job to another without any change in social status; 2) cultural dissemination that occurs without any change in social status (e.g., trends or fashions that move within economic classes).

Hormones — the chemical messengers, manufactured and secreted by the endocrine glands, that regulate metabolism and influence body growth, mood and sexual characteristics.

Hozho — a Navajo concept referring to harmony, peace of mind, goodness, ideal family relationships, beauty in arts and crafts and health of body and spirit.

Hue — the dimension of color space that captures the qualitative experience of the color of a light.

Human behavior genetics — the area of study that evaluates the genetic component of individual differences in behaviors and traits.

Human-potential movement — the therapy movement that encompasses all those practices and methods that release the potential of the average human being for greater levels of performance and greater richness of experience.

Humanistic perspective — a psychological model that emphasizes an individual's phenomenal world and inherent capacity for making rational choices and developing to maximum potential.

Hypnosis — an altered state of consciousness characterized by deep relaxation, susceptibility to suggestions and hypnotist-directed changes in perception, memory, motivation, and self-control.

Hypnotizability — the degree to which an individual is responsive to standardized hypnotic suggestion.

Hypothalamus — the brain structure that regulates motivated behavior (such as eating and drinking) and homeostasis.

Hypothesis — a tentative and testable explanation of the relationship between two (or more) events or variables; often stated as a prediction that a certain outcome will result from specific conditions.

I

Iconic memory — sensory memory in the visual domain; allows large amounts of information to be stored for very brief durations.

Id — the primitive, unconscious part of the personality that operates irrationally and acts on impulse to pursue pleasure.

Ideal culture — the beliefs, values, and norms that people in a society say they hold or follow.

Identification and recognition — two ways of attaching meaning to percepts.

Illusion — an experience of a stimulus pattern in a manner that is demonstrably incorrect but shared by others in the same perceptual environment.

Illusory contours — contours perceived in a figure when no contours are physically present.

Implicit uses of memory — the availability of information through memory processes without the exertion of any conscious effort to encode or recover information.

Implosion therapy — a behavioral therapeutic technique that exposes a client to anxiety-provoking stimuli, evoked by their own imagination, in an attempt to extinguish the anxiety associated with the stimuli.

Impression management — the process of providing information and cues to others to present oneself in a favorable light while downplaying or concealing one's less appealing qualities.

Imprinting — a primitive form of learning in which some infant animals physically follow and form an attachment to the first moving object they see and/or hear.

Impulsive aggression — emotion-driven aggression produced in reaction to situations in "the heat of the moment."

Incentives — external stimuli or rewards that motivate behavior, although they do not relate directly to biological needs.

Incest taboo — cultural norms and laws that forbid sexual relationship between close blood relatives, such as siblings, parent and child or uncle/aunt and niece/nephew.

Independent construals of self — conceptualization of the self as an individual whose behavior is organized primarily by reference to one's own thoughts, feelings, and actions, rather than by reference to the thoughts, feelings and actions of others.

Independent variable — in experimental settings, the stimulus condition whose values are free to vary independently of any other variable in the situation.

Induced motion — an illusion in which a stationary point of light within a moving reference frame is perceived as moving while the reference frame is perceived as stationary.

Inductive reasoning — a form of reasoning in which a conclusion is made about the probability of some state of affairs, based on the available evidence and past experience.

Inferences — missing information filled in on the basis of a sample of evidence or on the basis of prior beliefs and theories.

Inferential statistics — statistical procedures that allow researchers to determine whether the results they obtain support their hypotheses or can be attributed just to chance variation.

Informational influence — group effects that arise from individuals' desire to be correct and right and to understand how best to act in a given situation.

In-group — a social group commanding a member's esteem and loyalty whose identity in part derives from the rejection, ridicule or ostracism of an "outgroup" or opposition group.

In-group bias — an evaluation of one's own group as being better than others.

Inhibitory inputs — information entering a neuron that signals it not to fire.

Insanity — the legal (not clinical) designation for the state of an individual judged to be legally irresponsible or incompetent.

Insight therapy — A technique by which the therapist guides a patient toward discovering insights between present symptoms and past origins.

Insomnia — the chronic inability to sleep normally; symptoms include difficulty in falling asleep, frequent waking, inability to return to sleep and early-morning awakening.

Instincts — preprogrammed tendencies that are essential to a species' survival.

Instinctual drift — the tendency for learned behavior to drift toward instinctual behavior over time.

Instrumental aggression — cognition-based and goal-directed aggression carried out with premeditated thought to achieve specific aims.

Intelligence — the global capacity to profit from experience and go beyond given information about the environment.

Intelligence quotient (IQ) — an index derived from standardized tests of intelligence; originally obtained by dividing an individual's mental age by chronological age and then multiplying by 100; now directly computed as an IQ test score.

Interdependent construals of self — conceptualization of the self as part of an encompassing social relationship; recognizing that one's behavior is determined, contingent on and to a large extent organized by what the actor perceives to be the thoughts, feelings, and actions of others.

Interference — a memory phenomenon that occurs when retrieval cues do not point effectively to one specific memory.

Intergenerational mobility — the change in social class or types of jobs that occurs between generations (e.g., when parents ensure that their children will be better off than them).

Internal consistency — a measure of reliability; the degree to which a test yields similar scores across its different parts, such as on odd versus even items.

Internalization — 1) according to Vygotsky, the process through which children absorb knowledge from the social context; 2) the process of learning cultural behaviors and expectations so deeply that one automatically assumes they are correct and accepts them without question.

Interneurons — brain neurons that relay messages from sensory neurons to other interneurons or motor neurons.

Intersectional theory — meshes characteristics like gender and race or male and female to research.

Intersexual — when an individual, at birth, is not distinctly male or female; intersex individuals were previously referred to as hermaphrodites; however, the term is not commonly used today as it is considered to be stigmatizing or misleading.

Intimacy — the capacity to make a full commitment (sexual, emotional or moral) to another person.

Intragenerational mobility — the change in social class or types of jobs that occurs within a person's lifetime (e.g., moving from the working class to the middle class).

Ion channels — the portions of neurons' cell membranes that selectively permit certain ions to flow in and out.

IQ — see *Intelligence quotient.*

J

James-Lange theory of emotion — a peripheral-feedback theory of emotion; states that an eliciting stimulus triggers a behavioral response that sends different sensory and motor feedback to the brain and creates the feeling of a specific emotion.

Jigsaw classrooms — classrooms that use a technique, known as "jigsawing," in which each pupil is given part of the total material to master and then share it with the other group members.

Job burnout — syndrome of emotional exhaustion, depersonalization and diminished sense of personal accomplishment; often experienced by workers in high-stress jobs.

Judgment — 1) the process by which people form opinions, reach conclusions and make critical evaluations of events and people based on available material; 2) the product of said mental activity.

Just noticeable difference (JND) — the smallest difference between two sensations that allows them to be discriminated.

K

Kinesthetic sense — the sense concerned with bodily position and movement of the body parts relative to each other.

L

Language-making capacity — the innate guidelines or operating principles that children bring to the task of learning a language.

Language production — what people say, sign and write, as well as the processes they go through to produce those messages.

Latent content — in Freudian dream analysis, the hidden meaning of a dream.

Latent functions — functions in society or within an institution that are unintended or unrecognized (e.g., when a newspaper is used as a flyswatter); see *Manifest functions*.

Law of common fate — a law of grouping that states that elements moving in the same direction at the same rate are grouped together.

Law of effect — a basic law of learning that states that the power of a stimulus to evoke a response is strengthened when the response is followed by a reward and weakened when it is not.

Law of proximity — a law of grouping that states that the nearest elements are grouped together.

Law of similarity — a law of grouping that states that the most similar elements are grouped together.

Learned helplessness — a general pattern of nonresponding in the presence of noxious stimuli that often follows after an organism has previously experienced noncontingent, inescapable aversive stimuli.

Learning — a process based on experience that results in a relatively permanent change in behavior or behavioral potential.

Learning-performance distinction — the difference between what has been learned and what is expressed in overt behavior.

Lesions — injuries to or destruction of brain tissue.

Levels-of-processing theory — a theory that suggests that the deeper the level at which information was processed, the more likely it is to be retained in memory.

Liberation theology — a fusion of Christian principles with political activism, often Marxist in character.

Libido — the psychic energy that drives individuals toward sensual pleasures of all types, especially sexual ones.

Life-change units (LCUs) — in stress research, the measure of the stress levels of different types of change experienced during a given period.

Lightness constancy — the tendency to perceive the whiteness, grayness or blackness of objects as constant across changing levels of illumination.

Limbic system — the region of the brain that regulates emotional behavior, basic motivational urges, and memory, as well as major physiological functions.

Looking-glass-self — Cooley's assertion that the self is based on how others respond to us.

Longitudinal design — a research design in which the same participants are observed repeatedly, sometimes over many years.

Long-term memory (LTM) — memory processes associated with the preservation of information for retrieval at any later time.

Loudness — a perceptual dimension of sound influenced by the amplitude of a sound wave; sound waves with large amplitudes are generally experienced as loud and those with small amplitudes as soft.

Lucid dreaming — the theory that conscious awareness of dreaming is a learnable skill that will enable dreamers to control the direction and content of their dreams.

M

Macrosociology — examines large-scale and broader aspects of society (e.g., functionalist and conflict theories and, to some extent, feminism).

Magnetic resonance imaging (MRI) — a technique for brain imaging that scans the brain using magnetic fields and radio waves.

Major depressive disorder — a mood disorder characterized by intense feelings of depression over an extended time, lacking the manic high phase of bipolar depression.

Manic episode — a component of bipolar disorder characterized by periods of extreme elation, unbounded euphoria without sufficient reason and grandiose thoughts or feelings about personal abilities.

Manifest content — in Freudian dream analysis, the surface content of a dream which is assumed to mask the dream's actual meaning.

Manifest functions — functions that are intended or recognized (e.g., a newspaper being read to learn about the news); see *Latent functions*.

Marriage — a socially-approved mating relationship that people expect to be stable and enduring.

Marriage market — a process in which prospective spouses compare the assets and liabilities of eligible partners and choose the best available mate.

Masculine traits — aggressive, independent, dominant, competitive, active.

Mass media — form of communication designed to reach large numbers of people.

Master status — an ascribed or achieved status that determines a person's identity.

Material culture — the tangible objects that members of a society make, use and share; see *Nonmaterial culture*.

Matriarchal family system — a family system where the oldest females (usually grandmothers and mothers) control cultural, political and economic resources and consequently have power over the males.

Matrilocal residence pattern — newly married couples living with the wife's family.

Maturation — the continuing influence of heredity throughout development; the age-related physical and behavioral changes characteristic of a species.

Mean — the arithmetic average of a group of scores; the most commonly used measure of central tendency.

Measure of central tendency — a statistic, such as a mean, median or mode, that provides one score as representative of a set of observations.

Measures of variability — a statistic, such as a range or standard deviation, that indicates how tightly the scores in a set of observations cluster together.

Median — the score in a distribution above and below which lie 50 percent of the other scores; a measure of central tendency.

Meditation — a form of consciousness alteration designed to enhance self-knowledge and well-being through reduced self-awareness.

Medulla — the region of the brain stem that regulates breathing, waking and heartbeat.

Memory — the mental capacity to encode, store and retrieve information.

Menarche — the onset of menstruation.

Mental age — in Binet's measure of intelligence, the age at which a child is performing intellectually; expressed in terms of the mean age at which average children achieve a particular score.

Mental retardation — a condition in which individuals have IQ scores of 70 to 75 or below and also demonstrate limitations in their ability to bring adaptive skills to bear on life tasks.

Mental set — the tendency to respond to a new problem in the manner used to respond to a previous problem.

Meta-analysis — a statistical technique for evaluating hypotheses by providing a formal mechanism for detecting the general conclusions found in data from many different experiments.

Metamemory — implicit or explicit knowledge about memory abilities and effective memory strategies; cognition about memory.

Metamotivation — a term coined by Abraham Maslow to describe the motivation of individuals who are self-actualized and are striving to reach their full potential beyond the scope of their basic needs.

Microsociology — studies why people act in a certain way in particular situation (e.g., symbolic interactionism and, to some extent, feminism).

Mnemonics — strategies or devices that use familiar information during the encoding of new information to enhance subsequent access to the information in memory.

Mode — the score appearing most frequently in a set of observations; a measure of central tendency.

Monogamy — when one person is married exclusively to one other person.

Mood disorder — a mood disturbance such as severe depression or depression alternating with mania.

Morality — a system of beliefs and values that ensures that individuals will keep their obligations to others in society and will behave in ways that do not interfere with the rights and interests of others.

Mores — norms that members of a society consider very important because they maintain moral and ethical behavior.

Motivation — the process of starting, directing and maintaining physical and psychological activities; includes mechanisms involved in preferences for one activity over another and the vigor and persistence of responses.

Motor cortex — the region of the cerebral cortex that controls the action of the body's voluntary muscles.

Motor neurons — the neurons that carry messages away from the central nervous system toward the muscles and glands.

Multicultural — the coexistence of several cultures in the same geographic area without any one culture dominating the other; see *Cultural pluralism*.

Multiculturalism — promoting the equality and coexistence of many varied cultural traditions; the government's willingness to accommodate the widest possible cultural diversity (multilingualism, multi-religious, multicultural history, etc.); see *Pluralism*.

N

Narcolepsy — a sleep disorder characterized by an irresistible compulsion to sleep, often at inappropriate times (during the daytime) and places.

Natural selection — Darwin's theory that favorable adaptations to features of their environment allow some members of a species to perpetuate themselves more successfully over time than others.

Nature-nurture controversy — the debate concerning the relative importance of heredity (nature) and learning or experience (nurture) in determining development and behavior.

Need for achievement (n Ach) — an assumed basic human need to strive for the achievement of goals that motivates a wide range of behavior and thinking.

Negative punishment — when a behavior is followed by the removal of an appetitive stimulus, decreasing the probability of that behavior recurring.

Negative reinforcement — when a behavior is followed by the removal of an aversive stimulus, increasing the probability of that behavior recurring.

Neolocal residence pattern — when newly married couples have their own residence.

Neuromodulator — any substance that modifies or modulates the activities of the postsynaptic neuron.

Neuron — a cell in the nervous system whose function is to receive, process and/or transmit information to other cells.

Neuropathic pain — pain caused by the abnormal functioning or overactivity of the nerves; results from an injury or a disease of the nerves.

Neuroscience — the scientific study of the brain and the links between brain activity and behavior.

Neurotic disorder — a mental disorder in which a person does not have signs of brain abnormalities and does not display grossly irrational thinking or violate basic norms but does cause him or her to experience subjective distress; a category dropped from DSM-III; see *DSM*.

Neurotransmitters — chemical messengers released from neurons that cross the synapse from one neuron to another, stimulating the postsynaptic neuron.

Nociceptive pain — pain induced by a noxious external stimulus; specialized nerve endings in the skin send this pain message from the skin through the spinal cord to the brain.

No–fault divorce — state laws that do not require either partner to establish guilt or wrongdoing on the part of the other to get a divorce.

Nonconscious — information not typically available to consciousness or memory.

Nonprobability sample — a sample chosen with little or no attempt to get a representative cross-section of the population.

Non-REM (NREM) sleep — the period during which a sleeper does not show rapid eye movement; characterized by less dream activity than during REM sleep.

Nonmaterial culture — the shared set of meanings that people in a society use to interpret and understand the world. See also *Material culture.*

Nonverbal communication — communication using body movements, body gestures and facial expressions supporting, or in lieu of, speech.

Norms — written and unwritten rules, guidelines and expectations by which a society guides the behavior of its members (e.g., "right" and "wrong," proper social interaction).

Norm crystallization — the convergence of the expectations of a group of individuals into a common perspective as they talk and carry out activities together.

Normal curve — the symmetrical curve that represents the distribution of scores on many psychological attributes; allows researchers to make judgments of how typical or atypical an observation or result is.

Normative influence — group effects that arise from individual members' desire to be liked, accepted and approved of by others.

Normative investigations — research efforts designed to describe what is characteristic of a specific age or developmental stage.

Norms (social) — written and unwritten rules, guidelines, and expectations by which a society guides the behavior of its members (e.g., "right" and "wrong," proper social interaction).

Norms (testing) — standards based on measurements of a large group of people; used for comparing the scores of an individual with those of others within a well-defined group.

Nuclear family — also known as a "conjugal family," a family unit composed of one or more parents and their biological or adopted children.

O

Object permanence — the recognition that objects exist independently of an individual's action or awareness; an important cognitive acquisition of infancy.

Object relations theory — psychoanalytic theory that originated with Melanie Klein's view that the building blocks of how people experience the world derive from their relations to loved and hated objects (significant people in their lives).

Observational learning — the process of learning new responses by watching the behavior of another.

Observer bias — the distortion of evidence because of the personal motives and expectations of the viewer.

Obsessive-compulsive disorder (OCD) — a mental disorder characterized by obsessions (recurrent thoughts, images or impulses that recur or persist despite efforts to suppress them) and compulsions (repetitive, purposeful acts performed according to certain "rules" or in a ritualized manner).

Occipital lobe — the rearmost region of the brain; contains the primary visual cortex.

Olfactory bulb — the center where odor-sensitive receptors send their signals, located just below the frontal lobes of the cortex.

Operant — behavior emitted by an organism that can be characterized in terms of the observable effects it has on the environment.

Operant conditioning — learning in which the probability of a response is changed by a change in its consequences.

Operant extinction — when a behavior returns to the level of occurrence it had prior to operant conditioning and no longer produces the desired consequences.

Operational definition — a definition of a variable or condition in terms of the specific operation or procedure used to determine its presence.

Opponent-process theory — the theory that all color experiences arise from three systems, each of which includes two "opposing" elements (red versus green, blue versus yellow, black versus white).

Optic nerve — the axons of the ganglion cells that carry information from the eye toward the brain.

Organismic variables — the inner determinants of an organism's behavior.

Organizational psychologists — psychologists who study various aspects of the human work environment (e.g., communication among employees, socialization or enculturation of workers, leadership, job satisfaction, stress and burnout and overall quality of life).

Orientation constancy — the ability to perceive the actual orientation of objects in the real world despite their varying orientation in the retinal image.

Out-group — 1) a social or cultural group with which one feels they do not identify, are in competition with or in opposition to; 2) an outside group whose cultural practices are avoided or are behaved in contrast to (e.g., if Jewish Israelis constitute one's *in-group*, then Palestinians would be one's *out-group* and vice-versa).

Overregularization — a grammatical error usually appearing during early language development; when rules of the language are applied too broadly, resulting in incorrect linguistic forms.

P

Pain — the body's response to noxious stimuli intense enough to cause, or threaten to cause, tissue damage.

Panic disorder — an anxiety disorder in which sufferers experience unexpected, severe panic attacks that begin with a feeling of intense apprehension, fear or terror.

Parallel forms — different versions of a test used to assess test reliability; the change of forms reduces the effects of direct practice, memory or the desire of an individual to appear consistent on the same items.

Parallel processes — two or more mental processes that are carried out simultaneously.

Parasympathetic division — the subdivision of the autonomic nervous system that monitors the routine operation of the body's internal functions and conserves and restores body energy.

Parental investment — the time and energy that parents must expend raising their offspring.

Parenting practices — specific parenting behaviors that arise in response to particular parental goals.

Parenting styles — the manner in which parents rear their children; an authoritative parenting style, which balances demandingness and responsiveness, is seen as the most effective.

Parietal lobe — the region of the brain behind the frontal lobe and above the lateral fissure; contains somatosensory cortex.

Partial reinforcement effect — the behavioral principle that states that responses acquired under intermittent reinforcement are more difficult to extinguish than those acquired with continuous reinforcement.

Participant modeling — a therapeutic technique in which a therapist demonstrates the desired behavior and a client is aided, through supportive encouragement, to imitate the modeled behavior.

Participant observation — a data collection method where the researcher becomes a participant in a real-life research setting in order to observe what happens in that setting; its strengths are an in-depth understanding and flexibility; ideally, it doesn't disrupt the subjects' lives; its weaknesses are that it can be expensive and, in some settings, dangerous, or that there is little control over the data.

Pastoral counselor — a member of a religious order who specializes in the treatment of psychological disorders, often combining spirituality with practical problem-solving.

Patient — the term used by those who take a biomedical approach to the treatment of psychological problems to describe the person being treated.

Patriarchal family system — where the oldest men (grandfathers, fathers, uncles) control cultural, political and economic resources and consequently have power over the females.

Patrilocal residence pattern — newly married couples living with the husband's family.

Peace psychology — an interdisciplinary approach to the prevention of nuclear war and the maintenance of peace.

Perceived control — the belief that one has the ability to make a difference in the course or consequences of some event or experience; often helpful in dealing with stressors.

Perception — the processes that organize information in the sensory image and interpret it as having been produced by properties of objects or events in the external, three-dimensional world.

Perceptual constancy — the ability to retain an unchanging perception of an object despite variations in the retinal image.

Perceptual organization — the processes that put sensory information together to give the perception of a coherent scene over the whole visual field.

Peripheral nervous system (PNS) — the part of the nervous system composed of the spinal and cranial nerves that connect the body's sensory receptors to the CNS and the CNS to the muscles and glands.

Personality — the unique psychological qualities of an individual that influence a variety of characteristic behavior patterns (both overt and covert) across different situations and over time.

Personality disorder — a chronic, inflexible, maladaptive pattern of perceiving, thinking and behaving that seriously impairs an individual's ability to function in social or other settings.

Personality inventory — a self-report questionnaire used for personality assessment that includes a series of questions about personal thoughts, feelings, and behaviors.

Personality types — distinct patterns of personality characteristics used to assign people to categories; qualitative differences, rather than differences in degree, used to discriminate among people.

Persuasion — deliberate efforts to change attitudes.

PET scans — brain images produced by a device that obtains detailed pictures of activity in the living brain by recording the radioactivity emitted by cells during different cognitive or behavioral activities.

Phantom limb phenomenon — as experienced by amputees, the sensation of extreme or chronic pain in a limb that is no longer there.

Phenotype — the observable characteristics of an organism, resulting from the interaction between the organism's genotype and its environment.

Pheromones — chemical signals released by organisms that are instinctively perceived by other members of the species; often serve as long-distance sexual attractors.

Phi phenomenon — the simplest form of apparent motion; the movement illusion in which stationary lights going on and off in succession are perceived as a single moving light.

Phobia — a persistent and irrational fear of a specific object, activity or situation that is excessive and unreasonable, given the unlikelihood of the threatened "harm."

Phonemes — minimal units of speech in any given language that make a meaningful difference in speech production and reception (e.g., "r" and "l" are two distinct *phonemes* in English, but in Japanese, they are variations of one).

Photoreceptors — receptor cells in the retina that are sensitive to light.

Physical development — the bodily changes, maturation and growth that occur in an organism starting with conception and continuing throughout the lifespan.

Physiological dependence — the process by which the body becomes adjusted to and dependent on a drug.

Pitch — sound quality of highness or lowness; primarily dependent on the frequency of the sound wave.

Pituitary gland — located in the brain, the gland that secretes growth hormone and influences the secretion of hormones by other endocrine glands.

Place theory — the theory that different frequency tones produce maximum activation at different locations along the basilar membrane, with the result that pitch can be coded by the place at which activation occurs.

Placebo control — an experimental condition in which treatment is not administered; it is used in cases where it is thought a *Placebo effect* might occur.

Placebo effect — a change involving the anticipation of effects in the absence of actual experimental manipulation.

Placebo therapy — a therapy independent of any specific clinical procedures that results in client improvement.

Pluralism — a state in which independent cultures coexist while maintaining their cultural differences; see *Multiculturalism*.

Polyandry — a marriage where the wife has more than one husband simultaneously.

Polygamy — a marriage in which one spouse of either sex may have more than one mate at the same time; a family unit with more than two partners; see *Polyandry* and *Polygyny*.

Polygyny — a marriage where the husband has more than one wife simultaneously.

Pons — the region of the brain stem that connects the spinal cord with the brain and links parts of the brain to one another.

Popular culture — the beliefs, practices, activities, and products that are widely shared among a population in everyday life.

Population — the entire set of individuals about which generalizations can be made based on an experimental sample.

Positive punishment — a behavior is followed by the presentation of an aversive stimulus, decreasing the probability of that behavior recurring.

Positive reinforcement — a behavior is followed by the presentation of an appetitive stimulus, increasing the probability of that behavior recurring.

Possible selves — the ideal selves that a person would like to become, the selves a person could become and the selves a person is afraid of becoming; components of the cognitive sense of self.

Posttraumatic stress disorder (PTSD) — an anxiety disorder characterized by the persistent re-experience of traumatic events through distressing recollections, dreams, hallucinations or dissociative flashbacks; develops in response to rapes, life-threatening events, severe injuries, war-related trauma or natural disasters.

Preattentive processing — processing of sensory information that precedes attention to specific objects.

Preconscious memories — memories that are not currently conscious but that can easily be called into consciousness when necessary.

Predictive validity — how well a test or scale can foretell the measure of some criterion (e.g., when a cognitive test taken for an occupation is compared to a test-taker's later performance reviews); see *Criterion validity*.

Prefrontal lobotomy — an operation that severs the nerve fibers connecting the frontal lobes of the brain with the diencephalon, especially those fibers of the thalamic and hypothalamic areas; the best-known form of psychosurgery.

Prejudice — a learned attitude toward a target object involving negative affect (dislike or fear), negative beliefs (stereotypes) that justify the attitude and a behavioral intention to avoid, control, dominate or eliminate the target object.

Primacy effect — improved memory for items at the start of a list.

Primary reinforcers — biologically determined reinforcers such as food and water.

Priming — in the assessment of implicit memory, the advantage conferred by prior exposure to a word or situation.

Probability sample — a sample for which each person (or thing, such as an email address) has an equal chance of being selected because the selection is random.

Problem-solving — thinking that is directed toward solving specific problems and that moves from an initial state to a goal state by means of a set of mental operations.

Problem space — the elements that make up a problem: the initial state, the incomplete information or unsatisfactory conditions the person starts with; the goal state, the set of information or state the person wishes to achieve; and the set of operations, the steps the person takes to move from the initial state to the goal state.

Procedural memory — memory for how things get done; the way perceptual, cognitive and motor skills are acquired, retained and used.

Projective test — a method of personality assessment in which an individual is presented with a standardized set of ambiguous, abstract stimuli (e.g., Rorschach ink blots) and asked to interpret their meanings; the individual's responses are assumed to reveal inner feelings, motives, and conflicts.

Prosocial behaviors — behaviors that are carried out with the goal of helping other people.

Prototype — the most typical example of a class or category.

Proximal stimulus — the optical image on the retina; contrasted with the distal stimulus (the physical object in the world).

Psychiatrist — an individual who has obtained an M.D. degree and also has completed postdoctoral specialty training in mental and emotional disorders; may prescribe medications for the treatment of psychological disorders.

Psychic determinism — the assumption that mental and behavioral reactions are determined by previous experiences.

Psychoactive drugs — chemicals that affect mental processes and behavior by temporarily changing one's conscious awareness of reality.

Psychoanalysis — the form of psychodynamic therapy developed by Freud; an intensive and prolonged technique for exploring unconscious motivations and conflicts in neurotic, anxiety-ridden individuals.

Psychoanalyst — an individual who has earned either a Ph.D. or an M.D. degree and has completed postgraduate training in the Freudian approach to understanding and treating mental disorders.

Psychobiography — the use of psychological (especially personality) theory to describe and explain an individual's course through life.

Psychodynamic personality theories — theories of personality that share the assumption that powerful inner forces shape the personality and motivate the behavior.

Psychodynamic perspective — a psychological model in which behavior is explained in terms of past experiences and motivational forces; actions are viewed as stemming from inherited instincts, biological drives and attempts to resolve conflicts between personal needs and social requirements.

Psychological assessment — the use of specified procedures to evaluate the abilities, behaviors and personal qualities of people.

Psychological dependence — the psychological need or craving for a drug.

Psychological diagnosis — the label given to psychological abnormality by classifying and categorizing the observed behavior pattern into an approved diagnostic system.

Psychologist — an individual with a doctoral degree in psychology from an organized, sequential program in a regionally accredited university or professional school.

Psychology — the scientific study of the behavior of individuals and their mental processes.

Psychometric function — a graph that plots the percentage of detections of a stimulus (on the vertical axis) in relation to stimulus intensity (on the horizontal axis).

Psychometrics — the field of psychology that specializes in mental testing.

Psychoneuroimmunology — the research area that investigates interactions between psychological processes (e.g., responses to stress) and the functions of the immune system.

Psychopathological functioning — disruptions in emotional, behavioral or thought processes that lead to personal distress or block one's ability to achieve important goals.

Psychopharmacology — the branch of psychology that investigates the effects of drugs on behavior.

Psychophysics — the study of the correspondence between physical stimulation and psychological experience.

Psychosocial stages — proposed by Erik Erikson, successive developmental stages that focus on an individual's orientation toward the self and others; these stages incorporate both the sexual and social aspects of a person's development and the social conflicts that arise from the interaction between the individual and the social environment.

Psychosomatic disorders — physical disorders aggravated by or primarily attributable to prolonged emotional stress or other psychological causes.

Psychosurgery — a surgical procedure performed on brain tissue to alleviate a psychological disorder.

Psychotherapy — any of a group of therapies used to treat psychological disorders that focus on changing faulty behaviors, thoughts, perceptions, and emotions that may be associated with specific disorders.

Psychotic disorders — severe mental disorders in which a person experiences impairments in reality testing manifested through thought, emotional or perceptual difficulties; no longer used as a diagnostic category after DSM-III.

Puberty — the attainment of sexual maturity; indicated for girls by menarche and for boys by the production of live sperm and the ability to ejaculate.

Punisher — any stimulus that, when made contingent upon a response, decreases the probability of that response recurring.

Q

Qualitative research — research that examines non-numerical material and interprets it.

Quantitative research — research that focuses on a numerical analysis of people's responses or specific characteristics.

R

Race — a category composed of people who share certain inheritable phenotypical traits that members of a society deem socially significant.

Racism — discrimination against people based on their skin color or ethnic heritage.

Range — the difference between the highest and the lowest scores in a set of observations; the simplest measure of variability.

Rapid eye movements (REM) — a behavioral sign accompanying the phase of sleep during which the sleeper is likely to be experiencing dreamlike mental activity.

Rational-emotive therapy (RET) — a comprehensive system of personality change based on changing irrational beliefs that cause undesirable, highly-charged emotional reactions, such as severe anxiety.

Rational-legal authority — also known as "bureaucratic authority;" power legitimized by legally-enacted rules and regulations (e.g., the majority rules, the chain of command).

Rationalization of society — Max Weber's term for the historical change from tradition, emotion and spirituality to more scientifically based rationality as the dominant mode of human thought and decision making.

Real culture — the actual, everyday behavior of people in a society.

Reasoning — the process of thinking in which conclusions are drawn from a set of facts; thinking directed toward a given goal or objective.

Recall — a method of retrieval in which an individual is required to reproduce the information previously presented.

Recency effect — improved memory for items at the end of a list.

Receptive field — the visual area from which a given ganglion cell receives information.

Reciprocal altruism — the idea that people perform altruistic behaviors in the expectation that others will perform altruistic behaviors for them in turn.

Reciprocal determinism — a concept of Albert Bandura's social learning theory that refers to the notion that a complex reciprocal interaction exists among the individual and their behavior and environmental stimuli and that each of these components affects the others.

Reciprocity norm — expectation that favors will be returned (e.g., if something is done for someone, that person should do something in return).

Recognition — a method of retrieval in which an individual is required to identify stimuli as having been experienced before.

Reconstructive memory — the process of putting information together based on general types of stored knowledge in the absence of a specific memory representation.

Reflex — an unlearned response elicited by specific stimuli that have biological relevance for an organism.

Refractory period — the period of rest during which a new nerve impulse cannot be activated in a segment of an axon.

Reinforcement contingency — a consistent relationship between a response and the changes in the environment that it produces.

Reinforcer — any stimulus that, when made contingent upon a response, increases the probability of that response.

Relative motion parallax — a source of information about depth in which the relative distances of objects from a viewer determine the amount and direction of their relative motion in the retinal image.

Relative poverty — not having enough money to maintain an average standard of living.

Relaxation response — a condition in which muscle tension, cortical activity, heart rate, and blood pressure decrease and breathing slows.

Reliability — the degree to which a test produces a similar range of scores each time it is used; the stability or consistency of the scores produced by an instrument.

Religion — a social institution involving beliefs and practices based upon a conception of the sacred and the possible rituals that surround the sacred.

Representative sample — a subset of a population that closely matches the overall characteristics of the population with respect to the distribution of males and females, racial and ethnic groups and so on.

Representativeness heuristic — a cognitive strategy that assigns an object to a category on the basis of a few characteristics regarded as representative of that category.

Repression — the basic defense mechanism by which painful or guilt-producing thoughts, feelings or memories are excluded from conscious awareness.

Residual stress pattern — a chronic syndrome in which the emotional responses of posttraumatic stress persist over time.

Resistance — the inability or unwillingness of a patient in psychoanalysis to discuss certain ideas, desires or experiences.

Resocialization — the process of unlearning old ways of doing things and adopting new attitudes, values, norms, and behaviors.

Response bias — the systematic tendency as a result of non-sensory factors for an observer to favor responding in a particular way.

Resting potential — the polarization of cellular fluid within a neuron which provides the capability to produce an action potential.

Reticular formation — the region of the brain stem that alerts the cerebral cortex to incoming sensory signals and is responsible for maintaining consciousness and awakening from sleep.

Retina — the layer at the back of the eye that contains photoreceptors and converts light energy to neural responses.

Retinal disparity — the displacement between the horizontal positions of corresponding images in the two eyes.

Retrieval — the recovery of stored information from memory.

Retrieval cues — internally or externally generated stimuli available to help with the retrieval of a memory.

Reversal theory — a theory that explains human motivation in terms of reversals from one opposing metamotivational state to another; see *Metamotivation*.

Ritual healing — ceremonies that infuse special emotional intensity and meaning into the healing process.

Rods — photoreceptors concentrated in the periphery of the retina that are most active in dim illumination; rods do not produce the sensation of color.

Role — the behavior expected of someone who holds a particular status (i.e., expected behavior).

Role performance — the actual behavior of a person who occupies a particular status.

Role set — a number of roles that are attached to a single person (e.g., mother, wife, realtor, Cuban-American, Catholic, etc.).

Role strain — the frustrations and uncertainties a person experiences when having to cope with the requirements of two or more statuses.

Role taking — assuming someone else's perspective for learning purposes.

Rules — behavioral guidelines for acting in certain ways in certain situations.

S

Sample — a group of people or organisms that are representative of the population researchers wish to study.

Sanctions — rewards for good or appropriate behavior and/or penalties for bad or inappropriate behavior.

Sapir-Whorf hypothesis — a hypothesis stating that people perceive the world through the cultural lens of their unique language; habits of speech and reading create habits of perception and, to some extent, a unique reality.

Saturation — the dimension of color space that captures the purity and vividness of color sensations.

Scapegoat — a person or category of people, typically with little power, whom people unfairly blame for their own mistakes or inadequacy.

Schedules of reinforcement — in operant conditioning, the patterns of delivering and withholding reinforcement.

Schemas — general conceptual frameworks, or clusters of knowledge, regarding objects, people and situations; knowledge packages that encode generalizations about the structure of the environment.

Schemes — Piaget's term for cognitive structures that develop as infants and young children learn to interpret the world and adapt to their environment.

Schizophrenic disorder — a severe form of psychopathology characterized by the breakdown of integrated personality functioning, withdrawal from reality, emotional distortions and disturbed thought processes.

Scientific method — 1) the steps in the research process that include careful data collection, exact measurement, accurate recording and analysis of the findings, thoughtful interpretation of results and, when appropriate, a generalization of the findings to a larger group; 2) the set of procedures used for gathering and interpreting objective information in a way that minimizes error and yields dependable generalizations.

Scientific research — the effort to reduce uncertainty about some aspect of society through the science of observation.

Secondary analysis — a data collection method that examines the data collected by someone else; includes historical materials, public records, and official statistics; its strengths are that it is convenient and inexpensive; its weakness is that it may be difficult to gather all the information a researcher needs.

Secularization — the historical decline in the importance attached to the supernatural and the sacred; the declining influence of religion in everyday life.

Selective optimization with compensation — a strategy for successful aging in which one makes the most of gains while minimizing the impact of losses that accompany normal aging.

Selective social interaction theory — the view that suggests that, as people age, they become more selective in choosing social partners who satisfy their emotional needs.

Self — an awareness of one's social identity.

Self-actualization — a concept in personality psychology referring to a person's constant striving to realize their potential and to develop their inherent talents and capabilities.

Self-awareness — the top level of consciousness; cognizance of the autobiographical character of personally experienced events.

Self-concept — a person's mental model of their abilities and attributes.

Self-efficacy — the set of beliefs that one can perform adequately in a particular situation.

Self-esteem — a generalized evaluative attitude toward the self that influences both moods and behavior and that exerts a powerful effect on a range of personal and social behaviors.

Self-fulfilling prophecy — a prediction made about some future behavior or event that modifies interactions so as to produce what was expected.

Self-handicapping — the process of developing, in anticipation of failure, behavioral reactions, and explanations that minimize ability deficits as possible attributions for the failure.

Self-perception theory — the idea that people observe themselves in order to figure out the reasons they act as they do; people infer what their internal states are by perceiving how they are acting in a given situation.

Self-report measures — the self-behaviors that are identified through a participant's own observations and reports.

Self-serving bias — a class of attributional biases in which people tend to take credit for their successes and deny responsibility for their failures.

Semantic memories — generic, categorical memories, such as the meanings of words and concepts.

Sensation — the process by which stimulation of a sensory receptor gives rise to neural impulses that result in an experience or awareness of conditions inside or outside the body.

Sensory adaptation — a phenomenon in which receptor cells lose their power to respond after a period of unchanged stimulation; allows a more rapid reaction to new sources of information.

Sensory memory — the initial memory processes involved in the momentary preservation of fleeting impressions of sensory stimuli.

Sensory neurons — the neurons that carry messages from sense receptors toward the central nervous system.

Sensory physiology — the study of the way in which biological mechanisms convert physical events into neural events.

Sensory receptors — specialized cells that convert physical signals into cellular signals that are processed by the nervous system.

Serial monogamy — when individuals marry several people but one at a time.

Serial position effect — a characteristic of memory retrieval in which the recall of items at the beginning and at the end of a list is often better than the recall of items in the middle.

Serial processes — two or more mental processes that are carried out in order, one after the other.

Set — a temporary readiness to perceive or react to a stimulus in a particular way.

Sex chromosomes — chromosomes that contain the genes that code for the development of male or female characteristics.

Sex differences — biologically based characteristics that distinguish males from females.

Sexism — discrimination against people because of their sex.

Sexual arousal — the motivational state of excitement and tension brought about by physiological and cognitive reactions to erotic stimuli.

Sexual scripts — socially learned programs of sexual responsiveness.

Shamanism — a spiritual tradition that involves both healing powers and actual or assumed contact with the spirit world.

Shape constancy — the ability to perceive the true shape of an object despite variations in the size of the retinal image.

Shaping by successive approximations — a behavioral method that reinforces responses that successively approximate and ultimately match the desired response.

Short-term memory (STM) — memory processes associated with preservation of recent experiences and with retrieval of information from long-term memory; short-term memory is of limited capacity and stores information for only a short length of time without rehearsal.

Shyness — an individual's discomfort and/or inhibition in interpersonal situations that interferes with pursuing interpersonal or professional goals.

Signal detection theory (SDT) — a systematic approach to the problem of response bias that allows an experimenter to identify and separate the roles of sensory stimuli and the individual's criterion level in producing the final response.

Significant difference — a difference between experimental groups or conditions that would have occurred by chance less than an accepted criterion; in psychology, the criterion most often used is a probability of fewer than 5 times out of 100, or $p < .05$.

Situational variables — external influences on behavior.

Size constancy — the ability to perceive the true size of an object despite variations in the size of its retinal image.

Sleep apnea — a sleep disorder of the upper respiratory system that causes the person to stop breathing while asleep.

Socialization — the lifelong process of social interaction in which the individual acquires a social identity and ways of thinking, feeling and acting that are essential for effective participation in a society; the teaching and learning of culture, most of which is acquired in the early years.

Social categorization — the process by which people organize the social environment by categorizing themselves and others into groups.

Social-conflict approach — a framework for building theory based on the assumption that society is characterized by inequality and conflict that generate change; where functional theory addresses what works in a cultural group or society, social-conflict theory looks for the dysfunction, mostly the structures that reinforce inequality; see *Conflict theory*.

Social development — the ways in which individuals' social interactions and expectations change over their lifespan.

Social exchange theory — the perspective that says people, when interacting, act to maximize rewards and benefits and minimize punishments or cost.

Social intelligence — a theory of personality that refers to the expertise people bring to their experience of life tasks.

Social interactionist theory — a microsociological theory which states that shared-meaning orientations and assumptions form the basic motivation behind people's actions.

Social-learning theory — the learning theory that stresses the role of observing and imitating others' behaviors.

Social learning theories — approaches whose central notion is that people learn new attitudes, beliefs, and behaviors through social interaction, especially during childhood.

Social-learning therapy — a form of treatment in which clients observe models' desirable behaviors being reinforced.

Social mobility — a person's ability to move up and down the social ladder; see *Horizontal mobility*, *Intragenerational mobility*, and *Intergenerational mobility*.

Social norms — the expectation a group has for its members regarding acceptable and appropriate attitudes and behaviors.

Social perception — the process by which a person comes to know or perceive the personal attributes of themselves and other people.

Social phobia — a persistent, irrational fear that arises in anticipation of a public situation in which an individual can be observed by others.

Social psychology — the branch of psychology that studies the effect of social variables on individual behavior, attitudes, perceptions, and motives; also studies group and intergroup phenomena.

Social role — a socially defined pattern of behavior that is expected of a person who is functioning in a given setting or group.

Social stratification — ranking the members of a society into a pattern of superior and inferior ranks, such as wealth, prestige, power, etc. (e.g., caste or class systems).

Social support — resources (including material aid, socioemotional support, and informational aid) provided by others to help a person cope with stress.

Society — people who interact in a defined territory and share some facets of common interests and values (i.e., some aspects of culture and leadership that bring them together).

Socialization — the lifelong process whereby an individual's behavioral patterns, values, standards, skills, attitudes, and motives are shaped to conform to those regarded as desirable in a particular society.

Sociobiology — a research field that focuses on evolutionary explanations for the social behavior and social systems of humans and other animal species.

Sociocultural evolution — the Lenski's' term for the process of change that results from a society's gaining new cultural information, particularly technology, that may have a good and/or bad impact on the society.

Soma — the cell body of a neuron, containing the nucleus and cytoplasm.

Somatic nervous system — the subdivision of the peripheral nervous system that connects the central nervous system to the skeletal muscles and skin.

Somatosensory cortex — the region of the parietal lobes that processes sensory input from various body areas.

Specific phobias — phobias that occur in response to specific types of objects or situations.

Split-half reliability — a measure of the correlation between test-takers' performance on different halves of a test (e.g., odd- and even-numbered items).

Spontaneous recovery — the reappearance of an extinguished conditioned response after a rest period.

Spontaneous-remission effect — the improvement of some mental patients and clients in psychotherapy without any professional intervention; a baseline criterion against which the effectiveness of therapies must be assessed.

Standard deviation (SD) — the average difference of a set of scores from their mean; a measure of variability.

Standardization — a set of uniform procedures for treating each participant in a test, interview or experiment or for recording data.

Status — a social position and/or identity that a person occupies in a society; see *Status set*.

Status set — a collection of social statuses than an individual occupies at a given time (if one has a *Role set*, then they will often have a status set).

Stepfamily — a household in which two adults marry or cohabit and one or both of them have a biological or adoptive child/children from a prior relationship.

Stereotype — a set of overgeneralizations concerning some category of people in which the same characteristics are assigned to all members of a group; some positive stereotypes exist, but most are negative.

Stereotype threat — the threat associated with being at risk for confirming a negative stereotype of one's group.

Stigma — 1) a powerfully negative social label that radically changes a person's self-concept and social identity; 2) the negative reaction of people to an individual or group because of some assumed inferiority or source of difference that is denigrated.

Stimulus discrimination — a conditioning process in which an organism learns to respond differently to stimuli that differ from the conditioned stimulus on some dimension.

Stimulus-driven capture — a determinant of why people select some parts of sensory input for further processing; occurs when features of certain stimuli (objects in the environment) automatically capture attention, independent of the local goals of a perceiver.

Stimulus generalization — the automatic extension of conditioned responding to similar stimuli that have never been paired with the unconditioned stimulus.

Storage — the retention of encoded material over time.

Stress — the pattern of specific and nonspecific responses an organism makes to stimulus events that disturb its equilibrium and tax or exceed its ability to cope.

Stress moderator variables — variables that change the impact of a stressor on a given type of stress reaction.

Stressor — an internal or external event or stimulus that induces stress.

Structural-functional approach — a framework for building theory based on the assumption that society is a complex system whose parts work together to promote stability; that humans work toward functional organization, order, and stability, and that their cultural norms and institutions reflect that goal; therefore there are logical reasons for why people do the things they do and organize themselves the way they do; see *Functionalist theory*.

Structuralism — the study of the structure of mind and behavior; the view that all human mental experience can be understood as a combination of simple elements or events.

Subculture — cultural patterns that distinguish some segment of a society's population; variations within a society regarding some aspects of religion, language, traditions/customs or outward symbols/appearance that sets them apart from the mainstream or dominant culture (e.g., intercity gangs, the Amish of Pennsylvania, hippies of the 1960s, some African-American communities, etc.).

Superego — the aspect of personality that represents the internalization of society's values, standards, and morals.

Surveys — a data collection method that uses questionnaires and interviews; its strengths are that it can be inexpensive, easy to administer, have a fast turnaround, easy to acquire sensitive information; its weaknesses are its low response rate and the possibility of respondents giving inaccurate (or dishonest) answers.

Sustainable ecosystem — the human use of the natural environment to meet the needs of the present generation without threatening the prospects of future generations; economic growth without further or irrevocable damage to natural ecosystems.

Symbolic-interaction approach — a theoretical framework based on the assumption that society is the product of the everyday interactions of individuals, therefore the focus of research should be on the actual viewpoints, perspectives, and interpretations of people (the culture and its institutions as they see it, not necessarily as social scientists see it).

Symbolic interactionist theory — a theory that states that cultural symbols forge identities (that change over time), and that culture (such as norms and values) helps people merge into a society despite their differences.

Symbols — anything that stands for something else and has a particular meaning for people who share a culture (e.g., apple pie, American flag).

Sympathetic division — the subdivision of the autonomic nervous system that deals with emergency response and the mobilization of energy.

Synapse — the gap between one neuron and another.

Synaptic transmission — the relaying of information from one neuron to another across the synaptic gap.

Systematic desensitization — a behavioral therapy technique in which a client is taught to prevent the arousal of anxiety by confronting the feared stimulus while relaxed.

T

Taste-aversion learning — a biological constraint on learning in which an organism learns in one trial to avoid a food that results in illness.

Temporal lobe — region of the brain found below the lateral fissure; contains auditory cortex.

Tend-and-befriend response — a response to stressors that is hypothesized to be typical for females; stressors prompt females to protect their offspring and join social groups to reduce vulnerability.

Terminal buttons — the bulblike structures at the branched endings of axons that contain vesicles filled with neurotransmitters.

Testosterone — the male sex hormone secreted by the testes that stimulates the production of sperm and is also responsible for the development of male secondary sex characteristics.

Test-retest reliability — a measure of the correlation between the scores of the same people on the same test when given on two different occasions.

Thalamus — the brain structure that relays sensory impulses to the cerebral cortex.

Thematic Apperception Test (TAT) — a projective test in which illustrations of ambiguous scenes are presented to an individual who is encouraged to imagine "what you think is happening in this picture."

Theory — an organized set of concepts that explains a phenomenon or set of phenomena; an explanation of how two or more facts are related to one another

Theory of ecological optics — a theory of perception that emphasizes the richness of stimulus information and views the perceiver as an active explorer of the environment.

Think-aloud protocols — reports made by experimental participants of the mental processes and strategies they use while working on a task.

Thomas Theorem — W.I. Thomas's assertion that situations defined as real become real in their consequences, even if all of the facts are not taken into consideration.

Three-term contingency — the means by which organisms learn that, in the presence of some stimuli but not others, their behavior is likely to have a particular effect on the environment.

Timbre — the dimension of auditory sensation that reflects the complexity of a sound wave.

Tolerance — a situation that occurs with continued use of a drug in which an individual requires greater dosages to achieve the same effect.

Top-down processing — perceptual processes in which information from an individual's past experience, knowledge, expectations, motivations, and background influence the way a perceived object is interpreted and classified.

Traits — enduring personal qualities or attributes that influence behavior across situations.

Transduction — transformation of one form of energy into another (e.g., light is transformed into neural impulses).

Transfer-appropriate processing — the perspective that suggests that memory is best when the type of processing carried out at encoding matches the processes carried out at retrieval.

Transference — the process by which a person in psychoanalysis attaches to their therapist feelings formerly held toward some significant person who figured in a past emotional conflict.

Transgender — general term involving tendencies to diverge from the gender norm of a society; individuals who are transsexual or intersexual.

Transsexual — adjective describing someone who identifies with the physical sex different from what the person was assigned at birth.

Transvestites — people who cross-dress at times but do not necessarily identify with the opposite sex.

Trichromatic theory — the theory that there are three types of color receptors that produce the primary color sensations of red, green and blue.

Type A behavior pattern — a complex pattern of behaviors and emotions that involves excessive emphasis on competition, aggression, impatience, and hostility (hostility increases the risk of coronary heart disease).

Type B behavior pattern — as compared to Type A behavior pattern, a less competitive, less aggressive, less hostile pattern of behavior and emotion.

Type C behavior pattern — a constellation of behaviors that may predict which individuals are more likely to develop cancer or to have their cancer progress quickly; these behaviors include passive acceptance and self-sacrifice.

U

Unconditional positive regard — complete love and acceptance of an individual by another person, such as a parent for a child, with no conditions attached.

Unconditioned response (UCR) — in classical conditioning, the response elicited by an unconditioned stimulus without prior training or learning.

Unconditioned stimulus (UCS) — in classical conditioning, the stimulus that elicits an unconditioned response.

Unconscious — the domain of the psyche that stores repressed urges and primitive impulses.

Unconscious inference — Helmholtz's term for the perception that occurs outside of conscious awareness.

V

Validity — the extent to which a test measures what it was intended to measure.

Values — culturally-defined standards by which people judge desirability, goodness, and beauty and which serve as broad guidelines for social living as well as public policies; core values are the key values given high priority in society (e.g., individualism or personal freedoms in the U.S.).

Variable — in an experimental setting, a factor that varies in magnitude or value.

Variable-interval schedule — a schedule of reinforcement in which a reinforcer is delivered for the first response made after a variable period of time whose average is predetermined.

Variable-ratio schedule — a schedule of reinforcement in which a reinforcer is delivered for the first response made after a variable number of responses whose average is predetermined.

Vestibular sense — the sense that tells how one's own body is oriented in the world with respect to gravity.

Visual cortex — the region of the occipital lobes in which visual information is processed.

Volley principle — an extension of frequency theory which proposes that when peaks in a sound wave come too frequently for a single neuron to fire at each peak, several neurons fire as a group at the frequency of the stimulus tone.

W

Weber's law — asserts that the size of a difference threshold is proportional to the intensity of the standard stimulus.

Wellness — optimal health incorporating the ability to function fully and actively over the physical, intellectual, emotional, spiritual, social and environmental domains of health.

Wisdom — expertise in the fundamental pragmatics of life.

Within-subjects design — a research design that uses each participant as their own control; for example, the behavior of an experimental participant before receiving treatment might be compared to their behavior after receiving treatment.

Working memory — a memory resource that is used to accomplish tasks such as reasoning and language comprehension; consists of the phonological loop, the visuospatial sketchpad, and the central executive.

World system theory — a macro-scale approach to social analysis, developed by Immanuel Wallerstein, in which the world system (not nations themselves) is the means to understanding social changes and historical events; in this system there are "core" (First World) countries, "semi-periphery" (industrializing) countries and "periphery" (poorer) countries that interrelate, with some inevitably taking advantage of others.

Y

Yerkes-Dodson law — a correlation between task performance and optimal level of arousal.

Z

Zygote — the single cell that results when a sperm fertilizes an egg.

We want to hear from you

Your feedback is important to us because we strive to provide the highest quality prep materials. Email us if you have any questions, comments or suggestions, so we can incorporate your feedback into future editions.

Customer Satisfaction Guarantee

If you have any concerns about this book, including printing issues, contact us and we will resolve any issues to your satisfaction.

info@sterling-prep.com

We reply to all emails – please check your spam folder

Thank you for choosing our products to achieve your educational goals!

Made in the USA
Columbia, SC
11 November 2018